MT. HERMON AND THE
SEA OF GALILEE
Matson Photo Service
Alhambra, California

STUDIES IN
LUKE

BOOKS IN THE BIBLE STUDY TEXTBOOK SERIES

- ACTS MADE ACTUAL
- SACRED HISTORY AND GEOGRAPHY
- THE CHURCH IN THE BIBLE
- ROMANS REALIZED
- HELPS FROM HEBREWS
- THE GLORIOUS CHURCH OF EPHESIANS
- THE GOSPEL OF JOHN VOL. I
- GUIDANCE FROM GALATIANS
- THE GREATEST WORK IN THE WORLD
- PAUL'S LETTERS TO TIMOTHY AND TITUS
- SURVEY COURSE IN CHRISTIAN DOCTRINE VOL. I
- SURVEY COURSE IN CHRISTIAN DOCTRINE VOL. II
- LETTERS FROM PETER
- THINKING THROUGH THESSALONIANS
- STUDIES IN FIRST CORINTHIANS
- THE SEER, THE SAVIOUR, AND THE SAVED IN THE BOOK OF REVELATION
- SURVEY COURSE IN CHRISTIAN DOCTRINE VOL. III & IV

BIBLE STUDY TEXTBOOK

STUDIES IN

LUKE

T. R. Applebury

Professor of New Testament

Pacific Christian College

Long Beach, California

College Press, Joplin, Missouri

PREFACE

TO THE READER

These studies are the result of years of research and teaching in the Bible college and in church classes. My object in presenting them is to encourage the program of Bible study and to help meet the needs of the general Bible reader.

The analysis of each chapter is both an outline and, in many cases, a paraphrase of the Bible text. It is intended to be of help to the general reader and also to the teacher who may be leading a study group. The analysis will enable the reader to have a comprehensive view of the Gospel of Luke at a glance.

The printed text is the American Standard Version of the New Testament. I urge you, however, to use your own Bible in these studies. The *comments* should be of help regardless of the version you may use. Under no circumstances should comments be placed above the Bible text in importance. In some instances there are recognized differences of opinion. In all such cases, I ask that you do not accept my opinions. I urge you to study your own Bible and to do your own thinking that your conclusion may be your own. Every student should seek to learn what the Bible actually says and what it means.

The summary of each chapter will help the student to review the material covered in the commentary. *The questions at the end of each chapter* are designed to point out the significant issues of the chapter. For best results, the student should write out the answers to each question.

I am indebted to Don DeWelt, editor of the BIBLE STUDY TEXTBOOK series, with whom I served on the faculty of the San Jose Bible College, for his encouragement and assistance in preparing this work for publication.

It is my prayer that you may search the Scriptures as the Beroeans did and meditate on the meaning of God's Word day and night that you may translate it into life and share it with others.

Department of New Testament
Pacific Christian College
January, 1965   40528

CONTENTS

CHAPTER ONE

Outline

A. Luke writes to Theophilus (1-4).
  1. Why he is writing this story of Jesus (1-3a).
     a) Many had undertaken to write about the things that had been accomplished among them.
     b) Those who from the beginning were eyewitnesses and servants of the word had reported these things to Luke.
  2. His qualifications to undertake the task (3b).
     a) He had followed the reports with care.
     b) He had gone back to the beginning of the story.
  3. The nature of the account he is writing (3c-4).
     a) He planned to write a connected account of these things.
     b) He did so in order that Theophilus might know about the unshakable evidence that firmly supports the things about which he had been instructed.
B. He began by telling about the promised birth of John (5-25).
  1. The angel Gabriel appeared to Zacharias bringing him this message. (5-12).
     a) It was in the time of Herod the Great.
     b) Zacharias was a priest, and his wife whose name was Elizabeth was a daughter of Aaron.
     c) They were righteous people keeping all the commandments and ordinances of the Lord blamelessly.
     d) They were childless elderly people.
     e) Zacharias was preparing to burn incense in the temple, and the people were outside praying.
     f) Zacharias became frightened when he saw the angel of the Lord standing by the right side of the altar.
  2. The angel told Zacharias about the child (13-17).
     a) His prayer had been heard; Elizabeth was to bear a son whose name was to be John.
     b) Rejoicing would occur at his birth, for he was to be dedicated to the Lord from his birth.
     c) His mission was to turn many to the Lord; he was to go forth in the spirit and power of Elijah.
  3. The angel gave Zacharias a sign that this would happen (18-22).
     a) Zacharias asked how he would know this.

9

b) Gabriel said he would be unable to speak until the child was born.

c) As he came out of the temple, the people became aware of his having seen a vision.

4. Zacharias and Elizabeth returned home to await the coming of the child (23-25).

C. He told about the angel informing Mary that she was to bear a son and call his name Jesus (26-38).

1. The angel was sent from God to inform Mary (26-29).

a) He was sent to Nazareth, a city in Galilee.

b) Mary was a virgin betrothed to Joseph of the family of David.

c) He told Mary that she was highly favored of the Lord.

d) Mary wondered what this might mean.

2. The angel explained to Mary how the Lord would accomplish this.

a) Mary had found favor with God and was to conceive and bear a son and call his name JESUS.

b) He explained about the child.

(1) He was to be great and to be called the Son of the Most High.

(2) The Lord God would give him the throne of his father David.

(3) He was to reign over the house of Jacob forever; there would be no end to his kingdom.

c) He explained how this was to be accomplished.

(1) Mary asked how it could be since she did not know a man.

(2) The Holy Spirit and the power of the Most High would accomplish it.

(3) Because of this miracle of conception, "the holy thing which is begotten shall be called the Son of God."

(4) Elizabeth also was soon to bear a son for "no word from God shall be void of power."

(5) Mary responded: "Behold the handmaid of the Lord; be it unto me according to thy word."

D. He told about Mary's visit to Elizabeth (39-40).

1. She went in haste to the hill country to a city of Judah and

10

entered the house of Zacharias and greeted Elizabeth (39-40).
2. Elizabeth responded in inspired words of praise (41-45).
  a) Her unborn babe leaped, and she was filled with the Holy Spirit (41).
  b) What she said to Mary (42-45).
    (1) "Blessed art thou among women, and blessed is the fruit of thy womb."
    (2) She asked, "Why is it that the mother of my Lord should come to me?"
    (3) She told Mary that her own unborn babe had leaped for joy when Mary greeted her.
    (4) She praised Mary for believing the promise of the Lord, for He would fulfill it.
3. Mary's song of praise to God (46-55).
  a) She praised God for blessing her in her humble estate.
  b) She spoke of the might and holiness and mercy of God.
  c) She told how He had put down the proud and exalted the humble.
  d) She spoke of His help to Israel and His remembrance of His covenant with Abraham.
4. Mary stayed with Elizabeth three months and then returned to her home (56).
E. He told about the birth of John the Baptist (57-80).
  1. Elizabeth gave birth to a son; her neighbors and relatives rejoiced with her (57-58).
  2. Her child was named at the time of his circumcision (59-63).
    a) Some wanted him to be called Zacharias after his father, but Elizabeth said, "He shall be called John."
    b) The relatives protested and appealed to Zacharias. He wrote, "His name is John."
    c) All marvelled at this, but Zacharias was now able to speak after the period of silence imposed on him by the Lord.
    d) The people throughout the hill country of Judea heard about the child and said, "What then shall this child be?"
  3. Zacharias prophesied under the inspiration of the Holy Spirit (67-79).

11

    a) What God had done in the house of David (67-75).
        (1) Redemption, salvation, and mercy had been shown to His people.
        (2) He had remembered His covenant and promise to Abraham.
    b) What the child—John the Baptist—was to do (76-79).
        (1) As the prophet of the Most High, he was to go before the face of the Lord to make ready His ways and give knowledge of salvation and remission of sins to the people (76-77).
        (2) The mercy of God as shown in Christ was to guide those in darkness into the ways of peace (78-79).
  4. The child grew and became strong in spirit and lived in the deserts until the beginning of his ministry to Israel (80).

Luke Writes to Theophilus

Scripture

1:1-4 Forasmuch as many have taken in hand to draw up a narrative concerning those matters which have been fulfilled among us, 2 even as they delivered them unto us, who from the beginning were eyewitnesses and ministers of the word, 3 it seemed good to me also, having traced the course of all things accurately from the first, to write unto thee in order, most excellent Theophilus; 4 that thou mightest know the certainty concerning the things wherein thou wast instructed.

Comments

Forasmuch as many.—Many who had heard the words of Jesus and had seen the things He did had made a written record of them. Others had repeated them orally. In so doing, it is possible that variations in the wording, without change in thought, had taken place. Even the inspired writers—Matthew, Mark, Luke, and John—do not always use the same words, but in a very remarkable way they do express the same thoughts. Some of the written accounts were fragmentary. One person told about something he heard Jesus say; another described a miracle he had seen. Perhaps details were lacking in some cases. So we can see why God selected His inspired writers to give an accurate account of the things that Jesus did and taught.

Theophilus had been instructed in them, but Luke wanted him to have the complete and accurate account of these things.

matters that have been fulfilled among us.—In the Book of Acts which Luke also wrote to Theophilus, Luke gives his own statement about the content of the first letter. He says he had written about "all that Jesus began both to do and teach until the day in which he was received up, after that he had given commandment through the Holy Spirit unto the apostles whom he had chosen" (Acts 1:1-2). He recorded the historical facts after he had carefully researched the whole project.

they delivered them to us.—This is not a fictional story. Luke wrote an accurate account of things that were reported to him by those who saw and heard them. Of the four gospel writers, only Matthew and John were apostles who had seen and heard the things they wrote about. Mark could have heard them, but not Luke. That's why he checked every detail of this wonderful story. He wrote it because he was convinced that it was reliable history. More than that, he was certainly inspired by the Holy Spirit, for he had been with the apostle Paul and could easily have received this power through the laying on of the apostle's hands. See Acts 8:14-17; II Tim. 1:6.

eyewitnesses and ministers.—Luke rests his case on a solid foundation. The apostles were numbered among the eyewitnesses. See Acts 1:21-22; Heb. 2:3-4; I John 1:1-4. Paul was a witness of the risen Lord, although there is nothing to show that he witnessed the events of Jesus' ministry as the other apostles had done. See I Cor. 9:1. In writing about the resurrection (I Cor. 15:1-58) he did tell about the more than five hundred brethren—most of them were still alive—who had seen the risen Lord.

These eyewitnesses were ministers—servants who rendered faithful obedience to their Lord. See Paul's use of this word in I Cor. 4:1-2. He also calls the apostles stewards of the mysteries of God—that is, His revealed secret in the Word. See also I Tim. 6:20-21; II Tim. 2:1-2.

from the beginning.—How far back does this go? If we are to restrict it to the ministry of the apostles, then the beginning may well be the public ministry of Jesus. See Acts 1:21-22. But Luke must have talked with witnesses who had seen and heard the things with which he begins his story—the facts about the birth of John and of Jesus. It is significant that "the beloved physician" wrote the facts about the birth of Jesus in this reliable record of things that actually happened.

it seemed good to me also.—The writer does not give his name. For that matter, neither do the writers of the other three gospels. We are left to external evidence for this information. There is, however, internal evidence that the Gospel According to Luke and The Acts were written by the same person. Both of them are written to Theophilus. See Acts 1:1.

Luke "the beloved physician" (Col. 4:14) was a traveling companion of the apostle Paul. References in Acts suggest that he joined Paul at Troas on his second missionary journey and went with him to Philippi. See Acts 16:10. Evidently, he was with Paul on the last part of the third journey which took them to Jerusalem (Acts 20:5 and 21:15). He was with him when he left Caesarea for Rome (Acts 27:1). Two remarkable statements bring the story of Acts to a climax; they also show that the author of the Book was with Paul when he entered Rome. See them in Acts 28:14 and 16.

Luke's association with Paul on these journies sheds some light on the possible time during which he researched these important matters recorded in his gospel. The time they spent in Jerusalem and the long imprisonment of Paul in Caesarea (Acts 24:27) could have given him time to investigate the sources of the reports recounted by those who had actually seen and heard the things about which he was to write.

We do not know where he was when he wrote the gospel. It could have been at Caesarea or it could have been at Rome while Paul was there in prison. The closing words of Acts suggest that the outcome of Paul's trial was not known when Luke wrote the book. The closing words of the Gospel and the opening words of Acts suggest that Luke wrote them without any great lapse of time between the two. This tends to suggest that both were written at Rome. Luke was faithful to Paul to the last. When others for various reasons left him, Paul wrote to Timothy from Rome saying, "Only Luke is with me" (II Tim. 4:11).

having traced the course of all things accurately.—Many had written about some of the things in the life of Jesus. Luke carefully researched all the evidence in connection with the reports of the "eyewitnesses" of these things. What he wrote under the inspiration of the Holy Spirit is trustworthy.

from the first.—King James says, "from the very first," while R. S. V.

says, "for some time past." The Greek term is translated in various ways. It simply marks the starting point from which the action proceeds. Jesus said to Nicodemus, "except one be born anew—or from above—he cannot see the kingdom of God" (John 3:3). We think of it as the new birth or being born again.

Luke researched this project to the point at which he began the written account, that is, to the birth of John the Baptist and the birth of Jesus.

Why didn't Luke begin at the same point from which Matthew presents his account of the life of the Messiah? For one thing, Matthew evidently wrote to the Jews who were proud of their birth records. They kept them with great care and traced their ancestry back to the original twelve tribes of Israel. They were also fond of the Old Testament prophecies about the Messiah. Matthew caught the attention of his readers immediately with the genealogical table that shows Jesus' legal right to the throne of David. He traces the royal line of Jesus from David and Abraham through Solomon to Joseph the "husband of Mary of whom was born Jesus who is called Christ." He proved his claim that Jesus is Messiah by showing how He fulfilled the prophecies of the Old Testament.

It is altogether likely that Luke was familiar with Matthew's account of the Gospel of Christ. But Luke wrote to Theophilus, a Gentile. His background was different; he may not have been familiar with these prophecies. Luke evidently thought it best to put the genealogy of Jesus after the account of the birth and baptism of Jesus. He gave Theophilus evidence that Jesus is the Son of God before tracing His line (the blood line) through Nathan the son of David to Adam, the son of God.

But why didn't he go all the way back to the point at which John begins his account of the Word who became flesh and revealed the Father (John 1:1, 18)? John's "in beginning" reached to eternity as man views the past. It helps to understand what he meant when he wrote, "The Word became flesh." This is John's way of presenting the virgin birth of Jesus. Matthew and Luke give the complete details. It was Luke's purpose to write about the things that had been reported by eyewitnesses and which he had carefully examined so that Theophilus could be fully assured that Jesus is Son of God and Son of Man—He really is God and He really is man.

to write unto thee in order.—Luke did not give a chronological

15

account of the life of Jesus or a geographical report of His journies. He did write a logically connected account of the One whom he calls "Son of God" and "Son of Man." The arrangement of his materials differs in some cases from that of Matthew or Mark. This difference may be traced to the fact that Jesus repeated the things He taught on various occasions. For example, the Sermon on the Mount could have been delivered on many occasions. He could have changed the arrangement of the materials or the wording to suit the occasion. This may account for the differences between the report of Matthew in chapters five, six, and seven of his Gospel and what Luke says in chapter six of his account of the Life of Jesus. Luke's Gospel is an orderly, logically arranged account of the material he selected to give Theophilus something solid on which to base his belief in Jesus as the Son of God and the Son of Man.

Luke divides his materials into three sections. The first presents the evidence that shows Jesus to be the Son of God and the Son of Man (1:5-4:13). It begins with the birth narratives and continues through the accounts of Jesus' baptism and temptation. The second and largest section tells about Jesus' ministry of teaching and healing (4:14-21:38). It presents the Galilean ministry (4:14-9:50), the ministry of Jesus on the way to Jerusalem which included the Perean ministry (9:51-19:28), and the closing events of His ministry which occurred in Jerusalem (18:29-21:38). The third section centers around the crucifixion and resurrection (22:1-24:53). It tells about the arrest and trial (22:1-23:32), the crucifixion and burial (23:33-56), and His resurrection, appearances, and ascension (24:1-53).

most excellent Theophilus.—Who is Theophilus? His name suggests that he was a Gentile. It means friend of God or one whom God loved. The title "most excellent" suggests official rank; he was a man of some importance in his day. The fact that Luke says that he had been instructed in these matters about which he was writing suggests that he was a Christian, although some are in doubt about this point. When and where Luke first came in contact with him, we have no way of knowing. It is an interesting fact that about one-fourth of the New Testament—The Gospel of Luke and The Acts—was addressed to this man.

The Promise of the Birth of John

Scripture

1:5-25 There was in the days of Herod, king of Judae, a certain priest named Zacharias, of the course of Abijah: and he had a wife of the daughters of Aaron, and her name was Elisabeth. 6 And they were both righteous before God, walking in all the commandments and ordinances of the Lord blameless. 7 And they had no child, because that Elisabeth was barren, and they both were *now* well stricken in years.

8 Now it came to pass, while he executed the priest's office before God in the order of his course, 9 according to the custom of the priest's office, his lot was to enter into the temple of the Lord and burn incense. 10 And the whole multitude of the people were praying without at the hour of incense. 11 And there appeared unto him an angel of the Lord standing on the right side of the altar of incense. 12 And Zacharias was troubled when he saw *him,* and fear fell upon him. 13 But the angel said unto him, Fear not, Zacharias: because thy supplication is heard, and thy wife Elisabeth shall bear thee a son, and thou shalt call his name John. 14 And thou shalt have joy and gladness; and many shall rejoice at his birth. 15 For he shall be great in the sight of the Lord, and he shall drink no wine nor strong drink; and he shall be filled with the Holy Spirit, even from his mother's womb. 16 And many of the children of Israel shall he turn unto the Lord their God. 17 And he shall go before his face in the spirit and power of Elijah, to turn the hearts of the fathers to the children, and the disobedient *to walk* in the wisdom of the just; to make ready for the Lord a people prepared *for him.* 18 And Zacharias said unto the angel, Whereby shall I know this? for I am an old man, and my wife well stricken in years. 19 And the angel answering said unto him, I am Gabriel, that stand in the presence of God; and I was sent to speak unto thee, and to bring thee these good tidings. 20 And behold, thou shalt be silent and not able to speake, until the day that these things shall come to pass, because thou believedst not my words, which shall be fulfilled in their season. 21 And the people were waiting for Zacharias, and they marvelled while he tarried in the temple. 22 And when he came out, he could not speak unto them: and they perceived that he had seen a vision in the temple: and he continued making signs unto them, and remained dumb. 23 And

it came to pass, when the days of his ministration were fulfilled, he daparted unto his house.

24 And after these days Elisabeth his wife conceived; and she hid herself five months, saying, 25 Thus hath the Lord done unto me in the days wherein he looked upon *me,* to take away my reproach among men.

Comments

in the days of Herod.—This is Herod the Great, king of Judea. He died shortly after the birth of Jesus. He was an Idumean, that is, a descendant of Esau. Luke also mentions Herod the king in Acts 12:1 without saying that he was the grandson of this one mentioned in Luke 1:5. Theophilus must have been aware of these details and did not need to have them pointed out to him. His full title was Herod Agrippa I. He was the father of King Agrippa before whom Paul made his defense. Another son of Herod the Great was Archelaus who ruled in Judea after the death of his father (Matt. 2:22). Herod the tetrarch, another son of Herod the Great, ruled in Galilee and figured in the trial of Jesus (Lk. 23:7-12). This whole family from the grandfather who slew the babes at the birth of Jesus to the king before whom Paul made his defense seems to be arrayed against Christ and His church.

Herodias was the daughter of Aristobulus, another son of Herod the Great. She married her uncle, Philip I, but left him to marry another uncle, Herod the tetrarch. John the Baptist was beheaded by this Herod at the request of Salome the daughter of Herodias, because he condemned the marriage.

the course of Abijah.—In the days of David the priests were organized into twenty-four groups, the eighth of which was that of Abijah. Each group in turn performed the functions of the priesthood. The arrangement was still in force in the days of Zacharias.

Zacharias . . . Elizabeth.—This childless old couple were descendants of Aaron. They were "righteous before God." Luke says that in God's sight they lived a blameless life in accord with all the commandments and ordinances of the Lord. He doesn't say that they had never committed a sin, but they were not habitually sinning for they were blameless in the sight of the Lord.

John the Baptist had the good fortune to have parents who set the proper example for him. Every child has the right to have such a backround, but, unfortunately, very few do. Timothy, devoted servant of the Lord that he was, had two generations of faithful ones back of him (II Tim. 1:5). How we should thank the Lord for our godly parents! The return to God's standard for the home is one of the crying needs of this day.

It has been said repeatedly that no one could live up to the requirements of the law, but Luke affirms—and he had researched these reports so that he was sure of his ground—that the parents of John did. God has not required us to do the impossible, and all of us at all times should try to do all things He has told us in His Word to do. See James 1:18-25.

his lot to enter the temple of the Lord and burn incense.—the altar of incense stood before the curtain that separated the Holy Place from the Holy of Holies. While the priest was burning the incense, the people were outside praying. Some believe that a priest got to perform this task only once in a lifetime.

there appeared unto him an angel of the Lord.—Zacharias was greatly disturbed when he saw the angel standing at the right side of the altar. But the angel spoke reassuringly to him and told him that his prayer had been heard and that Elizabeth would bear a son and that he should name him John.

In the days of the fathers, God spoke on many occasions in many ways as He revealed His will to them. For example, the angel of the Lord spoke to Gideon in the days of the Judges (Judges 6:11-12). He does not speak to us in this manner, for at the end of these days of revelation He spoke with finality and completeness and authority in the One who bears the name Son (Heb. 1:1-2). We have that message—a message that is just as up-to-date now as it was when first spoken—in the Bible.

he shall be filled with the Holy Spirit.—What is said about John who was to be great in the sight of the Lord and drink no wine or strong drink reminds us of the Nazarite vow. The law of the Nazarite is given in Num. 6:1-8. Samson was a Nazarite; he was to be dedicated to the Lord all the days of his life (Judges 13:7). Hannah promised the Lord that she would give her son, Samuel, to the Lord all the days of his life and that no razor should touch his head (I Sam. 1:11). Apparently, John also conformed to this law, for he dedicated himself to the Lord all the days of his life.

This background sheds light on the meaning of the words about John's being filled with the Holy Spirit from the time of his birth.

19

Note the difference between this and what is said about Elizabeth's being filled with the Holy Spirit (1:41). She was given power by the Holy Spirit to speak words of praise. The same is true of Zacharias (1:67) and of the apostles and prophets (Acts 2:1-4; II Pet 1:21). But it cannot be said that John was inspired by the Holy Spirit to speak from the time of his birth. His inspiration as a prophet is accounted for in John 3:34. But John was filled with a spirit of dedication and consecration to the Lord from the time of his birth.

Luke says that Barnabas "was a good man, and full of the Holy Spirit and of faith" (Acts 11:24), but this does not indicate that he was inspired like Elizabeth or Zacharias. This may be the reason he went to Tarsus and found Saul—an inspired apostle—and brought him to Antioch where for a whole year they taught the people. The indwelling of the Holy Spirit in the believer, in all probability, implies not miraculous power but consecration to the Lord, for every baptized believer in the Lord is to live a life of dedication from the time of his new birth.

in the spirit and power of Elijah.—The prophecy of Elijah's coming is found in Mal. 4:5. When the Jews asked John, "Art thou Elijah?" he said, "I am not" for he was not literally Elijah. See John 1:21. But Jesus indicates that the prophecy of Malachi was fulfilled in John—that is, figuratively, he was Elijah. See Matt. 11:14 and 17:10-13. Luke says that John came in the spirit and power of Elijah and this explains why Jesus said he was Elijah. John was like Elijah in life and mission.

turn the hearts of the fathers to the children.—John's mission in preparing a people for the Lord involved turning the interest of the fathers to their children (Deut. 6:6-9) and the children to obey their parents (Ex. 20:12; Eph. 6:1-4; Mal. 4:4-6). Many people were turned to the Lord by John's preaching.

Whereby shall I know this?—Zacharias is not the only one to ask for evidence on which to base his belief: Gideon did; Thomas did. See Judges 6:36-40 and John 20:24-29. But since Zacharias didn't believe the word of the angel Gabriel, he was given a sign that would not only establish it in his mind but also cause the people to see that something unusual had happened while he was in the temple. John was a man sent from God (John 1:6).

The Promise of the Birth of Jesus

Scripture

1:26-38 Now in the sixth month the angel Gabriel was sent from God unto a city of Galilee, named Nazareth, 27 to a virgin betrothed to a man whose name was Joseph, of the house of David; and the virgin's name was Mary. 28 And he came in unto her, and said, Hail, thou that art highly favored, the Lord *is* with thee. 29 But she was greatly troubled at the saying, and cast in her mind what manner of salutation this might be. 30 And the angel said unto her, Fear not, Mary: for thou hast found favor with God. 31 And behold, thou shalt conceive in thy womb, and bring forth a son, and shalt call his name JESUS. 32 He shall be great, and shall be called the Son of the Most High: and the Lord God shall give unto him the throne of his father David: 33 and he shall reign over the house of Jacob for ever; and of his kingdom there shall be no end. 34 And Mary said unto the angel, How shall this be, seeing I know not a man? 35 And the angel answered and said unto her, The Holy Spirit shall come upon thee, and the power of the Most High shall overshadow thee: wherefore also the holy thing which is begotten shall be called the Son of God. 36 And behold, Elizabeth thy kinswoman, she also hath conceived a son in her old age; and this is the sixth month with her that was called barren. 37 For no word from God shall be void of power. 38 And Mary said, Behold, the handmaid of the Lord; be it unto me according to thy word. And the angel departed from her.

Comments

a virgin betrothed to a man whose name was Joseph.—Matthew and Luke clearly indicate that Joseph was not the father of Jesus; he was the husband of Mary of whom was born Jesus the Christ (Matt. 1:16). Matthew and Luke present the evidence of the miraculous conception of Our Lord. Matthew, using the words of Isaiah 7:14, says, "A virgin shall conceive and bear a son." But Matthew indicates that after the birth of Jesus, Mary's firstborn son, children were born to Joseph and Mary. See Matt. 1:25. Their names are given in Matt. 13:55-56.

of the house of David.—Joseph was the descendant of David and Solomon. The legal right to the throne of David, it seems, belonged to him. As the husband of Mary, these rights would legally belong

21

to Jesus, Mary's firstborn son. But Mary was also the descendant of David, for Paul says that Jesus "was born of the seed of David according to the flesh" (Rom. 1:3).

the virgin's name was Mary.—The purity of Mary is beyond question. The sinlessness of Jesus, however, does not depend on the purity of His mother, but on the fact that He "hath been tempted in all points like as we are, yet without sin" (Heb. 4:15).

thou shalt conceive.—The conception was a miracle. There is a difference between the birth of John and of Jesus. John was born as a result of a conception that was unusual but not miraculous, for he had a human father as well as a human mother. But the birth of Jesus was the result of the miracle of the Holy Spirit. Both Matthew and Luke explain it and John supports it (John 1:1, 14).

shalt call his name JESUS.—Jesus means savior, "for he shall save his people from their sins" (Matt. 1:21). Immanuel means "God with us." Christ means Anointed and refers to Jesus' office as prophet, priest, and king. Messiah is the Hebrew term for Christ.

the throne of his father David.—Israel was constituted a theocracy at Sinai; God was the Supreme Ruler of the holy nation. In the days of Samuel, the people asked to have a king like the nations about them. Samuel assumed that they were rejecting him as their judge, but God told him that actually they were rejecting Him as king. See I Sam. 8:4-8. Later, God told Samuel to anoint David to be king over His people (I Sam. 16:1). Then God promised David that one of his descendants would reign on his throne forever. See Psa. 89:3-4. In the course of events, Solomon succeeded his father. In I Kings 2:12 it is stated that "Solomon sat upon the throne of his father David." But in I Chron. 29:23 which describes the same thing, it is stated that "Solomon sat on the throne of the Lord instead of David his father." David's throne, then, was actually the throne of the Lord. Therefore when the angel said to Mary that the Lord God would give Jesus the throne of His father David, he was referring to the throne of God. On the Day of Pentecost, Peter declared that God's promise to David had been fulfilled in the resurrection and ascension of Jesus Christ to the right hand of the throne of God. See Acts 2:30-31.

His kingdom is spiritual. He refused to allow the people to make Him king after the feeding of the five thousand (John 6:14-15). He said to Pilate, "My kingdom is not of this world" (John 18:36).

of his kingdom there shall be no end.—No other king will succeed Him. Paul says, "Then cometh the end when he shall deliver up the kingdom to God" (I Cor. 15:24). He did not contradict the angel, for he was speaking of the end of the earthly phase of the kingdom. See Peter's reference to "the eternal kingdom of our Lord and Saviour Jesus Christ" (II Pet. 1:11).

I know not a man.—Both Luke and Matthew attest the belief in the purity of Mary.

the power of the Most High.—The miracle of conception was accomplished by divine power exercised through the Holy Spirit.

The fact that the Holy Spirit is often spoken of as the One through whom God's power is exercised does not suggest that the Spirit is merely the power of God. All the attributes of deity and of personality that are assigned to the Father and to the Son by the Scriptures, are also assigned to the Holy Spirit.

the holy thing which is begotten shall be called the Son of God.—A clear reference to the deity of Jesus. Before His coming into the world, He is called the Word (John 1:1). Son of God is applied to Him (1) at the time of His birth when He became Son of God; (2) at the time of His baptism and transfiguration when He was acknowledged by the Father as His Son (Lk 3:22; 9:35); and (3) at the time of His resurrection when God had proved conclusively that He is the Son of God (Acts 13:33). See also Rom 1:3-4.

For no word of God shall be void of power.—God demonstrated that His word about the birth and resurrection of Jesus was true. This gives us reason to trust His promises about the victory of Christ and His church (II Tim. 1:12; Rev. 11:15).

Mary Visited Elizabeth

Scripture

1:39-56 And Mary arose in those days and went into the hill country with haste, into a city of Judah; 40 and entered into the house of Zacharias and saluted Elisabeth. 41 And it came to pass, when Elisabeth heard the salutation of Mary, the babe leaped in her womb; and Elisabeth was filled with the Holy Spirit; 42 and she lifted up her voice with a loud cry, and said, Blessed *art* thou among women, and blessed *is* the fruit of thy womb. 43 And whence is this to me, that the mother of my Lord should come unto me? 44 For behold, when the voice of thy salutation came into mine ears, the

babe leaped in my womb for joy. 45 And blessed *is* she that believed;
for there shall be a fulfilment of the things which have been spoken
to her from the Lord. 46 And Mary said,

My soul doth magnify the Lord,

47   And my spirit hath rejoiced in God my Saviour.
48   For he hath looked upon the low estate of his handmaid:
     For behold, from hence forth all generation shall call me
     blessed.
49   For he that is mighty hath done to me great things;
     And holy is his name.
50   And his mercy is unto generations and generations
     On them that fear him.
51   He hath showed strength with his arm;
     He hath scattered the proud in the imagination of their heart.
52   He hath put down princes from *their* thrones,
     And hath exalted them of low degree.
53   The hungry he hath filled with good things;
     And the rich he hath sent empty away
54   He hath given help to Israel his servant,
     That he might remember mercy
55   (As he spake unto our fathers)
     Toward Abraham and his seed for ever.

56 And Mary abode with her about three months, and returned
unto her house.

Comments

into the hill country with haste.—The angel had informed Mary
that Elizabeth was to give birth to a son. Mary went in haste to visit
her relative and remained with her for about three months. The
home of Zacharias and Elizabeth was in a city of Judah in the hilly
country south of Jerusalem. The name of the city is not given.

Upon her return to Nazareth, Joseph learned that she was "with
child of the Holy Spirit" (Matt. 1:18).

Elizabeth was filled with the Holy Spirit.—What she said was not
an emotional outpouring of words, but words of truth spoken under
the control of the Holy Spirit.

Blessed art thou among women.—Elizabeth and Zacharias knew that
the child to be born to them would go before the Lord who would
give remission of sins to His people. Elizabeth also knew that the
child to be born to Mary would fulfill God's promise to redeem

man from the bondage to sin. She could properly call Mary "blessed" because she was to be the mother of Our Lord. In no other way is it suggested that she is to be elevated above other godly women. It is to her credit and that of others also that she was found in the company of believers after the resurrection of the Lord (Acts 1:14). *And Mary said.*—The words of Mary—beautiful poetic words full of meaning to all believers in Christ—are the expression of the humble handmaid of the Lord. They exalt God Our Savior for His mercy and power and His remembrance of His promise to Abraham. There is no hint here that Mary was anything more than the pure, humble servant of the Lord.

God my Savior.—A reference to God, not Jesus. See also I Tim. 1:1; 2:3; Titus 3:4 which also refer to God as Savior. But see Titus 2:13 which, in all probability, refers to Jeus Christ as "the great God and Our Savior."

all generations shall call me blessed.—We can join with the saints of all the ages to thank God that Mary was able to serve the Lord as she did. And since Christ came, having been "born of woman, born under the law, that he might redeem them that were under the law" (Gal 4:4), we may also join them who obey Him that they may have the rights of sonship bestowed on them by the heavenly Father.

Toward Abraham.—See Paul's explanation of the gospel promise to Abraham which was fulfilled through Christ (Gal. 3:8, 16, 29). Mary's understanding of this promise stands in bold contrast to that of many Jews who felt that being the literal descendants of Abraham was a guarantee of their right to enter the heavenly kingdom. See Matt. 3:9; 8:11-12; and John 8:31-46.

Elizabeth Gives Birth to a Son

Scripture

1:57-80 Now Elizabeth's time was fulfilled that she should be delivered; and she brought forth a son. 58 And her neighbors and her kinsfolk heard that the Lord had magnified his mercy towards her; and they rejoiced with her. 59 And it came to pass on the eighth day, that they came to circumcise the child; and they would have called him Zacharias, after the name of his father. 60 And his mother answered and said, Not so; but he shall be called John. 61 And they said unto her, There is none of thy kindred that is called

25

by this name. 62 And they made signs to his father, what he would have him called. 63 And he asked for a writing tablet, and wrote, saying, His name is John. And they marvelled all. 64 And his mouth was opened immediately, and his tongue *loosed,* and he spake, blessing God. 65 And fear came on all that dwelt round about them: and all these sayings were noised abroad throughout all the hill country of Judaea. 66 And all that heard them laid them up in their heart, saying, What then shall this child be? For the hand of the Lord was with him.

67 And his father Zacharias was filled with the Holy Spirit, and prophesied, saying,

68 Blessed *be* the Lord, the God of Israel;
For he hath visited and wrought redemption for his people,

69 And hath raised up a horn of salvation for us
In the house of his servant David

70 (As he spake by the mouth of his holy prophets that have
been from of old),

71 Salvation from our enemies, and from the hand of all that
hate us;

72 To show mercy towards our fathers,
And to remember his holy covenant;

73 The oath which he sware unto Abraham our father,

74 To grant unto us that we being delivered out of the hand of
our enemies
Should serve him without fear,

75 In holiness and righteousness before him all our days.

76 Yea and thou, child, shalt be called the prophet of the Most
High:
For thou shalt go before the face of the Lord to make ready his
ways;

77 To give knowledge of salvation unto his people
In the remission of their sins,

78 Because of the tender mercy of our God,
Whereby the dayspring from on high shall visit us,
death;

79 To shine upon them that sit in darkness and the shadow of
To guide our feet into the way of peace.

80 And the child grew, and waxed strong in spirit, and was in the deserts till the day of his showing unto Israel.

Comments

the Lord had magnified his mercy.—Zacharias and Elizabeth had been childless for a long time. The Lord showed mercy on them, and Elizabeth brought forth a son as the angel promised Zacharias. These godly parents considered it a privilege to rear a son to serve the Lord. Many parents feel the same way about it today. A revival of that wholesome attitude toward family life is needed in many instances today.

The angel of the Lord had instructed Zacharias to call him John. The name means "the Lord is gracious." It was to remind all who knew the facts about his birth that God's favor was soon to be made known through Christ, the One of whom John was to be the forerunner.

All who heard about these unusual things were filled with a sense of reverence for God. It was only natural that they should ask, "What then shall this child be?"

prophesied.—Zacharias was a devout man; but the expression "filled with the Spirit" refers to the fact that he was inspired by the Holy Spirit as he spoke about the mission of John and of Jesus.

He praised God who had provided redemption for His people. Redemption means release, and the New Testament it usually means release from the slavery of sin. Christ redeemed His people by His blood (Eph 1:7). He is also the "horn of our salvation," for it is by His power that salvation is brought to all who believe, whether Jew or Greek (Rom. 1:16). This horn of salvation was raised up in the house of God's servant David. The Bible repeatedly emphasizes this truth: Christ was born of the seed of David. See Psa. 89:3-4; Jer. 23:5; Rom. 1:3-4.

prophet of the Most High.—John was the last of the prophets who prophesied before Christ. Jesus, speaking about John, said that he was more than a prophet. He had the privilege of presenting Messiah to Israel. They had been waiting for Him so long (Lk 7:26; I Pet. 1:10-12). His coming was like the dawning of the new day. It brought light and life to those who sat in darkness—the darkness of sin and death.

the child grew.—The reference suggests the normal growth and development of the child. Nothing is known about his life or his parents during the period between his birth and his appearance to Israel. It is natural to suppose that the parents who were old when

27

he was born had died before he began his ministry. Perhaps his seclusion made his appearance in the wilderness as a prophet all the more startling to Israel.

Summary

Luke was ready to write to Theophilus. His papyrus roll was on his writing table. Before him were the records of his investigation into the thrilling story of Jesus the Son of God and the Son of Man. Perhaps Mark's Gospel and maybe Matthew's too were there before him. He was eager to write the whole story, for he was convinced that it would give Theophilus the confidence he needed in these things in which he had already been instructed.

As he thought of all the things that might be written and looked at the one papyrus roll, he knew that it would never hold all that he wanted to say. He would have to write a second letter to Theophilus, but just now he would tell about all the things that Jesus began both to do and to teach and bring the story to a climax with the account of His crucifixion, the evidence of His resurrection, and the story of His ascension that took place just after He had told His disciples to preach the gospel to all the nations, beginning at Jerusalem. In the second letter he would tell how the apostles preached the gospel of Christ in Jerusalm, then Judea and Samaria, and finally how Paul and his companions of whom Luke was one brought the gospel to Rome.

His first problem was to determine the point at which to begin. He probably knew how Mark had plunged into the story of the ministry of Jesus without telling about the birth of John or the birth and childhood of Jesus. He may have known that Matthew began with the birth record of Jesus Christ the son of David and the son of Abraham. But as he thought of Theophilus, who like himself was a Greek, he decided to begin at the first of the story and tell about the birth of John and the birth of Jesus who, as he had become thoroughly convinced, was the Son of God and the Son of Man.

Theophilus would need to be fully assured that the birth of Jesus was the result of a miraculous conception. He made his point clear with the presentation of the facts about which he had made careful investigation. And to make this even clearer, he told about the birth of John. John's parents were a childless elderly couple, but God showed His mercy toward them and sent the angel to tell

28

Zacharias that Elizabeth was to bear a son and that he was to name him John. But Jesus was born of the virgin Mary. The angel told her that although she knew no man, she would conceive and bear a Son and name His Jesus. The power of God exercised by the Holy Spirit would accomplish this. For that reason, the child would be called the Son of God.

Luke wanted Theophilus to be able to read the words of praise spoken by Mary, the humble servant of the Lord, as she thought of God's mercy toward her and toward His people. Her words magnified the Lord. He also told about the words spoken by Zacharias the father of John. He praised God for His tender mercy and for the light that was to shine upon those who sat in darkness waiting for the new day.

Questions

1. Why did Luke undertake the task of writing the Life of Christ?
2. How did he prepare for the task?
3. What was his aim in writing?
4. Who was Theophilus?
5. At what point did he begin his record of the Life of Christ?
6. Who was Herod?
7. What did Luke say about Zacharias and Elizabeth?
8. What was Zacharias doing when the angel appeared to him?
9. What did the angel say about the mission of John?
10. What is meant by "the spirit and power of Elijah"?
11. What effect would John's message have on the fathers?
12. What happened to Zacharias as a sign by which he knew that the promise of the angel would be fulfilled?
13. What evidence does Luke present to show his conviction that Jesus was born of the virgin Mary as the result of a miraculous conception?
14. What was Mary's relation, at the time of the angel's announcement, to Joseph?
15. Why, when, and how did Jesus receive the throne of David?
16. What was said about the duration of His kingdom?
17. Why was Jesus called the Son of God?
18. Where did Zacharias and Elizabeth live?
19. What did Luke mean when he said that Elizabeth was filled with the Holy Spirit?
20. Why was Mary to be called blessed among women?

29

21. What did Luke say about Mary's response to the announcement of the angel?
22. What promise made to Abraham was fulfilled by the coming of Jesus?
23. How does Luke carefully distinguish between the facts about the birth of John and the facts about the birth of Jesus?
24. What did the people say when they learned about the birth of John?
25. How is their question answered by the words spoken by Zacharias as he was inspired by the Holy Spirit?
26. What is known about John from the time of his birth to the time of his appearing as a prophet to Israel?

Outline

A. He told about the birth of Jesus (1-21).
   1. He began with the account of the trip from Nazareth to Bethlehem where the Child was to be born (1-7).
      a) It was at the time of the enrollment ordered by Caesar Augustus when Quirinius was governor of Syria (1-3).
      b) Joseph went from Nazareth to Bethlehem where the family of David had to go to be enrolled, taking with him Mary who was betrothed to him and who was soon to give birth to the Child (4-5).
      c) While there she gave birth to her firstborn Son and wrapped Him in swaddling clothes and laid Him in a manger (6-7).
      d) There was no room for them in the inn (7).
   2. He told the story of the angels and the shepherds (8-20).
      a) How the good news came to the shepherds (8-12).
         (1) They were keeping watch over their flocks at night when the angel of the Lord appeared to them (8-9).
         (2) The angel said, "I bring you good news of great joy for all the people, for there is born to you this day in the city of David a Savior who is Christ the Lord."
         (3) The angel gave them a sign by which they were to identify Him—they were to find the babe in swaddling clothes lying in a manger.
      b) Then the heavenly host sang praises to God and peace to men (13-14).
      c) The shepherds went to Bethlehem to confirm the angel's message (15-20).
         (1) They found Joseph and Mary, and the Child lying in the manger.
         (2) They told the amazing story of what they had learned about the Child.
         (3) Mary kept these things in her heart and thought about their meaning.
         (4) The shepherds went back to their flocks praising God that they had seen what the angel had told them.

31

3. He told about the naming of the Child (21).
   a) It was at the time of the circumcision on the eighth day.
   b) His name was called JESUS.
   c) This was the name the angel had told Mary to call Him.
B. He told about the presentation of the Child to the Lord (22-40).
   1. Mary and Joseph brought Him to Jerusalem to present Him to the Lord according to the law of Moses (22-24).
      a) It was after the days of purification prescribed by the law of Moses.
      b) They offered according to the law of the Lord a pair of turtledoves or two young pigeons.
   2. Simeon, inspired by the Holy Spirit, spoke about the Child (25-35).
      a) Some things about Simeon (25-29).
         (1) He was a righteous and devout man living in Jerusalem.
         (2) He had been looking for the consolation of Israel.
         (3) It had been revealed to him by the Holy Spirit that he would not die before he had seen the Lord's Christ.
         (4) He was in the temple when the parents brought the Child Jesus.
      b) What he said (28-35).
         (1) About the Child.
            (a) He was the fulfillment of the Lord's promise.
            (b) This Child was a light for revelation to the Gentiles and the glory of Israel.
         (2) To the parents as they marvelled at the things he had said about the Child.
            (a) He told Mary that the Child was set for the rising and falling of many in Israel and for a sign to be spoken against.
            (b) He told Mary that a sword was to pierce her soul that thoughts out of many hearts might be revealed.
   3. Anna spoke about the Child (36-38).
      a) Some things about Anna.

    (1) She was a prophetess who spent her time in the temple worshipping, fasting, and praying.

    (2) She was the daughter of Phanuel of the tribe of Asher.

    (3) She was an elderly widow.

  b) She spoke about Jesus to all who were looking for the redemption of Jerusalem.

  4. Following the presentation, they returned to Nazareth (39-40).

C. He told about the trip to Jerusalem at the passover feast when Jesus was twelve years old (41-52).

  1. After the parents started home, Jesus remained in Jerusalem hearing the teachers and asking questions that amazed them.

  2. The parents had supposed that He was with friends and relatives who had accompanied them, but on discovering that He was not with them they returned to Jerusalem and found Him in the temple.

    a) Mary said, "Son, why did you do this to us? Your father and I were looking for you, sorrowing."

    b) Jesus said, "Why did you look for me? Didn't you know that I must be in my Father's house?"

    c) They didn't understand what He meant.

  3. Jesus went with them back to Nazareth where He was subject to them, growing in wisdom and stature and in favor with God and man.

The Birth of Jesus

Scripture

2:1-21 Now it came to pass in those days, there went out a decree from Caesar Augustus, that all the world should be enrolled. 2 This was the first enrolment made when Quirinius was governor of Syria. 3 And all went to enrol themselves, every one to his own city. 4 And Joseph also went up from Galilee, out of the city of Nazareth, into Judaea, to the city of David, which is called Bethlehem, because he was of the house and family of David; 5 to enrol himself with Mary, who was betrothed to him, being great with child. 6 And it came to pass, while they were there, the days were fulfilled that she should be delivered. 7 And she brought forth her firstborn son; and she wrapped him in swaddling clothes, and laid him in a manger, because there was no room for them in the inn.

8 And there were shepherds in the same country abiding in the field, and keeping watch by night over their flock. 9 And an angel of the Lord stood by them, and the glory of the Lord shone round about them: and they were sore afraid. 10 And the angel said unto them, Be not afraid; for behold, I bring you good tidings of great joy which shall be to all the people: 11 for there is born to you this day in the city of David a Saviour, who is Christ the Lord. 12 And this *is* the sign unto you: Ye shall find a babe wrapped in swaddling clothes, and lying in a manger. 13 And suddenly there was with the angel a multitude of the heavenly host praising God, and saying,

14   Glory to God in the highest,
    And on earth peace among men in whom he is well pleased.
15 And it came to pass, when the angels went away from them into heaven, the shepherds said one to another, Let us now go even unto Bethlehem, and see this thing that is come to pass, which the Lord hath made known unto us. 16 And they came with haste, and found both Mary and Joseph, and the babe lying in the manger. 17 And when they saw it, they made known concerning the saying which was spoken to them about this child. 18 And all that heard it wondered at the things which were spoken unto them by the shepherds. 19 But Mary kept all these sayings, pondering them in her heart. 20 And the shepherds returned, glorifying and praising God for all the things that they had heard and seen, even as it was spoken unto them.

Comments

a decree from Caesar.—By order of the Roman Emperor all the people of the world who came under his authority were to be enrolled. It was a combined census and assessment with taxation as an important part of it.

Augustus reigned from 30 B. C. to 14 A. D. Historians point out that his reign was characterized by peace that extended to almost all parts of the world. But the most significant event that occurred during his reign, which was little noticed by the Romans at the time, was the birth of Jesus, the Prince of Peace. Luke shows himself as a reliable historian reporting two of the most important events of the first century, the life of Christ and the history of His church.

to the city of David.—The decree required each man to go to the city of his own family. In Joseph's case, it was necessary to go to Bethlehem, the city of David, for he was of the house and family of David.

The prophecy of Micah who lived some 700 years before the birth of Christ says that He was to be born in Bethlehem (Micah 5:2; Matt. 2:5-6). Now the kingdom of Rome was only in its infancy when Micah prophesied. How could Micah foresee the day when the mighty Caesar would be able to issue a decree that would cause Joseph to leave his home in Nazareth and with Mary his wife go to Bethlehem that her child might be born in the city of David? The Holy Spirit spoke through the prophet!

Joseph was fully aware of the responsibility he had assumed under the direction of the Lord (Matt. 1:20-25). He took Mary with him because he was aware of the nearness of the birth of the Child.

her firstborn son.—Jesus was the first child born to Mary. "Firstborn" does not necessarily imply that she gave birth to other children, but Matthew's statement about the relation of Joseph and Mary after the birth of Jesus does indicate clearly that they had other children. The names of Jesus' brothers are given in Matt. 13:55-56. His sisters are referred to in the same passage. Paul mentions James the Lord's brother whom he visited in Jerusalem (Gal. 1:19).

and laid him in a manger.—In simple language, Luke related the humble circumstances of the birth of the Savior. There was no room for them in the inn. The crowded condition of the city at the time of the enrollment made it necessary for Joseph to find quarters wherever possible. The fact that there was no place in the inn for them does not suggest that Bethlehem was rejecting the Christ. They who were His own people did later by deliberate action reject Him before Pilate and cry out for Him to be crucified. God held them accountable for that terrible deed (Acts 2:22-24), but not for any discourtesy which some assume was shown by the innkeeper to Mary and Joseph.

shepherds in the same country.—Humble shepherds were the first to hear about the birth of the Savior. But later, as Matthew relates, wise men came to see the new-born King and to worship Him with gifts of gold, frankincense, and murrh.

an angel of the Lord.—Angels announced the birth of the Lord to the shepherds. They ministered to Him after the temptation and in the Garden of Gethsemane. They were present at His resurrection and ascension. They will be with Him when He comes again. They are ministering spirits sent forth to do service for the sake of them who shall inherit salvation (Heb. 1:14), but they were never permitted to tell a sinner what to do to be saved. That message must be told by men.

I bring you good tidings.—The good news about the Savior is still the most thrilling message that can be given to the lost sinner. Luke is careful throughout his story of Jesus to set Him forth in His wonderful role as Savior.

Christ the Lord.—Christ or Messiah refers to His office as prophet, priest, and king. What does Lord mean? On the Day of Pentecost, Peter declared that God had made His both Lord and Christ, that is, this Jesus whom they had crucified and whom God had raised from the dead. Jews had long been used to pronouncing the word "Lord" when they read the word "Jehovah" (more properly YAHVEH) in the Old Testament Scriptures. When the Hebrew Scriptures were translated into Greek about 250 B. C., this Hebrew word "Yahveh" was translated "Lord." Jews were familiar with that translation in the days of Jesus and the apostles. When they heard Peter say that Jesus is Lord, they must have understood him to say that Jesus is the eternal living God. Luke has presented evidence of His deity in the facts about His birth and does not hesitate to tell Theophilus that He is the Son of God as well as the Son of Man. His authority is upheld in the word "Christ" for He is not only prophet, and priest, but also KING.

the sign unto you.—The angel gave the shepherds the sign which they could investigate and know that the child they found in the manger was the Christ.

on earth peace.—This is not merely the cessation of wars among men. It refers primarily to the peace that should exist between men and God, for sinful man in reality is at war with God. Peace may be had only by accepting the terms dictated by the Prince of Peace. See Acts 10:36; 11:18; 2:36-39. Peace is possible through the blood of Christ. "Being justified by faith, we have peace with God through our Lord Jesus Christ" (Rom 5:1). "Much more then, being justified by his blood, shall we be saved from the wrath of God through him. For it, while we were enemies, we were reconciled to God through the death of his Son, much more, being reconciled, shall we be saved by his life" (Rom 5:9-10). Enmity was destroyed and peace made possible at the cross (Eph. 2:15-16). God's peace that passes understanding guards the hearts and thoughts of those who have been reconciled to Him through Christ (Phil. 4:6-7). And this becomes the real foundation upon which peace between men on earth can be built (Isa. 2:2-4).

men in whom he is well pleased.—Commentators differ as to the meaning and rendering of this text. It probably should be rendered, "men of good will." But what does that mean? To say that it means men who are well disposed toward one another is to ignore the fact that the angels spoke of God's favor toward men in sending them the Savior, Christ the Lord. God is well disposed toward men, for although all have sinned and have fallen short of His approval He has provided the means of blotting out their sins and reconciling them to Himself. This in no way implies that He was pleased with their sins, but He was pleased to grant to them an opportunity to repent (Acts 11:18).

and the babe lying in a manger.—The shepherds went to Bethlehem on the day of His birth and found the babe lying in a manger. But when the wise men arrived in Bethlehem they "came into the house and saw the young child with Mary his mother" (Matt. 1: 11). This suggests that their visit was at a later date and that Joseph had found a house for his family, for they were no longer in the temporary quarters which they occupied when there was no place for them in the inn.

Mary kept all these things.—The memories of Mary the mother of Jesus were filled with those things about Him. She remembered the words of the angel as he told of the Child who was to be born. At the time she thought about the meaning of the heavenly message. And when the shepherds came telling her of the angel who spoke of the birth of the Savior who is Christ the Lord, Mary kept these things in her heart pondering their significance. And the words He spoke to her when He was twelve years old were also added to the memories she had kept in her heart. In all probability she did not fully understand them until that day when she stood at the foot of His cross and heard Him say, "Father, into thy hands I commend my spirit." At least, we know that she was with that little company of believers after the resurrection of Christ (Acts 1:14).

Did Luke learn of Mary's memories from her? He does not say. He could have—assuming that she was still alive when he was

37

checking every detail of this gospel story. They could have been given to him directly by the Holy Spirit.

when eight days were fulfilled for circumcising him.—Circumcision was given originally to Abraham and later to the Jews (John 7: 22). Since Jesus was born under the law, His parents complied with its requirements.

His name was called JESUS.—Both Mary and Joseph had been informed that they were to call His name JESUS. There was no problem about it as there had been with the relatives when John was named.

Presenting the Child to the Lord

Scripture

2:22-40 And when the days of their purification according to the law of Moses were fulfilled, they brought him up to Jerusalem, to present him to the Lord 23 (as it is written in the law of the Lord, Every male that openeth the womb shall be called holy to the Lord), 24 and to offer a sacrifice according to that which is said in the law of the Lord, A pair of turtledoves, or two young pigeons. 25 And behold, there was a man in Jerusalem, whose name was Simeon; and this man was righteous and devout, looking for the consolation of Israel: and the Holy Spirit was upon him. 26 And it had been revealed unto him by the Holy Spirit, that he should not see death, before he had seen the Lord's Christ. 27 And he came in the Spirit into the temple: and when the parents brought in the child Jesus, that they might do concerning him after the custom of the law, 28 then he received him into his arms, and blessed God, and said,

29 Now lettest thou thy servant depart, Lord,
    According to thy word, in peace;
30 For mine eyes have seen thy salvation,
31 Which thou hast prepared before the face of all peoples;
32 A light for revelation to the Gentiles,
    And the glory of thy people Israel.

33 And his father and his mother were marvelling at the things which were spoken concerning him; 34 and Simeon blessed them, and said unto Mary his mother, Behold, this *child* is set for the falling and the rising of many in Israel; and for a sign which is spoken against; 35 yea and a sword shall pierce through thine own

soul; that thoughts out of many hearts may be revealed. 36 And there was one Anna, a prophetess, the daughter of Phanuel, of the tribe of Asher (she was of a great age, having lived with a husband seven years from her virginity, 37 and she had been a widow even unto fourscore and four years), who departed not from the temple, worshipping with fastings and supplications night and day. 38 And coming up at that very hour she gave thanks unto God, and spake of him to all them that were looking for the redemption of Jersusalem. 39 And when they had accomplished all things that were according to the law of the Lord, they returned into Galilee, to their own city Nazareth.

40 And the child grew, and waxed strong, filled with wisdom: and the grace of God was upon him.

Comments

purification according to the law of Moses.—See Lev. 12:1-8 for this law of purification. It was a ceremonial purification in connection with the birth of a child. It had nothing to do with so-called "original sin." The reference to their cleansing does not suggest that Jesus had inherited the taint of Adams' sin. Adam's sin did involve all of his descendants in physical death (Rom. 5-12). But "as in Adam all die, so also in Christ shall all be made alive" (I Cor. 15:22).

holy to the Lord.—All of the firstborn were to be dedicated to the Lord, because He had saved them from death during the plague in Egypt (Ex. 13:1-6). Later, the Lord took the tribe of Levi instead of the firstborn (Num. 3:11-12). The law of redemption of the firstborn of man is given in Num. 18:15.

A pair of turtledoves.—The law provided for those who could not afford a lamb. They were allowed to take a pair of turtledoves or two young pigeons and offer them as a burnt offering and as a sin offering (Lev. 12:8). The fact that Mary and Joseph brought such an offering indicates something of their humble circumstances.

the consolation of the Lord.—Israel had been waiting for the coming of Messiah for a long time. They needed someone to help them in their weakness, someone to console them in their sorrow; they needed someone to save them from their sins.

Simeon had been told that he would not die until he had seen the Lord's Christ, for He is the consolation of Israel and the Savior of His people. The Holy Spirit who revealed this to him gave him the words he spoke to Mary and Joseph about the Child. He spoke of Him as salvation for the Lord's people, a light for revelation to the Gentiles, and the glory of Israel.

Christ provided salvation for His people through His death on the cross. He gives light that reveals the way through the preaching of His Word even to Gentiles. He is the glory—the presence of God—to Israel.

the falling and rising of many in Israel.—Christ was a stone of stumbling. Just as one might stumble over a protruding rock in his pathway, some stumbled over Christ. They were the ones who had their own idea about what Messiah should do for them: overcome the Roman bondage and restore their national dignity. But many who had fallen by the wayside because of sin were to be raised up and set on the highway of holiness and dignity in the sight of the Lord.

sign that is spoken against.—Men ridiculed Jesus as He was dying on the cross, but the cross was a sign of God's love for the world and His power to save the believer (I Cor 1:18-25). His resurrection is the cornerstone of our faith (Rom. 10:9-10). It is because the apostles preached the resurrection of the Lord that they were persecuted (Acts 4:1-4).

a sword shall pierce through thine own soul.—These words refer to the cross and to the sorrow of Mary as she watched Him there (John 19:25). No other experience is mentioned in the Gospels that can fulfill this prophecy of her grief. What memories flooded her mind in that tragic hour! How her grief must have been intensified by them! But that sorrow was turned into gladness when she knew that He had been raised from the dead.

looking for the redemption of Jerusalem.—The majority of the people were looking for someone to release them from Roman bondage. Some were looking for the Savior who would redeem them from the bondage to sin. This is what Christ came to do, but the Roman bondage continued until it reached its awful climax in the destruction of Jerusalem in 70 A. D.

to their own city Nazareth.—Matthew says that they went back to Bethlehem and from Bethlehem they went to Egypt where they stayed until Herod was dead. Then they came back to Judea, but because Archelaus was ruling instead of his father, Joseph was warned in a dream to go to Galilee (Matt. 2:13-23). Both Luke and Matthew agree that they went to Nazareth, but Luke does not

40

tell of the trip to Egypt. Luke usually gives these interesting side-lights, but in this case did not choose to do so.

At the Age of Twelve

Scripture

2:41-52 And his parents went every year to Jerusalem at the feast of the passover. 42 And when he was twelve years old, they went up after the custom of the feast; 43 and when they had fulfilled the days, as they were returning, the boy Jesus tarried be-hind in Jerusalem; and his parents knew it not; 44 but supposing him to be in the company, they went a day's journey; and they sought for him among their kinsfolk and acquaintance: 45 and when they found him not, they returned to Jerusalem, seeking for him. 46 And it came to pass, after three days they found him in the temple, sitting in the midst of the teachers, both hearing them, and asking them questions: 47 and all that heard him were amazed at his understanding and his answers. 48 And when they saw him, they were astonished; and his mother said unto him, Son, why hast thou thus dealt with us? behold, thy father and I sought thee sor-rowing. 49 And he said unto them, How is it that ye sought me? knew ye not that I must be in my Father's house? 50 And they understood not the saying which he spake unto them. 51 And he went down with them, and came to Nazareth; and he was subject unto them: and his mother kept all *these* sayings in her heart.

52 And Jesus advanced in wisdom and stature, and in favor with God and men.

Comments

the feast of the passover.—This is the sacrifice of the Lord's pass-over when He passed over the firstborn in the houses of the people of Israel and did not slay them when all the firstborn of the Egyptians were slain. See Ex. 12:27. The law required the men of Israel to appear before the Lord three times a year; one of those times was at the passover. Ex. 34:22-24. The parents of Jesus ob-served this custom and every year went to Jerusalem for the pass-over feast.

God promised the people of Israel that their lands would be pro-tected during these feasts when the men were away from home (Ex. 34:24). But it was at the passover time that the Romans besieged the city of Jerusalem and destroyed the temple and killed thousands of those who had gone there to worship according to that ancient custom. That awful retribution came upon them because they had forfeited their right to claim God's protection; they had crucified His Son, and the Son had warned them in these words: "Behold your house is left unto you desolate" (Matt. 23:38).

supposing him to be in the company.—Joseph had always exercised watchful care over Mary and the Child Jesus. There is no indication that he was negligent at this time. It was perfectly normal to suppose that Jesus was with the relatives and friends as the group made their way homeward. Mary seems to blame herself, for she said to Jesus, "Your father and I sought for you, sorrowing." This is not a case of delinquent parents who never care for their children. Both Mary and Joseph knew that they could trust Jesus, for he was now twelve years old and had always been obedient to them.

The incident shows a brief glimpse of Him as the Son of God who was concerned about the things of His Father.

all that heard him were amazed.—Not just a precocious twelve year old boy! We know that when He was mature all the treasures of wisdom and knowledge were hidden in Him (Col. 2:3). We are inclined to look upon Him even at the age of twelve as the One who revealed the wisdom of God (I Cor. 1:30). It must be admitted, however, that this reference alone would not necessarily indicate supernatural wisdom.

he was subject to them.—The parents were obedient to the law of Moses and to the instruction of the Lord in caring for this Child who had been entrusted to them. Jesus was obedient to loving parents who had demonstrated before Him what it meant to obey.

"Children, obey your parents in the Lord: for this is right. Honor thy father and thy mother (which is the first commandment with promise), that it may be well with thee, and that thou mayest live long on the earth" (Eph 6:1-3).

And Jesus advanced.—His development was normal for He grew intellectually, physically, spiritually, and socially.

Summary

With boldness born of complete confidence that what he was about to write was the truth, Luke told about the birth of Jesus.

The decree of Caesar had gone out and it had affected even the people who were living in the land where once David had reigned as king. Joseph was required to leave Nazareth and go to Bethlehem,

the city of David, to enroll himself with Mary his wife. And
while they were there, Mary gave birth to her firstborn Son and
wrapped Him in swaddling clothes and laid Him in a manger, for
there was no room for them in the inn.

Shepherds were watching their flocks by night, when suddenly a
brilliant light shone about them and they were greatly frightened.
The angel of the Lord was standing by them, and he said, "Be not
afraid; I bring you good news of great joy for all the people, for
unto you is born this day in the city of David a Savior who is
Christ the Lord." Then the choir of angels sang of glory to God in
the highest and of peace on earth among men of good will.

Mary and Joseph, as the law of Moses required, presented the
Child to the Lord in the temple at Jerusalem. There Simeon blessed
God for permitting his eyes to see the One who is the salvation of
all people, and Anna the prophetess spoke about Him to all who
were looking for the redemption of Jerusalem.

Luke had made careful investigation into all the reports and
records of the things about Jesus and must have known about the
flight into Egypt and return to Nazareth by way of Judea as Matthew
reports it. But he was hurrying with his story and merely said that
Mary and Joseph returned to Nazareth, for he wanted to tell Theophilus about another journey, the one that Jesus made with His
parents to Jerusalem when He was twelve years old.

Jewish families must have made a great thing out of such occasions, especially those who would be on the road several days
each way. Friends and relatives had gone with Mary and Joseph to
the passover feast. When it was over, they all started home, but
Jesus remained in Jerusalem. Sorrowing parents sought Him supposing He was with the group. But when they didn't find Him, they
returned to Jerusalem. There they found Him in the temple sitting
in the midst of the teachers, listening to them and asking them questions; and the teachers were amazed at His understanding and His
answers. To Mary's gentle rebuke—or was she blaming herself for
what had happened?—Jesus said, "Why did you seek me? Didn't you
know that I must be about my Father's business?" But Mary and
Joseph didn't understand Him.

We do not know what rejoicing was theirs when they joined the
group and journied on to their home. We do not know what resolu-
tions they may have made to guard the trust the Lord had committed to them more carefully. Luke simply says that Jesus went

with them to Nazareth and was obedient to them, and that Mary kept all these things in her heart. How precious were His mother's memories! In all probability, she is the one who shared them with Luke, and he with Theophilus, and we are blessed by the record that has been preserved for us.

Questions

1. Why did Joseph take Mary and go to Bethlehem?
2. What had Micah prophesied about the birthplace of Messiah?
3. What is known about the power of Rome at the time of Micah?
4. From the Christian point of view, what are the two most important events in the reign of Augustus?
5. What do the Scriptures say about the children of Mary and Joseph who were born after Jesus?
6. Why is He called Mary's firstborn Son?
7. What can be said about the fact that there was no room for them in the inn?
8. How does the story of the angels and the shepherds add to the evidence that proves that Jesus is the Son of God and the Son of Man?
9. What good news did the angel of the Lord bring?
10. What, in all probability, did the people understand the word "Lord" to mean when applied to Jesus?
11. What is meant by "peace on earth"?
12. What is meant by "men in whom he is well pleased"?
13. What do Matthew and Luke say about the time of the visit of the shepherds and the wise men to Bethlehem?
14. What does Luke say about the things that Mary kept in her heart?
15. Why did the parents observe the law of circumcision and presentation of the Child to the Lord?
16. What does the fact that they brought an offering of turtledoves or pigeons suggest?
17. What is meant by the consolation of Israel?
18. Who was Simeon?
19. What had the Holy Spirit revealed to him?
20. What did the Holy Spirit reveal about the Child in the words spoken by Simeon?
21. In what way was He set for the falling and rising of many?
22. What is the sign that is spoken against?

23. What is the sword that pierced Mary's heart?
24. Who was Anna?
25. What did she say about Jesus?
26. For what possible reason did Luke omit the account of the journey to Egypt?
27. What was the passover?
28. What was the custom of observing it in the days of Joseph?
29. What had the Lord promised the men of Israel who left their homes unguarded on these feast days?
30. Why, then, did the destruction of Jerusalem occur during their feast?
31. Why would Mary and Joseph suppose that Jesus was with the group when they started home?
32. Did they blame Jesus or themselves?
33. How explain Jesus' questions and answers before the teachers?
34. What lesson is there for parents in the experience of Mary and Joseph when Jesus was twelve years old?
35. What lesson for children?

CHAPTER THREE

Outline

A. Luke gives a brief account of the ministry of John the Baptist
(1-20).
  1. He told when it occurred in relation to the civil and the
religious rulers (1-2).
    a) He named the civil rulers of the time and gave their
territories.
      (1) It was in the fifteenth year of the reign of Tiberias
Caesar.
      (2) Pontius Pilate was governor of Judea.
      (3) Herod was tetrarch of Galilee.
      (4) Herod's brother Philip I was ruler of Iturea and
Trachonitis.
      (5) Lysanias was ruler of Abilene.
    b) He named the two high priests of the Jews: Annas and
Caiaphas.
    c) He indicated the place of John's ministry—The word
of God came to John the son of Zacharias in the wilderness.
  2. He told about John's message (3-9).
    a) He preached the baptism of repentance for remission of
sins.
    b) In so doing, he fulfilled what Isaiah had written (Isa.
40:3-5).
      (1) John's was the voice of one crying in the wilder-
ness.
      (2) That voice said:
        (a) Make ready the way of the Lord.
        (b) Make his paths straight.
      (3) Obedience to that voice would cause:
        (a) the valleys to be filled and the mountains to
be brought low,
        (b) and the crooked paths to be straightened and
the rough places to be smoothed.
        (c) And all people would see the salvation of
God.
    c) He rebuked the multitudes and warned them about the
thing they were facing.
      (1) He called them offspring of vipers and asked,

46

"Who warned you to flee from the wrath to come?"

(2) He told them to bring forth fruits worthy of repentance.

(3) He warned them not to rely on the fact that they were descendants of Abraham, for he said, "God can make these stones into Abraham's children."

(4) He likened Israel to a fruitless tree that was about to be cut down and burned.

3. He told what John said when the multitudes asked, "What then shall we do?"

   a) To the multitudes, he said, "Let the one who has two coats or food share with the one who has none."

   b) To the publicans, he said, "Collect no more tax than what is ordered."

   c) To the soldiers, he said,

      (1) "Don't force money out of anyone,"

      (2) "Don't accuse anyone wrongfully,"

      (3) "Be content with your wages."

4. He told how the people reacted to John's ministry (15-17).

   a) They were in a state of expectation, wondering if John were the Christ.

   b) John explained his relation to Christ by telling about his baptism and the two baptisms Christ would administer.

      (1) John, who acknowledged his inferiority to Christ, said, "I baptize in water."

      (2) Christ would baptize in the Holy Spirit and in fire.

         (a) He explained baptism in the Holy Spirit with the illustration of gathering the wheat into the granary.

         (b) He explained baptism in fire as the burning up of the chaff.

5. He gave a brief statement of the further activity of John (18-20).

   a) "With many other exhortations he preached good tidings to the people."

   b) He rebuked Herod for having married his brother's wife, and was imprisoned because of it.

47

B. Luke told about the baptism of Jesus (21-22).
 1. He was baptized when all the people were coming to have John baptize them.
 2. He was praying during His baptism.
 3. The heaven was opened, and the Holy Spirit descended upon Him in bodily form, as a dove.
 4. A Voice from heaven said, "Thou art my beloved son; in thee I am well pleased."
C. After having presented the evidence to prove that Jesus is the Son of God and the Son of Man, Luke gave the list of His ancestors (23-38).
 1. Jesus was about thirty years old when He began His ministry.
 2. Those who didn't know the facts supposed that He was the son of Joseph.
 3. To overcome this erroneous supposition, Luke traced the ancestry of Jesus through Nathan to David and Adam, then added, "the son of God."

The Ministry of John the Baptist

Scripture

3:1-20 Now in the fifteenth year of the reign of Tiberius Caesar, Pontius Pilate being governor of Judaea, and Herod being tetrarch of Galilee, and his brother Philip tetrarch of the region of Ituraea and Trachonitius, and Lysanias tetrarch of Abilene, 2 in the highpriesthood of Annas and Caiaphas, the word of God came unto John the son of Zacharias in the wilderness. 3 And he came into all the region round about the Jordan, preaching the baptism of repentance unto remission of sins; 4 as it is written in the book of the words of Isaiah the prophet,
 The voice of one crying in the wilderness,
 Make ye ready the way of the Lord,
 Make his paths straight.
5 Every valley shall be filled,
 And every mountain and hill shall be brought low;
 And the crooked shall become straight,
 And the rough ways smooth;
6 And all flesh shall see the salvation of God.
 7 He said therefore to the multitudes that went out to be baptized

48

of him, Ye offspring of vipers, who warned you to flee from the wrath to come? 8 Bring forth therefore fruits worthy of repentance, and begin not to say within yourselves, We have Abraham to our father: for I say unto you, that God is able of these stones to raise up children unto Abraham. 9 And even now the axe also lieth at the root of the trees: every tree therefore that bringeth not forth good fruit is hewn down, and cast into the fire. 10 And the multitudes asked him, saying, What then must we do? 11 And he answered and said unto them, He that hath two coats, let him impart to him that hath none; and he that hath food, let him do likewise. 12 And there came also publicans to be baptized, and they said unto him, Teacher, what must we do? 13 And he said unto them, Extort no more than that which is appointed you. 14 And soldiers also asked him, saying, And we, what must we do? And he said unto them, Extort from no man by violence, neither accuse *any one* wrongfully; and be content with your wages.

15 And as the people were in expectation, and all men reasoned in their hearts concerning John, whether haply he were the Christ; 16 John answered, saying unto them all, I indeed baptize you with water; but there cometh he that is mightier than I, the latchet of whose shoes I am not worthy to unloose: he shall baptize you in the Holy Spirit and *in* fire: 17 whose fan is in his hand, thoroughly to cleanse his threshing-floor, and to gather the wheat into his garner; but the chaff he will burn up with unquenchable fire.

18 With many other exhortations therefore preached he good tidings unto the people; 19 but Herod the tetrarch, being reproved by him for Herodias his brother's wife, and for all the evil things which Herod had done, 20 added this also to them all, that he shut up John in prison.

Comments

the reign of Tiberias Caesar.—If the outstanding thing that happened in the reign of Caesar Augustus was the birth of Christ, we may safely say that the outstanding thing that happened in the reign of Tiberias was the life, death, and resurrection of Christ.

Pontius Pilate was the governor of Judea during that eventful period of history. His claim to fame depends upon the fact that he presided over the trial of Jesus. Although he tried to wash his hands of responsibility in the case, he finally acceded to the demands of those who clamored for His death and gave orders for Him to be crucified.

Herod, also known as Antipas, was tetrarch of Galilee and Perea. The kingdom of Herod the Great was divided after his death and Antipas became ruler of a fourth part of it. That's why he was sometimes called Herod the tetrarch (Matt. 14:1). Not only is he known for his infamous deed of having John the Baptist beheaded, but also for the fact that he had some small part in the trial of Jesus.

Lysanias, though not related to the Herods, was tetrarch of the territory that lay to the north of the Sea of Galilee and east of Mount Hermon.

the highpriesthood of Annas and Caiphas.—Actually there was only one office of high priest. But through Roman manipulation the high priesthood of Annas had been given to his son-in-law, Caiaphas, and both men were looked upon by Jews as high priest. This is not the first time that the Mosaic law of succession had been set aside. According to that law, at the death of the high priest the oldest son was to be consecrated to the office. Evidently some did not accept the idea of having another appointed high priest during the lifetime of one whom they had recognized as their high priest. It may be that it was for that reason that the Jews led Jesus first to Annas when they brought Him to trial before their court (John 18:13). But before they took the case to the Roman governor, they met with Caiaphas and then decided on the course of action in presenting their case to Pilate.

the word of God came to John.—John is acknowledged in every way as a prophet of God. God's word came to the prophet while he was in the wilderness. The same formula is used to describe the Old Testament prophets, for it is said that the word of the Lord came to them, that is, their message was not their own, it was from the Lord.

Luke had to use a very cumbersome method to affix a date to the birth of Christ and to the ministry of John. He began with the Caesar, then told of the local rulers and finally gave the names of those who were filling the office of high priest of the Jews. Now a simple number that recalls the year of Our Lord significantly takes the place of the system Luke used.

baptism of repentance unto remission of sins.—Repentance is the decision that leads to a change of conduct. Through the preaching of John, the people were convinced that they needed to change their way of life and came to John to be baptized for the remission of their sins.

Isaiah the prophet.—The prophecy of Isaiah introduces the ministry of John the Baptist, and another word from the same prophet introduces the ministry of Jesus (Isa. 40:3-6; 61:1-2). While Matthew gives especial attention to the fulfillment of prophecy by Jesus, Mark and Luke do not neglect the matter. Paul also shows how the gospel is rooted in the Old Testament Scriptures, that is, "the gospel of God which he promised afore through his prophets in the holy scriptures concerning his Son" (Rom. 1:2-3).

The voice.—When the Jews sent a deputation from Jerusalem to John to ask, "Who are you?" he replied, "I am not the Christ." They asked, "Are you Elijah?" He said, "I am not." They tried again, "Are you the prophet?" He said, "No." With no success with the suggestions they had made, they said, "Who are you, that we may give answer to those who sent us?" He said, "I am the voice of one crying in the wilderness, Make straight the way of the Lord, as the prophet Isaiah said." See John 1:19-23.

Their questions were based on Deut. 18:15; Psa. 89:3-4; and Mal. 4:5. John answered them by quoting Isaiah, because it was his message and not his person that was of importance. In this he differs from Jesus, for who He was and what He taught were of great importance. A little later, John explained this to his disciples by saying, "He must increase, but I must decrease" (John 3:30). *Make ready the way of the Lord.*—John's task was to get the people to prepare themselves for the coming of the Lord. In the figure of Isaiah, this was like making a straight path for the Lord. Let the valleys be filled and the mountains be leveled and the curves straightened and the rough places smoothed. They would have to repent of their ways and be baptized for the remission of their sins.

All flesh shall see the salvation of God.—All peoples, not just the Jews, were to see the salvation God sent to them in the person of His Son. When Theophilus read this, he must have been deeply grateful that the grace of God had extended to the Gentiles too. Luke stressed the point again as he closed the letter by saying "that repentance and remission of sins should be preached in his name unto all the nations, beginning from Jerusalem" (Lk 24:47).

the multitudes that went out to be baptized.—The size of the crowds might have flattered some preachers, but not John. He greeted them with words intended to shock them into action. Repent! Make ready the way of the Lord! Generation of vipers, who warned you to flee from the wrath to come? You are a tree that has not been producing fruit; and like that tree, you are about to be cut down. Change your minds about your sinful ways and start producing righteous fruit.

We have Abraham to our father.—Since they were the descendants of Abraham, it was easy for them to assume that they were children of God. When they argued the same way with Jesus, He plainly told them that they were not Abraham's children because their attitude toward the Son of God proved that they were children of the devil. See John 8:31-44.

God is able of these stones.—Why didn't God turn the stones into Abraham's children? Why didn't He create people who were incapable of anything except faith and obedience? Evidently God wants those to be His children who will be like Abraham in faith and obedience because of their love for God. This, of course, calls for sinners to repent and be baptized for the remission of their sins and as an indication of their love for the Lord to conduct themselves as intelligent people who want to glorify the heavenly Father by living a life of faith and purity.

the axe also lieth at the root of the trees.—God was ready to destroy the fruitless trees. Sinners who were not producing the fruit of righteousness to the glory of God were facing certain doom unless they changed their minds about the issue of sin. Jesus also likens the nation of Israel to a tree that failed to produce fruit (Lk. 13:6-9). He also called on the people to repent. Jesus pronounced judgment on a tree that had no fruit on it although it did have leaves (Mark 11:12-25). The miracle seems to be a portent of what was about to happen to a nation that was getting ready to crucify the Son of God.

When then must we do?—John was an effective prophet. Little good is accomplished by telling people what to do before they are in a frame of mind to be advised. John's stern warning brought the people to the point where they wanted to do something to avoid the destruction that awaited them. The same thing happened on the day of Pentecost. Peter produced the evidence that let the people know that they were guilty of having crucified the Son of God. Because they were pricked to the heart by his message, they said to

Peter and the rest of the apostles, "Brethren, what shall we do?" Acts 2:37.

John was ready with the answer to the multitudes. He said, "He who has two coats, let him share with him who has none; and do likewise with food." This was not to encourage laziness, but rather to encourage concern for those who are really in need. The progress of the gospel is hindered today, not because God has not provided food for all the people of the world, but because we lack the ability and perhaps the willingness to properly distribute it. Christianity prompted the early Christians to share with any who had need (Acts 2:45) and even to feed a hungry enemy (Rom. 12:20).

publicans to be baptized.—The tax collectors were usually classed as sinners because of the common practice of taking advantage of their office by collecting more than authorized. But they were not all like that. The apostle Matthew reminds us that he was a publican (Matt. 10:3). Zacchaeus, a chief publican, is known for his desire to see Jesus (Lk 19:1-10). There is no indication that Matthew ever abused his office, but Zachaeus seems quite willing to admit that he may have been guilty of doing so. John gave the general order to the publicans: "Extort no more than that which is appointed you."

And soldiers also asked him.—There is no way of knowing whether these soldiers were in the service of some local government or of the Roman emperor. We do not know whether they were Jews or Romans. But John's message was so striking that these military men came to ask what they were to do.

Luke gives the account of at least three other military men who were attracted by Christ and His gospel: (1) the centurion who asked Jesus to heal his servant (Lk 7:2); (2) the centurion who commanded the soldiers who carried out Pilate's order to crucify Jesus (Lk 23:47); (3) Cornelius, the centurion to whom Peter preached the gospel (Acts 10:1).

John's instructions to the soldiers were directed toward things that were common problems of soldiers of that day. They were not to use violence for the sake of getting money; they were not to become informers with intent to injure the innocent or to gain personally from such activity; they were to be content with their wages. The soldier who was content with his wages wouldn't be trying to force people to give him money or informing on others for the same purpose.

the people were in expectation.—It had been a long time since Israel had a prophet living in their midst. When John came, there was a strange stirring in their hearts, wondering if this could be the Messiah. They had been taught about the days of David and the glory of the reign of Solomon. Perhaps they were now dreaming of a Messiah who would free them from the Roman yoke. It is possible, on the other hand, that some were tired of their sins and were wondering if John could be Christ who would lead them back to the glory their nation had once known. But John pointed them to Jesus and the salvation with which He would satisfy the longing of those who wanted to do the will of God.

I indeed baptize you with water.—John baptized in water, not with it. He immersed the people in the Jordan river. To translate "with water" is to suggest the action of sprinkling or pouring, neither of which are suggested by the word baptize.

This immersion in water was for the remission of sins. "John came, who baptized in the wilderness and preached the baptism of repentance unto remission of sins" (Mark 1:4). Repentance preceded the baptism, and without it baptism was meaningless. The same thought is suggested in Matthew's account: "I indeed baptize you in water unto repentance" (Matt. 3:11). This does not say that they were baptized so that they could repent, but that they were baptized with regard to repentance, that is, the repentance that John had demanded of them.

John was sent from God (John 1:6) and we may assume that the baptism he preached was commanded by God. It was for the remission of sins, but like all other provisions under the Old Covenant for remission of sins, it anticipated the sacrifice of Christ that actually blotted out sin (Heb. 9:15; Rom 3:25-26). We may safely assume that the Jews whom John baptized continued to offer the sacrifices required by the law of Moses.

Of the three thousand who were baptized on the day of Pentecost under the New Covenant, no doubt, many had been already baptized into John's baptism. On that day they were baptized in the name of Christ for the remission of sins in order to be in the body of Christ (Acts 2:38; Gal 3:27). Apparently, after the day of Pentecost, all who had been baptized by John were also required to be baptized in the name of the Lord Jesus. See Acts 19:1-7.

he shall baptize you in the Holy Spirit and in fire.—John baptized in water; Christ would baptize in two elements: (1) the Holy

Spirit, that is, in the power of the Holy Spirit; and (2) in fire.

John explained this with the illustration of the threshing floor. The gathering of the wheat into the grannery is like the thing that would be accomplished by those baptized in the Holy Spirit. The burning of the chaff is like the baptism in fire—the destruction of the wicked in hell (II Thes. 1:8-9).

Jesus also explained the baptism in the Holy Spirit when He spoke to the apostles just before His ascension (Acts 1:4-5, 8). They were baptized in the Holy Spirit on the day of Pentecost, and as a result of it they were able to tell the people what to do to be saved (Acts 2:1-4; and 2:37-38).

The "tongues parting asunder, like as of fire" which appeared in connection with the baptism of the apostles in the Holy Spirit should not be confused with the baptism in fire. That phenomenon, together with the sound like the rushing of a great wind, attracted the attention of the people. Then the apostles who were all filled with the Holy Spirit spoke to them in the people's own native languages.

With many other exhortations.—One papyrus roll was not enough to tell all that John said or did. Luke was saving space for those events in the ministry of Jesus that he wanted to tell Theophilus about. See how he made use of this expression in reporting the events of the day of Pentecost (Acts 2:40).

Herod the tetrarch.—This wicked son of a wicked father—he had slain the babes at the time of the birth of Jesus—was reproved by John for the evil things he had done including his marriage to the wife of his half brother, Philip I. For this, John was shut up in prison and before long was beheaded.

The Baptism of Jesus

Scripture

3:21-22 Now it came to pass, when all the people were baptized, that, Jesus also having been baptized, and praying, the heaven was opened, 22 and the Holy Spirit descended in a bodily form, as a dove, upon him, and a voice came out of heaven, Thou art my beloved Son; in thee I am well pleased.

Comments

when all the people were baptized.—For the purpose of this baptism, see comment on 3:16.

55

Jesus also having been baptized.—It is important to notice the distinction between the purpose of the baptism of the people and the purpose of the baptism of Jesus by John. Jesus said His was "to fulfill all righteousness"—that is, to do all things that meet the approval of God. See Matt. 3:15. John suggests two more reasons why Jesus was baptized. He had been told that the one upon whom he would see the Holy Spirit descending would be the one who would baptize in the Holy Spirit. Although John knew Jesus—he said, "I have need to be baptized by you"—he needed this evidence that came at the time of Jesus baptism to be able to reveal Him to the people as the Son of God. See John 1:29-34.

and praying.—Only Luke tells us that Jesus was praying when He was baptized. He also records a good many other things about the prayer life of Jesus.

the Holy Spirit descended.—This was the sign to John that Jesus was the One who would baptize in the Holy Spirit. Peter also refers to the fact that "God anointed him with the Holy Spirit and with power and that He went about doing good and healing all that were oppressed of the devil; for God was with him" (Acts 10:38).

a voice from heaven.—The One who was designated Son of God at the time of His conception is now publically recognized by the Father. The Voice of God was heard three times during the ministry of Jesus: (1) at His baptism; (2) when He prayed after the Greeks came to see Him (John 12:28); and (3) at the time of His transfiguration (Luke 9:35).

The List of Jesus' Ancestors

Scripture

3:23-38   And Jesus himself, when he began *to teach,* was about thirty years of age, being the son (as was supposed) of Joseph, the *son* of Heli, 24 the *son* of Matthat, the *son* of Levi, the *son* of Melchi, the *son* of Jannai, the *son* of Joseph, 25 the *son* of Mattathias, the *son* of Amos, the *son* of Nahum, the *son* of Esli, the *son* of Naggai, 26 the *son* of Maath, the *son* of Mattathias, the *son* of Semein, the *son* of Josech, the *son* of Joda, 27 the *son* of Joanan, Cosam, the *son* of Elmadam, the *son* of Er, 29 the *son* of Jesus, the *son* of Eliezer, the *son* of Jorim, the *son* of Matthat, the *son* of Levi, 30 the *son* of Symeon, the *son* of Judas, the *son* of Joseph, the *son* of Jonam, the *son* of Eliakim, 31 the *son* of Melea, the *son* of Menna, the *son* of Mattatha, the *son* of Nathan, the *son* of David, 32 the *son* of Jesse, the *son* of Obed, the *son* of Boaz, the *son* of Salmon, the *son* of Nahshon, 33 the *son* of Amminadab, the *son* of Arni, the *son* of Hezron, the *son* of Perez, the *son* of Judah, 34 the *son* of Jacob, the *son* of Isaac, the *son* of Abraham, the *son* of Terah, the *son* of Nahor, 35 the *son* of Serug, the *son* of Reu, the *son* of Peleg, the *son* of Eber, the *son* of Shelah, 36 the *son* of Cainan, the *son* of Arphaxad, the *son* of Shem, the *son* of Noah, the *son* of Lamech, 37 the *son* of Methuselah, the *son* of Enoch, the *son* of Jared, the *son* of Mahalaleel, the *son* of Cainan, 38 the *son* of Enos, the *son* of Seth, the *son* of Adam, the *son* of God.

Comments

And Jesus himself.—Luke has presented strong evidence in support of his claim that Jesus is the Son of God. The climax of that evidence is the report of God's public acknowledgment of His Son when He said, "Thou art my beloved Son; in thee I am well pleased." He is now ready to tell Theophilus about the ancestors of Jesus who is also the Son of Man. Matthew began the birth record with David and Abraham and traced it to Joseph, the husband of Mary of whom was born the Christ. But Luke—this is much more meaningful to a Gentile—began with Jesus and traced His lineage through Nathan to David and finally to Adam and then adds the final note, "the son of God."

as was supposed.—Two interesting items open the paragraph: (1) Jesus was about thirty years old when He began to teach; (2) It was assumed by those who didn't know the facts that He was the son of Joseph.

Why did He wait until He was thirty? Our impatience makes us wonder why He didn't begin much sooner. But God had waited until the "fulness of time" to bring His Son into the world. There are many things involved in that statement, but one thing is clear, the world was ready for Him; the Jewish people were in expectation; even Gentiles were glad when they heard the news of salvation through Him. The simple answer, of course, to the question is that Jews expected their teachers to have some maturity when they began. This does not bar a younger man who is prepared to undertake a ministry for the Lord today.

It was only natural for those who did not know the facts to suppose that Jesus was the son of Joseph. He grew up in Joseph's home and was obedient to Mary and Joseph. Of course, Mary and Joseph knew that He was the Son of God—how well they understood it may be a question—but there was no good way to tell others about it until after His ministry where He demonstrated it and His resurrection that proved it beyond a doubt. Even the Lord's brothers were not aware of the truth that He is Lord and Christ until after they had become convinced of it by the force of the evidence of the resurrection.

the son of Heli.—The names in this list differ somewhat from those given in Matt. 1:1-16. But both Matthew and Luke and Paul make it clear that Jesus, "according to flesh" was born of the seed of David (Rom. 1:3). Both Matthew and Luke make it clear that Joseph was not Jesus' father; the conception was a miracle and Paul affirms that the resurrection designated Him as Son of God. The difference in the two lists may be explained by assuming—we have no way of proving it—that Luke gives Mary's genealogy and Matthew gives Joseph's.

of Nathan, the son of David.—Matthew traced the line through Solomon, suggesting that Joseph was the legal heir to David's throne. Luke traces it through Nathan, suggesting the blood line of Mary of whom was born Jesus the Christ.

the son of Adam.—Adam was the head of the human race; Christ is the head of the new creation (I Cor 15:45-49). Adam was created by God and so was the son of God. But Jesus' relation to God is unique, for, as John says, "He was God" (John 1:1) and "became flesh" (1-14). Therefore, He can rightly be called "the only begotten Son of God" (John 1:18).

Summary

With this chapter Luke completes the evidence—with the exception of the account of the Temptation—that presents Jesus as the Son of God and the Son of Man who is ready to begin His ministry. He begins with a brief account of the ministry of John, then tells of the baptism of Jesus, and closes the chapter with the genealogy of Jesus.

John came with his stirring message at a time when all the people were in expectation, wondering if he could be the Messiah.

But he was not the Christ; he was the prophet of God sent to tell the people to make ready for the coming of the Lord. He had a harsh message, for they were sinners. They were like valleys that had to be filled, mountains that had to be leveled, and curves that had to be straightened so that their lives might be suitable for the Lord. They were a fruitless tree that was about to be cut down. He commanded them to repent; he baptized them in the Jordan for the remission of their sins.

John's message bore fruit. Crowds flocked to hear him from Jerusalem and the surrounding country. He baptized them as he saw that they were heeding his command to repent. Tax collectors came asking what they should do; soldiers wanted to know what to do. His answer was simple and direct: Repent and let your lives show that you have changed from your evil ways.

But John directed them to Jesus. He said, "I baptize you in water, but the One who is coming after me will baptize you in the Holy Spirit and in fire." By the baptism in the Holy Spirit He was to enable the apostles to tell men what to do to be saved and like wheat be gathered into the granary. But those who will not respond to their message will, like chaff that is burned up, be destroyed when Christ comes again.

Luke gave only a summary of what John did and taught. Among the many things which he did, John reproved Herod the tetrarch for the evil he had done, including his marriage to the wife of his brother. And for this, John was put in prison.

The climax of the evidence that presents Jesus as Son of God and Son of Man ready to begin His public ministry, came at the time of His baptism. John baptized Jesus because He said it was right to do the thing that God approves, and also that he might see the sign that shows Him as Son of God. At the baptism of Jesus, the Holy Spirit descended upon Him and the Father said to Him, "Thou art my beloved Son; in thee I am well pleased."

Not until this evidence had been presented was Luke ready to tell about the ancestry of Jesus. He traced the line from Jesus all the way to Adam and to God.

One more incident belongs to this section of Luke's story and that is the account of the temptation of Jesus which is in chapter four. It shows that Satan was unable to shake the evidence that proves that Jesus is the Son of God and the Son of Man.

59

Questions

1. What was the most important event, from the Christian's point of view, in the reign of Caesar Augustus?
2. For what things do we remember Herod the tetrarch?
3. How did it happen that both Annas and Caiaphas were high priests at the same time?
4. What is the significance of the statement that "the word of God came to John"?
5. What is meant by "baptism of repentance"?
6. What was the purpose of John's baptism?
7. How does Isaiah's prophecy fit the condition of John's time?
8. Why is John called "the voice of one crying in the wilderness"?
9. What Scriptures did the Jews have in mind when they asked if John was the prophet or Elijah?
10. How was John to prepare for the Lord?
11. What is there in the prophecy of Isaiah that indicates that the Gentiles were to share in the salvation through Christ?
12. What was John's attitude toward the multitudes who came to hear him?
13. Why did he liken them to a tree about to be cut down?
14. What did he mean by saying that "God is able of these stones to raise up children unto Abraham"?
15. What did John tell the crowds to do? the publicans? the soldiers?
16. What does Luke say about the attitude of the people at the time of John's appearing in the wilderness?
17. Why should we say that John baptized "in" water rather than "with" water?
18. How could John's baptism be "for remission of sins"?
19. Into what two elements was Jesus to baptize?
20. What was the purpose of the baptism in the Holy Spirit?
21. What is the baptism in fire?
22. With what illustration did John explain the two baptisms?
23. Why was John imprisoned?
24. Why was Jesus baptized?
25. What did the descent of the Spirit on Jesus mean to John?
26. What was Jesus doing when He was being baptized?

27. What is the significance of the fact that the Voice of God spoke at the baptism of Jesus?
28. Why did Luke wait until this point in his narrative to give the genealogy of Jesus?
29. How are we to understand the statement that Jesus was the son of Joseph (as was supposed)?
30. How account for the difference between Luke's list and Matthew's?
31. Why did Luke trace the genealogy to Adam?
32. What is the connection between the temptation of Jesus and what was said about Him at the time of His baptism?

CHAPTER FOUR

Outline

A. Luke told about Christ's victory over the devil's temptations (1-13).
    1. The circumstances under which the temptations were presented (1-2).
        a) Jesus, full of the Holy Spirit, returned from the Jordan. He had just been baptized; the Spirit had descended upon Him; and God had said, "This is my Son."
        b) He was led by the Spirit in the wilderness during forty days.
        c) He was tempted by the devil.
        d) He ate nothing during the forty days and was hungry at the end of the period.
    2. The three temptations (3-12).
        a) The temptation to change the stone into bread (3-4).
            (1) The devil's challenge: "If you are the Son of God."
            (2) The devil's proposition: "Command the stone to become bread."
            (3) Jesus' answer based on what is written in the Word of God, "Man shall not live by bread alone."
        b) The temptation to worship the devil (5-8).
            (1) The devil's offer: He showed Jesus all the kingdoms of the world and offered their authority and glory to Him.
            (2) The devil's terms: "If thou wilt worship before me, it shall all be thine."
            (3) Jesus' answer: "It is written, Thou shalt worship the Lord thy God, and Him only shalt thou serve."
        c) The temptation to cast Himself down from the pinacle of the temple (9-12).
            (1) The devil's challenge: "If you are the son of God."
                (a) The devil had led Him to Jerusalem and set Him on the pinacle of the temple.
                (b) The devil quoted from the Psalms about the care exercised by the angels (Psa. 91:11-12).
            (2) The devil's proposition: "Cast yourself down."

      (3) Jesus' answer: "It is said, Thou shalt not make trial of the Lord thy God."

  3. The devil's activity after Jesus' victory over him (13).

    a) He had completed every temptation.

    b) He departed from Jesus for a season.

B. Luke told about the beginning of Jesus ministry in Galilee (14-30).

  1. A general statement about the Galilean ministry (14-15).

    a) He returned to Galilee in the power of the Spirit.

    b) His fame spread throughout the whole region.

    c) He taught in the synagogues and was glorified by all.

  2. The rejection at Nazareth (16-30).

    a) Jesus went to the synagogue at Nazareth (16).

      (1) He had been reared at Nazareth.

      (2) His custom was to go to the synagogue on the sabbath.

      (3) He stood up and read from the book of Isaiah.

    b) It was the passage that told about His ministry (17-19).

      (1) The Spirit of the Lord was upon Him.

      (2) The Lord had anointed Him to preach good tidings to the poor.

      (3) He had sent Him to:

        (a) Proclaim release to the captives.

        (b) Recovering of sight to the blind.

        (c) Set at liberty them that are bruised.

        (d) Proclaim the acceptable year of the Lord.

    c) He explained that the prophecy was fulfilled that day in their hearing (20-21).

    d) He answered their objections (22-27).

      (1) They wondered at His words and asked, "Is not this Joseph's son?"

      (2) His answer:

        (a) Physician, heal thyself—referring to what had been done in Capernaum.

        (b) No prophet is acceptable in His own country.

          i) He reminded them of Elijah and the widow at Zarephath.

          ii) He reminded them of Elisha and the healing of Naaman the Syrian.

    e) He escaped from the mob that tried to kill Him (28-30).
- (1) They were filled with anger at His words.
- (2) They led Him to the brow of the hill, intending to cast Him down to His death.
- (3) Luke says, "But he passing through the midst of them went his way."

C. Luke told about His ministry in Capernaum and other parts of Galilee (31-44).
- 1. A general statement about Jesus going down to Capernaum (31-32).
  - a) Capernaum was a city of Galilee.
  - b) Jesus taught the people on the sabbath day.
  - c) They were astonished at the authority with which He taught them.
- 2. Healing the man with the spirit of an unclean demon (33-37).
  - a) The demon possessed man said:
    - (1) What have we to do with thee, Jesus thou Nazarene?
    - (2) Are you come to destroy us?
    - (3) I know who you are, the Holy One of God.
  - b) Jesus commanded the demon to come out of him.
  - c) People were amazed at what happened, and the report of Jesus' work spread to all the region.
- 3. The healing of Simon's mother-in-law (38-39).
- 4. The healing of many sick and demon possessed people as the sun was setting at the close of the sabbath day (40-41).
- 5. The plea of the people for Him to remain with them (42-44).
  - a) Jesus had gone to a desert place; the crowds came and asked Him to remain with them.
  - b) He explained that He had been sent to preach good tidings of the kingdom of God to other cities also.
  - c) He was preaching in the synagogues of Galilee.

Victory of Jesus Over Temptation

Scripture

4:1-13 And Jesus, full of the Holy Spirit, returned from the Jordan, and was led in the Spirit in the wilderness 2 during forty days, being tempted of the devil. And he did eat nothing in those days: and when they were completed, he hungered. 3 And the devil said unto him, If thou art the Son of God, command this stone that it become bread. 4 And Jesus answered unto him, It is written, Man shall not live by bread alone. 5 And he led him up, and showed him all the kingdoms of the world in a moment of time. 6 And the devil said unto him, To thee will I give all this authority, and the glory of them: for it hath been delivered unto me; and to whomsoever I will I give it. 7 If thou therefore wilt worship before me, it shall all be thine. 8 And Jesus answered and said unto him, It is written, Thou shalt worship the Lord thy God, and him only shalt thou serve. 9 And he led him to Jerusalem, and set him on the pinnacle of the temple, and said unto him, If thou art the Son of God, cast thyself down from hence: 10 for it is written,

He shall give his angels charge concerning thee, to guard thee:
11 and,

On their hands they shall bear thee up,

Lest haply thou dash thy foot against a stone.

12 And Jesus answering said unto him, It is said, Thou shalt not make trial of the Lord thy God.

13 And when the devil had completed every temptation, he departed from him for a season.

Comments

full of the Holy Spirit.—John was also said to be full of the Holy Spirit, meaning dedication to the service of the Lord. See 1:15. It probably means the same when referring to Jesus, for He was also dedicated to His Father's business. John as a prophet was also inspired by the Holy Spirit (John 3:34). Jesus was the Prophet; what He said and did were by the power of the Holy Spirit. Acts 1:2; Matt. 12:28.

led in the Spirit.—God through the Holy Spirit led Him from the baptism where He acknowledged Him as Son to the wilderness where the devil tempted Him because He was also Son of Man.

tempted of the devil.—He was tempted by the devil. Temptation is

65

a trial that presents an opportunity to choose between good and evil, between God and the devil. Man was tempted in the Garden because God said he was not to eat of the tree of knowledge of good and evil, but the devil said that it was good and would make man wise. To do what the devil says is to break the law of God, and that is sin. The temptation in itself is not sin; it is the submission to the devil's proposition that is sin. The submission need not go as far as the actual committing of the act; the longing desire for the evil thing is also sin. James says, "Each man is tempted when he is drawn away by his own lust—longing desire for evil—and enticed." James 1:14. Jesus said the same thing. "Ye have heard that it was said, Thou shalt not commit adultery; but I say unto you, that every one that looketh on a woman to lust after her hath committed adultery with her already in his heart" (Matt. 5:27-28).

When Jesus was tempted by the devil, He did not hesitate one fleeting moment to reject the evil suggestion.

he hungered.—He had been without food for forty days; He was really hungry; thought of food presented a challenge. The devil wouldn't try to tempt a man with the thought of food just after he had eaten. He always strikes at the weakest place. Judas' love for money made the thought of "thirty pieces of silver" a real temptation and it became his downfall.

Paul said, "Let him who thinketh he standeth, take heed lest he fall" (I Cor 10:12). Remember that Peter denied His Lord in a few short hours after boasting that he would be true even if all the other disciples should fail.

If you are the Son of God.—Jesus was tempted as man; He could not be tempted as God, for God cannot be tempted of evil (James 1:13). He also met temptation as man and overcame it as a man. He said, "Man shall not live by bread alone," quoting what God had caused to be written for man's direction (Deut. 8:3).

Why then did the devil say, "If you are the Son of God"? He knew He was; God had just acknowledged Him from heaven saying, "You are my beloved Son; in you I am well pleased." The devil's proposition to change a stone into bread that a hungry man might eat was real because as Son of God He could have done it. Otherwise there would have been no temptation at all. Then why didn't He do it? Because it would have violated what God had said, and that would have been sin!

The writer of Hebrews says that He was tempted in all points like we are, yet without sin. Heb. 4:15. Then let no one when he is tempted say that he must submit because he is just human; rather, let him use the same weapon that Jesus used, the Word of God, and with it overcome the devil.

command this stone that it become bread.—The devil presented three temptations in the Garden: (1) The tree was good for good; (2) it was a delight to the eyes; (3) it was to be desired to make one wise, like God. The same three temptations are seen in the propositions which the devil presented to Jesus: (1) food; (2) the sight of the worlds with their glory and authority; (3) be like God and defy God's law for man. John mentions the same three issues when he writes about "all that is in the world" of sin: (1) the lust of the flesh; (2) the lust of the eyes; (3) and the vainglory of life—man's reckless disregard for God. See I John 2:15-16.

The devil's ability to tempt man is limited. Man's ability to withstand temptation depends on doing what God had commanded (I Cor. 10:13). The victory of Jesus proves it. Paul said to put on the whole armor of God in order to withstand the devil. Take the shield of faith, for with it you can quench all the fiery darts of the evil one. Eph. 6:10-18.

To thee I will give all this authority.—The devil said it had been given to him to give to whomsoever he would. But he lied in the Garden, and Jesus said he is a liar and the father of liars (John 8:44). Why should anyone believe him? Jesus certainly didn't for He answered, "It is written, Thou shalt worship the Lord thy God, and Him only shalt thou serve."

the pinacle of the temple.—Some high point on the temple in Jerusalem. The devil suggested that Jesus use His divine power for self-glory and disregard God's law for man. He even attempted to use Scripture to support his evil suggestion. He seems to say, "Just jump off; you won't fall. God will take care of you." How many foolish things men have attempted to do because they have not considered all that God has said! But Jesus was not caught unawares, for He knew the whole Word of God. He said, "It is written, Thou shalt not make trial of the Lord thy God."

when the devil had completed every temptation.—This may refer to the three temptations which he had just presented to Jesus, or it may mean that every temptation of the devil can be put into these three categories.

he departed from him for a season.—The devil had been defeated in in each attempt to lead Jesus to sin. He left Him for a season, but returned again and again in many situations that presented temptations.

Matthew says that when the devil left Jesus, "angels came and ministered unto him" (Matt. 4:11).

The Beginning of Jesus' Ministry in Galilee

Scripture

4:14-30   And Jesus returned in the power of the Spirit into Galilee: and a fame went out concerning him through all the region round about. 15 And he taught in their synagogues, being glorified of all.

16 And he came to Nazareth, where he had been brought up: and he entered, as his custom was, into the synagogue on the sabbath day, and stood up to read. 17 And there was delivered unto him the book of the prophet Isaiah. And he opened the book, and found the place where it was written,

18 The Spirit of the Lord is upon me,
     Because he anointed me to preach good tidings to the poor:
     He hath sent me to proclaim release to the captives,
     And recovering of sight to the blind,
     To set at liberty them that are bruised,
19 To proclaim the acceptable year of the Lord.

20 And he closed the book, and gave it back to the attendant, and sat down: and the eyes of all in the synagogue were fastened on him. 21 And he began to say unto them, To-day hath this scripture been fulfilled in your ears. 22 And all bare him witness, and wondered at the words of grace which proceeded out of his mouth: and they said, Is not this Joseph's son? 23 And he said unto them, Doubtless ye will say unto me this parable, hysican, heal thyself: whatsoever we have heard done at Capernaum, do also here in thine own country. 24 And he said, Verily I say unto you, No prophet is acceptable in his own country. 25 But of a truth I say unto you, There were man widows in Israel in the days of Elijah, when the heaven was shut up three years and six months, when there came a great famine over all the land; 26 and unto none of them was Elijah sent, but only to Zarephath, in the land of Sidon, unto a woman that was a widow. 27 And there were many lepers in Israel in the time of Elisha the prophet; and none of them was

cleansed, but only Naaman the Syrian. 28 And they were all filled with wrath in the synagogue, as they heard these things; 29 and they rose up, and cast him forth out of the city, and led him unto the brow of the hill whereon their city was built, and they might throw him down headlong. 30 But he passing through the midst of them went his way.

Comments

And Jesus returned.—Up to this point Luke has been concerned with the evidence that presents Jesus as the Son of God and the Son of Man. Now he begins to tell about His ministry in which both His deity and His humanity will continue to be emphasized.

Luke told about the baptism and temptation without mentioning other details of Jesus early Judean ministry. See John 4:45.

Jesus returned to Galilee after He heard that John had been put in prison. Matt. 4:12.

in the power of the Spirit.—When He returned to Galilee, He began His ministry of teaching and healing in that district. He performed miracles by the power of the Holy Spirit. These miracles were His credentials as Son of God. They were performed to help people believe His message. See John 20:30-31; Acts 10:38.

Peter said that God anointed Him with the Holy Spirit and with power and that He went about doing good and healing those who were oppressed of the devil. See Acts 10:38. His first miracle was at Cana of Galilee, but He also performed miracles when He was in Jerusalem at the passover (John 2:13, and 23).

a fame went out concerning him.—It was only natural the distressed people should come to Him when they heard about all the things he was doing. See 4:40-41. This gave Him the opportunity to tell them about the kingdom of God.

he taught in their synagogues.—Everywhere the Jews had built their synagogues where they could gather for religious instruction. See Acts 15:21. Both Jesus and the apostles went to the synagogues where Jews were gathered on the sabbath day, and being Jews, they spoke, to those assembled, the gospel message that fulfilled the law of Moses and the prophets. Rom 3:21. Luke describes the order of service in 4:16-21 and also in Acts 13:14-43. It consisted in reading from the law and the prophets and the explanation of them for the benefit of the people.

Nazareth, where he had been brought up.—Nathanael had raised the question with Philip, "Can any good thing come out of Nazareth?" John 1:46. But in this humble village Jesus had grown to manhood and was known to the neighbors as Joseph's son. In such a place, everyone would know just about everything about the rest of the people. Undoubtedly no one in the synagogue that day when they handed Him the book of Isaiah had the slightest notion that He was the Son of God and the Son of Man, the One who fulfilled what the prophet had written about the Messiah.

as his custom was.—The synagogue was the center of the religious life of the community. Jesus had made it a habit to go to the synagogue on the sabbath day. He lived under the Old Covenant and kept the customs of the people who were under the Mosaic law. But Paul, whose ministry was of the New Covenant, went to the synagogue on the sabbath because there he found an audience that needed the gospel of Jesus the Savior.

stood up to read.—Jesus stood while reading the Scriptures and sat down to teach. Paul, at Antioch, sat down while the Scriptures were being read and stood up when he addressed the audience. Apparently there was not fixed rule in the matter. Matthew says that Jesus sat down when He delivered the Sermon on the Mount to the disciples and the multitudes, but Luke says that He stood on a level place when He spoke similar words—perhaps, on another occasion at another place. All these little sidelights tend to mark the genuineness of the sacred records.

the book of the prophet Isaiah.—Isaiah had prophesied about the ministry of John the Baptist. Isaiah's prophecy about the Messiah is an outline of Jesus' ministry.

The Spirit of the Lord is upon me.—The ministry of Jesus was under the direction of God through the Spirit. The prophets and priests of the Old Testament were consecrated to their office by the ceremony of anointing with oil. Jesus, as Prophet, Priest and King, was anointed with the Holy Spirit as He began His ministry. That ministry consisted in preaching good tidings to the poor, proclaiming release to the captives, giving sight to the blind, and liberty to those broken in heart and body. His ministry that fulfilled this prophecy marked Him as the Messiah. See Lk 7:22.

the acceptable year of the Lord.—that is, the season during which God's approval is given to those who accept the deliverance which Christ brought.

the eyes of all the synagogue.—Every eye was fixed on Him. He read the Scriptures with meaning that was genuine, for He was the fulfillment of the words He read. But they were not quite ready to accept it when He said, "Today this scripture has been fulfilled in your hearing."

the words of grace.—The words of Isaiah and the words of Jesus, as He explained that He was fulfilling them, were words about the grace of God that brought relief to the oppressed. Jesus spoke them with gracious concern for all who heard Him.

Is not this Joseph's son?—They didn't know the facts about Jesus' birth? What if Mary had tried to tell them? Who would have believed her then? But after the resurrection when God demonstrated that Jesus is His Son, the facts of His birth can be told as the only reasonable explanation of this One who is the Son of God and the Son of Man.

Physician heal thyself.—Jesus recognized the problem and suggested this to them, for this is what they were thinking. They had probably heard of the miracle of healing the nobleman's son at Capernaum while Jesus was at Cana (John 4:46). Why not do in His own home town what—according to reports—had been done elsewhere? But, of course, they didn't believe that He had performed such a cure. He answered, "No prophet is acceptable in his own country." That's why He had come back to Galilee (John 4:44). In Judea there was a rising storm of opposition because they knew He was a prophet (John 3:2). But in Galilee, they thought He was just "Joseph's son" and were not too concerned about His activities, even though the crowds followed Him wherever He went. In the end, He was to journey back to Jerusalem, for it was there that He was to suffer for the sins of the people (Lk 9:51; 13:33-35).

widows in Israel in the days of Elijah.—See I Kings 17:8-24. The one miracle that Elijah performed was sufficient to convince this Gentile woman, for she said, "Now I know that you are a man of God, and that the word of the Lord that is in your mouth is true." The implied conclusion is that the one miracle Jesus had performed in Capernaum should have caused these who were Jews to believe Him.

lepers in Israel in the time of Elisha.—See II Kings 5:1-27. This one miracle in Elisha's time was sufficient to establish the fact that there is no God in all the earth but in Israel and that Elisha was His prophet. Again the implied conclusion is that Jesus' one miracle should have caused them to believe in Him instead of asking, "Is not this Joseph's son?"

they were filled with wrath.—What made them so angry? They had been defeated in the debate by this One who had been reared in their midst, whom they had been accustomed to call "the carpenter's son." But more than that, He had drawn an unfavorable comparison between them and the two Gentiles who believed Elijah and Elisha. This was the unforgivable offense. Rather than consider the force of His argument, they determined to destroy Him.

led him to the brow of the hill.—It was mob violence with intent to kill; no doubt about it. This nearby precipice met their need as a place of execution. It would be swift; and in their madness they no doubt thought it would be easy.

he passing through their midst.—Instead of permitting them to cast Him headlong to His death, He simply passed through their midst and went on His way. Was it a miracle that delivered Him? Or was it the strength of this Person who, although He had grown up in their city, was beginning His ministry as the Lord's anointed? We cannot answer the question. I prefer to believe that, although He could have used divine power, He walked through that mob as a Man dedicated to His God. He was surely one of the most forceful persons every to walk on this earth.

His Ministry in Capernaum

Scripture

4:31-44   And he came down to Capernaum, a city of Galilee. And he was teaching them on the sabbath day: 32 and they were astonished at his teaching; for his word was with authority. 33 And in the synagogue there was a man, that had a spirit of an unclean demon; and he cried out with a loud voice, 34 Ah! what have we to do with thee, Jesus thou Nazarene? are thou come to destroy us? I know thee who thou art, the Holy One of God. 35 And Jesus rebuked him, saying, Hold thy peace, and come out of him. And when the demon had thrown him down in the midst, he came out of him, having done him no hurt. 36 And amazement came upon all, and they spake together, one with another, saying, What is this word? for with authority and power he commandeth the unclean spirits, and they come out. 37 And there went forth a rumor concerning him into every place of the region round about.

38 And he rose up from the synagogue, and entered into the house of Simon. And Simon's wife's mother was holden with a great fever; and they besought him for her. 39 And he stood over her, and rebuked the fever; and it left her: and immediately she rose up and ministered unto them.

40 And when the sun was setting, all they that had any sick with divers diseases brought them unto him; and he laid his hands on every one of them, and healed them. 41 And demons also came out from many, crying out, and saying, Thou art the Son of God. And rebuking them, he suffered them not to speak, because they knew that he was the Christ.

42 And when it was day, he came out and went into a desert place; and the multitudes sought after him, and came unto him, and would have stayed him, that he should not go from them. 43 But said unto them, I must preach the good tidings of the kingdom of God to the other cities also: for therefore was I sent.

44 And he was preaching in the synagogues of Galilee.

Comments

And he came down to Capernaum.—Capernaum became the center of Jesus' ministry in Galilee (John 2:12). It was located on the northwest shore of the Sea of Galilee. It was thus situated more than six hundred feet below sea level; that's why Luke says He came down to Capernaum. Jesus taught in the synagogues of Capernaum and performed miracles there. It became the object of His wrath because of the stubborn rejection of the evidence that should have led to repentance. He said, "And thou Capernaum, shalt thou be exalted unto heaven? thou shalt go down unto Hades: for if the mighty works had been done in Sodom which were done in thee, it would have remained unto this day" (Matt. 11:23). See also Lk 10:13.

astonished at his teaching.—Matthew calls attention to this same reaction after the Sermon on the Mount (Matt. 7:28-29). Jesus was unlike other teachers who had to rely on other sources for their authority; He spoke from His own authority, for He spoke the words of God.

a spirit of an unclean demon.—Demons are spiritual beings without bodies. They have all the attributes of personality. They are under the control of Beelzebub, the prince of demons (Lk 11:15). They are unclean. They have a desire to be in a body and did actually take

73

up residence in the bodies of living people. On one occasion, when driven out of the human body, they were permitted to enter the bodies of swine. They are thought by some to be evil angels, and by others, the spirits of the wicked dead.

Demon possession was manifested in at least three forms in biblical times: (1) extreme mental illness (Lk. 8:26-27); (2) physical illness such as blindness, inability to speak, epilepsy (Matt. 17:14-18); and (3) soothsaying powers (Acts 16:16-18).

If there is such a thing as demon possession today, it cannot be claimed with real assurance, for no one is equipped to accurately diagnose such a case. Jesus, of course, was able to distinguish between the effects of demon possession and the symptoms of physical or mental illness. It is worthwhile to note the difference between His technique in handling cases of demon possession and in miraculous cures of those who were physically or mentally ill.

he cried out with a loud voice.—This may suggest fear or a desire to be let alone. Coupled with the loud voice, this expression may indicate a symptom of mental illness, but there is insufficient evidence in this case of demon possession to classify it accurately.

what have we to do with thee?—These spirits or demons knew that they had nothing in common with the Lord, for their prince was the devil. The plural "we" may suggest that more than one demon was using the speech organs of the possessed man. See 8:30.

I know thee.—Demons recognized Jesus of Nazareth. They knew that He, in contrast to their prince, was the Holy One of God. They knew that they were destined for destruction. They knew that Jesus is the Son of God and they knew that He was the Christ (4:41). It is not strange that there is no record of a demon possessed person confessing that He is the Christ, for that would mean that the demon was acknowledging Him as Lord whereas the prince of demons is the devil.

Jesus rebuked him.—He rebuked the demon by saying, "Be quiet and come out of him." This is an order given to a being capable of understanding and obeying. When Luke says that He rebuked the fever (4:39), there is no suggestion that he considered the fever in the same light. It was, of course, by miraculous power that he instantly stopped the fever and caused the temperature to return to normal. But in the case of casting out the demon, He ordered the unclean spirit or demon to leave and it did.

demon had thrown him down.—Such convulsions seem to be common effects of demon possession (Lk. 9:42). By the order from Christ, the demon came out, having done the man no injury.

amazement came upon all.—The use of such divine power was intended to point out the deity of Jesus. In this case, Luke reminds us that those who witnessed the handling of the demon possessed man were amazed at what they saw. It also shows Jesus' concern for those unfortunate sufferers.

There is no indication that any demon possessed person was responsible for his condition. There was no word of condemnation for this man after the demon left him.

with authority and power.—Jesus had defeated Satan in the wilderness temptation by using the Word of God. But by the exercise of His divine power and authority, He defeated Satan's efforts to use demon possessed people to discredit Him before the crowds.

there went forth a rumor.—The story of Jesus' power and authority to heal was repeatedly heard throughout the whole region. This explains why the people brought all their sick and demon possessed to Him to be healed (4:41).

Simon's wife's mother.—Peter's mother-in-law was sick with a very high fever. By placing this account immediately after the miracle of casting out the demon, Luke shows the distinction between a miracle of healing and one dealing with demon possession.

immediately she rose up.—Luke was a trained physician. He had investigated these accounts and did not hesitate to show that a genuine miracle had taken place. She was able to minister to those present immediately after Jesus healed her.

when the sun was setting.—This was at the close of the sabbath day, and the people were free to bring their sick for Him to heal. But, of course, healing the sick on the sabbath was not breaking the sabbath as Jesus later proved (John 7:23).

he suffered them not to speak.—Jesus did not permit the demons to speak for Him. That was what the devil wanted them to do in order to make people believe that Jesus was in league with Satan, and thus discredit Him in their eyes. See Paul's attitude in a similar situation (Acts 16:17-18).

the multitudes sought after him.—No wonder they followed Him into the lonely place where He had gone to rest and pray. In their distress, they begged Him to stay with them. But it was necessary that He preach the gospel in other cities also. The purpose of His ministry was to prepare for the kingdom of God.

75

And he was preaching in the synagogues of Galilee.—These provi-
dentially prepared places of meeting enabled Jesus to carry on His
ministry of preaching the gospel of the kingdom. Luke did not have
enough room on one papyrus roll to give all the details of all these
incidents, but the ones he does tell about are sufficient to let us see
what an important place preaching held in the ministry of Jesus.

Summary

The chapter begins with the account of the complete victory of
Jesus over the devil. With it, Luke completes the first part of his
Life of Christ. In it he gives sufficient evidence to prove that Jesus
is the Son of God and the Son of Man. Not even the devil with his
three-fold temptation could destroy this evidence.

The temptations presented a choice between God's instructions
and the propositions of the devil. Jesus could have turned the stone
into bread, but without hesitation He said, "It is written, Man shall
not live by bread alone."

When the devil had completed every temptation, he left Jesus
for a season. But it is quite evident that he returned many times
during Jesus' ministry to renew his efforts to defeat Him. One such
instance may be seen in the effort of the people to make Him king
after the feeding of the five thousand.

God had led Jesus through the Holy Spirit into the wilderness
where He was tempted. Then Jesus returned to Nazareth to begin
His public ministry in the little village where He grew up. He
came with power performing miracles through the Holy Spirit to
prove that His message came from God.

In the synagogue at Nazareth, He read from the prophet Isaiah
the passage that outlined the ministry He was to undertake. When
He finished reading, He said to the people, "Today this Scripture is
fulfilled before you." But they said, "This is Joseph's son," for they
didn't know the facts in the case. It was for people like them that
Luke made a careful research of the facts and reported them to
Theophilus that no one may ever need to fall into that error again.

The irate people of Nazareth would not let this One, whom they
had known since He was a boy, compare them unfavorably with
Gentiles. They took Him to the cliff at the edge of the city to hurl
Him down to His death. But He walked through that mob as one
would swim through a turbulent stream and went on His way.

Jesus went down to Capernaum which became the center of His

activity for the greater part of His ministry. There He taught the people. They were astonished at the authority of His words. There He healed a demon possessed man. The report of His work spread throughout the whole district. He healed Peter's wife's mother. The people brought their demon possessed and sick to Him and He healed them all.

He withdrew to a lonely place, but the crowds followed and begged Him to stay with them. But He said, "I must preach good tidings of the kingdom of God to other cities also, for it was for that purpose that I was sent." He continued preaching in the synagogues of Galilee.

Questions

1. What is meant by "full of the Holy Spirit" when it refers to John? to Jesus?
2. What is meant by "led in the Spirit"?
3. What is temptation?
4. What is the difference between temptation and sin?
5. What did Jesus say about the longing desire for the thing God has forbidden?
6. Why was changing a stone into bread a temptation to Jesus?
7. Why did the devil say, "If you are the Son of God"?
8. What proof is given to show that Jesus overcame temptations as a man?
9. What did He use to defeat the devil?
10. How is the Christian equipped to defeat the devil?
11. Were other temptations presented to Jesus later?
12. What does John say about "all that is in the world"?
13. What are the three temptations in the wilderness?
14. What does Matthew say about the ministry of angels after the temptation of Jesus?
15. What is the significance of the fact that the temptation followed immediately after the baptism of Jesus?
16. What is the significance of the evidence presented in the first section of Luke's Gospel?
17. What is meant by "in the power of the Spirit" as it relates to Jesus' ministry?
18. What does Luke say about the fame of Jesus at this point?
19. Why did Jesus and the apostles preach in the synagogues?
20. What was the order of service in the synagogue?

21. Why did He read from Isaiah?
22. What was the response of the people to His reading? to His explanation?
23. Why did they say, "This is Joseph's son?"
24. Why did they try to kill Him?
25. How did He escape from the violence of the mob?
26. What place did Capernaum have in the ministry of Jesus?
27. What was the response of the people of Capernaum?
28. What is a demon?
29. What distinction does Luke show between the technique used by Jesus in casting out a demon and in healing a sick person?
30. What forms did demon possession take?
31. Is there demon possession today?
32. Why is there no record of a demon possessed person confessing that Jesus is the Christ?
33. What was the response of the people to the reports of His healing ministry?
34. Why did Jesus withdraw to a lonely place?
35. What did He say when the people begged Him to stay with them?

Outline

A. Luke told about two more incidents that happened in Galilee (1-16).
  1. The miraculous catch of fish (1-11).
    a) It happened at the lake of Gennesaret (1-2).
      (1) The crowd was pressing upon Jesus in order to hear the word of God.
      (2) Jesus was standing on the shore of the lake.
      (3) He saw two boats by the shore.
      (4) The fishermen had left them and were washing their nets.
    b) Jesus taught the people from one of the boats (3).
      (1) He got into Simon's boat and asked him to row it a little way from the shore.
      (2) He sat down and taught the people from the boat.
    c) By miraculous power, Jesus enabled the disciples to catch a "multitude of fish" (4-7).
      (1) He told Simon to put out into the deep and let down the nets for the catch.
      (2) Simon protested, "Master we toiled all night and caught nothing, but at your word we will let down the nets."
      (3) The miraculous catch of fish—so many that the nets were breaking and the filled boats were about to sink.
    d) The effect of the miracle on Simon Peter (8-10a).
      (1) He fell down at Jesus' knees and said, "Depart from me, for I am a sinful man, O Lord."
      (2) His partners, James and John, were also amazed.
    e) The lesson drawn from the miracle (10b-11).
      (1) Jesus said, "Fear not; from henceforth you will catch men."
      (2) The disciples brought their boats to land and, leaving all, followed Him.
  2. The healing of a leper (12-16).
    a) The man was "full of leprosy."
    b) When he saw Jesus, he fell on his face and said, "If you will, you can make me clean."

   c) Jesus touched him and said, "I will; be clean." And the leprosy left him.
   d) Jesus told him to tell no one, but to show himself to the priest as Moses had commanded.
   e) The effect of the miracle.
      (1) The report of it went everywhere.
      (2) The crowds came to hear and to be healed.
      (3) Jesus withdrew where He could be alone to pray.
B. He told of the beginning of the complaints against Jesus (17-39).
   1. The complaint about healing a paralytic (17-26).
      a) The circumstances of the miracle (17-20).
         (1) Jesus was teaching.
         (2) Pharisees and doctors of the law were present.
         (3) The power of the Lord was with Him to heal.
         (4) A paralytic was let down through the roof into the presence of Jesus.
         (5) Jesus said, "Man, your sins are forgiven."
      b) Jesus answered the complaint of the Pharisees (21-24).
         (1) They asked, "Who is this that speaks blasphemies? Who can forgive sins, but God?"
         (2) Jesus answered them.
            (a) He asked, "Why reason ye in your minds?"
            (b) He gave them something to think about: "Which is easier, to say, Thy sins are forgiven; or to say, Arise and walk?"
            (c) He had performed the miracle to show that the Son of Man has authority on earth to forgive sins.
            (d) Then He gave His command of authority, "Arise, take up your bed and go to your house."
      c) The effect of the miracle (25-26).
         (1) The man arose and departed glorifying God.
         (2) Amazement seized all, and they glorified God.
         (3) They were filled with fear and said, "We have seen strange things today."
   2. The complaint about associating with publicans (27-32).
      a) The circumstances (27-29).

80

    (1) Jesus saw Levi the publican and said to him, "Follow me."

    (2) Levi, whose other name was Matthew, arose and followed Him.

    (3) Levi gave a great reception for Jesus and invited a crowd of publicans and others.

  b) Jesus answered the complaint of the Pharisees (30-32).

    (1) The Pharisees and their scribes, muttering complaints, said to the disciples of Jesus, "Why do you eat and drink with publicans and sinners?"

    (2) Jesus answered them.

      (a) "They that are in health have no need of a physician; but they that are sick."

      (b) "I am not come to call the righteous, but sinners to repentance."

3. The complaint about fasting (33-39).

  a) The circumstances (33).

    (1) The Pharisees and scribes said, "John's disciples and the disciples of the Pharisees fast and pray."

    (2) Their complaint: "Your disciples eat and drink."

  b) Jesus answered them (34-39).

    (1) By reference to weddings: Men do not fast while the bridegroom is with them; but, when he is taken away.

    (2) By reference to a patch on a garment: Putting a new patch on an old garment or new wine into old wine skins—this is not done.

    (3) Those who have drunk the old wine will say that it is good—they do not want to see any change in the time-honored custom of fasting!

Fishers of Men

Scripture

5:1-11 Now it came to pass, while the multitude pressed upon him and heard the word of God, that he was standing by the lake of Gennesaret; 2 and he saw two boats standing by the lake: but the fishermen had gone out of them, and were washing their nets. 3 And he entered into one of the boats, which was Simon's, and asked him to put out a little from the land. And he sat down and taught the multitudes out of the boat. 4 And when he had left speaking, he said unto Simon, Put out into the deep, and let down your nets for a draught. 5 And Simon answered and said, Master, we toiled all night, and took nothing: but at thy word I will let down the nets. 6 And when they had done this, they inclosed a great multitude of fishes; and their nets were breaking; 7 and they beckoned unto their partners in the other boat, that they should come and help them. And they came, and filled both the boats, so that they began to sink. 8 But Simon Peter, when he saw it, fell down at Jesus' knees, saying, Depart from me; for I am a sinful man, O Lord. 9 For he was amazed, and all that were with him, at the draught of the fishes which they had taken; 10 and so were also James and John, sons of Zebedee, who were partners with Simon. And Jesus said unto Simon, Fear not, from henceforth thou shalt catch men. 11 And when they had brought their boats to land, they left all, and followed him.

Comments

multitudes pressed upon him.—The crowds, in their eagerness to hear Jesus, followed Him everywhere. He felt the pressure of the multitudes as they crowded around Him. The people of Nazareth marveled at the words of grace that came from His lips, but they were unable to accept them because they thought of Him only as Joseph's son. Elsewhere the eager multitudes listened to Him until the jealous Pharisees and their scribes planted doubt in their minds. This persistent opposition came to a climax at the trial of Jesus. The very people whom Jesus had so often befriended were stirred up by the leaders and led to cry out, "Let Him be crucified."

standing by the lake of Gennesaret.—Jesus often taught in the formal setting of the synagogue; but, for the most part, He taught in informal situations like this one. He was standing by the lake when the crowds came up to Him and urged Him to speak the word of God to them.

Luke uses "Lake Gennesaret" for "Sea of Galilee." Accuracy is a characteristic of his writings. "Gennesaret" is derived from the name of the plain that drains into the Sea of Galilee. It is probably a corrupted form of the name "Chinnereth." Another name was "Sea of Tiberias" (John 21:1), derived from the city of Tiberias which Herod Antipas built in honor of Tiberias Caesar. It was located on the southwest shore of the Sea. Its Old Testament name was "Chinnereth"—perhaps because the shape of the lake reminded people of a harp (Num. 34:11), or it may have come from the ancient city of the same name (Josh. 19:35).

he saw two boats.—Matthew reminds us that Peter and Andrew were casting their nets when Jesus first spoke to them (Matt. 4:18).

Luke takes up the account after they had left the boats and continues it as they washed the nets. Each writer emphasizes the point that is necessary for the purpose of his writing.

Some assume from the differences in the accounts that there were two different events. If there were, it does not affect the lesson presented in the Gospel record. Jesus used the miracle as an occasion to teach His disciples about becoming fishers of men. "From henceforth," He said, "You shall catch men."

Put out into the deep.—Peter knew that Jesus had the right to issue such a command, for Andrew had introduced him to Jesus the Messiah (John 1:40-43). He had seen the miracle when Jesus healed his wife's mother. And now, although it was against his experience and judgment as a fisherman, he was willing to obey the order.

Master.—Jesus is often called Lord, Teacher, Rabbi; but Luke adds another term, "Master." It is similar in meaning to Rabbi or teacher, but it adds to that title the right to command. They were in Peter's boat, but he recognized Jesus' right to give the orders.

I will let down the nets.—A remarkable demonstration of confidence in Jesus! But Jesus was not just interested in their catching fish; He was preparing them for the lesson He was about to teach about their becoming fishers of men.

Depart from me.—Simon was so impressed by the miracle that he fell down at Jesus' knees and said to Him, "Depart from me; for I am a sinful man, O Lord." Just how clear his understanding of the deity of Jesus was at this point, we are not able to tell. But there was something in the miracle, together with all that he had seen done by Jesus before this time, that made him recognize his own sinfulness and the exalted position of the One whom he had just called "Master." Now he addresses Him as Lord.

Peter should have asked the Lord to forgive his sin; but it may be that he was not aware of this possibility at the time. Such mistakes are bound to occur when men attempt to tell the Lord what to do instead of following the example of Saul of Tarsus who said, "What shall I do, Lord?" (Acts 22:10).

For he was amazed.—Astonishment seized Peter and the others with him when they saw the miracle take place before their eyes. They had caught so many fish that their nets were breaking; being fishermen, they knew that a miracle had taken place. At the close of Jesus' ministry, a similar miracle occurred to prove that He had risen from the dead. Peter at that time also spoke out and said to the others, "It is the Lord" (John 21:7).

partners.—James and John, the sons of Zebedee, were partners with Simon. When they saw the miracle, Peter and those in the boat with him beckoned to their partners to come and help them. The word for "partner" suggests sharing with others in a common task. This partnership is something in which all who are engaged in winning men to Christ can share.

thou shalt catch men.—The word catch suggests "taking alive"; but this is not the thing stressed in Jesus' remark. He was contrasting catching fish with catching men, that is, preaching the gospel by which men are taken for Christ. The net is the captivating message of good news of salvation through Christ, and the place of operation is the world. The resurrection of Christ is a basic issue of that message (Rom 10:9-10). The miraculous catch of fish at Tiberias convinced the apostles that the Lord had risen. It ought to help those who now seek evidence on which to base their faith.

they left all and followed him.—It was no part-time task to which Jesus called them. They were to leave all and give all that they might be ready to go into all the world as fishers of men.

Jesus Heals a Leper

Scripture

5:12-16   And it came to pass, while he was in one of the cities, behold, a man full of leprosy: and when he saw Jesus, he fell on his face, and besought him, saying, Lord, if thou wilt, thou canst make me clean. 13 And he stretched forth his hand, and touched him, saying, I will; be thou made clean. And straightway the leprosy departed from him. 14 And he charged him to tell no man: but go thy way, and show thyself to the priest, and offer for thy cleansing, according as Moses commanded, for a testimony unto them. 15 But so much the more went abroad the report concerning him: and great multitudes came together to hear, and to be healed of their infirmities. 16 But he withdrew himself in the deserts, and prayed.

Comments

a man full of leprosy.—Leprosy was one of the most dreaded diseases of Bible times. Medical science has made great progress in relieving the suffering of lepers, but in Bible times there was no cure for leprosy except a miracle of God. For the laws pertaining to leprosy see Lev. 13:1-14:47.

There are many parallels between leprosy and sin. Both are small in beginning, but deadly in the end. Sin, of course, can be overcome by the divine remedy only. Only the blood of Christ can blot out sin.

Priests were appointed to diagnose cases of leprosy and to pass on the cure. This accounts for the fact that Jesus, after healing a leper, directed him to the priest as the Law of Moses required.

At least three persons in Old Testament times were stricken with leprosy because of their sin: (1) Mirriam (Num. 12:9-15); (2) Gehazi (II Kings 5:25-27); and (3) Uzziah (II Chron. 26:16-21). This does not suggest that all lepers were being punished because of their sins.

full of leprosy.—The law required the leper to separate himself from the camp of the Israelites and to warn others who might approach him (Lk 17:12-13). This man, however, came into the presence of Jesus, for he was full of leprosy. Just what that meant is not known. There was a regulation in the Law for one whose whole body was covered with leprosy (Lev. 13:12-13). Such a person was "clean," but the leper who came to Jesus, quite evidently, was not. We can be sure of two things: (1) the dreadful plight of the leper, and (2) the gentle response of the merciful Master who touched him and said, "I will; be thou made clean."

And he charged him to tell no man.—Jesus did not come into the world for the primary purpose of healing lepers. "It is appointed unto man once to die" (Heb. 9:27). Jesus did heal many lepers and others who were sick. Even so, disease and death remain in this world; but in heaven, "death shall be no more" (Rev. 21:14).

Why did Jesus forbid him to tell about his cure? Such news would bring so many that He would not be able to go from city to city to preach the Kingdom of God, and that is what He came to do (4:43).

But so much the more went abroad the report.—More than once people disregarded the wishes of Jesus. There is no indication that

85

He blamed them, for when they brought their sick to Him He healed them.

a great multitude came together to hear, and to be healed.—See Matt. 4:23-24. Their cries for help were heard; and when He had healed their sick, He withdrew into a quiet place to pray.

and prayed.—Prayer for Jesus was just as natural as for a son to talk to his father. He was Son of God, but He was also Son of Man. As a man, He talked to His heavenly Father. He often deliberately slipped away from the crowds when the pressures of His ministry were heaviest in order to have time to talk to the Father. When He prayed, He spoke to the Father with reverence. He put the Kingdom of God first in His prayers. He didn't hesitate to tell the Father of His own needs. His trust in God leads others to trust Him. His thanksgiving for the blessings of God sets an example for all to follow when they pray. "Thy will be done" is basic in all His petitions, and should be in ours too.

Jesus Heals a Paralytic

Scripture

5:17-26   And it came to pass on one of those days, that he was teaching; and there were Pharisees and doctors of the law sitting by, who were come out of every village of Galilee and Judaea and Jerusalem: and the power of the Lord was with him to heal. 18 And behold, men bring on a bed a man that was palsied: and they sought to bring him in, and to lay him before him. 19 And not finding by what *was* they might bring him in because of the multitude, they went up to the housetop, and let him down through the tiles with his couch into the midst before Jesus. 20 And seeing their faith, he said, Man, thy sins are forgiven thee. 21 And the scribes and the Pharisees began to reason, saying, Who is this that speaketh blasphemies? Who can forgive sins, but God alone? 22 But Jesus perceiving their reasoning, answered and said unto them, Why reason ye in your hearts? 23 Which is easier, to say, Thy sins are forgiven thee; or to say, Arise and walk? 24 But that ye may know that the Son of man hath authority on earth to forgive sins (he said unto him that was palsied), I say unto thee, Arise, and take up thy couch, and go unto thy house. 25 And immediately he rose up before them, and took up that whereon he lay, and departed to his house, glorifying God. 26 And amazement took hold on all, and they glorified God; and they were filled with fear, saying, We have seen strange things to-day.

Comments

And it came to pass.—We lose something of the vividness of Luke's descriptions. He had studied these events of the ministry of Jesus until they seemed to be taking place before his eyes as he wrote. By diligent study of the record he left for us to read, we can make these incidents come to life in our minds too.

This incident is the first in a series of five in which Luke records the complaints of the Pharisees against Jesus because He helped the people in their needs (5:17-6:11).

that he was teaching.—The ministry of Jesus was one of teaching and healing; the miracles demonstrated to His hearers that His message was from God. His message, confirmed by His miracles, is the basis of our faith in Him. See Mark 16:20; Heb. 2:3-4; John 20:30-31.

Jesus taught in the synagogues; He taught by the sea; He taught wherever crowds were gathered together or where a single individual was ready to listen. He always taught with authority (Matt. 7:28-29).

The ministry of the apostles followed the same pattern. They taught the people on Pentecost. They continued to teach although they were threatened with death (Acts 4:18-20; 5:42). Paul taught in Ephesis, both publically and from house to house (Acts 20:20). He wrote to Timothy: "Till I come, give heed to reading, to exhortation, to teaching" (I Tim. 4:12). And again, "The things which thou hast heard from me among many witnesses, the same commit thou to faithful men, who shall be able to teach others also" (II Tim. 2:2). The gospel message must be taught (Matt. 28:18-20).

and there were Pharisees.—They were separatists, possibly implying separation from everything unclean. Paul said that they were the straightest sect of the Jew's religion (Acts 26:5). They believed in the resurrection and angels and spirits, but the Sadducees rejected all this (Acts 23:8).

The Pharisees led the opposition to Jesus, constantly complaining that He had broken the Law and that He was guilty of blasphemy. But they were never able to prove their charges.

and doctors of the law.—These law-teachers are called scribes by

Matthew and Mark (Matt. 9:3; Mk. 2:6). For an example of the work of the scribes see Ezra 7:6; 10:1; Heb. 8:1-8.

Various functions were performed by them in the time of Jesus. They were best known for their work of guarding and teaching the Law. But both scribes and Pharisees were condemned by Jesus for their hypocrisy in applying the law. They taught it, but failed to live by it (Matt. 23:1-36). But they were not all like that; for an example of a scribe who had a beter understanding of the Law, see Mark 12:28-34. And think of Nicodemus a Pharisee who dared to defend Jesus before the counsel and to identify himself with Jesus although He had been put to death on the cross—the Roman instrument of execution of criminals. See John 7:50-52; 19:39.

out of every village.—This incident took place in Capernaum (Mark 2:1). John suggests that the Pharisees had already begun the opposition to Jesus in Jerusalem (John 4:1). For that reason, He left Judea and came again into Galilee where the opposition was not so great. He said, "A prophet hath no honor in his own country" (John 4:43-45). In Galilee He was less likely to have difficulty with the leaders. There He could carry on His work of preparing the disciples to take the gospel into all the world (Lk. 24:46-47). They were not content, however, to let Him carry on a ministry in Galilee without keeping close watch on its progress lest His influence with the people become too great. Later, they complained that if they should leave Him alone, all men would believe in Him and the Romans would come and take away their place and their nation (John 11:47-48).

And seeing their faith.—Faith that is put into action can be seen. The friends of the sick man believed that Jesus had the power to heal him. The multitudes were blocking the entrance to the house where He was, but the men found a way to let him down through the roof into the presence of Jesus.

Man, thy sins are forgiven.—In this dramatic way, Jesus pointed out that His mission was to forgive the sinner and save the lost. He knew that the man had been put in His presence because they wanted Him to heal him. He exercised the power of the Lord that was with Him to heal in order to prove that the Son of Man had authority on earth to forgive sins.

Who is this that speaketh blasphemies?—It would have been blasphemy for a man to assume the prerogative of God and presume to forgive sins. They were correct in saying, "Who can forgive sins, but God alone?" They failed to see that the Son of Man was also the Son of God. He was not guilty of blasphemy, for He spoke with the authority from God. Nevertheless, the Jews kept up their complaint, and in the end condemned Him to death because they said He was guilty of blasphemy (Mark 14:64).

Why reason ye in your hearts?—Only God can forgive sins, and only God can look into the hearts of men and know their secrets. On the Day of Judgment, He will judge the secrets of mens hearts (Rom 2:16; Heb. 4:13). With the heart, man thinks (Matt. 9:4), reasons (Mark 2:8), believes (Rom 10:9-10), and understands (Matt. 13: 5). The Scriptural heart is the intellect on which the facts of the gospel make impact that results in belief (Rom. 10:9-10). It is the emotions that respond to the love of God (Rom. 5:8; I John 4: 19). It is the will, for with the heart man purposes and determines (II Cor. 9:7; I Cor. 7:37). The consideration of the goodness of God (Rom. 2:4) and godly sorrow for sin (II Cor. 7:10) and the knowledge of the coming judgment (Acts 17:30-31) lead the sinner to change his will and decide to serve Christ. That is repentance. The heart condemns, for it is the conscience. The blood of Christ can cleanse the conscience by blotting out the sin that otherwise would constantly remind the sinner of his guilt (Heb. 10:22; 9:14). Baptism, which Peter declares saves us through the resurrection of Jesus Christ, is the act of obedience by which the sinner asks God for a good conscience, one that commends rather than condemns (I Pet. 3:21).

Which is easier?—Jesus implies that it is just as easy to say, "Thy sins are forgiven" as to say—and actually cause it to be done— "Arise and walk." The power of the Lord was with Him to heal. Why didn't he heal the man first? Forgiveness of sins is of first importance! The miracle was to prove that the Son of Man had authority on earth to forgive sins.

the Son of man hath authority on earth to forgive sins.—In their reasoning, the Jews had linked this authority with God. "Son of Man" does not imply that He was merely human; He was also Son of God. Note the force of His argument in the trial before the Jews where they understood His reference to "Son of Man" to imply that He is also Son of God (Lk. 22:67-70).

glorifying God.—At the command of Jesus the paralyzed man immediately arose and went to his home glorifying God. It was a genuine miracle. Luke, the beloved physician, was convinced that the power of the Lord was with Him to heal. Those who say that Jesus was merely a master of psychology who relieved this man of psychosomatic symptoms disregard Luke's statement about the power of the Lord and the technique of Jesus in dealing with the case. The people also glorified God, for they had seen strange things, that is, things not based on normal experience.

Jesus Called Levi the Publican

Scripture

5:27-32   And after these things he went forth, and beheld a publican, named Levi, sitting at the place of toll, and said unto him, Follow me. 28 And he forsook all, and rose up and followed him.

29 And Levi made him a great feast in his house: and there was a great multitude of publicans and of others that were sitting at meat with them. 30 And the Pharisees and their scribes murmured against his disciples, saying, Why do ye eat and drink with the publicans and sinners? 31 And Jesus answering said unto them, They that are in health have no need of a physician; but they that are sick. 32 I am not come to call the righteous but sinners to repentance.

Comments

a publican, named Levi.—His other name was Matthew (Matt. 9:9). In His public ministry, Jesus came into contact with all classes of people, including Pharisees and their scribes, and publicans. Tax collectors and sinners were usually classed together, for as a group the publicans abused their offices. There is no indication that Matthew did. Jesus evidently selected men to be apostles because of their ability to carry out the task He had for them. Matthew, as one used to keeping records, had the talent and training that could be put to use as the Holy Spirit used him to write the Gospel According to Matthew. He must have been a man of influence, for a great crowd of publicans and others attended the feast he gave in honor of Jesus.

Others such as Roman and Jewish rulers, officers of the Roman army, Gentiles, Samaritans, rich and poor were attracted to Jesus. He came to save the lost, and they were found among all classes.

Follow me.—Levi's immediate response leaves us wondering if he had known Jesus before this time. We have no way of knowing many things that would be of interest, although not necessary to the understanding of the gospel story. It is possible that this was the very first time he had seen Jesus. If so, it indicates the remarkable power of Jesus to influence men. But through the ages men have been willing to leave all and follow Him.

And Levi made him a great feast.—Luke says that a great multitude of publicans and others were present. Matthew says that many publicans and sinners came and sat down with Jesus and His disciples (Matt. 9:10). Luke also shows that the Pharisees asked the disciples this question: "Why do ye eat and drink with publicans and sinners?"

Levi used the occasion as an opportunity to present Jesus to his associates. Every follower of Jesus would do well to follow this example. Every member of the church is to be an evangelist and help in the total work of the church by seeking to save the lost.

And Jesus answering.—Jesus had the answer for His critics. The healthy need no physician. Of course, the complainers looked upon themselves as spiritually healthy—righteous. But they were wrong about themselves and wrong about condemning the Great Physician who ministered to the sick in soul as well as body. Jesus said, "I am not come to call the righteous, but sinners to repentance." Some of them were the worst sort of sinners, but as long as they thought of themselves as righteous, nothing could be done for them.

The Complaint About Fasting

Scripture

5:33-39 And they said unto him, The disciples of John fact often, and make supplications; likewise also the *disciples* of the Pharisees; but thine eat and drink. 34 And Jesus said unto them, Can ye make the sons of the bride-chamber fast, while the bridegroom is with them? 35 But the days will come; and when the bridegroom shall be taken away from them, then will they fast in those days. 36 And he spake also a parable unto them: No man rendeth a piece from a new garment and putteth it upon an old garment; else he will rend the new, and also the piece from the new will not agree with the old. 37 And no man putteth new wine into old wine-skins; else the new wine will burst the skins, and itself will be spilled, and the skins will perish. 38 But new wine must be put into fresh wineskins. 39 And no man having drunk old *wine* desireth new; for he saith, The old is good.

Comments

They said unto him.—According to Matthew 9:14, it was the disciples of John who raised the question about fasting. The Pharisees took up the issue and asked, "Why do your disciples eat and drink? John's didn't and the Pharisees' didn't." They implied that Jesus and His disciples were doing wrong by eating and drinking with the publicans and sinners.

while the bridegroom is with them?—Jesus answered the complainers with the illustration of the wedding feast. It wouldn't be fitting to hold a fast at a wedding; even John's disciples would see the correctness of His position. The time for fasting would be when the bridegroom was taken away. Jesus is the Bridegroom, His disciples are the attendants. After the crucifixion, He was to ascend to the Father. It is appropriate for the disciples to fast while awaiting His return (Acts 13:2).

a piece from a new garment.—A second illustration enforces His argument. Fasting while Jesus was with them was just as much out of place as putting a piece from a new garment on an old garment. There is a tendency for people to resist change. Jesus said, "No man having drunk old wine desireth new." Jesus understood why they didn't want to see the time-honored custom of fasting set aside even while He was with them.

Summary

The chapter begins with the account of two dramatic incidents in Jesus' Galilean ministry of healing and teaching. It continues with the account of the beginnings of the tide of complaint against Him that reached its crest at Calvary.

On the shores of Lake Genessaret, a crowd had gathered to hear Jesus speak the word of God. He sat in Simon Peter's boat and taught the people. When He finished speaking, He said to Peter, "Put out into the deep and let down the nets for a catch." Peter, experienced fisherman that he was, said, "We toiled all night and took nothing, but if you say so we will let down the nets again." They did and the miracle took place! So many fish were caught that the nets were breaking and the boats were beginning to sink.

When Peter saw it, he fell on his knees before Jesus and said, "Depart from me Lord, for I am a sinful man." But Jesus said, "From now on you shall catch men." Then the disciples left all and followed Him.

A man who was full of leprosy came up to Jesus and said, "If you will, you can make me clean." Jesus said, "I will; be clean." And again a miracle happened; his leprosy was gone!

Jesus told him to tell no one, but go and show himself to the priest. Instead, he told everybody what happened, and crowds came to hear Jesus and to be healed. Then Jesus withdrew into a lonely place to pray.

The great popularity of Jesus was bound to arouse the opposition of the leaders of the Jews. He healed a paralytic after He had forgiven his sins, but they complained that He was speaking blasphemies. They reasoned that only God could forgive sins, but they were unaware of the deity of Jesus and that the Son of Man had authority on earth to forgive sins.

They complained about His association with publicans, but Jesus answered, "Those who are in good health do not need a physician, but the sick do." They complained that He did not observe the time-honored custom of fasting, but He answered by showing that fasting was out of place while He, the bridegroom, was present. The time would come, however, when fasting would be appropriate. He implied that He would not be with them always, for He was going to the Father.

His answers to the complaints were clear and adequate, but the enemy was interested only in destroying any confidence the people might have in Him. They kept it up until the people were persuaded at His trial to cry out, "Away with him; let Him be crucified."

Questions

1. Under what circumstances did Jesus teach the lesson about becoming fishers of men?
2. Where did Jesus do most of His teaching?
3. What are the other names for the Sea of Galilee?
4. What name did Luke use.
5. How did Jesus use the miracle of catching fish to teach the lesson about fishers of men?

6. Why did Peter protest when Jesus said, "Put out into the deep and let down the nets for a catch"?
7. What is the meaning of the word "master" which Peter used in addressing Jesus?
8. How does it differ in meaning from "Lord"?
9. How did Peter show his confidence in Jesus?
10. What did Peter say when he saw that a miracle had happened?
11. What basic mistake did he make?
12. What proof is there that it was a genuine miracle?
13. When did Jesus perform another miracle like it?
14. What was Peter's response at that time?
15. Who were the sons of Zebedee? What were they to Peter?
16. Although the word "catch" literally means "take alive," what point did Jesus make in using it?
17. What did the disciples do after they witnessed the miracle?
18. What are the facts about the cure of leprosy in Bible times?
19. In what ways is the disease of leprosy like sin?
20. What were the O. T. regulations about leprosy and its cure?
21. Who are the three O. T. characters who were stricken with leprosy because of their acts of sin?
22. What did the leper say to Jesus?
23. Why did Jesus forbid him to tell about his healing?
24. Why did he disobey?
25. Why do some disobey the gospel command to tell the good news to all the world?
26. What was Jesus' attitude toward all the sick who were brought to Him?
27. Why did He withdraw to a quiet place?
28. How was Luke able to write such vivid accounts of the ministry of Jesus?
29. What are some of the facts about Jesus' prayers?
30. How can the story of Jesus become a living reality to us?
31. What was the primary purpose of Jesus miracles?
32. Why did Jesus and the apostles teach in the synagogues of the Jews?
33. Who were the Pharisees?
34. What are the beliefs of the Pharisees and the Sadducees?
35. Who were the scribes? What was their work?
36. Where was the principal opposition to Jesus located?

37. Why did Jesus carry on the greater part of His ministry in Galilee?
38. What is meant by "seeing their faith"?
39. Why did Jesus forgive the sins of the paralytic before He healed him?
40. Explain the reasoning of those who said that Jesus had spoken blasphemies.
41. What is meant by the heart as the term is used in Scripture?
42. How does the gospel act upon the heart?
43. Which was easier for Jesus to say, "Your sins are forgiven" or "Arise and walk"?
44. Why did Jesus say to the paralytic, "Arise and walk"?
45. What was the reaction of the people to the miracle of healing the paralytic?
46. Who was Levi? What was his other name?
47. What did Levi do after becoming a follower of Jesus?
48. What was the attitude of the Pharisees when they saw Jesus at Levi's feast?
49. How did Jesus answer their complaint?
50. How did Jesus answer the complaint about fasting?
51. What was implied by His remark?
52. What does the Bible say about fasting on the part of Christians?

CHAPTER SIX

Outline

A. Luke completed the account of a series of five complaints against Jesus (1-11).
   1. The complaint about plucking grain of the sabbath (1-4).
     a) The circumstances.
       (1) The disciples of Jesus plucked and ate the grain.
       (2) They rubbed the heads of grain in their hands.
       (3) The Pharisees, assuming that this was work, asked, "Why do ye do that which is not lawful on the sabbath?"
     b) Jesus answered the complaint.
       (1) He asked, "Haven't you ever read about what David did?"
       (2) David took the showbread and ate it and gave it also to his men.
       (3) This was not lawful except for priests.
     c) Jesus reminded them that "the Son of Man is lord of the sabbath."
   2. The complaint about healing on the sabbath (6-11).
     a) The circumstances.
       (1) It was on another sabbath.
       (2) Jesus was teaching in the synagogue.
       (3) A man was there with a withered hand.
     b) The attitude of the scribes and Pharisees.
       (1) They were watching to see what He would do.
       (2) They were looking for an excuse to accuse Him.
     c) Jesus' bold action.
       (1) Knowing what they were thinking, He said to the man, "Get up and stand in the midst"—that is, where he could be seen by all.
       (2) He asked, "Is it lawful on the sabbath to do good or to do harm?"
       (3) He looked around the room at all of them, then said to the man, "Stretch forth your hand."
     d) The miracle: "His hand was restored."
     e) The effect of the miracle on the accusers of Jesus.
       (1) They were filled with senseless fury.
       (2) They talked over their problem: "What are we to do with Jesus?"

B. Luke told about Jesus selecting the twelve apostles (12-16).
  1. The circumstances (12-13).
    a) Jesus had gone into the mountain to pray.
    b) He continued in prayer throughout the night.
    c) When it was day, He called His disciples and chose twelve of them whom He called apostles.
  2. The twelve whom He selected (14-16).
    a) Simon and Andrew.
      (1) Simon was also called Peter.
      (2) Andrew was the brother of Peter.
    b) James and John.
    c) Philip and Bartholomew.
    d) Matthew and Thomas.
    e) James and Simon.
      (1) James is the son of Alphaeus.
      (2) Simon was called the Zealot.
    f) Judas and Judas.
      (1) The first of these having the same name was the son of James.
      (2) The second is Judas Iscariot, who became the traitor.
C. He told about Jesus teaching a large crowd of His disciples 17-49).
  1. The occasion (17-19).
    a) After choosing the twelve, Jesus came down with them and stood on a level place.
    b) The large crowd of His disciples.
      (1) They were from Judea and Jerusalem and from the coast of Tyre and Sidon.
      (2) They had come to hear Him and to be healed of their diseases.
    c) The healing of the multitudes.
      (1) Those who were troubled with unclean spirits were healed.
      (2) All the multitude sought to touch Him, for power came forth from Him, and He healed them all.
  2. A summary of what Jesus taught (20-49).
    a) The Beatitudes and the Woes (20-26).
      (1) The four classes included in the Beatitudes.
        (a) Those who were poor.

97

  (b) Those who hunger now.
  (c) Those who weep now.
  (d) Those who are hated for the sake of the Son of Man.
 (2) The four classes included in the Woes.
  (a) Those who are rich now.
  (b) Those who are full now.
  (c) Those who laugh now.
  (d) Those of whom all men speak well.
b) Regulations for proper conduct (27-38).
 (1) Toward enemies (27-35).
 (2) Toward others in general (36-38).
c) Some concise statements of truth (29-45).
 (1) Blind guides of the blind.
 (2) Disciple and his teacher.
 (3) Mote and beam.
 (4) Good and corrupt.
d) The necessity of obedience (46-49).
 (1) "Why call me Lord, Lord, and do not the things which I say?"
 (2) The lesson illustrated by house built on the rock and the house built on sand.

Plucking Grain on the Sabbath

Scripture

6:1-5 Now it came to pass on a sabbath, that he was going through the grainfields; and his disciples plucked the ears, and did eat, rubbing them in their hands. 2 But certain of the Pharisees said, Why do ye that which it is not lawful to do on the sabbath day? 3 And Jesus answering them said, Have ye not read even this, what David did, when he was hungry, he, and they that were with him; 4 how he entered into the house of God, and took and ate the showbread, and gave also to them that were with him; which it is not lawful to eat save for the priests alone? 5 And he said unto them, The Son of man is lord of the sabbath.

Comments

Now it came to pass on a sabbath day.—Many of the incidents described in the Gospel record occurred on a sabbath day. It was natural for the writers to tell about those occasions when the people gathered together for their regular synagogue services. But there was more than this to it. The enemies of Jesus frequently attacked Him for doing what they said was unlawful on the sabbath. They, of course, were never able to prove Him guilty on this charge. On one occasion, Jesus challenged them by asking, "Which of you convicteth me of sin?" John 8:46. Although they tried hard, they were never able to convict Him, for He was the sinless Son of God and Son of Man.

rubbing them in their hands.—This constituted work, in the minds of His accusers. It was not lawful on the sabbath, so they said.

Originally, no work was done on the sabbath. But Jesus reminded them that the Jews did many things on the sabbath which they did not consider work. They led their animals to water on the sabbath; they pulled the ox out of the ditch on the sabbath. But they considered this to be necessary, and not work.

Have you not read even this, what David did.—Jesus' answer to the charge of sabbath breaking carried a double thrust: First, they were ignorant of the Word, because they had not been reading it; second, they had neglected to read about Davids' taking the showbread and giving it to his hungry men. Who were they to sit in judgment over the Son of Man and His disciples? Before condemning the innocent, these self-appointed leaders should read their own law.

The incident to which Jesus referred is found in I Sam. 21:1-7. David was fleeing from Saul. He came to Abimelech the priest and asked for anything he might have on hand. But there was no bread except the loaves that were used in the worship of the Lord. After David had assured the priest of the purity of his men, he was given the bread that only priests ate. As Jesus put it, "It was not lawful to eat save for the priests alone." Evidently, such sacred regulations could be superceded by greater needs. Saving the lives of David and his men was, in the sight of God, more important than allowing only priests to use the bread. According to Matthew, Jesus added this important point, "If ye had known what this meaneth, I desire mercy and not sacrifice, ye would not have condemned the guiltless" (Matt. 12:7).

The Son of man is lord of the sabbath.—He who had ordained the Law at Sinai had authority over it, not the critics of Jesus. And that ended the discussion of a time.

Healing on the Sabbath

Scripture

6:6-11 And it came to pass on another sabbath, that he entered into the synagogue and taught: and there was a man there, and his right hand was withered. 7 And the scribes and the Pharisees watched him, whether he would heal on the sabbath; that they might find how to accuse him. 8 But he knew their thoughts; and he said to the man that had his hand withered, Rise up, and stand forth in the midst. And he arose and stood forth. 9 And Jesus said unto them, I ask you, Is it lawful on the sabbath to do good, or to do harm? to save a life, or to destroy it? 10 And he looked round about on them all, and said unto him, Stretch forth thy hand. And he did *so*: and his hand was restored. 11 But they were filled with madness; and communed one with another what they might do to Jesus.

Comments

and there was a man there, and his right hand was withered.—The setting is the familiar sabbath-synagogue scene. But this is different. All the elements of a trap baited with a sick man are present. Those who considered themselves to be the rightful teachers were jealous of Jesus popularity. They were ready to spring their trap. Let this "Teacher" dare to perform a work of healing on the sacred sabbath, and they would destroy Him!

It is characteristic of Luke to mention the fact that it was the man's *right* hand that was withered. The beloved physician would be interested in such details.

that they might find how to accuse him.—Their purpose was clear: They were interested in destroying the influence of Jesus with the people. Make them believe that He was breaking the sabbath, and they would return to their former teachers, the scribes and Pharisees. *But he knew their thoughts.*—Perhaps human intelligence could have seen through their trap. His enemies certainly thought of Him only as a man. But He was the Son of God, and God knows the reasoning of man's heart. Jesus knew what was in man (John 2: 25). The Pharisees had not said anything up to this point, and were not aware that Jesus knew what they were plotting. They were soon to find out both the strength and the courage of the One whom they were seeking to destroy.

100

4.0528.

According to Matt. 12:10, the Pharisees asked, "Is it lawful to heal on the sabbath?" It is difficult to say at what point their question was asked, but probably not before He had asked them, "Is it lawful to do good or harm on the sabbath?"

Rise up and stand forth in the midst.—One can't help wondering what effect this order from Jesus had on those who had planned to trap Him. Were they delighted that their scheme was going so well? Did they in the least suspect that He was aware of their evil purpose? Were they surprised by His courage as He accepted the challenge to heal the man?

What did the people think? Were they aware of what was going on? Were they glorying in the wisdom and courage and mercy of the Prophet who had arisen in their midst?

Let those who picture Jesus as a weakling ponder the boldness of His action. He could have avoided the clash with the time-honored leaders; He could have waited until the crowd was gone; but He didn't. He said, "Stand here in the midst." He wanted all to see exactly what He was doing. Everything was out in the open. What a contrast to the secret conniving of the Pharisees who were bent on destroying the Son of God!

And he arose and stood in the midst.—It is highly improbable that the man had the slightest idea of what was about to happen to him. It is also highly improbable that he knew anything of the plot of the Pharisees to use him to get rid of Jesus. A physical handicap like that may have made him timid, but at the command of the Teacher, he stood up where all could see him.

Is it lawful on the sabbath to do good, or to do harm?—Jesus was in complete command of the situation. He knew what His opponents had in mind; He knew what He was going to do. He wanted all who present on that sabbath day to see through the evil plot of the Pharisees.

He asked, "Is it lawful on the sabbath to do good, or to do harm?" There could be but one answer to the question: "To do good, not harm, on the sabbath." His enemies were planning the most evil deed: to kill the Son of God!

"To save a life, or destroy," that was the real issue before them. The people must have been moved by the logic of Jesus and by His mercy. In their hearts they must have answered, "Save a life."

But the second part of the question, "or destroy it?" Whose life?

101

That of the man with the withered hand? Or was it His own life, for He knew that they desperately wanted to destroy Him.

He looked round about on them all.—Jesus had upset their trap; He was now ready to expose their wicked plot. He knew what they were thinking; did they see what He was about to do? Mark 3:5 says, He looked round about on them with anger, being grieved at the hardness of their hearts.

John describes Him in Rev. 1:14 as the one whose eyes were as a "flame of fire." Did something of that flame show in His eyes that sabbath day in the synagogue while wicked men dared Him to heal the man with the withered hand? Did they dare look Him full in the face? Did the people see the wrath of the Righteous Judge as Jesus stood by the man He was about to heal? Or did they see in His face the mellow light of mercy for all who turn to Him?

Stretch forth thy hand.—The man did so, and his hand was restored. It was as simple as that. Instantly, this one who had not been able to use his withered right hand—we do not know for how long—stretched it forth in demonstration of the power of Jesus to do good on the sabbath, to save a life, not destroy it.

they were filled with madness.—Their fury knew no bounds. Their cleverly arranged trap had been turned against them. They couldn't answer the logic of Jesus, for before their very eyes stood the man whose withered hand had been restored.

There was but one thing left: They would destroy Jesus. They talked the matter over among themselves. Their only question was, "What shall we do with him?" "They took counsel against him, how they might destroy him" (Matt. 12:14).

Jesus Selects the Twelve Apostles

Scripture

6:12-16 And it came to pass in these days, that he went out into the mountain to pray; and he continued all night in prayer to God. 13 And when it was day, he called his disciples; and he chose from them twelve, whom also he named apostles: 14 Simon, whom he also named Peter, and Andrew his brother, and James and John, and Philip and Bartholomew, 15 and Matthew and Thomas, and James *the son* of Alphaeus, and Simon who was called the Zealot,

16 and Judas *the son* of James, and Judas Iscariot, who became a traitor.

he went into the mountain to pray.—In His prayer life, Jesus presents an example for His disciples to follow. He prayed before choosing the twelve; He prayed after the feeding of the five thousand; He prayed during His baptism. He prayed publically; He prayed alone. His private prayers sometimes lasted all night long; invariably, His public prayers were brief.

He prayed all night to God just before choosing the twelve. We are not told what He said. We only know something of the significance of the issues involved. On the shoulders of these men was to rest the responsibility of carrying on the work of preaching the gospel in all the world. The success of His earthly mission would depend on them. Some of them were weak. One would deny that he had ever known such a person as Jesus. Another would betray Him into the hands of His enemies. What better way to ponder the problems of preaching the gospel in all the world than to pray to God? Did that night seem long to Him, or did the morning light find Him still grateful for the privilege of talking to His heavenly Father? This we do know, when the night was over He was ready for the great decision.

he called His disciples; and he chose from them twelve.—Some of these men had been following Jesus from the beginning. John tells the story of Andrew bringing his brother Simon to Jesus. Luke has already mentioned their becoming fishers of men. Now they are to be formally selected from the many disciples and designated apostles.

An apostle is one who is sent on a mission. The apostles of Christ were selected by Him and sent by Him to carry the gospel into all the world. Later, He chose Paul to be an apostle also. See Acts 9:3-6; 22:7-21; 26:12-18. Matthias was chosen by the Lord to take the place from which Judas fell away (Acts 1:24-26).

The apostles were equipped to carry out their worldwide mission by being baptized in the Holy Spirit (Acts 1:5, 8; 2:1-4). Paul also had all the rights of an apostle, although he was not of the original twelve (II Cor. 12:12).

Others such as Barnabas and James the Lord's brother were referred to as apostles because of having been sent out by the church (Acts 13:1-3). They, of course, were not baptized in the Holy Spirit, for that was limited to the twelve on the Day of Pentecost.

The writer of Hebrew says, "Consider the Apostle and High Priest of our confession, even Jesus" (Heb. 3:1). He can be called "apostle" because the Father sent Him. Understanding the use of the term depends on the one doing the sending. Christ sent the twelve and Paul; the church sent out some for special duties; God sent the Christ.

Simon, whom he also named Peter.—Peter is named first in all four of the lists of apostles (Matt. 10:2-4; Mk. 3:16-18; Lk. 6:14-16; Acts 1:13). The fact that he is mentioned first has led some to assume that he is head of the apostolic group. No such idea is presented in the Scriptures, for prominence is not preeminence. Exactly the same authority was given to all the apostles that was given to Peter (Matt. 16:19; 18:18). Jesus said to all of His apostles that in the regeneration—this Christian age when men are being made new creatures through obedience to the Word—the apostles were to sit on *twelve* thrones judging the twelve tribes of Israel (Matt. 19:28).

For the account of changing Simon's name to Peter, see John 1:42. But Jesus continued to address him as Simon. See Matt. 16:17; Lk. 22:31; John 21:15.

Among the outstanding things for which Peter is remembered are: (1) the good confession (Matt. 16:16); (2) the tragic denial (Lk. 22:54-62; and (3) the powerful sermon on the Day of Pentecost (Acts 2:14-40). He wrote two epistles to strengthen his brethren in Christ.

and Andrew his brother.—Andrew was one of the two disciples of John the Baptist who heard him speak of Jesus saying, "Behold the Lamb of God." John 1:35-42. The first thing he did after becoming convinced of the truth of John's statement was to find his own brother Simon and say, "We have found the Messiah." He will always be remembered for the fact that he brought his own brother to Jesus. In his quiet way, Andrew must be considered as an effective worker for Christ even though the prominence of his brother sometimes overshadows him.

When Philip was confronted with the problem of the Greeks who wanted to see Jesus, he sought the help of Andrew, not Peter, in deciding what to do. John adds the significant statement: "Andrew cometh, and Philip, and they tell Jesus" (John 12:22).

James and John.—Mark says that Jesus nicknamed these sons of Zebedee "Boanerges" which means "Sons of thunder" (Mark 3:

104

17). Their wanting to call fire from heaven to burn up a Samaritan village might suggest a reason for this name. See Lk. 9:54. They were selfishly ambitious and often made the other disciples jealous. See Matt. 20:20-28. At one time they actually sent their mother to ask Jesus to let her two sons sit one on the right hand and one on the left hand in His kingdom—evidently thinking of His kingdom as an earthly one like that of David or Solomon.

There is some reason to believe that James and John were cousins of Jesus. A comparison of the names of the women who were present at the crucifixion of Jesus suggests this possibility. See McGarvey and Pendleton, *The Fourfold Gospel,* page 225. If they were cousins of Jesus, their request for special consideration in His kingdom becomes a little more understandable even if less admirable.

These two and Peter formed what is sometimes called "the inner circle" of Jesus' disciples. He often took them with Him while leaving the others behind. They were with Him at the raising of Jairus' daughter (Lk. 8:51); the Transfiguration (Lk. 9:28); and in Gethsemane (Matt. 26:37). But it is possible that He kept them closer because they needed to be watched more than the others.

James was the first of the apostles to suffer martyrdom (Acts 12: 1-2). For a reference to John's death, see John 21:21-23.

John was prominent in the work of the church in Jerusalem. See Acts 3:1; 4:13. He wrote the Gospel of John, the three epistles, and the Revelation. (Some do not accept this view of the authorship of the books commonly believed to have been written by John the apostle).

Philip and Bartholomew.—Except for their place in the list of the Twelve and, in Philip's case, the mention made in John 12:22, little is known about the work of these disciples. See also John 1:43 and 6:5-7.

Matthew and Thomas.—As to Matthew, see comments on Lk: 5:27-32. Thomas who was called Dydimys—the name means "Twin"— is generally thought of as "doubting" Thomas, a charge that cannot be supported by the recorded facts. He was, in fact, a great believer. But he was not one to accept evidence until he had investigated it. When Jesus told him to put his finger in the print of the nail in His hand, Thomas said, "My Lord and my God." John 20:24-29.

James the son of Alphaeus, and Simon who was called the Zealot.— James is sometimes identified with James the less (Mk. 15:40).

Simon whom Luke calls the Zealot is called the Cananean by both Matthew and Luke.

Judas the son of James and Judas Iscariot.—Such names as Judas, Simon, and James were quite common. It is difficult to clearly identify some of those who bore these names. But Judas Iscariot forever bears the stigma of the one who betrayed his Lord.

Jesus Teaching the Crowds

Scripture

6:17-19 And he came down with them, and stood on a level place, and a great multitude of his disciples, and a great number of the people from all Judaea and Jerusalem, and the sea coast of Tyre and Sidon, who came to hear him, and to be healed of their diseases; 18 and they that were troubled with unclean spirits were healed. 19 And all the multitude sought to touch him; for power came forth from him, and healed them all.

Comments

and he came down with them.—Matthew describes a similar incident, but clearly states that when Jesus saw the multiudes He went up into the mountain and sat down. Then His disciples came to Him and He taught them (Matt. 5:1-2). Is Luke just giving another version of the Sermon on the Mount (Matt. 5-6-7)? The similarities are many and striking, but the differences must be accounted for. Luke says that Jesus came down to a level place (perhaps on the mountain), but Matthew says that He went up into the mountain. Matthew presents eight beatitudes; Luke gives four beatitudes and four woes. And there are other differences.

While it is possible to view these as two accounts of the same incident, it seems more likely that Luke tells about another occasion when Jesus taught the multitudes using much of the material He had used before. This would account for the differences. What of the similarities? Surely Jesus repeated these basic truths many times in the course of His teaching ministry. It is natural to suppose that He would change the message to suit the needs of the audience. While these matters are interesting, we should not become so involved in trying to answer the problems that we lose sight of the lessons taught.

and a great number of people.—The report about Jesus' activity spread throughout the whole country from Judea to Tyre and Sidon (Matt. 4:24-25).

to hear him and to be healed.—People came to hear Jesus and to be healed of their diseases. The demon possessed were healed also.

all the multitudes sought to touch him.—He could have spoken the word and they would have been healed, but the touch of His hand gave them added assurance. The power went forth from Him and healed them all.

The Beatitudes and the Woes

Scripture

6:20-26 And he lifted up his eyes on his disciples, and said, Blessed are ye poor: for yours is the kingdom of God. 21 Blessed are ye that hunger now: for ye shall be filled. Blessed are ye that weep now: for ye shall laugh. 22 Blessed are ye, when men shall hate you, and when they shall separate you from their company, and reproach you, and cast out your name as evil, for the Son of man's sake. 23 Rejoice in that day, and leap for joy: for behold, your reward is great in heaven; for in the same manner did their fathers unto the prophets. 24 But woe unto you that are rich! for ye have received your consolation. 25 Woe unto you, ye that are full now! for ye shall hunger. Woe unto you, ye that laugh now! for ye shall mourn and weep. 26 Woe unto you, when all men shall speak well of you! for in the same manner did their fathers to the false prophets.

Comments

he lifted up his eyes.—A speaker normally looks at his audience, but Luke seems to suggest something more when he says that Jesus lifted up His eyes on the disciples. He saw them as men who needed the lesson He was about to give. There were blessings for some but woes for others. All of them must have been aware of the importance of what He was about to say as He swept the audience with His eyes.

Blessed.—Only from the context can the rich meaning of the word be grasped. See it in Psa. 1:1 "Blessed is the man"—and there follows the description of the fortunate man who meditates on the Word of God day and night. Jesus spoke of those who were so fortunate as to cause others to long for the same blessed state.

"Happy" seems very limited as a word to carry all that is implied by the word Jesus used.

ye poor.—What did the poor of His audience think when He congratulated them and called them fortunate? Usually the poor are to be pitied. "Poor in spirit" seems to refer to humble people. But Jesus said, according to Luke, "blessed are ye poor." It is possible that He intended to speak to those who were literally poor. It was a common thing for the poor to be mistreated by the rich. See James 2:6. Jesus came to preach good tidings to the poor (Lk. 4: 18). It can mean the poor in spirit and also the poor in material goods. The principles of the gospel if applied would banish poverty from this world. See Paul's word to the poverty stricken Macedonians in II Cor. 8:1-9.

ye that hunger now.—In the fourth beatitude as Matthew reports it, Jesus spoke of those who hunger and thirst after righteousness. Are we to read this concept into Luke's account? Is it possible that Jesus was speaking to those who were actually feeling the pangs of hunger? We do know that He was aware of the physical needs of His people also, for He fed them on loaves and fishes. But more than that, He provided for their spiritual sustenance by giving them the Bread of Life. See James' word about those who lack daily food (James 2:15). So often those who lack daily food also lack the food that satisfies the soul.

for yours is the kingdom of God.—The poor are to be comforted in that they may have a rich blessing for their souls in this life. But in addition to that, the kingdom of God—heaven itself—belongs to them. There will be no poverty there, even though "the poor ye have with you always" in this world.

Wherever the Word of Christ has been fully accepted, the hungry are filled both literally and figuratively. The answer to the needs of the world is not the doctrine of materialism but the gospel of Christ. The gospel in the hearts of men will cause them to share the produce of the world with the needy and also the Bread of Life that will abolish spiritual poverty. See II Cor. 9:10-15.

that weep now: for ye shall laugh.—According to Matthew, Jesus said, "they that mourn shall be comforted." Is this a reference to the grief of this life or to those whose godly sorrow leads to repentance? Luke seems to place emphasis on the issue of the present first and the future last. Those who weep now shall laugh in heaven, for there will be no tears there.

when men shall hate you.—Peter and John gave an example of the proper attitude for Christians under persecution. They preferred the approval of God rather than men. See Acts 4:19-21.

your reward is great in heaven.—It is possible that all these rewards are heavenly. Jesus said, "In this world ye have tribulations: but be of good cheer; I have overcome the world (John 16:33). See also Phil. 3:20-21; II Pet. 3:11-13; Rev. 21-4-5.

But woe unto you that are rich.—Not the possession, but the misuse of riches is condemned. The one who worships gold rather than God justly comes under this condemnation. See James 1:9-11 for the correct view that puts the riches of heaven above the temporary riches of this life.

ye have received your consolation.—Some men prayed to be seen of men, and when men saw them and spoke of them as religious people, they were paid in full. When one makes riches his goal, he must settle for the consolation that riches bring, but he should remember what the Lord said about the time when riches fail. See Lk. 12:20-21; 16:11.

full now.—The emphasis is on "now." Some people are perfectly satisfied with physical food and have no thought for the food of the soul. Many who ate the loaves and fishes merely wanted more of the same and were not interested in the Bread of Life. "Ye shall hunger" seems to look to the time when those who have contented themselves with material riches will realize that they should have given some attention to the spiritual life.

that laugh now.—The laughter of the wicked will become the cries of the lost. James says, "Clean your hands, ye sinners; and purify your hearts ye doubleminded. Be afflicted, and mourn, and weep: let your laughter be turned into mouring, and your joy into heaviness" (James 4:8-9).

Neither Jesus nor James prohibit Christian joy and laughter. There is no record of Jesus having laughed, but He did join in the festive occasions of the people. If He did laugh, it certainly was not at some filthy joke. Much of what passes for humor today illustrates what Jesus was talking about. The "jesting" which Paul forbids is of the same sort—a well turned phrase that suggests evil and causes some to laugh at the filth of the world. Christian people ought not to be guilty of such a thing.

when all men speak well of you.—We are not to assume that a good reputation was not to be desired, for God's people are "to take

thought for things honorable in the sight of all men" (Rom. 12:
17). But Jesus was speaking of those who flattered the false
prophets in order to be in their favor. The fathers of the Jews had
been guilty of this very thing. But Jesus was not influenced by the
flattery of men. For example, He wasn't moved by their efforts to
that of men will find that they may have to pay dearly for their
make Him their king. Those who prefer the approval of Christ to
loyalty to the Lord (II Tim. 3:12).

Regulations for Conduct

Scripture

6:27-38   But I say unto you that hear, Love your enemies do good
to them that hate you, 28 bless them that curse you, pray for them
that despitefully use you. 29 To him that smiteth thee on the *one*
cheek offer also the other; and from him that taketh away thy cloak
withhold not thy coat also. 30 Give to every one that asketh thee;
and of him that taketh away thy goods ask them not again. 31 And
as ye would that men should do to you, do ye also to them likewise.
32 And if ye love them that love you, what thank have ye? for
even sinners love those that love them. 33 And if ye do good to them
that do good to you, what thank have ye? for even sinners do the
same. 34 And if ye lend to them of whom ye hope to receive, what
thank have ye? even sinners lend to sinners, to receive again as
much. 35 But love your enemies, and do *them* good, and lend, never
despairing; and your reward shall be great, and ye shall be sons of
the Most High: for he is kind toward the unthankful and evil.
36 Be ye merciful, even as your Father is merciful. 37 And judge not,
and ye shall not be judged: and condemn not, and ye shall not
be condemned: release, and ye shall be released: 38 give, and it
shall be given unto you; good measure, pressed down, shaken together, running over, shall they give into your bosom. For with
what measure ye mete it shall be measured to you again.

Comments

Love your enemies.—Some of the things that Jesus said must have
seemed difficult if not impossible. "Love your enemies." But they
hate you and curse you and spitefully use you! They strike you on
the cheek and even take away your property. How can you love
them? The answer lies in the meaning of "love." Jesus did not say

"Have the same feeling toward an enemy as you have for a friend." Love, according to this context, requires one to bless one's enemies and pray for them and do good to them. Turn the other cheek, when one strikes you. If he takes your garment—it could be done by law Ex. 22:26—give also the one that he could not legally take.

These directives are difficult, but not impossible to comply with. In essence, they suggest God's love for the world, and Jesus' attitude toward those who mistreated Him. On the cross He prayed, "Father, forgive them for they know not what they do."

Paul defines love in I Cor. 13:4-8. Love suffers long and is kind. We can be kind to an enemy. And strangely, an act of kindness may sometimes change an enemy into a friend.

as ye would that men should do to you.—This suggests that it might be easier to be kind to an enemy—love him—if we would put ourselves in his place. An honest effort to understand the other person's viewpoint might help to remove the enmity. This rule was based on the law and the prophets (Matt. 7:12). Jesus went a step farther in His teaching to the apostles when He said, "A new commandment I give unto you, that ye love one another, even as I have loved you." See John 13:34. Peter also said, "Seeing ye have purified your souls in your obedience to the truth unto unfeigned love of the brethren, love one another from the heart fervently" (I Pet. 1: 22).

and ye shall be sons of the Most High.—Jesus illustrated the issue of love for enemies by the fact that God sends the rain on the good and the bad alike (Matt. 5:43-48). Then He said, "Ye therefore shall be perfect as your heavenly Father is perfect." Men say, "That's a worthy goal, but impossible of attainment." But did Jesus give a command that can't be obeyed? What does "be perfect" mean? In this context it means complete or mature. Just as the Father sent the rain on the good and the bad—there are no others—so His children are to love their friends and their enemies; and that is perfect in the sense of completeness, for there are no others.

Jesus did not mean "sinless" when He said, "Be perfect." As long as we live, we can—although we ought not to—commit sin (I Cor. 10:12).

The sermon that Luke reported was slightly different from the one Matthew reported. According to Luke, Jesus said, "Ye shall be sons of the Most High, for He is kind toward the unthankful and

111

evil." Then Jesus said, "Be merciful, even as your Father is merciful."

And judge not.—This is expanded in verses 41-45 and in Matt. 7: 1-5. Jesus was speaking of hypocritical judging. But He also said that you can tell false prophets by their fruits. On another occasion He said, "Judge not according to appearance, but judge righteous judgments" (John 7:24).

And why not judge? "For with what measure ye mete it shall be measured to you again."

Four Concise Statements

Scripture

6:39-45 And he spake also a parable unto them, Can the blind is not above his teacher: but every one when he is perfected shall be as his teacher. 41 And why beholdest thou the mote that is in thy guide the blind? shall they not both fall into a pit? 40 The disciple brother's ye, but considerest not the beam that is in thine own eye? 42 Or how canst thou say to thy brother, Brother, let me cast out the mote that is in thine eye, when thou thyself beholdest not the beam that is in thine own eye? Thou hypocrite, cast out first the beam out of thine own eye, and then shalt thou see clearly to cast out the mote that is in thy brother's eye. 43 For there is no good tree that bringeth forth corrupt fruit; nor again a corrupt tree that bringeth forth good fruit. 44 For each tree is known by is own fruit. For of thorns men do not gather figs, nor of a bramble bush gather they grapes. 45 The good man out of the good treasure of his heart bringeth forth that which is good; and the evil *man* out of the evil *treasure* bringeth forth that which is evil: for out of the abundance of the heart his mouth speaketh.

Comments

Can the blind guide the blind?—A solemn warning not to follow blindly those who are not qualified to lead. Jesus applied this to the Pharisees (Matt. 15:12-14; 23:16).

The disciple is not above his teacher.—As long as one is following his teacher, he will not get beyond the teacher. When he is fully taught—knows all the teacher can impart to him—he will be as his teacher.

Jesus was speaking of the people who were being corrupted by the teachers they were following. They could scarcely be expected to rise above their leaders—scribes and Pharisees.

It is different when it comes to Jesus, the Teacher. He taught the truth. What a goal for a disciple of His to be fully taught and to be like Him!

Thou hypocrite, cast out first the beam that is in thine own eye.—Jesus had drawn a verbal cartoon for His audience. The lesson was so plain no one could miss it. The man with a large timber in his eye couldn't possibly remove a speck from his brother's eye. But we try it over and over today!

For each tree is known by its own fruit.—Conduct indicates true character just as fruit shows the true nature of the tree that bears it.

out of the abundance of the heart his mouth speaketh.—What is in the heart will come out in the speech. See Matt. 15:18-20. Let him who would glorify the Lord in his speech fill his heart with the truth of God's Word. See Psa. 119:11; 19:7-14; Phil. 4:4-9.

The Necessity of Obedience

Scripture

6:46-49   And why call ye me, Lord, Lord, and do not the things which I say? 47 Every one that cometh unto me, and heareth my words, and doeth them, I will show you to whom he is like: 48 he is like a man building a house, who digged and went deep, and laid a foundation upon the rock: and when a flood arose, the stream brake against that house, and could not shake it: because it had been well builded. 49 But he that heareth, and doeth not, is like a man that built a house upon the earth without a foundation, against which the stream brake, and straightway it fell in; and the ruin of that house was great.

Comments

And why call ye me Lord, Lord.—See Matt. 7:22-23. Jesus called for sincerity and honesty in all human relationships. Hypocritical judging was forbidden. Those who followed Him were to have their heart in it. Unless you say it by your life, there is no use to call Him Lord with your mouth.

heareth my words and doeth them.—James said, "Be ye doers of the word, and not hearers only" (James 1:22). Failing to do so results in self-delusion. Jesus' graphic illustration of the two houses—one built on solid rock and the other with no foundation—shows the folly of failing to obey His word.

Special Note

THE SABBATH

A. The Jews and the sabbath.
    1. It is first mentioned in Ex. 16:26.
    2. Was it observed as an eternal principle by Adam? The fact that Gen. 2:2-3 states that God rested on the seventh day and hallowed it, leads some to assume that it was given to Adam and all his posterity. This view contradicts Moses' statement that no other nation—not even their fathers—had this law of which the sabbath law was a part (Deut. 4:8; 5:1-3; 4:13). Moses mentioned the sabbath when he gave the account of the creation because the Jews were keeping it when he wrote. God had given it to the Jews because it was on the seventh day that He had rested from His work.
    3. Why was it given to the Jews? The seventh day, rather than any other day, was given because on it God had rested (Ex. 20:11). It was given to commemorate the deliverance of Israel from Egypt (Deut. 5:15).
    4. What is the relation of the sabbath to the Old Covenant? The first important fact to remember is that the Old Covenant was the Ten Commandments of which the sabbath was the fourth (Ex. 34:28; Deut. 4:13). A second and equally important fact is this: The New Covenant supplanted the Old and the sabbath is nowhere found as a part of the New. See Jer. 31:31-34; Heb. 8:6-13; II Cor. 3:2-18; Gal. 4:21-31.
B. Jesus and the sabbath.
    1. Why did He, as His custom was, observe the sabbath? He was born under the Law to redeem those under the Law (Gal. 4:4). At the time of His birth, His parents complied with the Law of Moses (Lk. 2:22-24). When the leper was cleansed, He commanded him to comply with the Law (Matt. 8:4). During His ministry, when asked what to do to have eternal life, He pointed to the Ten Commandments as the answer (Mk. 10:17-22). On the Day of Pentecost, however, when Peter spoke by the Holy Spirit, he said, "Repent and be baptized for the remission of sins"

(Acts 2:38). This is the directive in connection with the New Covenant.

2. What proof is there that He never broke the Law, although he was charged with sabbath-breaking?

The Jews complained that He broke the sabbath when He healed the lame man at Bethesda, but He defended His action by saying, "My Father worketh until now and I work" (John 5:18). A year and a half later, He referred to this incident and reminded the Jews that they carried out the law of circumcision even on the sabbath (John 7:21-24). When two laws were in conflict, the lesser was suspended at the point of conflict. Then why condemn Jesus for making a man completely whole on the sabbath?

He appealed to common sense when He asked, "Is it lawful to do good or bad on the sabbath?" (Matt. 12:9-12) No one dared say that His miracles of healing were bad. He pointed out the inconsistency of their complaints against Him, for they were in the habit of loosing the ox or the ass and leading it to water on the sabbath. See Luke 13:15. Does this indicate that the law had been relaxed to some extent? See Num. 15:32-36. Again, He answered the complaint of the Jews by reference to their history, specifically, an incident that involved David. See Matt. 12:2-8. It was mercy and not sacrifice that pleased God.

C. The Christian and the sabbath.

1. Was it the appointed day of meeting of the church? The first day of the week, and not the sabbath, was the day of their meeting. See Acts 20:7; I Cor. 16:1-2.

2. Why did the apostles go to the synagogue on the sabbath? They went to preach the Gospel. See the account of Paul preaching in the synagogue on the sabbath in Antioch in Acts 13:14-52. They did some things as Jews which they refused to let others bind on Gentile Christians—for example, circumcision (Gal 2:3-5). At Cenchreae Paul kept the provisions of a Jewish vow (Acts 18:18) and later in Jerusalem he was prepared to make certain Jewish offerings (Acts 21:17-31). He did these things as Jewish customs, not as Christian obligations (Rom. 14:5-6).

3. Was the sabbath changed to the first day of the week? No. What about Constantine? He had nothing to do with it. The New Testament was written long before his time, and it indicates that the early church gathered on the first day of the week, not the sabbath (Acts 20:7).

4. Are Christians commanded to "keep the first day of the week as a holy day" and refrain from working on that day? That provision related to the sabbath, not the first day of the week, the Lord's day. On the first day of the week, Christians were to assemble, break bread, preach the Word, and present the offering; but every day of the week was a holy day for them.

5. Is the Lord's day the first day of the week? The expression is found only in Rev. 1:10. Acts 20:7 indicates that the first day of the week was the day of meeting for the church.

6. What, then, is the significance of the sabbath to the Christian? It is a type of rest in heaven. See Heb. 4:9.

Summary

In this chapter Luke gives a condensed statement of some of the most interesting and important events in the Galilean ministry of Our Lord. He completes his report on a series of complaints against Jesus. The two mentioned in this chapter are based on Jesus' supposed breaking of the sabbath. He tells of the selecting of the Twelve and the teaching of the multitudes. The lessons Jesus taught on that occasion are similar to those of the Sermon on the Mount as presented by Matthew.

The complaints about working on the sabbath are based on two different types of work. One was, according to the Jews, actual work on the holy day, for the disciples of Jesus pulled off the heads of grain and rubbed them in their hands to get the grain. But Jesus pointed out that they hadn't been reading the Bible or, if they had, they hadn't understood the meaning of David's action when he used the bread that according to law was for priests only and gave it to his men to keep them alive. The Son of Man who explained this Scripture to the Jews is also Lord of the sabbath and allowed His men to gather the grain for food on that holy day.

The other work was the merciful work of healing a man with a withered hand. Jesus knew what they were thinking, so He told the man to stand up in the midst of the group where everyone could see him. Then He commanded him to stretch forth his hand, and it was restored. The senseless fury of the complainers asked only, "What can we do to get rid of Him?"

Selecting the twelve apostles was one of the most important tasks in the ministry of Jesus. He spent all night in prayer before making the choice. Luke gives their names and tells something

116

about some of them, closing his report with Judas who became the traitor.

After choosing the twelve, Jesus came down with them and stood on a level place where a large crowd from Judea and Jerusalem and even from Tyre and Sidon had gathered. They had come to hear Him and to be healed of their diseases.

The lesson began with the four Beatitudes and the four Woes. Then Jesus spoke of conduct toward enemies and others. In four brief statements of truth, He warned against following blind guides, false teachers, hypocritical judging, and conduct that is like trees producing corrupt fruit.

He closed the lesson with a warning about the necessity of true obedience. He warned against calling Him "Lord, Lord" and not doing what He said. He showed them what this meant by the illustration of the two houses, the one built on rock, the other had no foundation.

Questions

1. What are the five complaints against Christ as given in chapters five and six?
2. On what issue were the two presented in this chapter based?
3. What was the original law about work on the sabbath?
4. What are the two types of work about which the complaints were made?
5. How does Jesus' reference to David justify His disciples conduct?
6. What did Jesus say about His own relation to the sabbath?
7. What was unusual about the presence of the man with the withered hand in the synagogue on that sabbath when Jesus was present?
8. For what were the Pharisees hoping?
9. How was the issue brought to the test?
10. What did Jesus tell the man to do? Why?
11. What question did Jesus ask?
12. What did He do just before He told the man to stretch forth his hand?
13. What effect did the miracle have on those who were hoping to find a cause to condemn Jesus?
14. What did the enemies of Jesus plan to do?
15. What did Jesus do before selecting the Twelve?

16. What are some of the facts about the prayer life of Jesus?
17. How long did Jesus pray on that occasion?
18. What is an apostle?
19. Why was Jesus called the Apostle?
20. What principle is to be observed in explaining the use of the word "apostle"?
21. In what sense did Paul refer to James the Lord's brother as an apostle?
22. Was Peter's authority as an apostle different from that of the other apostles?
23. What is known about Andrew?
24. Why did Jesus call James and John "Sons of thunder"?
25. What may be said of the three who are commonly thought of as being the "inner circle of apostles"?
26. What of the two named Judas?
27. What are some of the difference between Matthew's account of the Sermon on the Mount and Luke's report of the lessons Jesus taught after selecting the Twelve?
28. Why did the people want to touch Jesus?
29. What four classes are called blessed?
30. What is the distinction between them and the ones mentioned in the Beatitudes of Matt. 5:1-12?
31. On what four classes are the woes pronounced?
32. What did Jesus mean when He said, "Beware when all men speak well of you"?
33. How can you love your enemies?
34. What rule of conduct toward others did Jesus give?
35. Is it possible to obey Jesus' command about love?
36. What did He mean by the reference to blind guides?
37. What did He mean by saying that a disciple is not above his teacher?
38. What kind of judging did He forbid?
39. Why did He say that a tree is known by its fruits?
40. What did He say about calling Him "Lord, Lord"?
41. How did He illustrate the necessity of obeying His word?

CHAPTER SEVEN

Outline

A. Luke's account of two miracles in the healing ministry of Jesus (1-17).

   1. Healing the centurion's servant—a lesson in faith (1-10).

      a) It took place at Capernaum (1).

      b) The centurion appealed to Jesus (2-5).

         (1) His servant was dear to him and at the point of death.

         (2) He sent the elders of the Jews to ask Jesus to come and save his servant.

         (3) The elders urged Jesus to do so. They said:

            (a) He is worthy that you do this for him.

            (b) He loves our nation and built our synagogue.

      c) Jesus went with the elders (6-9).

         (1) As they neared the house, they met the friends of the centurion with a message for Jesus.

            (a) He did not feel worthy to have Jesus enter his house or even to come in person to ask Jesus to come.

            (b) His request: "Say the word and my servant shall be healed."

            (c) The centurion's insight into the power and authority of Jesus:

               i) As a man under authority he understood the power of giving orders.

               ii) He knew what it meant to have his orders obeyed.

         (2) Jesus marveled and said, "Not even in Israel have I found such faith."

      d) When the centurion's friends returned to the house, they found the servant in good health.

   2. Raising the widow's son—a demonstration of Jesus' compassion (11-17).

      a) The circumstances leading to the miracle (11-13).

         (1) Jesus and His disciples, accompanied by a great crowd, were nearing the city of Nain where they met the funeral procession.

         (2) The man that had died was the only son of a widowed mother.

(3) Many people from the city were with her.

(4) When the Lord saw her, He had compassion on her and said, "Don't cry."

  b) The gentle Jesus performed the mighty miracle (14-15).

    (1) He touched the bier and the bearers stood still.

    (2) He said, "Young man, I say to you, Arise."

    (3) The dead man sat up and began to speak.

    (4) Jesus gave him back to his mother.

  c) The effect of this miracle (16-17).

    (1) Fear held all in its grasp.

    (2) They glorified God saying, "A great prophet has arisen among us; God has visited His people."

    (3) The report went out to all Judea and surrounding country.

B. Luke's account of two incidents in the teaching ministry of Jesus (18-50).

  1. What He taught about John the Baptist—a lesson on true greatness (18-23).

    a) John had sent two of his disciples to ask Jesus (18-23):

      (1) "Are you the one that is to come, or are we to look for another?"

      (2) Jesus' answer:

        (a) Instead of answering "Yes" or "No," He showed them His power to heal many diseases and to restore the sight of the blind.

        (b) He said, "Go tell John what you have seen and heard."

        (c) He added, "Blessed is he whosoever he might be who is not ensnared by me."

    b) The lesson about John (24-35).

      (1) What did people expect to see in John? (24-26).

        (a) A reed shaken in the wind?

        (b) A man clothed in soft raiment?

        (c) A prophet? Yes, but more than a prophet.

      (2) The true greatness of John (27-28).

        (a) He was the messenger to prepare for the Lord.

        (b) Among those born of women there is none greater than John.

        (c) The one who is but little in the kingdom of God is greater than he.

    (3) The reaction to John's message (29-30).
        (a) Publicans justified God by being baptized by John.
        (b) The Pharisees and lawyers rejected the counsel of God, refusing to be baptized by John.
    (4) A contrast between John and Jesus (31-35).
        (a) The example of children playing games: Funeral or Wedding.
        (b) The people rejected both John and Jesus:
           i) They said John had a demon.
           ii) They accused Jesus of being a winebibber and a glutton.
        (c) The wise understood both John and Jesus, for "Wisdom is justified of all her children."

2. What He taught on the occasion of the anointing in the house of Simon the Pharisee—a lesson on love and forgiveness. (36-50).

a) Jesus was a guest in the house of Simon (36).
b) The anointing while He was at the table (37-38).
    (1) By a woman of the city, a sinner.
    (2) She knew that He was at the Pharisee's house.
    (3) She stood at His feet weeping; her tears wet His feet; she wiped them with her hair and anointed them with precious ointment.
c) The reaction of the Pharisee (39-47).
    (1) Simon was saying to himself, "If this man were a prophet—he was sure that He wasn't—he would have known what sort of woman was touching him. Simon knew her only as a sinner.
    (2) Jesus answered the question of Simon's mind and said, "Simon, I have something to say to you."
    (3) Simon answered, "Teacher, say it." (40)
    (4) Jesus told the story of two debtors, one owing five hundred denarii and the other, fifty. Their debts were cancelled when they couldn't pay them.
    (5) Jesus asked, "Which of them will love more?"
    (6) Simon answered, "I suppose the one to whom he forgave more."
    (7) Jesus said, "You have decided correctly." Then He

pointed out the contrast between what the woman did and what Simon neglected to do.

(8) Jesus said, "Her sins which are many are forgiven, for she loved much." But the one to whom little is forgiven, loves little—that was true of Simon.

d) The lesson of forgivness (48-50).

(1) He said to the woman, "Your sins are forgiven."

(2) The other guests said to themselves, "Who is this that even forgives sins?"

(3) Jesus said to the woman, "Your faith has saved you; go in peace."

Healing The Centurion's Servant

Scripture

7:1-10   After he had ended all his sayings in the ears of the people, he entered into Capernaum.

2 And a certain centurion's servant, who was dear unto him, was sick and at the point of death. 3 And when he heard concerning Jesus, he sent unto him elders of the Jews, asking him that he would come and save his servant. 4 And they, when they came to Jesus, besought him earnestly, saying, He is worthy that thou shouldest do this for him; 5 for he loveth our nation, and himself built us our synagogue. 6 And Jesus went with them. And when he was now not far from the house, the centurion sent friends to him, saying unto him, Lord, trouble not thyself; for I am not worthy that thou shouldest come under my roof: 7 wherefore neither thought I myself worthy to come unto thee: but say the word, and my servant shall be healed. 8 For I also am a man set under authority, having under myself soldiers: and I say to this one, Go, and he goeth; and to another, Come, and he cometh; and to my servant, Do this, and he doeth it. 9 And when Jesus heard these things, he marvelled at him, and turned and said unto the multitude that followed him, I say unto you, I have not found so great faith, no, not in Israel. 10 And they that were sent, returning to the house, found the servant whole.

Comments

After he had ended all his sayings.—that is, after the lesson recorded in chapter six. The incidents that follow, emphasize the healing ministry of Jesus. The place is Capernaum. See also Matt. 8:5-13.

a certain centurion's servant.—Theophilus, a Gentile, would be interested in this. Of course, by the time Luke was writing the account, the gospel had been preached to much of the Gentile world. The ministry of Jesus was largely to the "lost sheep of the house of Israel," but there were some Gentiles who shared in the blessings of the Son of God. Such incidents as this gave Gentiles as well as Jews grounds to hope in Him. See Matt. 12:21; Lk. 2:32.

This Roman soldier's servant was dear to him; this helps us to see what kind of a man he was. The cruel business of war often tends to harden the hearts of men; some officers have little regard for their men. But the centurion's concern for his servant commended him to Jesus.

sick and at the point of death.—The servant was in critical condition. The centurion's request was urgent. Nothing but a miracle could save him.

he heard concerning Jesus.—The people of the whole area had heard about the miracles of Jesus. See Lk. 4:37; 6:17-19. The news traveled fast, and the distressed people were eager to bring their sick for Him to heal. He never turned one away who called on Him for help.

he sent unto him elders of the Jews.—Matthew says that the centurion came to Jesus and told Him about the sick servant. In the light of Luke's statement, we assume that he did it through his agents, the elders of the Jews.

Not all leaders of the Jews were opposed to Jesus. These elders were respected men who, the centurion thought, would have influence with Jesus.

besought him earnestly.—The elders were evidently sincere in their desire to help the centurion. They presented a strong case: "He is worthy of this thing he asks you to do." "He loves the Jewish nation; he built our synagogue."

This is not the only Roman soldier to be commended in Luke's writings. Cornelius was a devout man and one who worshiped God with all his house. See Acts 10:1-8.

Gentiles were attracted to the nation of Israel because God had given them the revelation of His will in the Old Covenant (Deut. 4: 7-8; 5:2-3). He had promised them the Messiah who would "reign as king and deal wisely, and execute justice and righteousness in the land" (Jer. 23:5). Hope was kindled in the hearts of many who heard about Him. Gentiles who were without God and who had no hope in this world (Eph. 2:12) were strangely drawn to the people of God and the hope of all the world which is Christ. See Rom. 9:4-5.

But many Jews conducted themselves in such a manner as to cause Gentiles to blaspheme the name of God (Rom. 2:24). What a warning to Christians!

And Jesus went with them.—The Physician answered the call for help. The fact that a Gentile had turned to Him in his distress was not the point. Soon His gospel would be proclaimed in all the world with the message of salvation for all peoples.

the centurion sent his friends.—The genuine humility of the man made him realize that he was not worthy to have the Prophet enter his home. He sent his friends to ask Jesus to speak the word that his servant might live—such faith is the complement of such humility. Who were these friends? Jews or Gentiles? All we know is that they were friends. But his greatest Friend was the one whom some had called "the friend of sinners" (7:34).

say the word and my servant shall be healed.—John records a similar incident which should not be confused with this one (John 4:46-54). In both cases, however, Jesus spoke the word that brought healing to the sick without being in the immediate presence of the person to be healed. He was not limited either by time or by space, for He is God.

I also am a man set under authority.—As an officer of the Roman army, he knew what it meant to take orders as well as give orders. He knew what it meant to be obeyed when he spoke. Perhaps no one ought to give orders who does not know how to obey orders.

He believed that Jesus' authority extended to the realm of disease. He could give the order, and the centurion's servant would live. The soldier expected a miracle to take place.

when Jesus heard these things, he marvelled.—He marvelled because of the nature of the centurion's faith and because a Gentile had such faith in contrast to the lack of it in Israel. Jesus marvelled also because of the unbelief of the people of His own town (Mark 6:6).

found the servant.—Jesus spoke the word; the centurion's servant was healed, and his faith in Jesus was justified. The friends found the servant in good health when they returned to the house.

Luke describes this amazing miracle in such simple terms, but we should remember that it was "the work" of God.

Raising the Widow's Son

Scripture

7:11-17 And it came to pass soon afterwards, that he went to a city called Nain; and his disciples went with him, and a great multitude. 12 Now when he drew near to the gate of the city, behold, there was carried out one that was dead, the only son of his mother, and she was a widow: and much people of the city was with her. 13 And when the Lord saw her, he had compassion on her, and said unto her, Weep not. 14 And he came nigh and touched the bier: and the bearers stood still. And he said, Young man, I say unto thee, Arise. 15 And he that was dead sat up, and began to speak. And he gave him to his mother. 16 And fear took hold on all: and they glorified God, saying, A great prophet is arisen among us: and, God hath visited his people. 17 And this report went forth concerning him in the whole of Judaea, and all the region round about.

Comments

soon afterwards.—The footnote in some Bibles reminds us that many ancient manuscripts suggest that this event occurred on the next day, that is, the day following the healing of the centurion's son. Nain is some fifteen miles from Capernaum. It is possible that Jesus made the journey within the time limit. But more likely, Luke merely says that this miracle followed after the other one without specifying the exact day on which it occurred.

and a great multitude.—Large numbers of people witnessed this miracle. A crowd accompanied Jesus and His disciples, and another crowd from the city of Nain was with the funeral procession. With that many people having witnessed the miracle, Luke had no difficulty verifying the facts as he was preparing to write to Theophilus.

the only son of his mother.—Note the details which suggest the genuineness of this miracle: Luke tells of the exact spot where it occurred —"when He drew near the gates of the city." The dead man was young and the only son of a widowed mother.

when the Lord saw her.—Luke had become convinced of the deity of Jesus and didn't hesitate to refer to Him as the Lord. See Rom. 10:9-10.

he had compassion on her.—The word signifies a deep stirring of the emotions. Jesus had pity and sympathy for the distressed mother.

125

Literally, the word refers to the vital organs of the body: the heart, the liver, the intestines and others. We know that fear, anger, joy, anxiety affect the function of these organs. The language of the New Testament expresses it in a bold term. It means that Jesus was deeply affected by the sight that met His eyes; His pity and compassion were really felt.

Weep not.—Jesus put His compassion into words when He said, "Don't cry—don't go on weeping." How helpless, by contrast, we often find ourselves when we try to comfort the sorrowing. "Don't cry" has little effect unless the cause of grief is removed. That's exactly what Jesus did, for He raised the son from the dead and gave him back to his weeping mother.

"Don't go on crying" can have meaning to the Christian as he looks to the resurrection when the enemy which is death shall be abolished. Paul urged the Christians at Thessalonica not to sorrow as those who have no hope. He assured them that Christ will come and that the dead in Christ will be raised and the living will be caught up with them to meet the Lord in the air. These are indeed words of comfort. I Thes. 4:13-18; Rev. 14:13; I Pet. 1:3-5; I Cor. 15:50-58; II Cor. 4:16-5:8.

And he that was dead sat up.—Luke stresses this astounding thing: at the command of Jesus the dead man sat up and began to talk. Jesus gave him back to his mother.

Fear took hold on all.—The fear that held all in its grasp was not the fear that makes man a coward, but the fear that makes him bow in reverence before his God. They all praised God for what He had done, and they were all sure that God had raised up a Prophet in their midst.

God hath visited his people.—He had blessed them with the presence of Jesus the Son of God. The miracle that showed His compassion prepared them to accept His deity.

Reports about Jesus' activity quickly spread throughout all the country of Palestine—here called Judea—and the surrounding territory. These reports reached the ears of John's disciples.

About John the Baptist

Scripture

7:18-35   And the disciples of John told him of all these things. 19 And John called unto him two of his disciples sent them to the

Lord, saying, Art thou he that cometh, or look we for another? 20 And when the men were come unto him, they said, John the Baptist hath sent us unto thee, saying, Art thou he that cometh, or look we for another? 21 In that hour he cured many of diseases and plagues and evil spirits; and on many that were blind he bestowed sight. 22 And he answered and said unto them, Go and tell John the things which ye have seen and heard; the blind receive their sight, the lame walk, the lepers are cleansed, and the deaf hear, the dead are raised up, the poor have good tidings preached to them. 23 And blessed is he, whosoever shall find no occasion of stumbling in me.

24 And when the messengers of John were departed, he began to say unto the multitudes concerning John, What went ye out into the wilderness to behold? a reed shaken with the wind? 25 But what went ye out to see? a man clothed in soft raiment? Behold, they that are gorgeously apparelled, and live delicately, are in kings' court. 26 But what went ye out to see? a prophet? Yea, I say unto you, and much more than a prophet. 27 This is he of whom it is written,

Behold, I send my messenger before thy face,

Who shall prepare thy way before thee.

28 I say unto you, Among them that are born of women there is none greater than John: yet he that is but little in the kingdom of God is greater than he. 29 And all the people when they heard, and the publicans, justified God, being baptized with the baptism of John. 30 But the Pharisees and the lawyers rejected for themselves the counsel of God, being not baptized of him. 31 Whereunto then shall I liken the men of this generation, and to what are they like? 32 They are like unto children that sit in the market place, and call one to another; who say, We piped unto you, and ye did not dance; we wailed, and ye did not weep. 33 For John the Baptist is come eating no bread nor drinking wine; and ye say, He hath a demon. 34 The Son of man is come eating and drinking; and ye say, Behold, a gluttonous man, and a winebibber, a friend of publicans and sinners? 35 And wisdom is justified of all her children.

Comments

And the disciples of John.—Matthew informs us that John was in prison when this incident occurred (Matt. 11:2). Luke had referred to the imprisonment earlier in his account (Lk. 3:20). He also refers briefly to the death of John at the hands of Herod a little later (9:7-9).

Art thou he that cometh, or look we for another?—There are two views about the reason for asking this question. One suggests that John had become impatient and discouraged as a result of his imprisonment and was actually wondering whether or not Jesus was the Messiah. The other—this is the view presented here—holds that John sent his disciples to Jesus for their own sakes that their faith might be strengthened and that their loyalty might be centered Him.

This, of course, is a matter of opinion; but it is hard to believe that John's faith faultered in face of persecution. He had seen the Spirit descend and abide on Jesus. He had heard God say, "This is my Son." Was John more likely to forget than Peter and John who refused to obey the order of the Sanhedrin in the face of the threat of death? They had seen the Risen Lord and could not forget what they had heard from Him (Acts 4:19-20). John's disciples had been loyal to him to the point of jealousy over the popularity of Jesus. Some of them may have been slow to transfer their loyalty to Jesus. See John 3:22-30.

Go tell John the things which ye have seen and heard.—This does not necessarily suggest that John was in doubt about the matter; it may suggest that Jesus was presenting visable evidence of His claim to be the Messiah so that John's disciples could see for themselves. It would relieve John's anxiety over their loyalty to Jesus to have them tell of the proof of His Messiahship.

What Jesus said corresponds to Isaiah's prophecy about the Messiah which Jesus read in the synagogue in Nazareth at the beginning of His ministry (Lk. 4:16-20). He could have answered the question with a simple "yes," but it was better to present the evidence that permitted the disciples to arrive at the answer for themselves. Jesus not only pointed to the miracles as His credentials but also to the fact that the poor had good tidings preached to them—this was the mark of the Messiah.

And blessed is he whosoever shall find no occasion of stumbling in me.—Some were ensnared by what they saw in Jesus, largely because He did not come up to their expectations of Messiah. They saw Him at the feasts where publicans and sinners were gathered. They saw Him doing what they called work on the sabbath day. They heard Him reproach both the Pharisees and the lawyers. He rejected the kingly crown they offered to Him, but later was compelled to wear the crown of thorns in shameful mockery of the fact that He is the King of kings and Lord of lords. He was a stumbling block to Jews who sought signs from heaven, but ignored the works that proved Him to be the Christ (I Cor 1:22-25; John 10:31-38).

This was a word of encouragement, perhaps for John, and certainly for his disciples. And it is also for all who examine the evidence and accept Him as the Christ.

he began to say to the multitudes concerning John.—The coming of John's disciples gave Jesus an excellent opportunity to teach the people about true greatness as it was seen in John the Baptist. Was he a reed shaken by the wind, that is, a weakling? Far from it! John was known for his great courage as well as for his humility (Matt. 3:14; John 3:30). Was he a man clothed in soft raiment, that is, one like the pampered sons of the kings of that day? All who had seen him remembered his garments of camel's hair and the leather girdle about his waist. No, John was not a man of luxury and ease.

much more than a prophet.—John was a prophet as much so as Elijah or any other Old Testament man of God who spoke God's message to His people under the power of the Holy Spirit. But he was more than a prophet, for he actually presented Messiah to Israel. The others had foretold His coming (Deut. 18:15; John 5:46).

Among them that are born of women there is none greater than John.—John was great in dedication to the task God gave him. He was great in humility, gladly serving as the forerunner of the Christ. He was great in courage, boldly denouncing the sin of Herod the tetrarch. He was great in faith, accepting the evidence God gave to prove that Jesus was the Son of God (John 1:29-34).

yet he that is but little in the kingdom of God is greater than he.—The contrast is between one born of women and one in the kingdom of God who enters that kingdom by being born of the water and the Spirit (John 3:3-5). The least in the spiritual realm is greater than the greatest of the physical realm. The kingdom of God is spiritual, and those born into that kingdom are the children of God.

justified . . . rejected.—The people who heard the message of John acknowledged that God was right in condemning their sins. The

129

Pharisees and lawyers rejected God's advice given through John, because they imagined that they were already righteous. Mark 1:4. *Whereunto shall I liken the men of this generation?*—Jesus likened them to children playing in the market place. They were playing two kinds of games, one the exact opposite of the other. One was the wedding game; the other was like a funeral. "We piped unto you and you didn't dance—the wedding." "We wailed and you didn't mourn—the funeral." These games illustrate the attitude of the Pharisees and others who refused to accept either John or Jesus. John's message was like the mournful funeral game, and the Pharisees and lawyers refused to be baptized by him. Jesus' message was like the festive wedding game, but they called Him a gluttonous man and a winebibber, a friend of publicans and sinners. *a friend of publicans and sinners.*—The Pharisees sought to label Jesus and thereby discredit Him in the eyes of the people. In reality, He was the Lamb of God who took away the sins of the people.

The label was intended as an insult, but in reality it became a compliment, for He is the Friend of sinners who died to blot out their sins. The Pharisees said He was blaspheming when He said to a sinner, "Thy sins are forgiven."

They had implied that He was a sinner. His answer was, "They that are whole have no need of a physician, but they that are sick." He did not come to call the righteous, but sinners to repent. Matt. 9: 12-13.

And wisdom is justified of all her children.—Wisdom's children can see why it was necessary for John to do what he did, and also understand why Jesus ate with publicans and sinners. Folly rejected the counsel of God, refusing to respond to the preaching of either John or Jesus.

The Anointing in the House of Simon

Scripture

7:36-50   And one of the Pharisees desired him that he would eat with him. And he entered into the Pharisee's house, and sat down to meat. 37 And behold, a woman who was in the city, a sinner; and when she knew that he was sitting at meat in the Pharisee's house, she brought an alabaster cruse of ointment, 38 and standing behind at his feet, weeping, she began to wet his feet with her tears, and wiped them with the hair of her head, and kissed his feet, and anointed them with the ointment. 39 Now when the Pharisee that had bidden him saw it, he spake within himself, saying, This man, if he were a prophet, would have perceived who and what manner of woman this is that toucheth him, that she is a sinner. 40 And Jesus answering said unto him, Simon, I have somewhat to say unto thee. And he saith, Teacher, say on. 41 A certain lender had two debtors: the one owed five hundred shillings, and the other fifty. 42 When they had not *wherewith* to pay, he forgave them both. Which of them therefore will love him most? 43 Simon answered and said, He, I suppose, to whom he forgave the most. And he said unto him, Thou hast rightly judged. 44 And turning to the woman, he said unto Simon. Seest thou this woman? I entered into thy house, thou gavest me no water for my feet; but she hath wetted my feet with her tears, and wiped them with her hair. 45 Thou gavest me no kiss; but she, since the time I came in, hath not ceased to kiss my feet. 46 My head with oil thou didst not anoint: but she hath anointed my feet with ointment. 47 Wherefore I say unto thee, Her sins, which are many, are forgiven; for she loved much: but to whom little is forgiven, *the same* loveth little. 48 And he said unto her, Thy sins are forgiven. 49 And they that sat at meat with him began to say within themselves, Who is this that even forgiveth sins? 50 And he said unto the woman, Thy faith hath saved thee; go in peace.

Comments

And one of the Pharisees.—Luke mentions two other occasions when Jesus was a guest in the home of a Pharisee. One wonders why these Jewish leaders invited Him. Nicodemus was a Pharisee, but one who was interested in what Jesus had to say. The ones about whom Luke writes were openly antagonistic to Jesus.

This incident occurred at the height of Jesus' popularity; the Pharisee may have used it as an occasion to evaluate the claims of the Prophet for himself. It is evident that Simon didn't believe Him to be a prophet and perhaps sought to vindicate his judgment on the issue.

And behold, a woman who was a sinner.—We must be content to leave the woman unnamed as Luke does. All efforts to identify her with Mary Magdalene or any other known person of New Testament times are futile. Luke's designation, "a woman of the city, a sinner," is all that the account requires. Not the name of the woman, but the lesson Jesus taught is what matters. The lesson is this: Christ does forgive sinners, and those who really understand His merciful forgiveness love Him greatly.

There is no indication that Luke intended this story to illustrate the thought of verse 35, "Wisdom is justified of her children." It does show what the Pharisee thought of Jesus in contrast to the love shown toward Him by a sinner who found forgiveness because of His mercy.

when she knew that he was sitting at meat in the Pharisee's house.— Two things are evident: She must have known Jesus, and her love for the Savior prompted her to enter the Pharisee's house to anoint His feet. What finer place to show her love for Him than in the house of one who needed to know Him? Was her weeping a sign of shame for a sinful life she was leading, or was it a tears of joy over having found Him who had forgiven her sins? The further development of the story gives us the answer to these questions.

This man, if he were a prophet.—Simon was watching the woman as she washed Jesus' feet with her tears and anointed His feet with precious ointment. He assumed that Jesus neither knew the woman nor what sort she was. Details are missing about the time and place of her having found forgiveness through Christ. There is no doubt, however, about this being the motivating force that prompted her to express her great love and appreciation for what had been done by Him for her. Being unaware of this, Simon was already passing judgment on Jesus. He was saying to himself, "This man is no prophet; I knew it all along. No prophet would let a woman that is a sinner touch him."

And Jesus answering said unto him.—Simon had not said a word, but Jesus knew what he was thinking. Probably his digust could be seen in his face. His contempt for Jesus could scarcely be hidden.

Jesus said, "Simon, I have something to say to you." The scorn of the proud Pharisee must have shown through his half-polite permission for Jesus to speak: "Teacher, say it." Then Jesus told the little story of the two debtors and asked, "Which of them will love more?" It was a very simple story; anyone could answer the question. Simon's answer shows that he was completely unaware of the identity of the One who had asked it. He didn't know that Jesus was the Prophet about whom Moses had written (Deut. 18:15); Acts 3:22).

Thou hast rightly judged.—Although he answered with indifference, he answered correctly: "The one, I suppose, to whom he forgave more." Jesus turned to the woman and said to Simon, "Do you see this woman?" He had been quite sure of himself; he had judged her to be a sinner. Is it possible that the Pharisee was beginning to realize that he could have been mistaken? Was there something about the presence of this Teacher that was causing him to reexamine both the question and his answer?

Jesus began to point out the discourtesy—if not the insult—with which Simon had treated Him. He contrasted it with the thing which the woman "who was a sinner" had done. Then he added, with words that must have stung this proud Pharisee, "Her sins, her many sins, have been and remain forgiven."

The tense of the verb "are forgiven" indicates that this had already occurred at some past time and that the fact remained true at the time Jesus spoke. The point of Jesus' parable shows the same thing: the debtors had been forgiven, even though one debt was so slight as to mean little or nothing.

for she loved much.—According to Jesus' story of the debtors, the love followed the forgiveness. Love led her to anoint the feet of her Lord.

Who is this that even forgives sins?—They reasoned correctly when they said, "Only God can forgive sins"; but they were wrong when they assumed that Jesus was just a man and not God.

Thy faith hath saved thee.—that is, her faith had saved her at some point in the past and the fact remained at the moment when He was speaking to her. Her faith, not her love, was the cause of her being forgiven. Love followed forgiveness, just as in the story of the debtors.

go in peace.—More than just a dismissal, this is instruction to continue in the way of peace.

Summary

Four incidents of the ministry of Jesus are presented in this chapter. Two are of the healing ministry and two of the teaching ministry of the Lord. But the examples of healing were also used to teach; for teaching was primary in His ministry, miracles were worked to prove that He spoke from God.

Healing the centurion's servant gave Jesus the opportunity to point out the meaning of faith. The soldier knew how to give

133

orders, and he knew how to obey them. He believed that Jesus had the right to give the order and his servant would be healed. Jesus marvelled that a Gentile saw what Israel failed to see, the real meaning of faith.

The compassion of Jesus was shown in the miracle of raising the widow's son. People stood in awe when they saw it and glorified God saying, "A great prophet has arisen among us; God has visited His people."

The disciples of John asked Jesus, at John's suggestion, the burning question, "Are you the one that is to come, or are we to look for another?" Jesus answered by telling them to look at what He was doing. It was the fulfillment of the prophet's description of the work of the Messiah.

Jesus spoke of the greatness of John, but pointed out that the least in the kingdom of God is greater than the greatest born of woman. But there was wisdom in John's approach to the work he was to do, and there was also wisdom in what Jesus did, although many misunderstood both John and Jesus.

He taught the great lesson on love and forgiveness when He was a dinner guest in the house of Simon the Pharisee. The woman of the city, a sinner, had been forgiven at some time before this incident. Out of her great love for the Lord who had forgiven her sins, she entered the house of the Pharisee who didn't believe that He was the Prophet of God and before all the guests poured out the expression of her love on Him. Her sins were forgiven as shown by her love; but, as in Simon's case, little appreciation for forgiveness is accompanied by little love.

Questions

1. What does the New Testament say about the various Gentiles who were attracted to Jesus?
2. What caused the centurion to appeal to Jesus?
3. What was his reputation among the Jews?
4. Why did he ask the elders of the Jews to speak for him?
5. When and why did he decide that Jesus should not enter his house?
6. How did he explain his reason for saying to Jesus, "Say the word and my servant shall live"?
7. Why did Jesus marvel at what he said?
8. What are the circumstances of the raising of the widow's son?

9. What was Jesus' attitude toward the widowed mother?
10. What are some of the Scriptures that give hope to the Christian in the face of death?
11. What was the effect of the miracle on the people who witnessed it?
12. What did John do when he heard about all these things?
13. What question did John's disciples ask Jesus? Why?
14. How did Jesus answer?
15. Why did some find an occasion of stumbling in Jesus?
16. What questions did Jesus ask the people about John?
17. How explain what Jesus said about the greatness of John in contrast to the least in the kingdom of God?
18. What did Jesus mean by His reference to the games played by the children?
19. Why did they call Jesus a friend of publican and sinners?
20. How did He show the wisdom of His ministry and of John's.
21. Why did the Jewish leaders invite Jesus to their homes?
22. What does John say about the attitude of Nicodemus toward Jesus?
23. What was the name of the Pharisee in whose house the anointing took place?
24. What are the facts about the woman who anointed Him?
25. Why did she enter the Pharisee's house?
26. What was the Pharisee thinking while she was anointing the feet of Jesus?
27. What story did Jesus tell the Pharisee?
28. How did he treat it?
29. What lesson did Jesus teach from it?
30. What did He say about the woman's sins?
31. What had her dramatic demonstration of love proved?
32. Why do some have only little love for the Lord?

CHAPTER EIGHT

Outline

A. Luke told more about the teaching ministry of Jesus (1-21).
  1. On one of the tours of Jesus (1-3).
    a) He went through the cities and villages bringing the good tidings of the kingdom of God.
    b) Those who accompanied Him:
      (1) The twelve.
      (2) Certain woman who had been healed of evil spirits and other infirmities.
        (a) Mary Magdalene from whom seven demons had gone out.
        (b) Joanna, the wife of Chuzas who was Herod's steward.
        (c) Susanna and many others.
      (3) These women ministered to them out of their material possessions.
  2. The parable of the sower: How to understand the Word 4-15).
    a) Jesus spoke the parable to a crowd that assembled from every city.
    b) Results of sowing the seed:
      (1) On the wayside, the birds got it.
      (2) On the rocky soil, it withered for lack of moisture.
      (3) On the thorny soil, the thorns choked it out.
      (4) On the good soil, it produced a hundredfold.
    c) Jesus warned: "He that hath ears to hear, let him hear."
    d) Jesus explained the parable to the disciples.
      (1) The disciples were to understand the secrets of the kingdom, although others did not.
      (2) The seed is the Word that was heard by four classes.
        (a) On the wayside, those who hear and do not understand. The devil takes away what was heard.
        (b) On the rocky soil, those who hear but have no depth in themselves. They fall when temptation comes.

      (c) On the thorny soil, those who hear but allow the cares of the world and pleasures to choke out the Word.

      (d) On the good soil, those who heed the word and hold it fast and produce the harvest with patience.

3. The parable of the lamp: The Word is to be understood (16-18).

  a) A lighted lamp isn't covered up, but placed where it enables people to see.

  b) "Nothing is hid," that is, Jesus' teaching is to enable men to understand.

  c) Jesus warned, "Take heed how you hear." Hearing can add to understanding or cause one to lose what he thinks he has.

4. Spiritual kinship: The result of hearing and understanding the Word (19-21).

  a) Jesus' mother and brothers were trying to reach Him, but couldn't for the crowd.

  b) When He was told that they were seeking Him, He said, "My mother and my brethren are those who hear the Word of God and do it."

B. Luke told more about the healing ministry of the Master (22-56).

1. Stilling the tempest (22-25).

  a) The circumstances.

    (1) It happened on "one of those days."

    (2) Jesus and His disciples entered a boat and He said, "Let's go to the other side of the lake."

    (3) They set out for the other side, and Jesus fell asleep.

    (4) A wind storm came down upon them, filling the boat with water and putting their lives in jeopardy.

    (5) The disciples awoke Jesus and said, "Master, Master, we are perishing."

  b) The miracle.

    (1) Jesus awoke and rebuked the wind and the waves.

    (2) The wind ceased blowing; the waves stopped tossing; a calm set in.

  c) Then the Master taught the lesson on faith.

    (1) He asked, "Where is your faith?"

   (2) In reverence and wonder, they said to one another, "Who is this who gives orders to the winds and the waves and they obey Him?"

2. The Gerasene demoniac (26-39).
  a) The circumstances.
   (1) It was in the country of the Gerasenes on the opposite side of the lake from Galilee.
   (2) A naked demon-possessed man who lived in the tombs met Jesus as He landed.
   (3) He fell down before Jesus and in a loud voice said, "What have I to do with you Jesus, Son of the Most High God?"
  b) Casting out the demons (29-33).
   (1) The fact that Jesus was commanding them to come out had caused the man to cry out as he did.
   (2) No one had been able to keep him under guard, for the demons drove him into the desert places.
   (3) Jesus asked him, "What is your name?"
   (4) He said, "Legion," for many demons had entered him.
   (5) The demons begged not to be ordered to depart into the abyss.
   (6) Jesus granted them permission to enter into the swine that were feeding nearby.
   (7) When they did, the swine rushed down the steep bank and were drowned in the sea.
  c) The effect of the miracle (24-39).
   (1) The herdsmen fled and told the story in the city and country, for they were afraid.
   (2) Those who came to investigate found Jesus and the man sitting at His feet, clothed and in his right mind, and they were afraid.
   (3) The Gerasenes asked Jesus to leave their country, for they were seized with a great fear.
   (4) Jesus entered the boat and returned, for He was rejected by those who lost their possessions.
   (5) The man wanted to go with Jesus, but He sent him to his own house and city to tell about the great things God had done for him.

3. Two more miracles of mercy (40-56).

a) A twelve year old girl was dying (40-42a).
    (1) A crowd that had been waiting for Jesus welcomed Him when He returned.
    (2) Jairus, a ruler of the synagogue and father of the dying girl, asked Jesus for help.
b) A miracle that happened while He was on the way to Jairus house (42b-48).
    (1) As the people crowded around Him, a woman who had suffered from a flow of blood for twelve years touched Him and it stopped.
    (2) Jesus, knowing that power to heal had gone forth from Him, said, "Who touched me?"
    (3) The woman, in the presence of all the people, told why she had touched Him and how she had been healed.
    (4) Jesus said to her, "Daughter, your faith has saved you. Go in peace."
c) Raising Jairus' daughter from the dead (49-56).
    (1) As He was speaking to the woman, there came one from Jairus' house to say, "Your daughter is dead; do not trouble the Teacher."
    (2) Jesus said, "Believe and she shall be saved."
    (3) He permitted only Peter, John and James, and the father and mother of the child to enter the house with Him.
    (4) To the mourners within, He said, "Stop weeping. She is not dead, she is sleeping."
    (5) They laughed Him to scorn for they knew that she was dead.
    (6) Jesus took her by the hand and said, "Child, arise."
    (7) Her spirit returned and she arose.
    (8) Jesus had them give her some food, but told the parents to say nothing of what had happened.

Those Who Accompanied Jesus

Scripture

8:1-3 And it came to pass soon afterwards, that he went about through cities and villages, preaching and bringing the good tidings

of the kingdom of God, and with him the twelve, 2 and certain
women who had been healed of evil spirits and infirmities: Mary
that was called Magdalene, from whom seven demons had gone out,
3 and Joanna the wife of Chuzas Herod's steward, and Susanna,
and many others, who ministered unto them of their substance.

Comments

And it came to pass soon afterwards.—Luke indicates that this is a
continuous story about the teaching ministry of Jesus and the miracles He performed to confirm His preaching. Our chapter divisions
sometimes keep us from seeing the connection between the incidents
he selected to make up his logically arranged story of the Life of
Christ.

that he went about through the cities and villages.—Jesus went
where the people were. He did not remain at the temple in Jerusalem, but visited even the little towns and villages that all might
have an opportunity to hear Him.

Jesus and the apostles, of course, did not overlook the importance
of preaching in the great centers of population. Jerusalem was one
of those centers, and some of Jesus greatest discourses were delivered
there. Antioch of Syria and Ephesus became radiating centers from
which the gospel was heard. While Paul was at Ephesus all Asia
Minor heard about the gospel. It was his plan to preach where no
one had ever told the story of Jesus. Finally, he realized his dream
to preach the gospel in Rome also. Wherever he went, he preached
the whole counsel of God, publically and from house to house. In
doing so, he was following the pattern of Jesus's ministry of teaching
and healing.

The methods that proved so effective in the ministries of Jesus
and of the apostles are, where they are being tried, proving effective
today. Church buildings for the assembly of the saints are necessary,
but so many of those who are lost never set foot inside of them.
Just as Paul did, the church must teach the Word in all the homes
where permission can be had to do so. Many practical aids are available to assist those who want to share in this task. The assembly of
the saints is designed, among other things, to give encouragement
to the people of God, to instruct them in the Word, and to help
them to know how to share the gospel with others. See Jesus' emphasis on this very thing in verses 38-39.

preaching and bringing good tidings of the kingdom.—Preaching on current issues on which the people may be as well or even better informed than the preacher tends to make the whole experience useless. The authoritarian approach of the preacher—this is entirely different from preaching the authoritative Word of God—often points to the importance of the preacher, but fails to help the people in the task of sharing the good news with those who so desperately need it. When Jesus preached, He proclaimed the good news about God's rule in the hearts of men. He trained His apostles and sent them out to preach "repentance and remission of sins." Luke 24: 46-47. In this day when we demand—and rightly so—that there shall be relevance in preaching, is there anything more relevant to the sinner than the message of salvation? In this sinful age, can we do better than point to Jesus whose very name indicates that He came to save His people from their sins? There was need for social reform in Jesus day. His answer to the problem was to proclaim God's rule in the hearts of men that their lives might be transformed, for a transformed life is the only sure way of transforming the social structure of any day.

certain women who had been healed.—Jesus meant something to those who faithfully followed and ministered to His and the apostles' needs. The reason for their devotion is to be found in their appreciation for what Jesus had done for them. Church people may need to reexamine their own relation to the Lord. Has He done anything for them? Does salvation from sin mean much to many who make up the churches today? Or is the church composed of nice people whose company is enjoyed by those who join?

Every sinner—every one who has transgressed God's law—is in desperate need of the salvation and forgiveness that Christ alone can give (Acts 4:12). Devotion to the Lord Jesus Christ depends on the awareness of what it means to be saved from eternal death. Great as release from demon possession was, it does not compare with the importance of release from slavery to sin.

Mary that was called Magdalene.—She was called Magdalene because she was from Magdala, a town near Tiberias on the southwest shore of the Sea of Galilee. Matthew mentions a town by the name of Magadan (Matt. 15:39), and Mark speaks of Dalmanutha (Mark 8:10) in connection with the journies of Jesus. There is not sufficient evidence to identify either with the home of Mary Magdalene, although some assume that Magadan may be a variant of Magdala.

Luke says that seven demons had gone out from Mary Magdalene.

141

Mark states that Jesus had cast them out (Mk. 6:9). Her demon possession is the basis of the totally unfounded tradition that Mary Magdalene is the "woman of the city" mentioned in Luke 7:37. There isn't the slightest evidence in the record that would indicate that she was responsible for the demon possession or that it in any way proves that she was a sinner. Mary's great loyalty to Jesus evidently grew out of her sincere appreciation for what He had done for her. Her loyalty did not lag, for she was among those who were at the cross when Jesus died for the sins of the world (Mk. 15:44-47). After His resurrection, He appeared first to Mary Magdalene (Mk. 16:9; John 19:1-18). She was with the women who brought the news of the resurrection to the apostles (Lk. 24:10).

the wife of Chuzas Herod's steward.—The Herodian family arrayed itself against Christ and the church, but the wife of one of Herod's servants was among those who ministered to Jesus and His apostles.

who ministered unto them of their substance.—This answers in part the question about Jesus' source of support. He and His disciples had not time to "make a living." These women contributed to the support of the Teacher and His disciples, for teachers were highly regarded by the people; and this was particularly true of Jesus and the people for whom He had done so much.

The Parable of the Sower

Scripture

8:4-15 And when a great multitude came together, and they of every city resorted unto him, he spake by a parable: 5 The sower went forth to sow his seed: and as he sowed, some fell by the way side; and it was trodden under foot, and the birds of the heaven devoured it. 6 And other fell on the rock; and as soon as it grew, it withered away, because it had no moisture. 7 And other fell amidst the thorns; and the thorns grew with it, and choked it. 8 And other fell into the good ground, and grew, and brought forth fruit a hundredfold. As he said these things, he cried, He that hath ears to hear, let him hear.

9 And his disciples asked him what this parable might be. 10 And he said, Unto you it is given to know the mysteries of the kingdom of God: but to the rest in parables; that seeing they may not see, and hearing they may not understand. 11 Now the parable

is this: The seed is the word of God. 12 And those by the way side are they that have heard; then cometh the devil, and taketh away the word from their heart, that they may not believe and be saved. 13 And those on the rock *are* they who, when they have heard, receive the word with joy; and these have no root, who for a while believe, and in time of temptation fall away. 14 And that which fell among the thorns, these are they that have heard, and as they go on their way they are choked with cares and riches and pleasures of *this* life, and bring no fruit to perfection. 15 And that in the good ground, these are such as in an honest and good heart, having heard the word, hold it fast, and bring forth fruit with patience.

Comments

he spake by a parable.—Crowds gathered to hear Jesus wherever He went. This is not the first time He used parables in His teaching. But this is unusual because He used a series of parables to present the lessons about the kingdom.

A parable is a comparison or illustration. Usually it is something that happens in a natural way that permits the teacher to point to its counterpart in the spiritual realm. They were not used because they were so simple that everybody could easily understand them. In fact, the disciples of Jesus didn't understand the parable of the sower until He explained it to them. Many who heard didn't understand and didn't take the pains to ask the Teacher what He meant by the parables.

The emphasis in this series of parables is on the necessity of understanding the Word. Parables helped those who wanted to understand what Jesus was saying, but were of no value to those who were not concerned about His message.

The sower went forth to sow.—The four types of soil represent the reaction of four types of hearers. Some who heard allowed the devil to snatch away the implanted Word. James says, "Wherefore putting away all filthiness and overflowing of wickedness, receive with meekness the implanted word, which is able to save your souls" (James 1:21). Others, like the seed that fell on the rocky soil, had no depth in themselves. They received the word with joy, but their convictions were not deep-rooted. Because they couldn't stand the trials of life, they fell away. Still others, like the ground that produced the thorns, allowed the cares of the world and the deceitfulness of riches to choke out the Word. But those who heard and understood were like the good soil that produced a rich harvest.

He that hath ears to hear, let him hear.—There was more to be learned in the parables than appeared on the surface. This phrase is repeated in each of the seven letters to the churches of Asia (Rev. 2:7).

And his disciples asked him what this parable might be.—Of this group of parables, Jesus explained only two: The Sower and The Tares. On the basis of His explanation of these two, the disciples were able to understand the others (Matt. 13:51-53).

All figurative language of Scripture is to be explained in the light of the plain statements. This is true of the figurative language of *Revelation.* John explains many of the symbols used in the book, and on the basis of his explanations many other figures of speech that are not explained are made understandable.

Since we now have the complete and final and authoritative revelation of God in the Bible (Heb. 1:1-2), we should let the whole Bible interpret any particular passage that may not appear to be clear. The Lord intended His Word to be read and understood (Eph. 3:4).

Unto you it is given to know the mysteries of the kingdom of God. —"Mysteries" refer to that which was not known until the secret was told. The secrets of the kingdom are told in the Bible, and they can be understood; but it takes effort to search the Scriptures (Acts 17:11), time to meditate on their meaning (Psa. 1:2), and a sincere desire to translate them into life to really know the sacred writings that can save those who believe in Jesus Christ (II Tim. 3:14-15).

The seed is the word of God.—Thus makes the parable meaningful to all who really want to know God's will for man. See also James 1:18; 22-25; Eph. 6:17; Psa. 119:9-16.

The Parable of the Lamp

Scripture

8:16-18 And no man, when he hath lighted a lamp, covereth it with a vessel, or putteth it under a bed; but putteth it on a stand, that they that enter in may see the light. 17 For nothing is hid, that shall not be made manifest; nor *anything* secret, that shall not be known and come to light. 18. Take heed therefore how ye hear: for whosoever hath, to him shall be given; and whosoever hath not, from him shall be taken away even that which he thinketh he hath.

Comments

that they that enter may see.—The purpose of the lamp is to let the light shine so that people may see. The parables of Jesus were intended to give light to their pathway. They were not to obscure the truth for anyone who wanted to understand.

By placing the parable of the lamp after the parable of the sower, Luke suggests that the Word of God—the seed—was like a lamp to give understanding to all who are willing to accept it. See Psa. 119:105; II Pet. 1:12-21.

For nothing is hid, that shall not be made known.—What was hid from the disciples by the parable was made plain to them by the explanation which Jesus gave.

Take heed therefore how ye hear.—The disciples were to hear with the intention of understanding and being enlightened by the lesson Jesus taught. That person who hears only to criticize will not be helped.

for whoever hath, to him shall be given.—See Matt. 13:12-13 for a similar statement. To the one who has a desire to understand, more will be given, that is, the matter will be explained so that he may understand. But the one who did not have the desire to understand will soon forget that he had heard the parable, for it had no meaning to him.

In this connection, Matthew quotes from Isa. 6:9-10 which seems to suggest that some had deliberately closed their eyes and stopped their ears so that they wouldn't hear and understand.

Spiritual Kinship

Scripture

8:19-21   And there came to him his mother and brethren, and they could not come at him for the crowd. 20 And it was told him, Thy mother and thy brethren stand without, desiring to see thee. 21. But he answered and said unto them, My mother and my brethren are these that hear the word of God, and do it.

145

Comments

Thy mother and thy brethren.—Mark reminds us that some of Jesus' friends thought that He was "beside himself" with the dream of messiahship. They tried to rescue Him from the crowds that followed Him (Mark 3:21). It is possible that His brothers felt the same way about Him, for John says that they did not believe on Him (John 7:5). But they were concerned about Him, for they had grown up with Him and must have had a very high regard for Him as their older brother. Of course, they did not know the facts about His birth that could not be shared with them by their mother until after His resurrection. It was the force of the resurrection that compelled them to believe that He was truly the Messiah. The Epistle of James begins with this statement: "James, servant of God and of the Lord Jesus Christ." If we are correct in assuming that this is "James the Lord's brother" (Gal. 1:19), we have in this remarkable statement the genuine faith of Jesus' brothers after they had become convinced that He was the Son of God.

What a wonderful older brother He must have been to them; what a wonderful Lord He became to them!

My mother and my brethren are these that hear the word of God.— The parable of the sower shows us how to understand the Word of God. The parable of the lamp indicates that it can be understood. The lesson on spiritual kinship shows the results of hearing the Word of God and obeying it. Once, only the little family at Nazareth knew Jesus as their older Brother; now all who obey the word spoken by Him can enjoy this privilege. See Heb. 2:11-12.

Stilling the Tempest

Scripture

8:22-25 Now it came to pass on one of those days, that he entered into a boat, himself and his disciples; and he said unto them, Let us go over unto the other side of the lake: and they launched forth. 23 But as they sailed he fell asleep: and there came down a storm of wind on the lake; and they were filling *with water,* and were in jeopardy. 24 And they came to him, and awoke him, saying, Master, master, we perish. And he awoke, and rebuked the wind and the raging of the water: and they ceased, and there was a calm. 25 And he said unto them, Where is your faith? And being afraid they marvelled, saying one to another, Who then is this, that he commandeth even the winds and the water, and they obey him.

Comments

on one of those days.—Crowds gathered around the Master wherever He went. On one of those days He got into a boat with the disciples and said, "Let's go to the other side of the lake." And as they crossed the lake, "the Master of ocean and earth and skies" fell asleep, relaxing from the pressures of His busy ministry. On another occasion, He said to the disciples, "Come ye apart into a desert place and rest a while" (Mark 6:31).

His desire to go to the other side of the lake reveals a perfectly normal human desire, for He was the Son of Man; but His command to the winds and waves that obeyed His voice just as clearly reveals Him as the Son of God.

and there came down a storm of wind on the lake.—The Sea of Galilee is some 682 feet below sea level; sudden storms on the lake are not uncommon. The disciples knew what they were facing and cried out to Jesus, "Master, we are perishing." They were sure that they were about to lose their lives in the storm. At the command of Jesus, the winds ceased blowing; the waves stopped tossing; a calm set in.

Where is your faith?—They had willingly followed Him. They had carried out orders even when they were against their own better judgment (Lk. 5:5). But they had not yet learned what it meant to be in the presence of the Son of God who upholds all things through the word of His power (Heb. 1:3). But there came the time when they did trust Him even in the threat of death (Acts 5:40-42).

Who then is this, that he commandeth even the winds and the water?—Their question was not one of unbelief, but one of beginning faith that led them to acknowledge Him as the Son of God.

The Gerasene Demoniac

Scripture

8:26-39 And they arrived at the country of the Gerasenes, which is over against Galilee. 27 And when he was come forth upon the land, there met him a certain man out of the city, who had demons; and for a long time he had worn no clothes, and abode not in any house, but in the tombs. 28 And when he saw Jesus, he cried out, and fell down before him, and with a loud voice said, What have I to do with thee, Jesus, thou Son of the Most High God? I beseech thee, torment me not. 29 For he was commanding the unclean spirit to come out from the man. For oftentimes it had seized him: and he was kept under guard, and bound with chains and fetters; and breaking the bands asunder, he was driven of the demon into the deserts. 30 And Jesus asked him, What is thy name? And he said, Legion, for many demons were entered into him. 31 And they entreated him that he would not command them to depart into the abyss. 32 Now there was there a herd of many swine feeding on the mountain: and they entreated him that he would give them leave to enter into them. And he gave them leave. 33 And the demons came out from the man, and entered into the swine: and the herd rushed down the steep into the lake, and were drowned. 34 And when they that fed them saw what had come to pass, they fled, and told it in the city and in the country. 35 And they went out to see what had come to pass; and they came to Jesus, and found the man, from whom the demons were gone out, sitting, clothed and in his right mind, at the feet of Jesus: and they were afraid. 36 And they that saw it told them how he that was possessed with demons was made whole. 37 And all the people of the country of the Gerasenes round about asked him to depart from them; for they were holden with great fear: and he entered into a boat, and returned. 38 But the man from whom the demons were gone out prayed him that he might be with him: but he sent him away, saying, 39 Return to thy house, and declare how great things God hath done for thee. And he went his way, publishing throughout the whole city how great things Jesus had done for him.

Comments

the country of the Gerasenes.—Both Mark and Luke say "Gerasenes," but Matthew says "the country of the Gadarenes." See Matt. 8:28 and Mark 5:1. It is possible that the country belonging to Gadara —the city itself was situated several miles southeast of the Sea of Galilee—reached to the shores of Galilee. Luke locates the incident on the banks of the Lake opposite the territory of Galilee.

a certain man out of the city, who had demons.—Matthew says there were two demoniacs (Matt. 8:28). Luke tells of only one of them.

That this is a genuine case of demon possession manifesting itself as extreme mental illness—note the psychotic symptoms—cannot be questioned. Luke, a trained physician, says the demon was an "unclean spirit." Further proof that this was demon possession is indicated by the following: (1) Jesus conversed with the demons; He asked the man, "What is your name?" He said, "Legion," for many demons had entered him. (2) Jesus commanded the unclean spirit to come out of the man. (3) The demons begged Jesus not to send them into the abyss, but to allow them to enter the bodies of the swine. (4) When they entered the swine, the herd rushed headlong into the sea and were drowned.

at the feet of Jesus.—When the report of the miracle reached the people of the city and surrounding country, they came to Jesus and found the man whom they had often tried to subdue sitting at the feet of Jesus. The storm that once raged in his wretched life had ceased. He was as calm as the sea after Jesus had rebuked the winds. He was clothed and in his right mind, that is, the demons were gone, and he was in control of his mental powers.

and they were afraid.—The miracle of the Lord caused them to fear, for they were sinful people. Peter reacted the same way after he witnessed the miracle of catching fish (Lk. 5:8). Adam and Eve hid themselves from God, because they knew they had disobeyed Him.

asked him to depart.—They were seized with a great fear. Fear, not the loss of property, caused them to make the request. Sinners will always hide from God unless they can become convinced that He has commended His love toward them by the fact that Christ died for them while they were yet sinners. Rom. 5:8.

prayed him that he might be with him.—At the request of the people, Jesus was leaving their shores. But the man from whom the demons had gone out, wanted to be with Him. Jesus said, "Go back to your home and tell how great the things are that God has done for you," for this is the secret of being with Him.

Jairus' Urgent Request

Scripture

8:40-42a And as Jesus returned, the multitude welcomed him; for they were all waiting for him. 41 And behold, there came a man named Jairus, and he was a ruler of the synagogue: and he fell down at Jesus' feet, and besought him to come into his house; 42 for he had an only daughter, about twelve years of age, and she was dying.

Comments

Jairus' a ruler of the synagogue.—Jesus had begun His ministry in the synagogue in Nazareth. He often found an audience in the synagogues, and sometimes He found those who need healing in these Jewish assemblies. But He did not always meet with a friendly reception there, especially from the leaders; but even the leaders had been known to ask His help in times of distress. We have no knowledge of Jairus after this incident, but Luke tells of another ruler of the synagogue whose name was Crispus who believed the gospel of Christ as Paul preached it in Corinth and was baptized. Acts 18:8.

and he fell down at Jesus' feet.—His respect for the Teacher, the urgency of the case, and his great distress caused him to fall at the feet of Jesus and ask Him to come and save his dying daughter.

A Woman in the Crowd Healed

Scripture

8:42b-48   But as he went the multitudes thronged him.
43 And a woman having an issue of blood twelve years, who had spent all her living upon physicians, and could not be healed of any, 44 came behind him, and touched the border of his garment: and immediately the issue of her blood stanched. 45 And Jesus said, Who is it that touched me? And when all denied, Peter said, and they that were with him, Master, the multitudes press thee and crush thee. 46 But Jesus said, Some one did touch me; for I perceived that power had gone forth from me. 47 And when the woman saw that she was not hid, she came trembling, and falling down before him declared in the presence of all the people for what cause she touched him, and how she was healed immediately. 48 And he said unto her, Daughter, thy faith hath made thee whole; go in peace.

Comments

the multitudes thronged him.—The crowd was waiting for Him and welcomed Him as He returned from the other side of the Sea of Galilee. They followed Him as He went with Jairus.

And a woman having an issue of blood twelve years.—Luke gives the medical history of this woman. She had spent everything, but no one could cure her. Mark says that after spending everything, she was no better, but rather grew worse (Mk 5:25-26).

touched the border of his garment.—The reports of the miracles that Jesus had worked must have led her to believe that even touching the hem of His garment would do what all others had failed to do. The flow of blood stopped immediately. What a contrast that was to the twelve years during which she had been treated without success by her physicians.

Who touched me?—Peter had a ready answer, but evidently failed to see why Jesus had asked the question. Jesus was aware of the multitudes who were pressing upon Him. He was aware that power had gone forth from Him. Why the question? Luke does not tell us, but it seems clear that He asked it to call attention to the miracle and to encourage the woman to let it be known.

And when the woman saw that she was not hid.—Her timidity caused her to try to hide the great favor, but at the word from the Master she came trembling, and falling down before Him she declared in the presence of all the people that she had touched Him and that she had been healed immediately.

Daughter, thy faith hath made thee whole; go in peace.—She had a right to believe that He would heal her, for she knew that He had been healing all who came to Him. This is entirely different from the faith through which miracles were performed by those to whom such power had been given. See comment on Luke 9:37-45 for further explanation of faith in connection with performing miracles.

Her faith in Christ was rewarded, for she was made well. She no longer needed to fear. The gentle Healer said, "Go in peace."

Raising Jairus' Daughter From the Dead

Scripture

8:49-56 While he yet spake, there cometh one from the ruler of the synagogue's house, saying, Thy daughter is dead; trouble not the Teacher. 50 But Jesus hearing it, answered him, Fear not: only believe, and she shall be made whole. 51 And when he came to the house, he suffered not any man to enter in with him, save Peter,

151

and John, and James, and the father of the maiden and her mother.
52 And all were weeping, and bewailing her: but he said, Weep
not; for she is not dead, but sleepeth. 53 And they laughed him
to scorn, knowing that she was dead. 54 But he, taking her by the
hand, called, saying, Maiden, arise. 55 And her spirit returned,
and she rose up immediately: and he commanded that something
be given her to eat. 56 And her parents were amazed: but he
charged them to tell no man what had been done.

Comments

While he yet spake.—Jesus was still speaking to the woman who
had just been miraculously healed when one came from Jairus' home
to give him the tragic news, "Thy daughter is dead." Perhaps we
now see why Jesus had not let that miracle go unnoticed. The messengers said hopelessly, "Do not trouble the Teacher."

But Jesus hearing it, answered him.—He had already given them a
reason to hope. Now He said, "Fear not; only believe, and she shall
be made well." He wanted them to believe what they had seen
and to have hope that He would perform this miracle also.

And when he came to the house.—He allowed only Peter, John, and
James, and the father and mother of the child to enter the house
with Him. The crowd had already seen the wonder of healing the
woman in their midst. Jesus did not work miracles merely to be
spectacular. His miracles were done primarily to prove that the
message He taught came from God. See Heb. 2:3-4.

All were weeping.—Inside the house, He met the usual mourning
that accompanied death. He said to the mourners, "Stop crying. She
did not die, she is sleeping." That turned their mourning to scornful
laughing, for they knew she was dead.

But he, taking her by the hand.—Without further rebuke, Jesus
gently took the hand of the dead child and said, "Child, arise."
Luke simply adds, "Her spirit returned, and she rose up immediately,
and He directed them to give her food."

And her parents were amazed.—Nothing is said about those who
had laughed at Him in the presence of death. Did anyone of them
have the grace to apologize to the Lord? Were they ashamed of
what they had done? Did they acknowledge the miracle as the woman in the crowd had done? "The parents were amazed." Thus in
simple words, Luke tells about the effect of this wonderful miracle.

Their gratitude must have been unlimited, but Jesus told them to say nothing of what had happened.

Summary

Jesus and His disciples were on one of the many tours that took them through the villages and towns of Galilee. Certain women whom He had healed accompanied them and ministered to the group.

On one occasion a crowd gathered and He taught them in parables. The parable of the sower showed them that the Word of God is the seed. Four classes of hearer were described by Jesus, but the ones who heard and understood produced the harvest.

The parable of the lamp explained that Jesus intended them to understand His words, for a lamp lets people see. He warned them to be careful how they heard.

On another occasion when He was teaching, His mother and brothers asked for Him; but He said that those who hear the word of God and do it are the members of His family.

The pressures of His busy ministry made it necessary for Him to get away for some rest from time to time. Jesus and the disciples got into a boat, and Jesus said, "Let's go to the other side." As they set out, He fell asleep. A sudden storm was about to sink their boat. The fearful disciples awoke Him. He rebuked the winds and waves and a calm set in. In reverent wonder they said, "Who is this who speaks to the winds and waves and they obey Him?"

They were met by a demon-possessed man as they landed on the other side of the Sea of Galilee. Jesus cast out the legion of demons and allowed them to enter a herd of swine that was feeding nearby. The swine rushed over the cliff and drowned in the sea. People came to see what had happened and were amazed to find this one whom they had never been able to control sitting calmly at Jesus' feet. Fear seized them and they asked Jesus to leave. As He was getting into the boat, Jesus said to the man, "Go to the people of your house and city and tell them about the great things God has done for you."

The daughter of a ruler of the synagogue was dying. Jairus, the father, asked Jesus to come to his home and help him.

On the way, a woman from the crowd that was following touched Him and was immediately healed.

On arriving at the home of Jairus, they were told that the child was dead. Jesus took Peter, James and John and the parents and entered the house. Taking the girl by the hand, He said, "Child, arise." Her spirit returned and she arose. He said, "Give her something to eat, but say nothing to anyone about what has happened."

Questions

1. Where did Jesus conduct His teaching ministry?
2. What do the Scriptures indicate about preaching in the great centers of population?
3. What did Jesus and the disciples preach?
4. How were they supported?
5. What are the known facts about Mary Magdalene?
6. How explain her loyalty to Christ?
7. What is a parable?
8. Why did Jesus speak in parables?
9. What do the four types of soil represent?
10. What is represented by the seed?
11. How did the disciples learn the meaning of the parable of the sower?
12. What bearing does this have on understanding figurative language of the Bible?
13. What is meant by "mysteries of the kingdom"?
14. What lesson is taught by the parable of the sower?
15. How does the parable of the Lamp continue the lesson of the parable of the Sower?
16. What lesson is taught by the parable of the Lamp?
17. What was the attitude of Jesus' brothers toward Him during His ministry?
19. Why did Jesus and the disciples start across the sea?
18. What changed their view?
20. What lesson did Jesus teach about spiritual kinship?
21. What is known about storms on the Sea of Galilee?
22. What effect did the miracle of stilling the storm have on the disciples?
23. Why did Jesus ask, "Where is your faith?"
24. Where is the country of the Gerasenes?
25. What proof that the man was demon-possessed?
26. Why did the people ask Jesus to leave?
27. What did Jesus say to the man who wanted to go with Him? Why?

154

28. Who was Jairus?
29. What did he ask Jesus to do?
30. What happened on the way to his house?
31. Why did the woman in the crowd have faith that Jesus could heal her?
32. How does this differ from the lack of faith that kept the disciples from casting out the demon from the epileptic boy?
33. Why did Jesus ask, "Who touched me?"
34. When did they learn that the daughter of Jairus was dead?
35. Why did He say, "Fear not; only believe, and she shall be made well"?
36. Why did He limit those permitted to enter the home?
37. What did He do in raising the child from the dead?
38. What was the effect of the miracle on the parents?
39. What restriction did Jesus place on them? Why?
40. What about those who had laughed at Him in the presence of death?

CHAPTER NINE

Outline

A. Luke told about the extension of Jesus ministry (1-17).
   1. The first mission of the twelve (1-6).
      a) He called them together and gave them power and authority over all demons and to cure diseases.
      b) He sent them forth to preach the kingdom of God and to heal the sick.
      c) He gave them instructions for the journey: Take no staff, wallet, bread, money or extra clothes; go to someone's house and stay there until time to depart; if any reject your message, shake the dust off your feet to show your disapproval and their responsibility.
      d) They went throughout the villages, preaching the gospel and healing everywhere.
   2. The reaction of Herod to His ministry (7-9).
      a) He was perplexed by the rumors that John the Baptist had been raised from the dead, or that Elijah had appeared, or that one of the old prophets had risen.
      b) He had beheaded John, but who was Jesus? He wanted to see Him.
   3. Feeding the five thousand (10-17).
      a) The circumstances.
         (1) It was after the apostles had returned and told Him what they had done that He took them and went to a city called Bethsaida.
         (2) The multitudes were aware of it and followed.
         (3) He welcomed them and spoke to them of the kingdom of God and cured those in need of healing.
      b) The problem the twelve faced and what Jesus did about it.
         (1) As the day began to wear away, they came to Him and urged that the crowds be sent to the villages to find food and lodging.
         (2) He said, "You give them something to eat," but they had only five loaves and two fish. Should they

go and buy food for all these people, about five thousand men?

(3) Jesus told the disciples to have the people sit down in groups of fifty. Then He took the loaves and the fish and blessed and broke them and gave them to the disciples to set before the multitudes.

c) The result of the miracle.

(1) They ate and were filled.

(2) There was taken up of what remained of the broken pieces, twelve baskets.

B. Luke told how Jesus prepared His disciples for their ministry (18-62).

1. The necessity of the cross (18-27).

a) The cross in the mission of the Messiah (18-22).

(1) Jesus was praying; the disciples were with Him.

(2) He asked, "Who do the multitudes say that I am?"

(3) They answered, "John the Baptist, Elijah, or one of the old prophets risen again."

(4) He asked, "But who do you say that I am?"

(5) Peter answered, "The Christ of God."

(6) Jesus made His point after charging them to tell this to no man by saying, "The Son of Man must be rejected by the leaders and be killed, and on the third day be raised up."

b) The cross in the life of His followers (23-27).

(1) He said, "If any man would come after me let him deny himself and take up his cross and follow me."

(2) He explained, "For whosoever would save his life shall lose it, but whosoever shall lose his life for my sake, this one shall save it."

(3) He asked, "What, indeed, is a man profited by gaining the whole world and losing himself?"

(4) He explained this loss: "Whosoever shall be ashamed of me and my words, the Son of Man shall be ashamed of him when He comes in glory that is His and the Father's and of the holy angels."

(5) In contrast to that coming, He said that some of those present would not taste death till they should see the kingdom of God.

2. Complete dependence on Christ (28-45).
   a) Revealed in the Transfiguration (28-36).
      (1) It occurred about eight days after the lesson about the cross when Jesus took Peter, John and James and went into the mountain to pray.
      (2) As He was praying, a change came over His face and His garments became white, flashing like lightning.
      (3) Then Moses and Elijah appeared to Him, speaking about His departure to be accomplished at Jerusalem.
      (4) Peter and the others had been asleep, but when they were fully awake, they saw His glory and the two who stood with Him.
      (5) Peter proposed that they put up three tents, one for each of them, not realizing that they were not needed.
      (6) A cloud overshadowed them; they were afraid as they entered the cloud; a Voice said, "This is my my Son, my chosen; Hear ye Him!"
      (7) After the Voice spoke, Jesus was alone. The disciples told no one what they had seen.
   b) Demonstrated in the cure of the epileptic boy (37-45).
      (1) On the next day when they had come down from the mountain, a man from the crowd asked Jesus to help his demon-possessed son.
      (2) The disciples hadn't been able to cast it out.
      (3) Jesus said, "O faithless generation, how long shall I be with you?" Then He said, "Bring your son here."
      (4) The demon convulsed the boy, but Jesus rebuked it and healed the boy and gave him back to his father.
      (5) All were astonished at the majesty of God.
      (6) While they were marvelling, Jesus said to the disciples, "Listen carefully, The Son of Man shall be betrayed into the hands of men."
      (7) They didn't understand, but were afraid to ask Him what He meant.

3. Necessary principles to direct them (46-62).
  a) True greatness explained (46-50).
    (1) The little child in their midst (46-48).
      (a) The disciples were arguing about which of them was the greatest.
      (b) Jesus, pointing to the child, said, "The least among you is the one who is great."
    (2) The unknown miracle worker (49-50).
      (a) He was casting out a demon in Jesus name.
      (b) John said, "We forbade him because he didn't follow with us."
      (c) Jesus said, "Don't forbid him; he that is not against you is for you."
  b) Rashness forbidden (51-55).
    (1) Jesus, approaching the time of the ascension, set out to go to Jerusalem.
    (2) He sent messengers into the Samaritan village to prepare for Him.
    (3) They didn't receive Him because He was going to Jerusalem.
    (4) James and John asked, "Lord, shall we call fire from heaven and consume them?"
    (5) Jesus rebuked their rashness, and they went to another village.
  c) Complete dedication demanded (57-62).
    (1) A volunteer who failed to realize the necessity of following Him unselfishly.
    (2) One who was invited to follow who failed to realize the need to follow unconditionally.
    (3) Another volunteer who failed to realize the need to follow Him unintermittently.

The Mission of the Twelve

Scripture

9:1-6 And he called the twelve together, and gave them power and authority over all demons, and to cure diseases. 2 And he sent them forth to preach the kingdom of God, and to heal the sick. 3 And he said unto them, Take nothing for your journey, neither staff, nor wallet, nor bread, nor money; either have two coats. 4 And into whatsoever house ye enter, there abide, and thence depart. 5 And as many as receive you not, when ye depart from that city, shake off the dust from your feet for a testimony against them. 6 And they departed, and went throughout the villages, preaching the gospel, and healing everywhere.

Comments

And he called the twelve together.—The account of choosing the twelve is given in 6:12-16. They are now being sent out on their first mission. The Master not only chose them, but He also instructed them and sent them out to share in the work that not even He could do alone. This became a training experience for the greater task of carrying the gospel into all the world (Mk. 16:15-16).

power and authority over all demons.—The message they would speak would be given them by the Holy Spirit (Matt. 10:20). The miracles were their credentials, proving the God spoke through them.

Jesus gave them power and authority to exercise it in casting out demons and curing diseases. Some, such as Jewish exorcists and some "faith healers" today, to whom no such power has been given have tried to exercise authority in these areas. Luke gives at least two examples of the utter failure of all such unauthorized efforts. See Acts 19:13-16 and Jesus reference to Jewish exorcists in Lk. 11:19.

to preach the kingdom of God.—They were to proclaim God's rule in the hearts of men. People needed to let God direct their lives. This is the same message John had preached. It must be proclaimed to every generation.

Take nothing for your journey.—On this first mission, they were to go among Jewish brethren who understood the meaning of hospitality and respect for teachers. But rejecting their message meant rejecting Christ; rejecting Him meant rejecting God's rule in their hearts.

The wallet or traveling bag was used for various purposes, sometimes to carry extra clothing or food. Since they were to have no extras, not even two coats, they didn't need the bag. Deissmann, in *Light From the Ancient East* (page 109), mentions a bag that was carried by pagan priests as they went about begging. But this could not apply to Christ's disciples since they were to go to the lost sheep of the house of Israel and be taken care of by them. They did face some dangers, however, for some would not believe their message.

160

Jesus pointed this out so that they might be prepared for it (Matt. 10:16-23).

And as many as receive you not.—The unwelcomed guests were to leave not only because of the lack of hospitality but also because the message of the kingdom of God was being rejected. They were to shake the dust from their feet and in this dramatic way indicate the unworthinesss of those who did not accept their message. The responsibility for rejecting God's rule was left with those who refused to be taught by Christ's messengers.

preaching the gospel and healing everywhere.—The good news of the kingdom was accompanied by the miracles of healing which served to prove that they spoke from God. Mark says that "they preached that men should repent" (Mark 6:13). Matthew adds that Jesus said, "Ye shall not have gone through the cities of Israel, till the Son of man be come" (Mt. 10:23). They were on an urgent mission. Jesus would meet them before they had time to finish this task. This, of course, is not a reference to His second coming.

The Reaction of Herod the Tetrarch

Scripture

9:7-9 Now Herod the tetrarch heard of all that was done: and he was much perplexed, because that it was said by some, that John was risen from the dead; 8 and by some, that Elijah had appeared; and by others, that one of the old prophets was risen again. 9 And Herod said, John I beheaded: but who is this, about whom I hear such things? And he sought to see him.

Comments

he was perplexed.—Herod who had beheaded John the Baptist was disturbed by the reports he was hearing about the miracles of Jesus. Some tried to explain them by assuming that He was Elijah or one of the old prophets who had been raised from the dead (Mal 4:5; Deut. 18:15). Some were saying that He was John who had risen. Herod seems to have accepted this view for a time, for his disturbed conscience was searching for an answer to its guilt. He decided to kill Jesus too, assuming that that would ease his conscience (Lk. 13:31). The only thing, however, that cleanses an evil conscience is the blood of Christ that was shed on Calvary (Heb. 9:14; 10:22; I Pet. 3:21).

161

But Herod's conscience didn't bother him very long, for when Pilate sent Jesus to him during the trial "he was exceeding glad: for he was of a long time desirous to see him, because he had heard concerning him; and he hoped to see some miracle done by him" (Lk. 23:8).

Feeding the Five Thousand

Scripture

9:10-17 And the apostles, when they were returned, declared unto him what things they had done. And he took them, and withdrew apart to a city called Bethsaida. 11 But the multitudes perceiving it followed him: and he welcomed them, and spake to them of the kingdom of God, and them that had need of healing he cured. 12 And the day began to wear away; and the twelve came, and said unto him, Send the multitude away, that they may go into the villages and country round about, and lodge, and get provisions: for we are here in a desert place. 13 But he said unto them, Give ye them to eat. And they said, We have no more than five loaves and two fishes; except we should go and buy food for all this people. 14 For they were about five thousand men. And he said unto his disciples, Make them sit down in companies, about fifty each. 15 And they did so, and made them all sit down. 16 And he took the five loaves and the two fishes, and looking up to heaven, he blessed them, and brake; and gave to the disciples to set before the multitude. 17 And they ate, and were all filled: and there was taken up that which remained over to them of broken pieces, twelve baskets.

Comments

a city called Bethsaida.—It is generally agreed that this is Bethsaida Julias, a city located on the east side of the Jordan near the point where it empties into the Sea of Galilee.

According to Mark 6:45 and 53, Jesus sent the disciples back across the lake after feeding the five thousand, and they landed at Genessaret, the west side of the lake. John says that it occurred on the other, that is, east side of the sea of Galilee and that after the miracle the disciples went down to the sea and got into the boat to go over the sea to Capernaum (John 6:1, 17). It was at Capernaum on the next day that the multitudes came to Jesus and asked, "Rabbi, when camest thou here?" (John 6:24-25). These Scriptures seem to indicate that the miracle took place on the northeast shore of the Sea of Galilee and that after the miracle the disciples returned to Capernaum which was located on the northwest side of the sea.

But the multitudes perceiving it followed him.—By this time the popularity of Jesus was reaching its climax; people were following Him everywhere He went. Even when He tried to get away for a little rest, they followed Him; and He "welcomed them and spake to them of the kingdom of God and them that had need of healing he cured."

Send the multitude away.—As evening drew on, these practical men realized that something had to be done for the welfare of the people. "Send them away" to the stores and places of lodging was all they could think to do. They knew that the "two hundred shillings" —all that they had—wouldn't buy enough to begin to feed them even if there had been a place where they could buy food.

But Jesus said, "You give them something to eat." At His suggestion, they took stock and found that they had only five loaves and two fish—just a lunch that belonged to a boy in the crowd (Mk. 6:38; John 6:9). What was that for so many? Were they to go and buy food for them? Apparently it didn't occur to them that Jesus could solve the problem, even though they had seen Him perform many wonders by this time.

Make them sit down in companies, about fifty each.—Jesus knew what He would do. In that desert place where there was virtually no food, He was the only one who could supply the need. The crowd was to sit down in groups of about fifty so that no one would be overlooked. He would provide the food; but the apostles were to do the rest, for that was within their ability. Organization was necessary to the success of the task.

Jesus took the loaves and the fish and looking up to the heavenly Father He blessed them and broke them and gave them to the disciples to give to the people. Was anyone in the crowd aware that a miracle was taking place? They were slow to grasp the lesson about the Bread of Life which He taught them when they came to Him after the miracle that had fed them physically.

remained over of the broken pieces, twelve baskets.—The miracle had demonstrated that He was the Creator, for "all things were made through him; and without him was not anything made that hath been made" (John 1:3). Gathering the broken pieces conserved the food, but more than that it demonstrated that a genuine miracle had taken place. The people said, "This is of a truth the prophet that cometh into the world" (John 6:15). But they didn't see that He was the Bread of Life (John 6:41). Their real selfishness is revealed in their reference to the manna which their fathers had eaten for the forty years in the wilderness; Jesus had fed them just once. And it was not Moses, but the Father who had sent the manna; Christ was the true bread that the Father had sent to those who believe on Him.

The Necessity of the Cross

Scripture

9:18-27   And it came to pass, as he was praying apart, the disciples were with him: and he asked them, saying, Who do the multitudes say that I am? 19 And they answering said, John the Baptist; but others say, Elijah; and others, that one of the old prophets is risen again. 20 And he said unto them, But who say ye that I am? And Peter answering said, The Christ of God. 21 But he charged them, and commanded them to tell this to no man; 22 saying, The Son of man must suffer many things, and be rejected of the elders and chief priests and scribes, and be killed, and the third day be raised up. 23 And he said unto all, If any man would come after me, let him deny himself, and take up his cross daily, and follow me. 24 For whosoever would save his life shall lose it; but whosoever shall lose his life for my sake, the same shall save it. 25 For what is a man profited, if he gain the whole world, and lose or forfeit his own self? 26 For whosoever shall be ashamed of me and of my words, of him shall the Son of man be ashamed, when he cometh in his own glory, and the glory of the Father, and of the holy angels. 27 But I tell you of a truth, There are some of them that stand here, who shall in no wise taste of death, till they see the kingdom of God.

Comments

And it came to pass.—Luke was aware of many things that he did not include in his narrative. See Mark 6:45-9:1. His purpose was to present Jesus as the Son of God and the Son of Man, and it did not take all that He did to establish the claim. But all that he did write concerned Jesus' work and teaching (Acts 1:1-2). John suggests that "even the world itself could not contain the books that should be written" if the complete record were made (John 21:25).

as he was praying.—Jesus constantly communicated with the Father about all that He did. Just before Peter expressed the conviction of the apostles that He was the Christ, Jesus was praying. Matthew reminds us that this incident occurred in the region of Caesarea Philippi.

Who do men say that I am?—This question was designed to lead the disciples to think clearly about Jesus and to prepare them to see that He must go to the cross. The cross was not only necessary for Him, it was also necessary in the life of each of His followers.

And they answered, John the Baptist.—Herod and others were saying this (Matt. 14:1-2). Others were saying that he was Elijah, basing their claim on the prophecy of Malachi 4:5 which said, "Behold, I will send you Elijah before the great and terrible day of the Lord comes." Others were explaining Jesus' powers by saying that He was one of the old prophets who had risen. After the feeding of the five thousand, the people came to take Him by force and make Him king, for they said, "This is of a truth, the prophet that cometh into the world" (John 6:14-15). Later, Peter positively identified Him as the prophet about whom Moses had written (Acts 3:20-24).

But who say ye that I am?—Peter said, "The Christ of God." Christ means anointed and refers to His office of prophet, priest and king. According to Peter's confession as given in Matthew 16:16, he added the words, "the Son of the living God." This explains His person, for He is Son of God as well as Son of Man. He was often called "Son of David" referring to Him as Messiah, that is, Christ.

According to Matthew, Jesus said to Peter, "Thou art Peter, and upon this rock I will build my church; and the gates of Hades will not prevail against it" (Matt. 16:18). The rock upon which the church was to be built is the truth expressed in Peter's confession that Jesus is the Christ, the Son of the living God. Perhaps the best proof of this is Peter's own statement in which he quotes Isaiah's prophecy and shows that Jesus Christ is the foundation of the spiritual temple, the church. See I Pet. 2:3-8. See also Paul's statement in I Cor. 3:11.

The gates of Hades refer to the power of death. In this context, Jesus was speaking about His own death which was to take place in Jerusalem (Matt. 16:21; Lk. 9:21-22). Peter explained this when he quoted the sixteenth Psalm, on the Day of Pentecost (Acts

165

2:24-31). The antecedent of "it" (Matt. 16:18) is not "church" but
"rock." The truth that He is the Christ, the Son of the Living God
is the rock that could not be destroyed by the powers of Hades.
He was to be put to death, but He was to be raised from the dead
to prove that He was Prophet, Priest, and King. If He had not been
raised, He could not have been any one of these. The victory of the
church over death depends on Christ (I Cor. 15:22-26), but this is
not in the context of Matthew sixteen.

tell this to no man.—A similar order is given after the transfiguration with the added word, "until the Son of man be risen from the
dead" (Matt. 17:9). The apostles were to wait until they had
positive evidence that could be shared with others before telling
of their conviction that Jesus is the Christ. The resurrection established it beyond doubt. See Acts 4:2, 10-11, 19-20; Rom. 10:9-10.

take up his cross daily.—The cross was necessary for Jesus in His
office of Prophet, Priest, and King. The cross was necessary in the
daily life of His followers as they went out to preach the Word
of the Cross.

The meaning of the cross for the follower of Christ depends on
the meaning of the cross to Him. His cross is a symbol of death to
sin. Then the cross to His disciples must be more than some burden
to be patiently borne. Paul says, "our old man was crucified with
him, that the body of sin might be done away" (Rom. 6:6). Those
who belong to Jesus Christ "have crucified the flesh with the passions
and the lusts thereof" (Gal. 5:24). See also Col. 2:20-3:17; Gal.
2:20; 6:14.

The cross, death to sin, must be taken up daily by those who
follow Him. Peter said that "Christ left us an example that we
should follow in his steps who did no sin" (I Pet. 2:21-22).
Should we stumble, as Peter did, there is the gracious provision of
the loving Father for the cleansing of the erring Christian (I John
2:1-2). But habitual sinning cannot be practiced by the Christian
(Rom 6:1-4). The standard of Christ is high, but not impossible.
His commandments are not grievous (I John 5:3).

Self-denial is not merely denying oneself of some material thing.
It means to disown self, to act in a completely selfless manner. Paul
is a good example: All that he had once counted dear, he set aside
for the privilege of gaining Christ (Phil. 3:7-11). Jesus illustrated
this in the parable of the Pearl of Great Price. The man who
sought goodly pearls had to sell all in order to gain the one pearl

of great price. Nothing short of complete dedication to Christ will satisfy the demand of self-denial.

save his life shall lose it.—This is Jesus' own explanation of what He had just said about self-denial. Lose it for Christ, if you would save your life! There is no diluting this to mean partly save, or partly lose; it means complete dedication.

For what is a man profited?—Jesus explained what He meant by losing or saving life. What profit is it if you gain the whole world but lose your life? Reason tells us He is right! The Bible gives us true perspective so that our sense of values may not be limited by what we see at the moment. See Psa. 37:1-40; 73:16-17.

ashamed of me and of my words.—The one who is ashamed of the Christ of the cross or of the Word of the cross will not be recognized by Christ when He comes to judge the world. See also Matt. 7:22-23. Mere profession of obedience is not enough; Jesus demands sincerity in relation to Him. James warns, "Be ye doers of the word, and not hearers only, deluding your own selves (James 1:22).

when he cometh in his own glory.—that is, at the last judgment. See Matt. 25:31-46; Heb. 9:27; Rev. 20:11-15.

till they see the kingdom of God.—This is in contrast to what He had just said about the final judgment. All will be present on that day. But some of those who heard Him speak were to be present on another occasion, that is, when they would see the kingdom of God. The kingdom, the earthly phase of it, came on the Day of Pentecost when Jesus was proclaimed both Lord and Christ, reigning at the right hand of the throne of God (Acts 2:33-36).

Some have assumed that Jesus and the apostles expected His second coming within the lifetime of some of those who heard Him speak. But the language of this context shows the contrast He made between His coming at the Judgment and His coming in the kingdom on the Day of Pentecost. Paul wrote II Thessalonians to correct the mistaken view that the coming of Christ was to be expected in his day (II Thes. 2:1-3). His kingdom did come on Pentecost; He will come at the end of the age. "Amen: come, Lord Jesus."

The Transfiguration

Scripture

9:28-36 And it came to pass about eight days after these sayings, that he took with him Peter and John and James, and went up into the mountain to pray. 29 And as he was praying, the fashion of his countenance was altered, and his raiment *became* white *and* dazzling. 30 And behold, there talked with him two men, who were Moses and Elijah; 31 who appeared in glory, and spake of his decease which he was about to accomplish at Jerusalem. 32 Now Peter and they that were with him were heavy with sleep: but when they were fully awake, they saw his glory, and the two men that stood with him. 33 And it came to pass, as they were parting from him, Peter said unto Jesus, Master, it is good for us to be here: and let us make three tabernacles; one for thee, and one for Moses, and one for Elijah: not knowing what he said. 34 And while he said these things, there came a cloud, and overshadowed them: and they feared as they entered into the cloud. 35 And a voice came out of the cloud, saying, This is my Son, my chosen: hear ye him. 36 And when the voice came, Jesus was found alone. And they held their peace, and told no man in those days any of the things which they had seen.

Comments

about eight days after.—Matthew and Mark say, "And after six days' (Matt. 17:1; Mark 9:2). Luke says *about* eight days. If we count the day on which Jesus had been speaking plus an interval of six days and add the day on which the Transfiguration took place, it would make the eight days, that is, about a week as they counted time.

he took with him Peter and John and James.—Peter gives his own version of the transfiguration in II Peter 2:16-18. This was not a cleverly fabricated tale, but the testimony of an eyewitness of the majesty of Jesus Christ. He heard the Voice that brought honor and glory to Jesus when the Father said, "This is my beloved Son, in whom I am well pleased; Hear ye Him." This is more reliable than the "cunningly devised fables" of the men who sought to deny the Master who bought them (II Pet. 2:1).

and went into the mountain to pray.—Since Matthew says that they were in the vicinity of Caesarea Philippi, it is reasonable to assume that the mountain, although not named by any of the writers, was Mount Hermon which has an elevation of some 9100 feet. Luke alone says that He went into the mountain to pray and that He was praying when the transfiguration took place. This was an important example for the apostles, for they would need to keep in constant

168

contact with the Father through the Lord Jesus Christ in their mission of spreading the gospel in all the world.

the fashion of his countenance was altered.—The change of His face and the gleaming white garments are a fitting symbol of the honor and approval which He received from the Father (II Pet. 1:17).

there talked with him two men.—How the disciples were able to recognize Moses and Elijah is not stated. They were in glory but had not lost their identity. They were talking about Jesus' "decease" which He was to accomplish at Jerusalem. He was soon to leave this earthly experience and return to "the glory which He had with the Father before the world was" (John 17:5). It is fitting that these two representatives of the Old Testament should be speaking to Christ about His death and the glories that were to follow since that is the message of the Law of Moses and the Prophets (I Pet. 1:10-12; Lk. 24:44-47).

Now Peter and they that were with him were heavy with sleep.—On another occasion these same men were found sleeping while the Master was undergoing the agony of Gethsemane (Matt. 26:36-44; Lk. 22:45-46). Before condemning them too harshly, we might do well to examine our own lack of alertness at prayer meeting. But because they were asleep, they were not prepared for what they saw when they were fully awake. As Moses and Elijah were departing, Peter proposed that they make three booths or tents, one each for Jesus, Moses, and Elijah. Apparently he didn't realize that Moses and Elijah were not remaining with them permanently or that Jesus was soon to be taken from them, although He had told them several times that He would be. The suggestion that Peter was placing Jesus on the level with Moses and Elijah in importance and honor does not seem to agree with the context. He really didn't know what he was proposing, but out of fear felt that he had to say something (Mark 9:6).

And a voice came out of the cloud.—This was the voice from the Majestic Glory, the voice of God who said, "This is my Son, my chosen: hear ye him." God's approval of His Son and the assurance to the apostles who heard Him speak form the two-fold purpose of the Transfiguration. When the Voice came, Jesus was found alone. In this dramatic way, God showed the men that they were to hear His Son.

and told no man.—They obeyed the instruction Jesus gave them, but they did discuss the coming of Elijah (Matt. 17:9-13). This led

169

Jesus to tell them how John fulfilled the prophecy about the coming of Elijah (Mal. 4:5).

The Epileptic Boy
Scripture

9:37-45   And it came to pass, on the next day, when they were come down from the mountain, a great multitude met him. 38 And behold, a man from the multitude cried, saying, Teacher, I beseech thee to look upon my son; for he is mine only child: 39 and behold, a spirit taketh him, and he suddenly crieth out; and it teareth him that he foameth, and it hardly departeth from him, bruising him sorely. 40 And I besought thy disciples to cast it out; and they could not. 41 And Jesus answered and said, O faithless and perverse generation, how long shall I be with you, and bear with you? bring hither thy son. 42 And as he was yet a coming, the demon dashed him down, and tare *him* grievously. But Jesus rebuked the unclean spirit, and healed the boy, and gave him back to his father. 43 And they were all astonished at the majesty of God.

But while all were marvelling at all the things which he did, he said unto his disciples, 44 Let these words sink into your ears: for the Son of man shall be delivered up into the hands of men. 45 But they understood not this saying, and it was concealed from them, that they should not perceive it; and they were afraid to ask him about this saying.

Comments

a great multitude met him.—Jesus and the three disciples had been in the mountain; the crowds were waiting for Him to return. Their anticipation was evidently heightened by the failure of the disciples to meet the request of the distressed father.

Teacher, I beseech thee.—The father turned to Jesus for help, for his only son was demon-possessed and in desperate need of help. Luke calls the demon an unclean spirit. The symptoms were those of epilepsy, but Luke says it was demon-possession. The technique which Jesus used in dealing with the case shows that it was not the ordinary disease, but real demon-possession. He, of course, had power to cast out demons as well as heal diseases.

I besought thy disciples.—Why couldn't they cast out the demon? Jesus, according to Mark, said that this kind came out only by prayer and fasting (Mark 9:29). He also said that it was because of their little faith (Matt. 17:20). If their faith had been as much as a grain of mustard seed, they could have removed mountains. This case clearly called for a miracle, and the least amount of faith that had to do with the power to perform miracles could have accomplished it. To assume that this refers to mountains of difficulty that can be removed by trust in Jesus is to overlook the meaning of Jesus' explanation. He had given them power over demons, but they lacked the faith—not faith like that of the woman in the crowd—by which that power was made operative. Had they, in the absence of Jesus, attempted to cast out the demon without relying on Him? Without the faith that kept them in contact with the power they were utterly unable to perform the miracle. See *Studies in First Corinthians,* pages 224-25 and 238, for additional comment of faith to remove mountains.

O faithless and perverse generation, how long.—Jesus had already given ample evidence of His deity, but many were looking at the cure—understandably so—and not at the evidential value of the miracle (John 20:30-31). Jesus was nearing the climax of His earthly ministry and knew that He would not be with them much longer. His complaint seems to be that they had not yet, even at this late date, grasped the truth about Him.

astonished at the majesty of God.—Jesus cast the demon out and gave the boy back to the.father. As usual, the crowds were astonished; but this time, at the majesty of God.

But while they were marvelling.—They marvelled at the miracle, but Jesus reminded the disciples that He was soon to be delivered up into the hands of men to be crucified. That's why He had asked, "How long shall I be with you?" It was important that they realize that His mission called for the cross by which He was to destroy the power of the devil (Heb. 2:14). He said, "Let these words sink into your ears." Don't let them go in one ear and out the other.

But they understood not this saying.—There seemed to be no place in their thinking for the cross. They had their minds centered on the kind of kingdom that they wanted Him to establish—an earthly kingdom. They were afraid to ask what He meant, lest it be the end of their dream. See Luke 24:21.

True Greatness

Scripture

9:46-48   And there arose a reasoning among them, which of them

171

was the greatest. 47 But when Jesus saw the reasoning of their heart, he took a little child, and set him by his side, 48 and said unto them, Whosoever shall receive this little child in my name receiveth me: and whosoever shall receive me receiveth him that sent me: for he that is least among you all, the same is great.

Comments

which of them was the greatest.—Peter's prominence and avowed loyalty to Jesus may have given him some notion that he was of special importance. James and John who may have been relatives of Jesus were evidently hoping to be elevated to positions of importance in the kingdom when Jesus established it (Matt. 20:20-21).

he took a little child.—Jesus took this an occasion to teach His disciples a much needed lesson on true greatness. He said, "Whosoever shall receive this little child in my name receiveth me." Then He made the point, "He that is least among you all is the one who is great." See also Mark 10:43-45 for Jesus' own example of true greatness.

The Unknown Miracle Worker

Scripture

9:49-50   And John answered and said, Master, we saw one casting out demons in thy name; and we forbade him, because he followeth not with us. 50 But Jesus said unto him, Forbid *him* not: for he that is not against you is for you.

Comments

one casting out demons in thy name.—They had just gone through the experience that taught them that no man could cast out demons except in relation to Jesus. This one whom they had forbidden was casting out a demon in His name. It, therefore, was not pretense as in the case of certain Jewish exorcists (Acts 19:13).

we forbade him, because he followeth not with us.—Their pride was offended. It was not a question of relieving the demon-possessed person; it was simply that he did not follow with these disciples.

Jesus said unto him, forbid him not.—Since he was doing the work in the name of Christ, he was not to be forbidden. This is the real

172

basis for unity of action, each one acting in the name of Christ. And to act in the name of Christ is to act by His authority. "He that is not against you is for you." Even the one who does such a lowly task as giving a cup of cold water because he belongs to Christ shall not lose his reward (Mark 9:41).

The Inhospitable Samaritans

Scripture

9:51-55　And it came to pass, when the days were well-nigh come that he should be received up, he stedfastly set his face to go to Jerusalem, 52 and sent messengers before his face; and they went, and entered into a village of the Samaritans, to make ready for him. 53 And they did not receive him, because his face was *as though he were* going to Jerusalem. 54 And when his disciples James and John saw *this,* they said, Lord, wilt thou that we bid fire to come down from heaven, and consume them? 55 But he turned, and rebuked them.

Comments

that he should be received up.—That is, the closing days of His ministry that led to the ascension (Acts 1:9). But the incident of sending the seventy shows that the ascension, while approaching, was still several months away. According to John's record, Jesus went first to the Feast of Tabernacles (John 7:1-2) and later to the Feast of Dedication (John 10:22). Why did Luke include this section which is not given by Matthew and Mark? It was to give Theophilus information which Luke considered important as he reassured him of the things in which he had been instructed.

entered into a village of the Samaritans.—This was not the first time that Jesus had been in Samaria. See John 4:1-4. See II Kings 17:24-28 for the origin of the Samaritans. The old controversy over the correct place to worship continued from the rebuilding of Jerusalem after the Babylonian captivity until the days of Jesus (John 4:20-24). The Samaritans held to the Pentateuch as their sacred scriptures, disregarding the other portions of the Old Testament which mention Jerusalem and the place or worship.

And they did not receive him.—The fact that He was going to Jerusalem—probably to the feast of Tabernacles—stirred the old prejudice and led them to refuse lodging to Jesus and His disciples. But see John 4:39-42 for their reaction to the invitation of the woman at the well, and Acts 8:5-40 for the account of Philip's ministry in Samaria.

bid fire come down from heaven.—James and John were not nick-named "sons of thunder" without cause (Mark 3:17). Their rash proposal was met with prompt rebuke by Jesus. There were other villages in which to spend the night. Violence seldom serves to abolish prejudice. By contrast, Luke shows the power of preaching Christ to bring joy to the lives of the people in the city of Samaria (Acts 8:4-8).

Dedication Demanded

Scripture

9:57-62 And as they went on the way, a certain man said unto him, I will follow thee whithersoever thou goest. 58 And Jesus said unto him, The foxes have holes, and the birds of the heaven *have* nests; but the Son of man hath not where to lay his head. 59 And he said unto another, Follow me. But he said, Lord, suffer me first to go and bury my father. 60 But he said unto him, Leave the dead to bury their own dead; but go thou and publish abroad the kingdom of God. 61 And another also said, I will follow thee, Lord; but first suffer me to bid farewell to them that are at my house. 62 But Jesus said unto him, No man, having put his hand to the plow, and looking back, is fit for the kingdom of God.

Comments

I will follow thee.—Jesus had already said that whoever would come after Him would have to deny himself and take up his cross daily and follow Him. Later, He challenged them with the necessity of counting the cost of discipleship, for anything short of complete dedication would not do (Luke 14:25-35). This volunteer failed to realize the necessity of following Him unselfishly.

And Jesus said unto him, The foxes have holes.—Foxes have dens, birds have roosts, but the Son of Man did not have a place to lay His head. The Samaritans had just refused Him lodging; His own home town, much earlier, had rejected Him; before Him loomed the cross.

And he said to another, Follow me.—The first man had volunteered,

174

but Jesus challenged this one to follow Him. He wanted first to go bury his father. If the father was actually dead, why wasn't he attending to the arrangements for the funeral? He said "Let me go bury my father." In all probability the father was old and the dutiful son wanted to be present when death came so that he might properly care for his burial. He put this first, but the followers of Christ must do so unconditionally.

Leave the dead to bury the dead.—Those who were spiritually dead could take care of the physically dead. The greater task was to publish abroad the kingdom of God. This will raise the dead in trespasses and sin to a new life in Christ. See Eph. 2:5-6; Rom. 6:4-5.

I will follow thee, but.—Another volunteer; he wanted time to say goodby to those at his house. But those who follow Christ must do so unintermittently.

No man, having put his hand to the plow.—The plow in that day was a forked stick and difficult to handle at best. Undivided attention was necessary to do a good job. The one with the hand to the plow who looks back is not fit for the kingdom of God.

The three cases—two volunteers and one who was invited—may be summarized as follows: To the first one, Jesus is saying, "Think it through first;" to the second, "Let nothing interfere with your following Me;" and to the third, "Stay with it to the end."

Summary

The incidents recorded in this chapter may be gathered up under two general headings: (1) Those things which Jesus did to extend the influence of His ministry, and (2) what He did to prepare His disciples for their work after His ascension. The importance of this preparation is seen in the fact that He was depending on them to take His gospel into all the world.

The mission of the Twelve to the lost sheep of the house of Israel was a training experience to prepare them for their worldwide mission.

Rumors of Jesus' miracles reached the ears of Herod the tetrarch. An aroused conscience asked, "Who is this?" Herod answered, "John the Baptist whom I beheaded." His only thought was, "Kill him too." A little later, the Pharisees warned Jesus to leave the district, for, they said, "Herod wants to kill you."

People by the thousands were following Jesus wherever He went.

In a lonely place where no food was to be found except a boy's lunch, He fed the five thousand on the loaves and fish. Even though He had worked such a miracle, He reminded the disciples that there was a cross to be borne, a cross for Him and a cross that meant self-denial for all who would follow Him.

The Twelve were completely dependent on Him. In the Transfiguration they were taught the necessity of obeying Him. In the cure of the epileptic boy they learned the meaning of faith in Him who had given them power to perform miracles. He taught them the meaning of true greatness, and stopped their wrangling over which one was to have first place among them. He rebuked their rashness that would have destroyed the Samaritan village and left the door open for the preaching of the gospel by Philip the evangelist.

Jesus dramatically demonstrated what His demand for complete dedication meant. He rejected the volunteer who offered to follow Him but who had not counted the cost. He rejected another whom He had invited to follow Him when he said, "Yes, but first let me bury my father." A third one volunteered, but Jesus demanded full-time service, for, He said, "the one who puts his hand to the plow and looks back is not fit for the kingdom of God."

Questions

1. How did Jesus extend the effectiveness of His ministry?
2. How did He train His disciples for the task of carrying the gospel into all the world?
3. What made the difference between the power of the disciples to cast out demons and the attempts of the Jewish exorcists to do so?
4. What were the disciples to preach on their first mission?
5. Why take nothing for the journey?
6. What did they mean by shaking the dust off their feet?
7. What did Jesus say He would do before they finished the task he gave them on this first mission?
8. Why did Herod think that Jesus was John the Baptist?
9. What can cleanse an evil conscience?
10. How does the feeding of the five thousand show the influence of Jesus' ministry?
11. Where did it take place?
12. What lesson did Jesus teach the people after it was over?
13. Why did Jesus tell the apostles to give the crowd something to eat?

14. How did Jesus demonstrate the necessity of organization in carrying out His work?
15. Why gather up the broken pieces?
16. What was Jesus doing just before Peter made the good confession?
17. Why did He ask, "Who do men say that I am?"
18. Why would some say "John the Baptist, Elijah, or one of the old prophets"?
19. What does "Thou art the Christ" mean?
20. What does "Son of God" mean?
21. On what was the church built?
22. Why did Jesus mention the gates of Hades? What is Hades?
23. Why did Jesus restrain them from telling others that He is the Christ?
24. Why was the cross necessary for Jesus?
25. What does the cross mean in the life of His followers?
26. How did He explain self-denial?
27. What of the one who is ashamed of Jesus and His words?
28. How was it possible for some to see the kingdom of God before they died?
29. Whom did Jesus take with Him into the mountain where He was transfigured?
30. What is the name of the mountain?
31. What did Peter write about his experience in that mountain?
32. Why had Jesus gone into the mountain?
33. What was the meaning of the Transfiguration to Christ? to the apostles?
34. Why were Moses and Elijah permitted to appear with Jesus?
35. What did they talk about?
36. Why did Peter want to build the three tabernacles?
37. What is the significance of the message of the Voice that came out of the cloud?
38. What explanation did Jesus make about the disciples' question concerning the coming of Elijah?
39. What had the disciples tried to do while Jesus was in the mountain?
40. Why did they fail?
41. What is the difference between the faith of the woman in the crowd and the faith which the apostles lacked?

42. Why did Jesus refer to "the faithless generation"?
43. Why didn't the disciples understand Jesus' prediction of His crucifixion?
44. Why did the disciples discuss the issue of greatness?
45. How did Jesus answer their problem?
46. Why did Jesus tell them not to forbid the unknown miracle worker?
47. Why did the Samaritans refuse lodging for Jesus and the disciples?
48. What did James and John propose that justifies their nickname, "Sons of thunder"?
49. How did Jesus' attitude affect the Samaritan situation later?
50. Why did Jesus reject the man who volunteered to follow Him?
51. What does this mean: "Let the dead bury the dead"?
52. Why did putting the hand to the plow and looking back make one unfit for the kingdom of God?

CHAPTER TEN

Outline

A. Luke told about the mission of the Seventy (1-24).
  1. Their appointment and work (1-16).
    a) The circumstances (1-2).
      (1) Jesus appointed seventy others (in addition to the twelve).
      (2) He sent them out two by two.
      (3) He sent them to the cities where He was soon to come.
      (4) He reminded them of two things:
        (a) The harvest was great, the laborers few.
        (b) They were going forth as lambs in the midst of wolves.
    b) The instruction for their journey (4-11).
      (1) Take no purse, traveling bag, or shoes.
      (2) Don't stop to greet people along the way.
      (3) Greet those into whose house you enter; if you are not welcomed, your greeting will return to you.
      (4) Accept such hospitality as may be offered, for the laborer is worthy of his hire; but do not go from house· to house.
      (5) Heal the sick and say, "The kingdom of God has come near you."
      (6) Where you may be rejected say, "The dust from our feet, we wipe off against you, but know that the kingdom of God has come near."
    c) The judgment on those cities that reject them (12-16).
      (1) It will be more tolerable in the Day of Judgment for Sodom.
      (2) Woe to Chorazen and Bethsaida; if the mighty works done in these cities had been done in Tyre and Sidon, they would have repented.
      (3) It will be more tolerable for Tyre and Sidon in the Judgment.
      (4) "Capernaum, will you be exalted to heaven? You will be brought down to Hades."
      (5) Why? "He who hears you hears me; he who rejects you rejects me and him who sent me."

179

2. Their return and report to Jesus (17-20).
   a) The demons were subject to them in His name.
   b) He said, "I was observing Satan as he fell like lightning from heaven."
   c) They were not to rejoice over their power which He
   had given, but over the fact that their names were
   written in heaven.
3. The prayer of Jesus at that time (21-24).
   a) He rejoiced in the Holy Spirit over the things the Father
   had revealed.
   b) The Father is known by the Son and him to whom the
   Son reveals Him.
   c) His disciples are to be congratulated on seeing what
   many prophets and kings desired to see.
B. Luke reported the incident that led to Jesus' telling the story
   of the Good Samaritan (25-37).
   1. A lawyer asked Jesus a question to embarrass Him (25-29).
      a) The question: "Teacher, what shall I do to inherit
      eternal life?"
      b) Jesus answered by asking, "What is written in the
      law? How does it read to you?"
      c) The lawyer answered, quoting from the Law of Moses,
      'Thou shalt love the Lord thy God with all thy heart,
      and with all thy soul, and with all thy strength, and
      with all thy mind, and thy neighbor as thyself."
      d) Jesus said, "You have answered correctly; do this and
      you shall live."
      e) But the embarrassed lawyer said, "And who is my
      neighbor?"
   2. Jesus answered his question by telling the story of the
      Good Samaritan (30-37).
      a) A man going from Jerusalem to Jericho fell among
      robbers who beat him and left him half dead.
      b) A priest and a Levite happened along but ignored it.
      c) A Samaritan came by and gave him aid, and took to the
      inn where he cared for him.
      d) He arranged for further care for which he promised to
      pay when he came again.
      e) Jesus' question requiring the lawyer to answer his own

own question, "Which of the three, do you think, proved
neighbor to the man who fell among the robbers?"

f) He answered, "He who showed mercy on him."

g) Jesus said, "You go and do likewise."

C. Luke told of Jesus' visit to the home of Martha and Mary (38-42).

1. Martha welcomed Him into her home; Mary, her sister, sat
at His feet listening to Him.

2. Martha complained, "Lord, doesn't it concern you that my
sister has been leaving me to serve alone? Tell her to
help me."

3. The Lord said, "Martha, Martha, you are worried and dis-
tracted about many things."

4. Then He added, "One thing is needed; Mary has chosen the
good part which shall not be taken away from her."

The Mission of the Seventy

Scripture

10:1-24 Now after these things the Lord appointed seventy others,
and sent them two and two before his face into every city and place,
whither he himself was about to come. 2 And he said unto them,
The harvest indeed is plenteous, but the laborers are few: pray ye
therefore the Lord of the harvest, that he send forth laborers into
his harvest. 3 Go your ways; behold, I send you forth as lambs
in the midst of wolves. 4 Carry no purse, no wallet, no shoes;
and salute no man on the way. 5 And into whatsoever house ye
shall enter, first say, Peace *be* to this house. 6 And if a son of peace
be there, your peace shall rest upon him: but if not, it shall turn
to you again. 7 And in that same house remain, eating and drinking such things as they give: for the laborer is worthy of his hire.
Go not from house to house. 8 And into whatsover city ye enter,
and they receive you, eat such things as are set before you: 9 and
heal the sick that are therein, and say unto them, The kingdom
of God is come nigh unto you. 10 But into whatsoever city ye
shall enter, and they receive you not, go out into the streets thereof
and say, 11 Even the dust from your city, that cleaveth to our feet,
we wipe off against you: nevertheless know this, that the kingdom
of God is come nigh. 12 I say unto you, It shall be more tolerable in that day for Sodom, than for that city. 13 Woe unto thee,

Chorazin! woe unto thee, Bethsaida! for if the mighty works had been done in Tyre and Sidon, which were done in you, they would have repented long ago, sitting in sackcloth and ashes. 14 But it shall be more tolerable for Tyre and Sidon in the judgment, than for you. 15 And thou, Capernaum, shalt thou be exalted unto heaven? thou shalt be brought down unto Hades. 16 He that heareth you heareth me; and he that rejecteth you rejecteth me; and he that rejecteth me rejecteth him that sent me.

17 And the seventy returned with joy, saying, Lord, even the demons are subject unto us in thy name. 18 And he said unto them, I beheld Satan fallen as lightning from heaven. 19 Behold, I have given you authority to tread upon serpents and scorpions, and over all the power of the enemy: and nothing shall in any wise hurt you. 20 Nevertheless in this rejoice not, that the spirits are subject unto you; but rejoice that your names are written in heaven.

21 In that same hour he rejoiced in the Holy Spirit, and said, I thank thee, O Father, Lord of heaven and earth, that thou didst hide these things from the wise and understanding, and didst reveal them unto babes: yea, Father; for so it was well-pleasing in thy sight. 22 All things have been delivered unto me of my Father: and no one knoweth who the Son is, save the Father; and who the Father is, save the Son, and he to whomsover the Son willeth to reveal *him*. 23 And turning to the disciples, he said privately, Blessed *are* the eyes which see the things that ye see: 24 for I say unto you, that many prophets and kings desired to see the things which ye see, and saw them not; and to hear the things which ye hear, and heard them not.

Comments

the Lord appointed seventy others.—It was impossible for Jesus to accomplish everything alone. He was able to reach more people, however, by effective organization and distribution of responsibility first to the twelve and then to the seventy (or seventy-two according to some texts). The seventy were selected, equipped for their mission, carefully instructed, and sent out two by two to do the work for which Christ commissioned them.

The value of organization had been demonstrated in Moses' day. At one time he attempted to care for all the problems of the nation of Israel, but Jethro wisely pointed out that it was too much for him. He advised Moses to appoint rulers over the people who were to be divided into groups of thousands, hundreds, and tens (Ex. 18:13-27).

When the twelve apostles attempted to carry the total burden of the church in Jerusalem, they soon found out that some of the people were being neglected. So they had the congregation select seven men whom they appointed to care for the distribution of food to the widows who were dependent on the church for support (Acts 6:1-6). The apostles gave themselves to the task of preaching the Word. Later, they appointed elders in all the churches (Acts 14: 23). And for a list of other workers see I Cor 12:28; Eph. 4:11-13.

Jesus maintained control over both the twelve and the seventy, for they were under the immediate direction of the Holy Spirit. He maintains His authority over His church today through the direction given to it in the New Testament (Matt. 28:18-20).

The harvest is plenteous.—Then as now, the harvest was great, but the laborers few. Crowds were following Jesus; why didn't He send all of them? The story of the rejected volunteers suggests that all did not have the required dedication for the task (Luke 9:57-61).

Workers should be carefully selected for the specialized tasks in the kingdom today. A call for volunteers is often answered by unqualified people. Often those who could be trained to do the work do not feel worthy to volunteer. The responsible leaders of the church—ministers, evangelists, elders, deacons and others—should constantly watch for those who are capable of being trained for the tasks necessary for the progress of the gospel. It should be the goal to have every member engaged in the work of the Lord. Some may not be qualified to teach, but the importance of their serving in other ways should not be overlooked.

pray ye therefore the Lord of the harvest.—The task was to be done under the direction of the Lord of the harvest. He sent them forth. *Go your ways.*—Too often people are told to go, but given no instruction as to ways to proceed or message to proclaim. Such generalized efforts accomplish little for the work of Christ. Many, no doubt, would go if they were told how and where and what to do.

lambs in the midst of wolves.—They were to go to their Jewish brethren, the lost sheep of the house of Israel. They could expect the hospitality normally accorded teachers in that day. But some would not accept them; they were to be on guard against such. See Luke 22:35-38 for Jesus instruction to the twelve when He sent them into all the world to preach the gospel.

183

Salute no man on the way.—Instructions for the Seventy were about the same as for the Twelve when they were sent out on their first mission. They were on urgent business for the King. They were not to lose time by visiting along the way. They would find it difficult to get their task done before Jesus came to them, for He was moving toward the climax of His ministry which was the cross and the ascension.

When they did enter some home, they were to say, "Peace be to this house." If a son of peace was there, a peace loving person, their blessing was to remain with him. But if he was not one characterized by peace, the blessing would return to the one who tried and failed to share the message of peace with him.

such things as they give.—The Seventy were not to move from house to house, for it would be time consuming and it would accomplish little. They were to become one of the family that gave them a place to stay and eat what was set before them. Just what was involved in the reference to diet may not be clear. Was it a matter of "clean and unclean" foods? Jews made much of this issue. Paul gave similar instruction to the Christians at Corinth about eating what was set before them (I Cor. 10:23-30). Jesus told the Seventy to eat what the family did, for it was one of the best ways of becoming identified with people whom they were to help with the gospel of the kingdom of God.

the laborer is worthy of his hire.—See also Matt. 10:10; I Tim. 5: 18; and I Cor. 9:14. See *Studies In First Corinthians,* pages 159-163 on Paul's argument for the support of the ministry.

and they receive you not.—The Seventy were forewarned that not all would accept their message. The Lord Himself was rejected by many and crucified by the very people He tried to help. His workers can expect to be rejected by some, but there are those who will gladly accept the message of salvation. Timothy was to face hardship as a good soldier of Jesus Christ, but there would be victories for his encouragement in the service of the Lord also.

If the Seventy met with rejection, they were to shake the dust from their feet and move to others who might respond to God's message.

It shall be more tolerable in that day.—Sodom fell under the terrible judgment of God because of its wickedness, but the city that rejected the messengers of Jesus was to fare worse in the Day of Judgment than Sodom. Chorazin, Bethsaida and Capernaum were warned about the fate that was awaiting them. If the mighty works of Jesus had been done in those other cities which had long since perished, they would have repented. But Capernaum which was the center of Jesus' whole Galilean ministry, would it be exalted to heaven? Jesus addressed the city and said, "You shall be brought down unto Hades." The ruins that mark the places where those proud but sinful cities once stood give silent testimony to the truth of Jesus' prophecy concerning them.

The kingdom of God is come nigh unto you.—This message was to be given both to those who received Jesus' messengers and to those who rejected them. To those who received the message of Christ, the kingdom came with blessing; to those who rejected, it came in judgment.

Jesus identified Himself with His messengers. To reject them was to reject Him; to reject Him was to reject the Father who sent Him. The kingdom of God came near with blessings for those who were willing to receive them, but judgments for those who refused God's rule in their lives.

I saw Satan fallen as lightening from heaven.—The Seventy reported to Jesus that the demons were subject to them in His name. The response of Jesus is rendered differently in the various versions. The King James reads, "I beheld Satan as lightning fall from heaven." This suggests that Jesus saw Satan fall from heaven. The American Standard puts it this way, "I beheld Satan fallen as lightning from heaven." This suggests that Jesus said that He saw Satan after he had fallen. R. S. V. reads, "I saw Satan fall like lightning from heaven." Jesus was observing when Satan fell, and his fall was like lightning from heaven. It was sudden, swift, and positive.

To what does this fall refer? Some, basing their views on Isa. 14:12 and Rev. 12:7-12, suggest that it was when Satan literally fell from his original state. But the Isaiah passage, according to Isa. 14:4, refers to the king of Babylon. The passage in Revelation shows that Satan was defeated before he began his attack on God's people on earth. They overcame him by the blood of the Lamb and the word of their testimony and by the fact that they loved not their lives even unto death. Others suggest that it was the defeat of Satan in the wilderness temptation of Our Lord. That was a signal victory for the Son of Man who was tempted in all points as we are but without sin (Heb. 4:15). But Jesus related this fall of Satan to the victory of the Seventy. They had just told Him that the demons were subject to them in His name; but He was aware of it before they told Him, for He was observing the battle as Satan fell before the power of the Lord's army.

he rejoiced in the Holy Spirit.—that is, He spoke these words of rejoicing and thanksgiving by the Holy Spirit. Luke also says that the words of the comand given by Jesus to His apostles were spoken through the Holy Spirit (Acts 1:2; Matt. 28:18-20).

The Seventy had cast out demons by the power of the Holy Spirit. They were not to rejoice that demons were subject to them, but that their names were written in heaven. All this was the occasion for Jesus' rejoicing.

I thank thee, O Father, Lord of heaven and earth.—Jesus usually addressed God as "Father" in His prayers. This is the longest recorded statement of address used by Him.

The Seventy were ordinary people, yet it pleased the Father to reveal the things of the Kingdom to them. They in turn told others about the kingdom of God. But those who were satisfied in their own wisdom did not welcome this revelation from God.

no one knoweth who the Son is.—At the baptism of Jesus, the Father had said, "This is my Son." The way to know the Father is to know His Son. When the disciples asked Jesus to show them the Father, He replied, "If you had recognized me, you would have known the Father" (John 14:7-11). This explains the statement of John 1:18, "No man has seen God at any time; the only begotten Son, who is in the bosom of the Father, he has declared Him"—that is, He has unfolded the story of the Father. That story is given in the Gospel of John. John 20:30-31 is the conclusion of the story, but John 1:18 is the statement of its purpose.

Blessed are the eyes which see the things that you see.—Just before Jesus explained the Parable of the Sower, He said to the disciples, "Blessed are your eyes, for they see; and your ears, for they hear" (Matt. 13:16). Many prophets and righteous men had desired to see and hear these things about Jesus. Those who had the privilege of hearing Him were to be congratulated. Peter wrote that the prophets and even the angels had desired to look into these things (I Pet. 1:10-12). The Old Testament message pointed to the coming of the Messiah. The disciples of Jesus were in the presence of the One about whom the prophets had spoken. The hope of Christians, based on the testimony about His life, death and resurrection, is in His coming again (Phil. 3:20-21; Heb. 9:27; I Thes. 4:13-18).

The Story of the Good Samaritan

Scripture

10:25-37   And behold, a certain lawyer stood up and made trial of him, saying, Teacher, what shall I do to inherit eternal life? 26 And he said unto him, What is written in the law? how readest thou? 27 And he answering said, Thou shalt love the Lord thy God with all thy heart, and with all thy soul, and with all thy strength, and with all thy mind; and thy neighbor as thyself. 28 And he said unto him, Thou hast answered right: this do, and thou shalt live. 29 But he, desiring to justify himself, said unto Jesus, And who is my neighbor? 30 Jesus made answer and said, A certain man was going down from Jerusalem to Jericho; and he fell among robbers, who both stripped him and beat him, and departed, leaving him half dead. 31 And by chance a certain priest was going down that way: and when he saw him, he passed by on the other side. 32 And in like manner a Levite also, when he came to the place, and saw him, passed by on the other side. 33 But a certain Samaritan, as he journeyed, came where he was: and when he saw him, he was moved with compassion, 34 and came to him, and bound up his wounds, pouring on them oil and wine; and he set him on his own beast, and brought him to an inn, and took care of him. 35 And on the morrow he took out two shillings, and gave them to the host, and said, Take care of him; and whatsoever thou spendest more, I, when I come back again, will repay thee. 36. Which of these three, thinkest thou, proved neighbor unto him that fell among the robbers? 37 And he said, He that showed mercy on him. And Jesus said unto him, Go, and do thou likewise.

Comments

a certain lawyer.—This incident is similar to the story of the Rich Young Ruler (Lk. 18:18-29), but there are striking differences. The ruler was evdently sincere in his desire to know what he had to do to have eternal life. The lawyer was deliberately trying to trap Jesus. Perhaps he was trying to get Jesus to set aside the Law of Moses or at least say something that could be used to condemn Him.

What shall I do to have eternal life?—Under the Law of Moses the answer was simple and should have been understood by the lawyer,

187

as his response shows. Paul says, "Moses writeth that the man that doeth righteousness which is of the law shall live thereby" (Rom. 10:5; Gal. 3:12). The law, of course, could not forgive the sinner who broke the law (Gal. 3:21). Only the blood of Christ could provide forgivness which is made available under the New Covenant to the obedient believer in Christ through the grace of God (Rom. 3: 21-26). This explains the difference between the answer of the lawyer which Jesus approved and the answer given on the Day of Pentecost to those who asked what to do for remission of their sins (Acts 2:36-38).

What is written in the law?—Jesus was born under the law, and His ministry was carried out during the period in which the Law of Moses still held jurisdiction over God's people. The Old Covenant did not give place to the New until the Day of Pentecost. Naturally, when He was asked about eternal life, He pointed to the Law of God for the age in which He lived.

Jesus answered the lawyers question by asking another, for He wanted him to think about it. He was aware of the purpose the lawyer had in asking it. So Jesus said, "What is written in the law? How does it read to you?"

Thou shalt love the Lord thy God.—The lawyer's statement first summarized the Law of Moses with reference to duties to God. The manner in which they were to be carried out is stressed in these details: (1) with all your heart; (2) with all your soul; (3) with all your strength; and (4) with all your mind. Then he added the statement that summarizes the duties toward man: "Love your neighbor as yourself."

desiring to justify himself.—The embarrassed lawyer who had deliberately tried to embarrass Jesus asked, "Who is my neighbor?" Jesus answered his question by telling the story of the Good Samaritan. A man went down from Jerusalem to Jericho and fell among robbers, but he was ignored by a priest and a Levite. Of all people, these should have gone to his rescue. But a Samaritan—they were despised by the Jews—came along and gave him aid. Then he took him to the inn where he could be cared for until he got well. As he was leaving, he said to the inn keeper, "Whatever else you spend, I'll repay when I return."

Which of these three?—Jesus' question made the lawyer answer his own. There could be no doubt about it. The one who had shown mercy to the distressed and beaten man was the neighbor. Was the proud lawyer ready to be taught? The Master said, "Go and do likewise."

Jesus at the Home of Mary and Martha

Scripture

10:38-42   Now as they went on their way, he entered into a certain village: and a certain woman named Martha received him into her house. 39 And she had a sister called Mary, who also sat at the Lord's feet, and heard his word. 40 But Martha was cumbered about much serving; and she came up to him, and said, Lord, dost thou not care that my sister did leave me to serve alone? bid her therefore that she help me. 41 But the Lord answered and said unto her, Martha, Martha, thou art anxious and troubled about many things: 42 but one thing is needful: for Mary hath chosen the good part, which shall not be taken away from her.

Comments

he entered a certain village.—Luke did not name the village, but John says that Lazarus, with his sisters Mary and Martha, lived in Bethany (John 11:1). Luke does not give all the geographical details necessary to enable us to reconstruct all the journies of Jesus in the closing months of His ministry. There can be little doubt, however, that He was in Bethany of Judea. Afterwards, He went again into Perea, "beyond the Jordan" (Jo. 10:40).
Martha received him into her house.—No mention is made of Lazarus. It is idle to speculate about this ommission. The important fact is that Mary, Martha's sister, was sitting at the feet of Jesus and learning the lessons the Master taught.
But Martha was cumbered.—The contrast does not encourage the neglect of household duties and hospitality to guests. It does stress the importance of giving first place to what the Teacher has to say. Martha, in her distress, said to Jesus, "You tell her to help me."
anxious and troubled about many things.—John tells something about her faith in Christ and hope of the resurrection (John 11:18-27). Jesus' gentle rebuke seems to say that it was not necessary to do so much to entertain Him.
one thing is needful.—Did this refer to food? Hardly. The one thing needful—food could be forgotten for a time (John 4:32-34)—

189

was the lesson Jesus was teaching. That was spiritual food, and it could not be neglected. Mary had chosen the good part, and it would not be denied her.

Summary

In addition to selecting, instructing and sending out the twelve apostles, Jesus appointed seventy others to go with the message of the kingdom of God into all the villages where He was about to come. The harvest was great, the laborers were few.

Their task was urgent; they would be working among their own people; they, therefore, were to make no elaborate preparations for this journey. There was but little time to get the work done.

On their return they reported to Jesus that the demons had been subject to them in His name. But He said, "I was observing as Satan fell like lightning from heaven." Instead of rejoicing over their power to cast out demons, they were to rejoice that their names were written in heaven. Jesus Himself rejoiced in the Holy Spirit that the Father had revealed these things to men who trusted Him.

The victories of Jesus were of various kinds. A lawyer challenged Him with the question, "Teacher, what shall I do to inherit eternal life?" Because they were living under the Law of Moses, Jesus said, "How does the Law of Moses read to you?" But the lawyer persisted, "Who is my neighbor?" Then Jesus told the story of the Good Samaritan. The meaning of "neighbor" was made plain. Jesus said, "You go and do likewise."

Jesus' journies took Him to many places. The details of these trips are not always given. The visit to the home of Martha and Mary gives a fleeting glimpse of an important teaching situation. Mary had chosen to sit at His feet and learn from Him; this privilege was not to be taken from her.

Questions

1. Why did Jesus appoint the Seventy?
2. What did He do for them before sending them out?
3. What does the Bible teach about the value of organization?
4. What can be done to enlist a larger number of church members in the Lord's work?
5. Should we pray for workers today?
6. In what ways does the sending of the Seventy help us to prepare for the work of evangelism today?

7. What dangers were they to face?
8. Why were they not to salute men on their way?
9. What greeting were they to give those who invited them into their homes?
10. What were they to do if they were rejected?
11. How were they to conduct themselves in the homes where they were to stay?
12. What does the New Testament teach about support for those who work in the gospel?
13. Why would it be more tolerable in the judgment for Sodom than for the cities of Jesus' time?
14. What is meant by the expression, "The kingdom of God is come near you"?
15. What are the various ways in which Jesus' remarks about Satan are stated?
16. What did His remark mean?
17. Why say that Jesus rejoiced in the Holy Spirit?
18. For what did Jesus thank the Father?
19. What did Jesus mean by the statement that no one knows who the Son is except the Father?
20. Why did Jesus say, "Blessed are your eyes"?
21. Who else had desired to see what the disciples were seeing?
22. What are the similarities and differences in the stories of the lawyer and of the Rich Young Ruler?
23. How did Jesus get the lawyer to answer His own question?
24. Why didn't He give a direct answer?
25. How does the lawyer's answer summarize the whole law?
26. Why didn't the apostles give the same answer on the Day of Pentecost?
27. Why had the lawyer asked the question in the first place?
28. Why was he embarrassed at the turn of events?
29. Why did he ask, "Who is my neighbor?"
30. How does the story of the Good Samaritan answer his question?
31. What did Jesus tell him to do?
32. Where was the home of Martha and Mary?
33. Why did Luke omit some of the details about the journies of Jesus?
34. What was Martha's problem?
35. What is "the one thing needful"?
36. Why was Mary not to be denied the part she had chosen?

CHAPTER ELEVEN

Outline

A. Luke told how Jesus met the problems of the disciples and of the crowds (1-36).
  1. The problem about prayer (1-13).
    a) A request for help: "Teach us to pray" (1).
    b) An example to follow: The Lord's Prayer (2-4).
      (1) How to address God.
      (2) What to put first—the kingdom of God.
      (3) When to mention material needs—daily bread.
      (4) Why mention forgivness.
      (5) Where to ask that God lead.
    c) A story that explained: The Friend at midnight (5-13).
      (1) When in need, don't be ashamed to ask God.
      (2) God answers prayer: Ask, seek, knock.
      (3) Praying is like talking to a father (11-13).
        (a) A father gives good gifts to his children: Bread, not a stone; fish, not a serpent; egg, not a scorpion.
        (b) The Heavenly Father gives the Holy Spirit to those who ask Him.
  2. The charge about casting out demons (14-26).
    a) The circumstances (14-16).
      (1) Jesus had cast out a demon.
      (2) When the demon was gone out of him, the dumb man spoke, and this caused the crowds to marvel.
      (3) Some said He had cast out the demon by Beelzebub, the prince of demons.
      (4) Others, to embarrass Him, wanted Him to show them a sign from heaven.
    b) The three-fold answer (17-23).
      (1) The divided kingdom.
        (a) A divided kingdom is brought to desolation.
        (b) Satan's kingdom can't stand if it is divided.
        (c) If demons are cast out by Satan's power, his kingdom is divided.
      (2) The reference to their own sons.
        (a) Question: If I do it by Beelzebub, by whom do your sons cast them out?

192

        (b) Let them be your judges.

        (c) If I by the finger of God cast out demons, then is the kingdom of God come upon you.

    (3) The strong man.

        (a) It takes a stronger man to overcome a strong one. Jesus is stronger than Satan, for He had cast out the demon.

        (b) The lesson: "He that is not with me is against me; and he that gathereth not with me scattereth."

  c) The unclean spirit and the empty house (24-26).

    (1) The unclean spirit left a man, went through waterless places and returned to the same man.

    (2) Finding the place empty, he took seven other spirits more evil than himself and entered and dwelt in the man.

    (3) The last state of the man was worse than the first.

3. The praise for the mother who bore Him (27-28).

  a) A woman from the crowd said, "Blessed is the womb that bore you and the breasts from which you took nourishment."

  b) But Jesus said, "Blessed are they who hear the word of God and keep it."

4. The demand for a sign (29-36).

  a) The Sign of Jonah and the Sign of the Son of Man (29-32).

    (1) The sign-seeking evil generation would be given the sign of Jonah.

    (2) Jonah was a sign to the Ninevites; the Son of Man would be a sign to them.

    (3) A two-fold contrast that condemned that generation.

        (a) The queen of the south and the wisdom of Solomon.

        (b) The men of Ninevah and the preaching of Jonah.

  b) The parable of the lighted lamp (33-36).

    (1) A lamp is to enable men to see.

    (2) The lamp of the body is the eye.

    (3) Warning lest the light become darkness.

B. Luke told how Jesus answered the criticism of the Pharisees and the lawyers (37-54).
  1. The criticism of the Pharisees (37-44).
    a) The occasion: a Pharisee who had invited Jesus to have lunch with him marvelled that He did not first "bathe Himself" before eating (37-38).
    b) The answer: What makes a thing clean (39-40)?
      (1) He said, "You Pharisees cleanse the outside of the cup, but your inward part is full of wickedness."
      (2) This was foolish, for the one who made the outside made the inside too.
      (3) He added, "Give for alms those things which are within, and all things are clean to you."
    c) He pronounced three woes upon the Pharisees (41-44).
      (1) Their abuse of tithing.
      (2) Their love of chief seats.
      (3) Their likeness to "tombs that appear not."
  2. The criticism of the lawyers (45-52).
    a) The occasion: One of the lawyers at the luncheon said, "When you say this about the Pharisees, you reproach us also" (45).
    b) He pronounced three woes upon the lawyers (46-52).
      (1) Their loading men with burdens.
      (2) Their building the tombs of the prophets.
      (3) Their taking away the key of knowledge.
  3. When they came out, the scribes and Pharisees angrily tried to provoke Him to say things that would enable them to condemn Him (53-54).

Teach Us to Pray

Scripture

11:1-13 And it came to pass, as he was praying in a certain place, that when he ceased, one of his disciples said unto him, Lord, teach us to pray, even as John also taught his disciples. 2 And he said unto them, When ye pray, say, Father, Hallowed be thy name. Thy kingdom come. 3 Give us day by day our daily bread. 4 And forgive us our sins; for we ourselves also forgive every one that is indebted to us. And bring us not into temptation.
5 And he said unto them, Which of you shall have a friend, and

shall go unto him at midnight, and say to him, Friend, lend me three loaves; 6 for a friend of mine is come to me from a journey, and I have nothing to set before him; 7 and he from within shall answer and say, Trouble me not: the door is now shut, and my children are with me in bed; I cannot rise and give thee? 8 I say unto you, Though he will not rise and give him because he is his friend, yet because of his importunity he will arise and give him as many as he needeth. 9 And I say unto you, Ask, and it shall be given you; seek, and ye shall find; knock, and it shall be opened unto you. 10 For every one that asketh receiveth; and he that seeketh findeth; and to him that knocketh it shall be opened. 11 And of which of you that is a father shall his son ask a loaf, and he give him a stone? or a fish, and he for a fish give him a serpent? 12 Or if he shall ask an egg, will he give him a scorpion? 13 If ye then, being evil, know how to give good gifts unto your children, how much more shall your heavenly Father give the Holy Spirit to them that ask him?

Comments

as he was praying.—The prayer life of Jesus must have made a profound impression on His disciples. Many strange, unscriptural, and sometimes fanatical things have been taught about prayer with the result that it has been almost completely discredited by many people. But what Jesus taught about prayer is sensible, understandable, and entirely practical. There is no better way to learn what prayer really means than to give attention to what Jesus said on the subject and to follow the example He set in His own prayer life.

Lord, teach us to pray.—While it is natural for man to pray under certain circumstances, the fact remains that we must be taught to pray if we are to do so intelligently and in accord with the Scriptures. The Old Testament, particularly the Psalms, gives us many examples of prayer and shows us how to pray. Jesus' instruction and examples of prayer show us that prayer is the privilege that God gives to His children to talk to Him about anything at any time anywhere. The prayers of the apostles and the early church which are given in the book of Acts add helpful information on the subject. A study of the prayers of Paul for the church—for example, those in Ephesians and Colossians and Romans—will enlighten us on this very important phase of the Christian life. Paul reminds us that we do not know how to pray as we ought (Rom. 8:26). He says that the Holy Spirit helps our weakness—the separation from the immediate presence of God because of sin—by making intercession for us. Christ is also our intercessor (8:34). The book of Revelation has much to say about prayer. One of the most significant prayers recorded in it is the closing words of John as he prayed, "Come, Lord Jesus."

as John also taught his disciples.—It seems strange that we have no recorded prayer of John the Baptist in the Bible. His disciples must have been greatly impressed by his prayers, for they said to Jesus, "Teach us to pray, as John taught his disciples." The account of his ministry stresses his stern warnings and harsh judgments on the very wicked men to whom he preached. He called on sinners to repent. His disciples reveal another side of John, for he also taught his disciples to pray.

John the Baptist was like Elijah in many ways. Elijah sternly rebuked king Ahab for his wicked ways, and ridiculed the nonsense of fanatical prophets of Baal for the demonstration of what they called prayer. But there is no greater example of prayer given in the Old Testament than the prayer of Elijah when he said, "O Lord, God of Abraham, Isaac, and of Israel, let it be known this day that thou art God in Israel, and that I am thy servant, and that I have done all these things at thy word. Answer me, O Lord, answer me that this people may know that thou, O Lord, art God, and that thou hast turned their hearts back." I Kings 18:36-37. God answered that prayer, and the erring people said, "The Lord, he is God."

When ye pray, say.—Jesus told them how to address God. As children, they were to speak to the heavenly Father with respect that arises from love and reverence. They were to think of His kingdom first, for His rule must always have first places in the hearts of His people. "Thy will be done" explains the meaning of the kingdom in the heart of the individual. Paul admonished the church to let the peace of Christ rule in their hearts and the word of Christ dwell in them richly (Col. 3:14-15). His kingdom—the church—that came on the Day of Pentecost was to be made up of saints who really let Him rule in their lives. Every Christian should examine his own heart often to make sure that God does rule in every area of it.

Jesus taught them that God was concerned about their daily bread. In simple language they were to say, "Give us day by day our daily bread." The heavenly Father constantly gives an abundant supply of food. Then why is it that so many people of the world go hungry all their lives? Can it be because men do not do His will on earth? There are economic, political, and social aspects to the problem. The only solution to them seems to be the transforming power of the rule of God in the hearts of men.

Jesus taught the disciples to pray for forgivness as they had forgiven those indebted to them. See Matt. 18:21-35 for His instruction on the extent to which this principle is to be carried out. Many find it difficult to practice forgivness. Too often, it is a matter of words and not heart. Forgivness means to remember the offense no more (Heb. 8:12). Unwillingness to actually forgive may come from our unwillingness to believe that God really forgives sins. The misery caused by an uneasy conscience may often be expressed in aggressive and hostile attitudes toward others, with or without provocation. But Jesus makes it clear that if you do not forgive, neither will the heavenly Father forgive you.

The petition, "And bring us not into temptation" causes a problem since God does not tempt man. James 1:13. But Jesus and James say exactly the same thing. The prayer is for God to lead; His leading does not take us into temptation, it delivers us from evil. The providential leading of God will never lead one to sin. It may allow us to undergo trials which genuine faith in the Lord Jesus Christ will enable us to endure. See James 1:2-4 and I Cor. 10:12-13.

Which of you shall have a friend.—The parable of the Friend at Midnight shows that God's children need not be ashamed to ask Him for help when in need. The parable of the Widow and the Judge teaches the lesson of persistency in prayer (Luke 18:1-8).

The word translated "importunity" really suggests that the man whose company came at midnight was not ashamed to tell his friend that he had nothing to set before them. It does not say that he kept pounding on the door until his friend, to stop the annoyance, got up and gave him what he wanted. Neither should we be ashamed to tell the heavenly Father just what our problem is, for He knows what it is before we ask Him.

Ask, seek, knock.—The man of the parable did knock on the door of his friend; he did seek help; he did ask for the bread he needed. This is but the common sense thing to do. Apply the same principle in prayer, for God answers prayer.

And which of you that is a father.—God knows how to answer prayer

197

far better than any human father. No father gives a stone when his son asks for bread. If you know how to give good gifts to your children, how much more does God know how to answer the requests of His children?

give the Holy Spirit.—According to Matt. 7:11, Jesus said that the Father gives "good things" to them that ask Him. The Holy Spirit is the agent through whom He gives the good things. Luke, by using a figure of speech—metonymy—stresses the agent, but Matthew emphasized the good things given through the Holy Spirit.

Casting Out Demons by Beelzebub

Scripture

11:14-26   And he was casting out a demon that was dumb. And it came to pass, when the demon was gone out, the dumb man spake; and the multitudes marvelled. 15 But some of them said, By Beelzebub the prince of the demons casteth he out demons. 16 And others, trying him, sought of him a sign from heaven. 17 But he, knowing their thoughts, said unto them, Every kingdom divided against itself is brought to desolation; and a house divided against a house falleth. 18 And if Satan also is divided against himself, how shall his kingdom stand? because ye say that I cast out demons by Beelzebub. 19 And if I by Beelzebub cast out demons, by whom do your sons cast them out? therefore shall they be your judges. 20 But if I by the finger of God cast out demons, then is the kingdom of God come upon you. 21 When the strong man fully armed guardeth his own court, his goods are in peace: 22 but when a stronger than he shall come upon him, and overcome him, he taketh from him his whole armor wherein he trusted, and divideth his spoils. 23 He that is not with me is against me; and he that gathereth not with me scattereth. 24 The unclean spirit when he is gone out of the man, passeth through waterless places, seeking rest, and finding none, he saith, I will turn back unto my house whence I came out. 25 And when he is come, he findeth it swept and garnished. 26 Then goeth he, and taketh to him seven other spirits more evil than himself; and they enter in and dwell there: and the last state of that man becometh worse than the first.

Comment

a demon that was dumb.—Demon possession in this case caused the man to lose his ability to speak. When it was gone, the dumb man spoke and the crowds marvelled.

By Beelzebub.—He is the prince of demons or Satan (11:18). Demons were under the control of the devil. Some were attempting to suggest that Jesus was in league with the devil because He cast out the demon. Others were demanding a sign from heaven. The fact that the dumb man spoke was not enough for them, for they had no intention of believing anything that proved Him to be the Son of God. There will still be unbelievers when the Son of Man comes in His glory with the angels of heaven, but it will be too late to change the inevitable result of willful unbelief in this life.

But he, knowing their thoughts.—Recognizing their insincerity, Jesus proceeded to answer their false charge with a three-fold argument.

(1) The divided kingdom. A divided kingdom cannot stand. If Jesus was casting out demons by Beelzebub, then Satan was working against himself and his kingdom could not stand.

(2) Their sons. If Jesus' work—He had demonstrated his power to cast out the dumb demon—was accomplished by Satan's power, by whose power did the Jewish exorcists pretend to cast out demons? For proof that they did not really cast out demons see Luke's account of the seven sons of Sceva (Acts 19:14-18). If they claimed that it was by divine power, they were making God inferior to Satan. Their charge was absurd. "Let them be your judges," said Jesus, for they would have to admit the superiority of His work. Jesus added, "If I by the finger of God—that is, the Spirit of God (Matt. 12: 28)—cast out demons, then is the kingdom of God come upon you." The genuine miracle of Jesus proved that the Father was working through Him. This was evidence of God's rule over them which meant judgment to those who rejected it.

(3) The strong man's house. The one who overcomes a strong man—Jesus did not question the strength of Satan—and destroys his goods must be stronger than the one he overcomes. Jesus, the Son of God, is stronger than Satan. He proved it by casting out the demon that was controlled by Beelzebub.

He that is not with me is against me.—Jesus demanded open allegience to Him. To reject His miracles and demand "signs from heaven" was to be against Him. There is no neutral position.

The unclean spirit.—After passing through waterless places where nothing could rest, the unclean spirit came back to the house which it had left and found it empty. Taking seven other spirits more evil

199

than himself, he entered the house and dwelt there. This seems to explain the state of those who are against Jesus, for He said, "He that gathereth not with me scattereth."

Could this refer to the man from whom Jesus had just cast out the demon? Those possessed with demons were never charged with responsibility for their plight. According to Matt. 12:44-45, Jesus applied it to that "evil generation" that refused to believe in Him. They were then planning to crucify Him, and for that awful deed they would suffer the most terrible destruction ever to be brought on a city (Matt. 24:21).

Praise for the Mother who Bore Him

Scripture

11:27-28   And it came to pass, as he said these things, a certain woman out of the multitude lifted up her voice, and said unto him, Blessed is the womb that bare thee, and the breasts which thou didst suck. 28 But he said, Yea rather, blessed are they that hear the word of God, and keep it.

Comments

a certain woman of the multitude.—The crowd had just witnessed the remarkable miracle of casting out the dumb demon. The woman paid tribute to Christ in an indirect way by voicing her praise for His mother. It was a perfectly natural thing for her to do. The words in no way tend to praise Mary beyond the suggestion of appreciation for the mother of Him who had been such a blessing to the distressed man. Mary herself had said that all generations would call her blessed. That was because she was to have the privilege of giving birth to the Savior of the world.

Yea rather, Blessed are they that hear the word of God.—Jesus approved the praise for His mother. But He said that those who hear the word of God and keep it are to be congratulated. All who do God's will are to share in the praise that belongs to His servants.

Seeking a Sign

Scripture

11:29-36   And when the multitudes were gathering together unto him, he began to say, This generation is an evil generation: it seeketh after a sign; and there shall no sign be given to it but the sign of Jonah. 30 For even as Jonah became a sign unto the Ninevites, so shall also the Son of man be to this generation. 31 The queen of the south shall rise up in the judgment with the men of this generation, and shall condemn them: for she came from the ends of the earth to hear the wisdom of Solomon; and behold, a greater than Solomon is here. 32 The men of Nineveh shall stand up in the judgment with this generation, and shall condemn it: for they repented at the preaching of Jonah; and behold, a greater than Jonah is here.

33 No man, when he hath lighted a lamp, putteth it in a cellar, neither under the bushel, but on the stand, that they which enter in may see the light. 34 The lamp of thy body is thine eye: when thine eye is single, thy whole body also is full of light; but when it is evil, thy body also is full of darkness. 35 Look therefore whether the light that is in thee be not darkness. 36 If therefore thy whole body be full of light, having no part dark, it shall be wholly full of light, as when the lamp with its bright shining doth give thee light.

Comments

it seeketh after a sign.—Jesus called that generation evil because it was seeking after a sign. See Paul's comment on this attitude of the Jews in I Cor. 1:22-25. It was not wrong to want genuine proof before accepting even the word of Christ; the wrong lay in the fact that sign after sign had already been given and still they refused to believe. They wanted some sign from heaven, but they said His miracles were of the devil.

the sign of Jonah.—A sign is a mark that points out the distinction between persons or things. It may be the exhibition of divine power used to establish the claims of God's messengers. See John 20:30-31. Jesus explained "the sign of Jonah" by saying that Jonah became a sign to the Ninevites. The experience he had before coming to Ninevah marked him as a prophet of God. Because of it, they believed the thing he was preaching about the destruction of Ninevah.

But "as Jonah was three days and three nights in the belly of the whale, so the Son of Man would be three days and three nights in the heart of the earth" (Matt. 12:40). His resurrection was to be the sign that would mark Him as The Prophet (Acts 3:22-26).

a greater than Solomon is here.—more correctly, *something* greater

201

than Solomon. The queen of the South, the queen of Sheba, came to see the wisdom of Solomon (I Kings 10: ,-7; 3:10-28). In the Judgment, she would condemn that generation, because they were privileged to see something greater than the wisdom of Solomon. That was the wisdom of Christ. Paul calls Him "wisdom from God" and says that in Him "are all the treasures of wisdom and knowledge are hidden" (Col. 2:3; I Cor. 1:30).

a greater than Jonah.—that is, something greater than Jonah had offered as evidence to cause the men of Ninevah to believe. That something was the resurrection of Christ. When Jonah preached judgment to Ninevah, the men of Ninevah repented, that is, changed their minds about the thing he preached. That repentance was expressed by sitting in sackcloth and ashes and turning away from their evil ways. The generation to which Jesus preached should have changed their minds about judgment. Instead of saying that they were Abraham's children and assuming that nothing could ever happen to them, they should have been aware that they were like trees ready to be cut down and burned. On the Day of Pentecost, three thousand of them did repent and get themselves baptized in the name of Jesus Christ for the remission of their sins (Acts 2:38).

No man, when he hath lighted a lamp.—The parable of The Lamp illustrates the meaning of Jesus' words about signs. He did not come to leave people in the dark about Himself. He was about to light the lamp of truth about Himself by His resurrection.

The eye is like a lighted lamp that is placed where people can see. But that evil generation was not willing to see the light of evidence in His miracles that proved Him to be the Son of God. They only saw evil; He cast out the dumb demon, but they only saw the power of Beelzebub. The light of the resurrection is the last great proof to lead men to believe in Him as Lord (Rom. 10: 9-10).

Christ Criticized by Pharisees and Lawyers

Scripture

11:37-54 Now as he spake, a Pharisee asketh him to dine with him: and he went in, and sat down to meat. 38 And when the Pharisee saw it, he marvelled that he had not first bathed himself before dinner. 39 And the Lord said unto him, Now ye the Pharisees cleanse the outside of the cup and of the platter; but your inward part is full of extortion and wickedness. 40 Ye foolish ones, did not he that made the outside make the inside also? 41 But give for alms those things which are within; and behold, all things are clean unto you.

42 But woe unto you Pharisees! for ye tithe mint and rue and every herb, and pass over justice and the love of God: but these ought ye to have done, and not to leave the other undone. 43 Woe unto you Pharisees! for ye love the chief seats in the synagogues, and the salutations in the marketplaces. 44 Woe unto you! for ye are as the tombs which appear not, and the men that walk over them know it not.

45 And one of the lawyers answering saith unto him, Teacher, in saying this thou reproachest us also. 46 And he said, Woe unto you lawyers also! for ye load men with burdens grievous to be borne, and ye yourselves touch not the burdens with one of your fingers. 47 Woe unto you! for ye build the tombs of the prophets, and your fathers killed them. 48 So ye are witnesses and consent unto the works of your fathers: for they killed them, and ye build their tombs. 49 Therefore also said the wisdom of God, I will send unto them prophets and apostles; and some of them they shall kill and persecute; 50 that the blood of all the prophets, which was shed from the foundation of the world, may be required of this generation; 51 from the blood of Abel unto the blood of Zachariah, who perished between the altar and the sanctuary: yea, I say unto you, it shall be required of this generation. 52 Woe unto you lawyers! for ye took away the key of knowledge: ye entered not in yourselves, and them that were entering in ye hindered.

53 And when he was come out from thence, the scribes and the Pharisees began to press upon him vehemently, and to provoke him to speak of many things; 54 laying wait for him, to catch something out of his mouth.

Comments

a Pharisee asketh him to dine with him.—This was not the earliest meal of the day nor the latest. Luke makes a difference between the two in 14:12. The Pharisee had probably invited Jesus to have lunch with him. Why did they continue to invite Him to their homes, since they used the occasions to criticize Him?
had not first bathed himself.—See Mark 7:3-4 for the customs of the Jews. Jesus did not observe this ceremonial washing. He was

criticized for His failure to conform. The Pharisees also criticized His disciples for the same thing (Matt. 15:1-20). In neither case was it a matter of sanitation. The Jews were offended because He did not observe their traditions. He condemned them because they made God's word void by their traditions.

And the Lord said unto him.—He had an answer for their criticism. He said that the Pharisees were more interested in outer cleanliness than in inward purity. He left no chance for them to misunderstand; He was talking about their impure hearts. He was aware of their motives in inviting Him to dine with them. He knew that they were full of extortion and wickedness. His judgment was severe. He said, "You foolish ones, don't you know that he that made the outside of the cup made the inside also?" They were not using good sense. It was just as important to keep the inside clean as the outside. This was a blow against their hypocritical display of righteousness.

But give for alms those things which are within.—When you give something to help the poor, give what is within and all things are clean unto you. This was His answer to the issue of cleanliness. What He was giving was out of a pure heart. His motives were pure in helping such as the man with the dumb demon. If they had invited Him from a pure motive, they would not have been critical about ceremonial cleanliness. But their purpose was to condemn; it came out of an inward part that was full of extortion and wickedness.

But woe unto you Pharisees.—The three woes condemn the Pharisees for (1) abuses in the matter of tithing, (2) pride expressed in the desire to have the chief seats in the synagogue, and (3) their contaminating influence over the people.

They were careful to give a tithe of those things that were relatively insignificant, but passed over such matters as justice and love of God. They loved the exalted places in the synagogues and the salutations in the market places that showed their power over the people. But the worst criticism was the last, for they were like tombs that men walk over without realizing that the tombs were there. But they were ceremonially contaminated even though they were unaware of it. They had come in contact with death, and were "unclean." In the same way, they were being contaminated by the Pharisees without realizing what was happening to them.

And one of the lawyers.—"Teacher, when you say this about the

204

Pharisees, you are condemning us too." Jesus didn't hesitate to accept the challenge; He pronounced three woes on the lawyers also. They were loading burdens on men that were hard to bear, but refused to touch them with a finger. See also Matt. 23:4. They were building the tombs of the prophets. This is slightly different from the charge aaginst the Pharisees whom He likened to hidden tombs. The lawyers were building the tombs of the prophets ostensibly in their honor, but they were joining with the Pharisees who were seeking a cause to kill The Prophet. Their hypocritical display simply proved that they were true children of those who had been guilty of murdering the prophets of God. The responsibility for shedding innocent blood, from Abel to Zachariah, was to fall on that generation which was soon to crucify the Son of God.

for ye took away the key of knowledge.—They had taken away the key to salvation which is the knowledge of the Scriptures. They had done it by their traditions, teachings, and practices. They had not entered the door of salvation that God had opened for His people, and they were hindering others who wanted to do so.

the scribes and Pharisees began to press upon him vehemently.— They were waiting for the opportunity to condemn Him. Their anger had been aroused by the rebuke He had administered. They were waiting to get even. Their provocative attack was designed to cause Him to say something that would give them cause to condemn Him.

Summary

The lessons which Jesus taught stimulated His disciples and the crowds to ask questions. The disciples wanted Him to teach them how to pray. He answered with an example, an illustration, and some additional explanatory remarks. The Lord's Prayer showed them how to use the elements of prayer; the story of the Friend at Midnight showed them the right approach to make; the remarks that followed showed that prayer is like the requests of a son for his father to give him the things he needs.

Not everyone was interested in learning from the Teacher; many only watched for an opportunity to criticize Him. The miracle of casting out the dumb demon caused some to say that He had performed it by the power of Beelzebub. But others ignored it and demanded a "sign from heaven."

Jesus answered their false charge by a three-fold argument: (1) the divided kingdom, (2) the work of Jewish exorcists, and (3) the story of the strong man. His devastating rebuttal led to the verdict: "He that is not with me is against me, and he that gathereth not with me scattereth." Indeed, they were like the empty house occupied by a demon and seven others worse than himself; their last state would be worse than the first. Rejecting Him would lead to their destruction.

Their demand for a sign was to be answered in the "sign of Jonah." The resurrection would establish His claims, for by it He was to be designated the Son of God.

A Pharisee had invited Him to have lunch with him. Jesus did not observe the ceremonies of these self-appointed leaders. He answered their criticism by showing the need for purity within, something they so evidently lacked.

The lawyers who were present took up the debate and accused Him of condemning them also. Jesus answered with a list of hypocritical practices of which they were guilty. By their example and by their teaching, they had taken away the knowledge of God's Word which is the key to salvation.

As He left the Pharisees house, the scribes and Pharisees continued to harass Him, hoping to find some excuse to condemn Him.

Questions

1. What led the disciples to ask Jesus to teach them to pray?
2. How did He teach them?
3. Where else may we find information on this important subject?
4. What is known about the prayer life of John the Baptist?
5. What may we learn from the contrast between the prayers of the prophets of Baal and the prayer of Elijah?
6. What are some of the things Jesus taught the disciples to say when they prayed?
7. Why pray for forgivness?
8. What is the point of the parable of the Friend at Midnight?
9. Why did Jesus say, "Ask, seek, knock"?
10. What does the reference to a son's requests to his father teach about prayer?
11. What part does the Holy Spirit have in answering prayer?
12. Why did some charge that Jesus was casting out demons by Beelzebub?

13. What were the three answers Jesus gave to this false charge? What is meant by each of them?
14. Why did He say, "He that is not with me is against me"?
15. What is the lesson of the unclean spirit?
16. Why did the woman from the crowd speak words of praise about His mother?
17. Why did Jesus answer her by speaking about those who hear the word of God?
18. What kind of a sign were some seeking?
19. What is meant by the "sign of Jonah"?
20. Why is the resurrection of vital importance to us?
21. What did Jesus mean by saying that something greater than Solomon is here?
22. How does the parable of the Lamp explain Jesus' answer to their request for signs?
23. Why did the Pharisee invite Jesus to dine with him?
24. Why did he criticize Jesus?
25. How did Jesus meet the criticism?
26. What did He mean by giving those things for alms that are within?
27. On what issues did He condemn the Pharisees?
28. What was the reaction of the lawyers to His criticism of the Pharisees?
29. What did He say to the lawyers?
30. What was the key of knowledge?
31. How had they taken it away?
32. What did the Pharisees and scribes do as Jesus left the house?

CHAPTER TWELVE

Outline

A. Luke told about Jesus' warnings and encouragements for His disciples (1-12).
   1. The circumstances: Opposition of the Pharisees (1).
   2. The warning: Beware of the leaven of the Pharisees (1-3).
      a) The leaven of the Pharisees is hypocracy.
      b) Their hypocracy would be exposed; nothing was covered up that would not be uncovered.
      c) The exposure would be complete: Things whispered in darkness would be heard in the light; things heard in the inner chamber would be shouted from the housetop.
   3. The encouragement (4-12).
      a) As friends, He told them of God's protective care (4-7).
         (1) Do not fear those who can kill the body—the Pharisees were plotting His death.
         (2) Rather fear Him who has power to cast into hell.
         (3) God cared for the sparrows, but they were of more value than many sparrows.
   4. Another warning: Confessing and denying Him (8-9).
      a) Those who acknowledge Him before men, He will acknowledge before the angels of God.
      b) Those who deny Him, He will deny before the angels.
      c) One speaking against the Son of Man may be forgiven, but blaspheming the Holy Spirit will not be forgiven.
   5. Added encouragement when brought before authorities (10-12).
      a) Do not be anxious about what to say.
      b) The Holy Spirit would teach them in that very hour what to say.
B. Luke told about the man who came to Jesus about his inheritance (13-21).
   1. The circumstances (13-15).
      a) He asked Jesus to tell his brother to divide the inheritance with him.
      b) Jesus said, "Man, who made me a judge or divider over you?"

    c) Then He warned: "See that you keep yourselves from all covetousness, for life doesn't depend on the abundance of your possessions."

  2. The parable of the Rich Fool which Jesus used to illustrate His point (16-20).

    a) A rich man's land produced well. He asked himself, "What am I to do, for I have no place to store the harvest?"

    b) He answered his own question, "I'll build bigger barns and store the grain; then I'll say to myself, You have plenty for many years; take a good rest, eat, drink, and enjoy life."

    c) God asked a question, "Fool, they are requiring your life from you tonight; and the things you have prepared, whose will they be?"

    d) Jesus said, "That's the way it is with the one who lays up treasure for himself and is not rich toward God."

C. Luke told how Jesus continued teaching His disciples the meaning of being rich toward God (22-53).

  1. He told them not to be anxious about food and clothing (22-34).

    a) God's care made it unnecessary (22-28).

      (1) Life is more important than food and clothing.

      (2) God cares for the birds and the flowers; how much more for you, "O you of little faith?"

    b) God's kingdom must have first place (29-34).

      (1) The pagans seek for these things, but the Father knows about your needs.

      (2) God's way: "Seek His kingdom, and these things will be added unto you."

      (3) His encouragement: "Fear not little flock, it is the the Father's good pleasure to give you the kingdom."

      (4) His directive: "Sell what you have, give alms; and you will have treasure in heaven."

      (5) The secret: "Where your treasure is, there will your heart be also."

  2. He told them to be alert concerning the Lord's coming (35-48).

    a) It will be at an unknown time (35-40).

        (1) Be prepared as servants who have the lamps burning as they watch for master's return.

        (2) As no one knows when a thief may come, so "in an hour that you think not, the Son of man is coming."

    b) It will be a time of giving rewards (41-48).

        (1) In response to Peter's question, He told about the reward for the faithful.

        (2) Then He told of punishment for the unfaithful according to their responsibility: many stripes, few stripes.

  3. He urged them to be aware of the purpose of His mission (49-53).

    a) It was like kindling a fire, but He had a baptism that He must undergo (49-50).

    b) He warned that He had not come to give peace, but division even between members of a family (51-53).

D. Luke told how Jesus chided the multitudes for being unable to read the signs of the coming storm (54-59).

  1. Why can't you interpret this time? (54-56).

    a) They were able to read the weather signs.

    b) Why couldn't they see the coming storm about which He had just given warning?

  2. Why can't you make the right decision about the thing you face?

    a) He illustrated His meaning by showing that it is good sense to settle out of court before the case goes against you.

    b) He pointed out the impossibility of escaping after the decision has been rendered by the Judge.

The Leaven of the Pharisees

Scripture

12:1-12 In the meantime, when the many thousands of the multitude were gathered together, insomuch that they trod one upon another, he began to say unto his disciples first of all, Beware ye of the leaven of the Pharisees, which is hypocrisy. 2 But there is nothing covered up, that shall not be revealed; and hid, that shall not be known. 3 Wherefore whatsoever ye have said in the dark-

210

ness shall be heard in the light; and what ye have spoken in the ear in the inner chambers shall be proclaimed upon the housetops. 4 And I say unto you my friends, Be not afraid of them that kill the body, and after that have no more that they can do. 5 But I will warn you whom ye shall fear; Fear him, who after he hath killed hath power to cast into hell; yea, I say unto you, Fear him. 6 Are not five sparrows sold for two pence? and not one of them is forgotten in the sight of God. 7 But the very hairs of your head are all numbered. Fear not: ye are of more value than many sparrows. 8 And I say unto you, Every one who shall confess me before men, him shall the Son of man also confess before the angels of God: 9 but he that denieth me in the presence of men shall be denied in the presence of the angels of God. 10 And every one who shall speak a word against the Son of man, it shall be forgiven him: but unto him that blasphemeth against the Holy Spirit it shall not be forgiven. 11 And when they bring you before the synagogues, and the rulers, and the authorities, be not anxious how or what ye shall answer, or what ye shall say: 12 for the Holy Spirit shall teach you in that very hour what ye ought to say.

Comments

In the meantime.—This warning followed the incident of the Pharisees and lawyers confronting Jesus as He came out of the house where He had been a guest of a Pharisee. His disciples could expect the same kind of treatment, for He had not called them to an easy task.

the many thousands.—Many things had attracted the crowds to Jesus, but the thing that caused them to gather at this time seems to have been the open discussion that was going on between Jesus and the Pharisees. One wonders if they really saw through the hypocracy of the Pharisees? Perhaps not. See 12:57.

he began to say unto his disciples first of all.—The lessons recorded in this chapter were primarily directed to the disciples, but the multitudes overheard what He was saying. At the close of the lesson, Jesus directed a warning to the crowds about interpreting the times.

the leaven of the Pharisees, which is hypocrisy.—Leaven is nearly always used in the Scriptures as a symbol of evil. At the time of the Passover, all leaven was excluded from the homes of the faithful people of Israel. Paul used this fact to teach that the whole Christian life was to be observed "not with old leaven, neither with the leaven of malice and wickedness, but with the unleavened bread of sincerity and truth" (I Cor. 5:7-8).

But leaven is also used in the parable of the Leaven to indicate the effective working of the gospel message. The reason it can be used in both ways is seen in the manner in which it works. It has the power to transform whatever it touches. To expose oneself to the hypocritical teaching of the Pharisee was to run the risk of becoming like the Pharisees. On the other hand, to come in contact with the message of Christ is to come under the transforming power of the Gospel with the hope of becoming like Him (II Cor. 3:18).

nothing covered up.—The leaven of the Pharisees, said Jesus, is hypocracy. When they spoke, it was as if they were speaking from under a mask of pretense at speaking the truth. They spoke falsehood under the guise of truth. But there was nothing that they covered up that would not be uncovered. Jesus had unmasked the Pharisees and the lawyers at the luncheon when He pointed out what they really were. See 11:37-52. Just so, hypocracy was to be unmasked whenever it was confronted with the truth of Christ.

Jesus' own teaching was not intended to be made a secret thing, for it was to be shouted from the house tops that everyone might know what He taught (Matt. 10:26-27).

Be not afraid of them that kill the body.—The conversation had arisen out of the attack of the enemies of Jesus who were trying desperately to find an excuse for killing Him. His disciple also would face persecution. But they were not to fear those who might kill the body, but rather fear God for He alone could punish the wicked by casting them into eternal punishment. That this is a reference to God and not the devil seems evident from the remarks that follow encouraging the disciples to remember God's tender care for them. The devil, of course, can afflict the saints of God. He can bring trials upon them to prove their faith, but the genuine thing in their faith enables them to endure the trial (James 1:2-3, 12). Jesus did two things to encourage at this point: (1) He called them friends and (2) He reminded them that God was watching over them.

five sparrows sold for two pence?—On another occasion Jesus used the same thought and spoke of two sparrows that were sold for a penny (Matt. 10:29). Jesus repeated His lessons with variations from time to time. If we carefully note the context when such variations occur, it will avoid the supposition that mistakes were made in reporting the incidents of the teaching ministry of Jesus.

The point of the lesson is this: the disciples of Jesus are of much more value than many sparrows. Not a single sparrow is forgotten in God's sight; He won't forget the friends of His Son.

But the very hairs of your head are all numbered.—This indicates the meticulous care exercised by the Father over the friends of Jesus. Why, then, should they fear those who would destroy the body?

Every one who shall confess me before men.—If they were to be known as friends of Jesus, they would have to acknowledge their allegience to Him in the face of threats from those who might even kill the body. In his second letter to Theophilus, Luke reports instances in which that very thing was done (Acts 4:19-21; 5:33-42).

The disciples were to acknowledge Him as the Christ of God (Luke 9:20). The Son of Man acknowledges them as His friends. But to disown Christ before men would mean that He will disown them before the angels of God. Did Peter remember this when he disowned Jesus at the trial? Did the remorseful Judas think of it as he was about to take his own life after he had betrayed his Friend into the hands of the enemy?

And every one who shall speak a word against the Son of man.—Even the heinous sin of speaking against the Son of Man can be forgiven. But forgiveness involves repentance which is produced by responding to the Spirit-breathed Word of God. But there is one sin that cannot be forgiven.

blasphemeth against the Holy Spirit it shall not be forgiven.—Were the Pharisees and lawyers whom Jesus had just reproved guilty of this sin? Jesus spoke by the Spirit, a fact that cannot be overlooked without failing to see why He mentions blasphemy of the Spirit in connection with forgiving those who speak against the Son of Man. Forgiveness depends on hearing and obeying the words He spoke by the Spirit (Acts 1:3; Luke 10:21-22). Rejecting this message constitutes an eternal sin when the rejection is final and complete. It is a sin that can be committed in this life, for Jesus said that it has no forgiveness in this life or in the life to come (Mark 3:28-30; Matt. 12:31-32). The reason is plain: Forgiveness depends on faith and repentance that must issue in obedience to the Word. The mind can be closed to the truth about Christ; the will can reach the place

213

where it can no longer respond to the appeal of God's love. Such a person is "past feeling." "It is impossible to renew such a one to repentance." See Eph. 4:17-19; Heb. 6:4-6.

Since it was blasphemy against the Holy Spirit to attribute the miracles of Jesus to the power of the devil, some say that the sin cannot be committed today. But this overlooks the fact that the miracles He performed by "the finger of God," that is, the Holy Spirit, were done to prove that He was speaking the truth of God. Rejecting this evidence was the fatal step. Jesus, of course, knew that these hardhearted men had completely and finally closed their minds to the truth.

when they bring you before the synagogues.—Just as Jesus had been put on trial by His oppressors so His disciples were to be brought before the authorities in the synagogues. But they did not need to fear such experiences, for the Holy Spirit was to enable them to speak the necessary words of truth in that hour (Acts 4:8, 13, 19-20). This promise was made to the apostles and not to the people in general. The Holy Spirit did guide the apostles into all the truth and enable them to leave the written record of it in the Bible (John 16:13-14; 20:30-31). When we face difficulties and trials, we can speak the truth by correctly using the message God gave us in the Bible.

To take this specific promise which Jesus made to the apostles and attempt to make it apply to believers in general is to disregard the fact that Jesus exercised special control over the apostles through the Holy Spirit. Jesus explained the function of the Holy Spirit to the apostles when He said, "He shall not speak for himself; but what things soever he shall hear, these shall he speak; and he shall declare unto you the things that are to come. He shall glorify me, for he shall take of mine and shall declare it unto you" (John 16: 13-14).

The Bible is the guidebook which we are expected to follow today (Rom. 2:16; II Tim 3:14-17).

The Man God Called a Fool

Scripture

12:13-21   And one out of the multitude said unto him, Teacher, bid my brother divide the inheritance with me. 14 But he said unto him, Man, who made me a judge or a divider over you? 15 And

214

he said unto them, Take heed, and keep yourselves from all covetousness: for a man's life consisteth not in the abundance of the things which he possesseth. 16 And he spake a parable unto them, saying, The ground of a certain rich man brought forth plentifully: 17 and he reasoned within himself, saying, What shall I do, because I have not where to bestow my fruits? 18 And he said, This will I do: I will pull down my barns, and build greater; and there will I bestow all my grain and my goods. 19 And I will say to my soul, Soul, thou hast much goods laid up for many years; take thine ease, eat, drink, be merry. 20 But God said unto him, Thou foolish one, this night is thy soul required of thee; and the things which thou hast prepared, whose shall they be? 21 So is he that layeth up treasure for himself, and is not rich toward God.

Comments

And one out of the multitude.—The lessons of this section were primarily for the disciples, but the crowds were listening also. This incident became the occasion for further instruction to the disciples on being rich toward God.

A man from the crowd asked Jesus to tell his brother to divide the inheritance with him. Jesus did not become involved in the family problem, for there was another issue before them that was of vastly greater importance. The eternal inheritance was being neglected. What He said about that became the basis upon which the man could settle his own problem with his brother. Jesus was the Savior, not just a social reformer; but in saving man from his sins, He pointed to the only effective way to overcome all kinds of injustice, social or otherwise. When we let the Word of Christ rule in our hearts we will be ready and willing to treat all men as God intended that they should be treated (Matt. 7:12; Col. 3:16).

for a man's life consisteth not in the abundance of the things he possesseth.—Jesus had just reminded the one who volunteered to follow Him that the Son of Man had no place to lay His head. He had also taught the disciples that God was mindful of their physical needs and that they were to ask Him for their daily bread. The point of Jesus' lesson was this: There is more to life than a material inheritance; life is not made up of possessing things. This life is temporary; the eternal inheritance is infinitely more important. To illustrate His point, Jesus told about the man God called a fool.

What shall I do?—He was completely selfish; he had not thought for the needs of others. The only thing he could think of was to build larger barns and store up more grain.

take thine ease, eat, drink, be merry.—Jesus did not say that the possession of wealth was wrong; it was the wrong use of it that He condemned. Neither is there anything wrong about rest, food, and proper enjoyment of life unless this be the only end in view. The rich fool prepared for the earthly life as if it were to continue forever.

Thou foolish one, this night is thy soul required of thee.—God called him "fool" because he had taken no thought for this eventuality. He had neglected the basic truth for all men, "It is appointed unto man once to die and then cometh the judgment" (Heb. 9: 27). In the very night in which he was prepared to live forever on this earth they were requiring him to give account of his life.

whose shall these be?—This question seems to be directed to the man who had asked Jesus to settle his problem about his inheritance. What if he did get the brother to divide their inheritance? A more important question: Was he rich toward God?

How to be Rich Toward God

Scripture

12:22-34 And he said unto his disciples, Therefore I say unto you, Be not anxious for *your* life, what ye shall eat; nor yet for your body, what ye shall put on. 23 For the life is more than the food, and the body than the raiment. 24 Consider the ravens, that they sow not, neither reap; which have no store-chamber nor barn; and God feedeth them: of how much more value are ye than the birds! 25 And which of you by being anxious can add a cubit unto the measure of his life? 26 If then ye are not able to do even that which is least, why are ye anxious concerning the rest? 27 Consider the lilies, how they grow: they toil not, neither do they spin; yet I say unto you, Even Solomon in all his glory was not arrayed like one of these. 28 But if God doth so clothe the grass in the field, which to-day is, and to-morrow is cast into the oven; how much more *shall he clothe* you, O ye of little faith? 29 And seek not ye what ye shall eat, and what ye shall drink, neither be ye of doubtful mind. 30 For all these things do the nations of the world seek after: but your Father knoweth that ye have need of these things. 31 Yet seek ye his kingdom, and these things shall be added unto you. 32 Fear not, little flock; for it is your Father's good pleasure to give you the kingdom. 33 Sell that which ye have, and give alms; make for yourselves purses which wax not old, a treasure in the heavens that faileth not, where no thief draweth near, neither moth destroyeth. 34 For where your treasure is, there will your heart be also.

Comments

Be not anxious for your life.—The man of the parable was overly anxious about eating and drinking and the enjoyment of this life. The disciples could be concerned about the kingdom of God, for they were to enjoy the providential care of God in this life. That did not mean that they didn't have to work, but it did mean that they could trust God who provides abundantly for all His creatures. The soul is more important than the food, and the body than the clothing it must have. To illustrate His point, Jesus called attention to God's care for the birds. They do not plant or reap or have barns in which to store food, but God cares for them. He added, "You are of much more value than the birds."

add a cubit unto the measure of his life.—Anxiety may shorten life, but lengthening it is another thing. Why then be anxious over things? Jesus illustrated this thought by pointing to the lilies of the field and to the fact that Solomon in all his glory was not arrayed like one of them.

cast into the oven.—Dried grass and flowers were used as fuel for the oven where wood may not have been plentiful. God clothes the grass with such glory even though it is to last for a few short months; but how much more will He care for the saints who are destined to live forever with Him in the heavenly kingdom?

but your Father knoweth that ye have need of these things.—Jesus did not advocate the extremes of asceticism. He reminded the disciples that the Father knew of their needs and told them what to do that they might be met.

Yet seek ye his kingdom.—The kingdom of God is eternal and must have first place in the lives of the disciples of Our Lord. It was the good pleasure of the Father to give this kingdom to those who trusted in Him. Jesus challenged them to sell their possessions and give alms, for they were to be concerned about the treasure in heaven that does not fail. When life is over—for that is the point of the lesson based on the parable of the Rich Fool—it will be clear why Jesus urged this course upon His disciples in contrast to giving attention to things that perish and do not make one rich toward God.

For where your treasure is, there will your heart be also.—Is your heart set on the things of God or on the things of this life? To be rich toward God is to have the heart set on the glories of His kingdom and the life eternal which the faithful will inherit.

The Coming of the Son of Man

Scripture

12:35-48　Let your loins be girded about, and your lamps burning; 36 and be ye yourselves like unto men looking for their lord, when he shall return from the marriage feast; that, when he cometh and knocketh, they may straightway open unto him. 37 Blessed are those servants, whom the lord when he cometh shall find watching: verily I say unto you, that he shall gird himself, and make them sit down to meat, and shall come and serve them. 38 And if he shall come in the second watch, and if in the third, and find *them* so, blessed are those *servants.* 39 But know this, that if the master of the house had known in what hour the thief was coming, he would have watched, and not have left his house to be broken through. 40 Be ye also ready: for in an hour that ye think not the Son of man cometh.

41 And Peter said, Lord, speakest thou this parable unto us, or even unto all? 42 And the Lord said, Who then is the faithful and wise steward, whom his lord shall set over his household, to give them their portion of food in due season? 43 Blessed is that servant, whom his lord when he cometh shall find so doing. 44 Of a truth I say unto you, that he will set him over all that he hath. 45 But if that servant shall say in his heart, My lord delayeth his coming; and shall begin to beat the menservants and the maidservants, and to eat and drink, and to be drunken; 46 the lord of that servant shall come in a day when he expecteth not, and in an hour when he knoweth not, and shall cut him asunder, and appoint his portion with the unfaithful. 47 And that servant, who knew his lord's will, and made not ready, nor did according to his will, shall be beaten with many *stripes*; 48 but he that knew not, and did things worthy of stripes, shall be beaten with few *stripes*. And to whomsoever

much is given, of him shall much be required: and to whom they commit much, of him will they ask the more.

Comments

Let your loins be girded.—This is the familiar figure of one gathering up the long flowing robes worn in that day and binding them about the body so as to be able to move without hindrance. It came to be a symbol of alertness and readiness for action. Jesus warned of the need to be alert, since His coming is at an unknown time.

The rich fool of the parable is still under consideration, for he illustrates the one who is not prepared for the future life. The account of the marriage feast and the coming of the bridegroom as given in Matt. 25:1-13 illustrates the point.

in what hour the thief was coming.—Paul used this figure in relation to the Second Coming: "For yourselves know perfectly that the day of the Lord so cometh as a thief in the night" (I Thes. 5:2). Since His coming is at an unknown hour, it is necessary to watch and be ready at all times. The rich fool of the parable did not know when his life would end or when he would be called upon to give account of himself to God. The Lord has delayed His coming through this time of God's longsuffering, but no one knows when it will end or when his time to prepare will be over. Of one thing we are sure: the Lord is coming! "Be ye also ready."

unto us, or even unto all?—Peter's question had to do with the story of the thief at night that showed the necessity of faithfulness in view of the unknown time of Christ's coming. Did it refer to the apostles or to all the people?

Jesus did not answer directly with "no" or "yes." He did answer in a manner that let Peter know that He was talking primarily to the apostles. They were to be wise stewards taking care of the Master's household while He was away. See I Cor. 4:1-2 for Paul's lesson on the necessity of faithfulness on the part of the apostles and others who share the responsibility of caring for the church of the Lord.

But if that servant shall say in his heart.—Jesus often presented both sides of an issue. His disciples were to be faithful and wise stewards, but if they should be unfaithful there was punishment awaiting them. Did Peter remember this lesson when he denied that he had never known such a person as Jesus?

many stripes . . . few stripes.—The degrees of punishment have to do with the servants: willful unfaithfulness merits many stripes; ignorance, few. But all unfaithfulness is punishable.

Does this passage teach degrees of punishment in hell? No wise servant should have to learn the lesson by experience. That punishment is too awful for the mind to fully appreciate just how terrible it is. The wise person will do all that is necessary to avoid it completely. Hell is prepared for the devil and his angels. No one who commits himself to the Lord and remains faithful will experience its pain and anguish, for there is the crown of life for those who are faithful to the Lord until death (Rev. 2:10).

The Parable of the Pounds (Luke 19:11-27) suggests that there will be a difference in the rewards to the faithful, perhaps that they are to be in proportion to the ability to enjoy them. But to be in the kingdom of heaven will be reward enough (II Pet 1:10-11).

The Mission of the Son of Man
Scripture

12:49-53   I came to cast fire upon the earth; and what do I desire, if it is already kindled? 50 But I have a baptism to be baptized with; and how am I straitened till it be accomplished! 51 Think ye that I am come to give peace in the earth? I tell you, Nay; but rather division: 52 for there shall be from henceforth five in one house divided, three against two, and two against three. 53 They shall be divided, father against son, and son against father; mother against daughter, and daughter against her mother; mother in law against her daughter in law, and daughter in law against her mother in law.

Comments

I came to cast fire.—The lesson about the purpose of His mission came directly out of what He had just said about faithfulness. It was no easy task to which His servants had been called. Some, no doubt, thought that the reign of the Messiah would be one of peace and easy living. Some were looking for a temporal kingdom that would provide an abundance of food—they had a sample when He fed them on the loaves and fish. But actually for many His kingdom was to be marked by persecution, bitterness, hardship, want and death. See Paul's description of what it meant for him to serve Christ (II Cor. 4:7-11; 11:23-28).

Fire is used as a symbol of purification in some instances, but in this context Jesus meant the destructive power of fire. There was to be strife in families because of Him; some would be for Him and others would oppose Him bitterly.

if it is already kindled?—Jesus came to cast fire upon the earth. That fire was already kindled, for people were taking sides for or against Him. Some of the Pharisees were plotting to kill Him. But He continued to challenge His disciples to a life of complete dedication to Him. Many were responding by taking up their cross daily and following Him.

But I have a baptism.—Jesus' mission was to start men thinking about Him. The sacrifice on the cross was one thing He still had to accomplish. There were many things pressing upon Him which He had to care for before He could do this last thing the Father had given to accomplish (John 10:18; 17:4; 19:30). For one thing, He had to prepare His disciples for their mission of taking the Word of the Cross into all the world.

Jesus reminded the disciples that they must share His experience (Mark 10:38). There was a cross in the mission of the Master, and there was a cross in the mission of His servants.

Signs of the Coming Storm

Scripture

12:54-59 And he said to the multitudes also, When ye see a cloud rising in the west, straightway ye say, There cometh a shower; and so it cometh to pass. 55 And when *ye see* a south wind blowing, ye say, There will be a scorching heat; and it cometh to pass. 56 Ye hypocrites, ye know how to interpret the face of the earth and the heaven; but how is it that ye know not how to interpret this time? 57 And why even of yourselves judge ye not what is right? 58 For as thou art going with thine adversary before the magistrate, on the way give diligence to be quit of him; let haply he drag thee unto the judge, and the judge shall deliver thee to the officer, and the officer shall cast thee into prison. 59 I say unto thee, Thou shalt by no means come out thence, till thou have paid the very last mite.

Comments

When you see a cloud rising.—Jesus had just been telling the disciples what His earthly mission would do to their lives and to the

221

lives of others who would take sides for or against Him. He also warned the crowds about the coming storm.

People were able to read weather signs, why couldn't they interpret the signs that pointed to the rejection of the Son of God and the resulting destruction that was coming upon Jerusalem? The setting of this whole lesosn is the bitter opposition to Jesus expressed by the Pharisees and lawyers (11:52-12:1).

And why even of yourselves judge ye not what is right?—With all the evidence about them, why couldn't they make the right decision by themselves? That decision called for them to align themselves with Christ; for if they let the matter go before God the Judge of heaven, they would lose their case. And many of them did just that (Luke 19:42). Before Pilate they rejected their King, and on the Day of Pentecost the Holy Spirit spoke through the apostles and charged them with the guilt of having crucified Him whom God made both Lord and Christ (Acts 2:23, 36).

with thine adversary before the magistrate.—The crowds were in danger of considering Christ as their adversary. He appealed to them to settle the issue before it was too late.

In Matt. 5:25, the same figure is used, but there it refers to the necessity of brethren adjusting their differences before attempting to approach God in worship.

Thou shalt by no means come out.—A person in debtor's prison had no possible way of earning money to effect his release. There is no escape from the final state of punishment into which sinner must go.

Summary

The scribes and Pharisees continued their attack on Jesus after leaving the house where He had dined with the Pharisee. This became the occasion for His warning to the disciples. The false teaching of the Pharisees was like leaven, transforming all who came in contact with it into hypocrits like the Pharisees. But their hypocracy was exposed by Jesus.

For the encouragement of the disciples, Jesus told them about God's protective care. He called on them to acknowledge Him even in face of all the threats of their enemies. He reminded them that the Holy Spirit would teach them what to say in the hour of need.

A man came to Jesus asking Him to tell his brother to divide their inheritance. Jesus told the story of the man God called a fool. He pointed out that life does not consist in possessions; the important thing is to be rich toward God. Jesus explained they could be rich in this way: it meant putting the kingdom of God first, for He said, "where your treasure is, there will be your heart also."

Since life is temporary, it is necessary to be alert to avoid being caught unprepared when the Lord comes again. When He comes, He will reward the faithful and punish the wicked.

His mission was like kindling a fire. Already there was the struggle going on between members of one's own family over their relation to Him.

Jesus chided the multitudes for their inability to see what was about to happen to them. He urged them to agree with Him before it was too late, for there will be no escape from punishment on the Judgment Day for those who fail to acknowledge Him before men.

Questions

1. What was the occasion of Jesus' warning about the leaven of the Pharisees?
2. What was it that had caused the crowds to gather at this time?
3. Why did Jesus say that the leaven of the Pharisees was hypocracy?
4. What important lesson did Paul teach using the figure of leaven to illustrate it?
5. How can leaven be used as a symbol of false teaching and also of teaching that is true?
6. What effect does the truth of the Gospel have on those who hear it and obey it?
7. What did Jesus do about the hypocritical teaching of the Pharisees?
8. What did Jesus tell the apostles to do about what He taught them?
9. Why did He say that they were not to be afraid of them that kill the body?
10. Of whom were they to be afraid? Why?
11. What lesson did He teach by calling attention to the sparrows?
12. What lesson did He teaching by calling attention to the fact that the hairs of their heads were numbered?

13. Why did Jesus demand allegience from His disciples?
14. What examples are given in the Scriptures of men confessing their faith in Him even in face of death?
15. Why could a word spoken against the Son be forgiven when blasphemy against the Holy Spirit couldn't?
16. What is this unforgivable sin?
17. What would the Holy Spirit do for the apostles when they were brought before the authorities of the synagogues?
18. How does God provide for the answers we may be called on to give today?
19. What was the request of the man from the crowd?
20. Why didn't Jesus do as the man requested?
21. What important lesson did Jesus teach by the story of the man God called a fool?
22. What foolish thing was the man doing?
23. What was his fatal mistake?
24. What does it mean to be rich toward God?
25. What is one to do to become rich toward God?
26. What did Jesus tell the disciples that would keep them from being anxious about food and clothing?
27. What can anxiety to for life? What can't it do?
28. What is the Father's concern about man's need for food and clothing?
29. How does one seek first the kingdom of God?
30. What did Jesus say about the heart and treasure?
31. What is meant by "Let your loins be girded"?
32. Why did Jesus liken His coming to a thief in the night?
33. Why did Peter want to know if Jesus was talking to all or just to the apostles?
34. How did He answer Peter's question?
35. What is the lesson of the unfaithful servant?
36. What about degrees of punishment?
37. What did Jesus mean by casting fire upon the earth?
38. In what way was it already kindled?
39. What did He mean when He said, "I have a baptism"?
40. What warning did Jesus give the crowds which He based on their ability to read the weather signs?
41. What storm warnings should they have been able to see?
42. What did He mean by saying that they should agree with their adversary?

CHAPTER THIRTEEN

Outline

A. Luke continued the account of Jesus' ministry of teaching and healing (1-21).
   1. The lesson on repentance (1-9).
      a) It was based on two tragic incidents (1-5).
         (1) The Galileans whose blood Pilate mingled with their sacrifices (1-3).
            (a) The question: "Were they sinners more than all Galileans?"
            (b) The answer: "No, but unless you repent you will likewise perish."
         (2) The eighteen on whom the tower of Siloam fell (4-5).
            (a) The question: "Were they offenders more than all others who dwelt in Jerusalem?"
            (b) The answer: "No, but unless you repent you will likewise perish."
      b) It was illustrated by the parable of the Fig Tree (6-9).
         (1) Time to repent: A man came seeking fruit for three years; finding none, he ordered it cut down.
         (2) The limit to God's longsuffering: The vinedresser said, "Give it special care for one more year; then if it doesn't bear fruit, cut it down."
   2. Healing the woman with a spirit of infirmity (10-17).
      a) The circumstances (10-13).
         (1) She had had it for eighteen years.
         (2) Jesus said, "Woman you are freed from your weakness."
         (3 Jesus laid His hands on her and immediately she was able to stand up straight and praise God.
      b) The reaction of the ruler of the synagogue (14).
         (1) He complained that the miracle had been performed on the sabbath.
         (2) The indignant ruler said, "There are six days in which work is to be done; on those days come and be healed, but not on the sabbath."
      c) The Lord's answer to the complaint (15-16).

225

  (1) He called attention to their hypocritical actions, for they led their animals to water on the sabbath.

  (2) He pointed out that this woman, a daughter of Abraham whom Satan had bound eighteen years, should be set free on the sabbath day.

 d) The effect of His remarks (17).

  (1) The adversaries were put to shame.

  (2) The people rejoiced for the glorious things that were done by Jesus.

 3. A question about the kingdom: What is it like? (18-21).

  a) It is like a grain of mustard see that grew into a tree large enough for birds to build nests in.

  b) It is like leaven which was hid in the meal until all of it was leavened.

B. Luke continued the account of Jesus' journeys that led Him to Jerusalem (22-35).

 1. The question: Are there few that are saved? (22-30).

  a) The circumstances (22-23).

   (1) Jesus was teaching as He went through the cities and villages on His way to Jerusalem.

   (2) Someone asked, "Lord, are they few that are saved?"

  b) The answer (24-25).

   (1) "Strive to enter by the narrow door."

   (2) But many would try to enter after the door was shut.

  c) The tragic state of those who were too later to enter (26-29).

   (1) Their pitiful plea: We ate and drank in your presence; we taught in your streets.

   (2) The just sentence: Depart from me, all you workers of iniquity.

   (3) The tragic state of the lost: Weeping and gnashing of teeth.

   (4) The glorious state of the saved: Many from the east and west, from the north and the south sitting at the heavenly banquet in the kingdom of God.

  d) The lesson summarized: Jesus said, "There are those who are last that will be first; and first that will be last."

2. The Pharisees' warning: Herod would like to kill you. (31-35).
    a) They urged Him to leave the area because of Herod's threat.
    b) Jesus' answer, "Take this message to that fox: I am casting out demons and performing cures today and tomorrow, and on the third day I am finished with my work."
    c) It was His intention to go to Jerusalem, for no prophet perishes outside of Jerusalem.
    d) Jesus mourned over the city as He thought how they were guilty of killing the prophets; their house would be left desolate, but some would say, "Blessed is he that comes in the name of the Lord."

Repent or Perish

Scripture

13:1-9 Now there were some present at that very season who told him of the Galilaeans, whose blood Pilate had mingled with their sacrifices. 2 And he answered and said unto them, Think ye that these Galilaeans were sinners above all the Galilaeans, because they have suffered these things? 3 I tell you, Nay: but, except ye repent, ye shall all in like manner perish. 4 Or those eighteen, upon whom the tower in Siloam fell, and killed them, think ye that they were offenders above all the men that dwell in Jerusalem? 5 I tell you, Nay: but, except ye repent, ye shall all likewise perish.

6 And he spake this parable; A certain man had a fig tree planted in his vineyard; and he came seeking fruit thereon, and found none. 7 And he said unto the vinedresser, Behold, these three years I come seeking fruit on this fig tree, and find none: cut it down; why doth it also cumber the ground? 8 And he answering saith unto him, Lord, let it alone this year also, till I shall dig about it, and dung it: 9 and if it bear fruit thenceforth, well; but if not, thou shalt cut it down.

Comments

Now there were some present.—This section continues the lesson which Jesus had been giving the people while meeting the complaints of the Pharisees (11:53; 12:54). Care must be exercised to keep the chapter divisions from letting us assume that a new subject begins with the new chapter. Sometimes this is true, but there are times—as in this case—when the thought runs over into the new chapter.

Jesus had been speaking of judgment from which there is no escape. Apparently, in answer to His remarks, the people told about those Galileans whose blood Pilate mingled with their sacrifices as an example of the kind of punishment He had described. But they had missed the point. Jesus said, "Do you think that these Galileans were worse than other sinners?" He had just told them about the necessity of settling cases out of court before it was too late to escape punishment. He had also spoken of the sin of failing to acknowledge Him before men (12:8-9). Those who wait until He comes again will find that it is too late. The case of the Galileans seems to suggest that it was not that they were worse sinners, but that they had reached a point where repentance was impossible, since repentance must be observed before death, not after.

whose blood Pilate had mingled with their sacrifices.—No details are given about how this happened. It is well known that the Roman soldiers were used to put down riots. They were none too careful about how they did it. It is possible that some disturbance had occurred while the people were offering their sacrifices. The soldiers may have killed the trouble makers on the spot. Their blood could have mingled easily with the blood of the animals which they were sacrificing.

sinners above all Galileans.—It seems to be admitted that those Galileans were sinners; what they had done that was wrong is not stated. The point is: they were not worse than other Galileans who were sinners. While others might not share the fate of those whom Pilate destroyed, they, nevertheless, were facing certain destruction that called for immediate action if they were to avoid it.

except ye repent.—Repentance is the change of the will that leads to changed conduct. In this case, the thing that should have led to that change of mind was the threat of punishment which would be worse than that which Pilate had inflicted.

The Scriptures point out at least three motivating forces that are designed to lead men to repentance, that is, change their minds and decide to do something about their situation. They are (1) the goodness of God (Rom. 2:4), (2) godly sorrow for sin (II Cor. 7:10), and (3) the judgment to come (Acts 17:30-31).

To those who had failed to acknowledge Him, Jesus said, "Repent or perish." It was an urgent matter; there was no time for delay.
the tower of Siloam fell.—This is a case of accidental death; there was no apparent connection between it and any particular thing they had done. Were they worse sinners than others? No. But they did face the future that involved eternal punishment if they failed to acknowledge Christ before men.

And he spake this parable.—This parable illustrates the fact that God does give men time to repent. We are reminded of the long-suffering of God in the days of Noah (I Pet. 3:20). He is long-suffering, for He does not wish that any should perish but that they should repent (II Pet. 3:9). The church at Ephesus was warned to repent or have their candlestick removed (Rev. 2:5). The history of Israel suggests that God will not tolerate the sinful conduct of men forever (Heb. 3:7-4:13; I Cor. 10:5-10).

these three years I come seeking fruit.—There is no lesson to be drawn from this time reference. It was probably the normal time to wait for the tree to produce, or it could suggest that the tree should have been producing all that time but hadn't done so. The tree represents the nation of Israel that was not producing the fruits of righteousness. They had been given ample time, for prophet after prophet had tried to bring them to repentance. The time of judgment was at hand; all that was left for the tree was expressed by the owner of the tree, "Cut it down."

Lord, let it alone this year also.—This is a plea for longsuffering toward a sinful people. One more year, and then if there is no fruit let it be cut down. Special care was given the tree. The year of unusual care may be the unusual privilege of the Israel to have the Lord in their midst to teach them what they should do to be pleasing to God and encourage them in every way to do it. He taught them; He healed their sick; He warned them of judgment to come; He revealed the loving Father to them; He even told them that He was to offer Himself for the sins of the people. What more could be done? And if they failed to respond, their fate would be worse than that of the Galileans or the eighteen on whom the tower fell.

Healing a Woman

Scripture

13:10-17 And he was teaching in one of the synagogues on the sabbath day. 11 And behold, a woman that had a spirit of infirmity eighteen years; and she was bowed together, and could in no wise lift herself up. 12 And when Jesus saw her, he called her, and said to her, Woman, thou art loosed from thine infirmity. 13 And he laid his hands upon her: and immediately she was made straight, and glorified God. 14 And the ruler of the synagogue, being moved with indignation because Jesus had healed on the sabbath, answered and said to the multitude, There are six days in which men ought to work: in them therefore come and be healed, and not on the day of the sabbath. 15 But the Lord answered him, and said, Ye hypocrites, doth not each one of you on the sabbath loose his ox or his ass from the stall, and lead him away to watering? 16 And ought not this woman, being a daughter of Abraham, whom Satan had bound, lo, these eighteen years, to have been loosed from this bond on the day of the sabbath? 17 And as he said these things, all his adversaries were put to shame: and all the multitude rejoiced for all the glorious things that were done by him.

Comments

teaching in one of the synagogues.—Luke reports a good many such incidents, but there is a reason for doing so in each case. This miracle had a two-fold purpose: (1) To teach a lesson about the kingdom of God and (2) to help a person whom Satan had bound for all those eighteen years.

a woman that had a spirit of infirmity.—This is probably another case of demon possession, for the woman had a spirit of weakness, that is, the spirit had caused her to be weak. It was impossible for her to straighten up, and she had been that way for eighteen years. Satan had bound this daughter of Abraham, a faithful person in spite of her affliction.

Woman, thou art loosed from thine infirmity.—Jesus laid His hands on her and immediately she was able to straighten up. But she had already been set free from the infirmity. A person who had been for so long in her condition would scarcely be expected to realize that it was possible to straighten up. The old habit would have to be overcome. The touch of the Master's hand gave the necessary encouragement. Jesus did the same for the demon possessed boy (Mark 9:27).

And the ruler of the synagogue.—The woman glorified God for what He had done for her, but the ruler of the synagogue indignantly condemned Jesus because He had done this on the sabbath. Was this just a pious attempt to discredit Jesus so that he might hold his own power over the people? At any rate, Jesus made his remarks look rather foolish.

the Lord answered him.—He was the Lord of the sabbath and knew why the regulation had been given. It was not just for pious pretense or hypocritical display. He said, "You hypocrites, does not each one of you on the sabbath loose his ox or his ass from the stall and lead him to water?" Then shouldn't this daughter of Abraham whom Satan had bound these eighteen years be loosed on the sabbath? Who could say "no"?

all his adversaries were put to shame.—They were seemingly placing more value on animals than human beings. They should have been ashamed. But the people rejoiced over the glorious thing that had been done.

Man's work could be done in six days; but there was no time limit for the glorious work of God. And what better day was there to loose a faithful daughter of Abraham whom Satan had bound?

What is the Kingdom Like?

Scripture

13:18-21   He said therefore, Unto what is the kingdom of God like? and whereunto shall I liken it? 19 It is like unto a grain of mustard seed, which a man took, and cast into his own garden; and it grew, and became a tree; and the birds of the heaven lodged in the branches thereof.

20 And again he said, Whereunto shall I liken the kingdom of God? 21 It is like unto leaven, which a woman took and hid in three measures of meal, till it was all leavened.

Comments

He said therefore.—The response of the people to the miracle of healing the woman suggested the growth of the kingdom as illustrated by these parables. It is true that Matthew records them in another context which simply shows that Jesus used the parables more than once.

It is like unto a grain of mustard seed.—The seed is small but the plant that grows from it is large enough for birds to build their nests in. Jesus had planted the seed of the kingdom, the Word of God; the people were already beginning to praise God for the things that He was doing for them.

When the kingdom was ushered in on the Day of Pentecost, the beginning was in reality small, for only three thousand out of the many that had heard the Lord or who may have heard the apostles responded to the gospel. Soon the number came to be about five thousand; then a great company of the priests became obedient to the faith (Acts 6:7). Ultimately, it will be a countless number that will wash their robes in the blood of the Lamb and make them white (Rev. 7:9-17). In triumph, the voices of heaven said, "The kingdom of the world is become the kingdom of our Lord and His Christ, and he shall reign for ever and ever" (Rev. 11:15).

It is like unto leaven.—While the parable of the Mustard Seed shows the visible, outward growth of the kingdom as presented in the history of Acts and the prophecy of Revelation, the parable of the Leaven shows how this growth is to be accomplished. See note on 12:1. The teaching of Jesus was already transforming the lives of people. The record in Acts shows how the gospel as it was preached by the apostles transformed lives of men and women. The transforming power of the gospel is equally effective today. But the gospel must be preached, for the leaven must be hid in the meal. The church loses sight of its mission when it turns aside to any other issue than the effective implanting of the leaven of God's Word in the minds and hearts of people.

Are the Saved Few?

Scripture

13:22-30 And he went on his way through cities and villages, teaching, and journeying on unto Jerusalem. 23 And one said unto him, Lord, are they few that are saved? And he said unto them, 24 Strive to enter in by the narrow door: for many, I say unto you, shall seek to enter in, and shall not be able. 25 When once the master of the house is risen up, and hath shut to the door, and ye begin to stand without, and to knock at the door, saying, Lord, open to us; and he shall answer and say to you, I know you not whence ye are; 26 then shall ye begin to say, We did eat and drink in thy presence, and thou didst teach in our streets; 27 and he shall say, I tell you, I know not whence ye are; depart from me, all ye workers of iniquity. 28 There shall be the weeping and the gnashing of teeth, when ye shall see Abraham, and Isaac, and Jacob, and all the prophets, in the kingdom of God, and yourselves cast forth without. 29 And they shall come from the east and west, and from the north and south, and shall sit down in the kingdom of God. 30 And behold, there are last who shall be first, and there are first who shall be last.

Comments

Lord, are they few that are saved?—Just why the disciples asked this question, Luke does not say. It could have come about from various causes. The demands that Jesus made on His disciples were such that some wouldn't follow Him. The thought of the cross and self-denial was too much for some. Opposition to Christ was great, for most of the leaders were against Him. Great wickedness prevailed then as now in the lives of the many. Jesus had said that many go through the wide gate to destruction.

Strive to enter in by the narrow door.—The point is: make sure that you enter by the door that leads to salvation. That door is narrow, suggesting that few enter through it (Matt. 7:14). Some will expect to enter on their own terms, but will be unable to do so. Some will be too late.

and hath shut the door.—It may appear strange that Jesus would ever close the door of salvation. Some presume on His grace and mercy and do nothing about entering while the narrow door of salvation is open. The time will come when the door will be closed, and no one may enter then.

God did shut the door of the ark in the days of Noah. He did close the door of entrance to the Promised Land to the rebellious Israel. The day of God's longsuffering will end; when it does it will be too late to ask for admittance into the heavenly kingdom.

Lord open to us.—The pitiful plea of the procrastinator will not avail once the door is closed. The fact that people attended the feasts when Jesus was eating with them in His day will not be sufficient grounds for entrance to the heavenly banquet.

233

Depart from me, all ye workers of iniquity.—Is this harsh? Yes. But workers of iniquity are not fit for the kingdom of heaven. The very nature of heaven excludes them. See Rev. 21:8; 22:14-15. The time to put off the works of darkness is now (Rom. 13:11-14). It is necessary to put on the Lord Jesus Christ, if we expect to be a part of the company in the heavenly banquet.

weeping and gnashing of teeth.—The anguish of those who might have been in heaven with the Lord is awful to contemplate.

when ye shall see Abraham, and Isaac, and Jacob.—Part of the punishment of the wicked will be to see what they have missed. The language seems to indicate that Abraham, Isaac, and the prophets will be recognized in heaven. If they will be, we may assume that all the saints will be recognizable in heaven. The individual will not lose his identity through the change that takes place in passing from this life to the presence of the Lord.

yourselves cast forth without.—Sin separates the saints from the sinners in this life even though they are like the wheat and tares that grow in the same field. But the separation will be made distinct after death. See 16:26.

And they shall come from east and west.—The mission of Jesus was to the lost sheep of the house of Israel. He sent the Twelve and the Seventy to the same group. But after His death, He sent the apostles into all the world with the eternal good tidings. Those who respond from east, west, north or south will sit down in the heavenly banquet with the saints of all the ages. The number will be like the multitude that no one could number (Rev. 7:9). But this is "few" in comparison to the many who neglect the great salvation.

last who shall be first.—These words are used in a different context in Matt. 19:30. There the question was about the relation of the apostles who left all to follow Jesus to others who might follow Him. Those who bore the load in the first days of the kingdom will not be ahead of the last faithful Christian who dedicates his life to Christ before the end of the day of salvation comes. The parable of the Vineyard given by Matthew shows this to be so (Matt. 19:16).

The context in Luke, however, indicates that Jesus was thinking of the nation of Israel who had been first in God's consideration but were to be rejected because they were failing to produce the fruits of righteousness. Others, however, would be invited and the banquet table would be filled (14: 23-24). The gospel invitation reads, "Whosoever will may come" (Rev. 22:17). Jesus said to the Jews,

"The kingdom shall be taken away from you, and shall be given to a nation bringing forth the fruits thereof" (Matt. 21:43). It would be a mistake to say that that nation is made up of Gentiles, for it is a nation of believers, whether Jews or Gentiles. See Gal. 3:28; Eph. 2:14-18; Col. 3:10-11.

The Warning From Herod

Scripture

13:31-35 In that very hour there came certain Pharisees, saying to him, Get thee out, and go hence: for Herod would fain kill thee. 32 And he said unto them, Go and say to that fox, Behold, I cast out demons and perform cures today and tomorrow, and the third day I am perfected. 33 Nevertheless I must go on my way today and tomorrow and the day following: for it cannot be that a prophet perish out of Jerusalem. 34 O Jerusalem, Jerusalem, that killeth the prophets, and stoneth them that are sent unto her! how often would I have gathered thy children together, even as a hen gathereth her own brood under her wings, and ye would not! 35 Behold, your house is left unto you desolate: and I say unto you, Ye shall not see me, until ye shall say, Blessed is he that cometh in the name of the Lord.

Comments

In that very hour.—There is a close connection between this incident and the one in which Jesus answered the question about whether few are saved. The warning came in the very hour when He was teaching.

The threat of Herod raised another question, since some thought of Jesus as a temporal king. If Herod should kill Him, how could the kingdom become the mighty force which He had described in the parables of the Mustard Seed and the Leaven? But His kingdom was spiritual and He had no fear of the threats of petty rulers like Herod or even the mighty Caesars.

Herod would fain kill thee.—This is Herod Antipas, ruler of Galilee and Perea. Jesus was operating in Perea at this time. The father of this ruler had tried to kill Jesus at His birth. Herod Antipas had caused John the Baptist to be beheaded. Perhaps the Pharisees were aware of all this and thought there was some real threat to Jesus' safety in the matter. It may be, of course, that they were trying to discourage people from following Him. At any rate, Jesus was unmoved by the warning.

Go say to that fox.—He called Herod a fox because he was cunning like a fox.

Today, tomorrow, and the third day.—No threat of violence from any ruler could stop the program of the Son of God. He intended to go on casting out demons and performing cures. He was waging war against the devil and all who were associated with him, Herod included.

The suggestion about today, tomorrow and the third day simply indicates that Jesus was moving steadily toward the goal for which He came into the world. There is no reference in the remark to the years of His ministry or the time of His resurrection. See John 10:18 for Jesus' own view of His mission which He would accomplish in Jerusalem.

and the third day I am perfected.—That is, I am finished with my earthly task. See John 17:4; 19:30.

no prophet perish out of Jerusalem.—He had set His face to go to Jerusalem (9:51; 13:22; Matt. 20:17). Jerusalem was the center of the nation. The temple was there; the sacrifices for the sins of the people were continually being offered there. Jerusalem was the place where He would offer Himself as the Lamb of God to take away the sins of the people. See Heb. 9:11-15; 10:1-10; 13:10-14. Jerusalem was the city "that killeth the prophets and stonest them that are sent unto her."

O Jerusalem, Jerusalem.—According to Matthew, the lament occurred after the Triumphal Entry and shortly before the death of Jesus (Matt. 23:37-39). Luke indicates that Jesus first uttered these words as He was approaching Jerusalem while still in Herod's territory. Some find it difficult to believe that He could have spoken these deeply emotional words more than once. But who can say that He didn't? Luke had made a careful study of all that he wrote. He was in a better position to know than today's critics. Since Jerusalem was the heart of the nation that Jesus had tried so hard to win back to God, why should it be thought impossible that their rejection and plan to kill Him should cause such extreme sorrow? He had tried to gather them under His protective care but they would have none of it.

Behold, your house is left unto you.—The word *desolate* is given in italics in the American Standard Version to indicate that it is

236

supplied by the translators to make the meaning complete. R. S. V. supplies "is forsaken" for the same purpose. Whether He meant the temple or the nation, Jesus said your house is left to you. There was nothing more He could do for them. Within a few short years the invading armies of Rome would bring desolation to Jerusalem. *Blessed is he that cometh in the name of the Lord.*—The words are quoted from Psa. 118:26. According to Matthew, they were uttered after the Triumphal Entry, but Luke has them before. Assuming that Jesus could have spoken them on two different occasions, the problem is to determine the meaning in each context.

According to Luke, Jesus was anticipating His triumphal entry into Jerusalem, for at that time the people did say, "Blessed is the King that cometh in the name of the Lord (19:38). According to Matthew, they may anticipate a time of acceptance after the death and resurrection of Jesus (Matt. 22:39). There are many who are acknowledging Him as King in the period that began on Pentecost and will end with His Second Coming.

Summary

Things were happening fast in the busy ministry of Jesus. He was meeting the opposition, teaching the disciples and the crowds, and healing the sick. He was hurrying to Jerusalem, for no prophet would perish outside of Jerusalem.

He taught a lesson on repentance. It was based on two tragic events, the death of the Galileans and of those on whom the tower of Siloam fell. But these were not worse sinners than all other, for all will perish who do not repent. The lesson of the fig tree showed that time was running out; the warning was: "Repent or perish."

Jesus clashed again with the ruler of the synagogue when He healed a woman on the sabbath. Ridiculously, the ruler held that there were six days for work to be done but not on the sabbath; he called the healing "work." Jesus' answer drew a sharp contrast between their attitude toward the ox or the ass and the woman, a daughter of Abraham, whom He had loosed from Satan's bonds. The people were with Him, for they glorified God for what they had seen that day.

The growth of the kingdom was presented in two parables. Like the mustard seed, it would grow to great proportions; like the leaven,

237

the gospel of the kingdom would transform those who hide that Word in their hearts.

As He was going on the way to Jerusalem, someone asked Him, "Lord, are there few that are saved?" The answer seemed to say, "Yes," but all should strive to enter the kingdom and be one of them.

Word came about Herod's threat to kill Him. Jesus said to tell "that fox" that nothing could interfere with His program. But as He thought of Jerusalem where He was to die, He mourned over the city that was rejecting her King.

Questions

1. How does Luke indicate the continuity between the events reported in this chapter and those of the previous chapters?
2. Why was the question raised about those whose blood Pilate had mingled with their sacrifices?
3. What lesson did Jesus teach from it?
4. Why mention those on whom the tower of Siloam fell?
5. What lesson did Jesus teach from this incident?
6. What is repentance?
7. What are the forces that lead to repentance?
8. What will happen to those who do not repent of their sins?
9. Does accidental death suggest that God is punishing the one involved?
10. What do the Scriptures teach about the longsuffering of God?
11. What lesson did Jesus teach from the parable of the Fig Tree?
12. What is represented by the three years mentioned in the parable?
13. What is represented by the year of special care given the tree?
14. What was the purpose of healing the woman in the synagogue?
15. What was her difficulty? How long standing?
16. Why did Jesus say, "You are loosed from your infirmity?"
17. Why is it called a "spirit of infirmity?"
18. Why did Jesus lay His hands on the healed woman?
19. What did the ruler of the synagogue say about the miracle?
20. What is the point of the contrast between what Jesus had done and the custom of the Jews?
21. Why did Jesus refer to the woman as a daughter of Abraham?
22. What effect did Jesus' answer have on the adversaries?

23. What was the reaction of the people?
24. Why did Jesus speak of the growth of the kingdom at this point?
25. How does the parable of the Mustard Seed illustrate the nature of the growth of the kingdom?
26. What do the Scriptures say about the ultimate growth of the kingdom?
27. What lesson does the parable of the Leaven teach about the growth of the kingdom?
28. What must be done with the Word in order for it to transform the life of an individual?
29. Why did they ask if the saved are few?
30. What did Jesus' answer imply?
31. What do the Scriptures say about the limit God places on the "Day of Salvation"?
32. Why is the door to salvation called "narrow"?
33. What will happen to the "workers of iniquity" who come too late?
34. Why "weeping and gnashing of teeth"?
35. What do the Scriptures teach about recognition of persons in heaven?
36. What does being on the outside and looking in on the heavenly banquet suggest as to the nature of punishment of the wicked?
37. Why did Jesus speak of those coming from east, west, north, and south?
38. How are all these to be invited?
39. What is meant by saying that the last shall be first?
40. Why did Jesus refer to Herod as a fox?
41. Was this a real threat or were the Pharisees trying to frighten Jesus?
42. What was Jesus' answer to the reported threat?
43. What did Jesus mean by reference to the third day?
44. Why was He going to Jerusalem?
45. Why did He mourn over Jerusalem?
46. What was to happen to "their house"? Why?
47. Where is the quotation about the coming of the Lord found?
48. To what does it refer?

CHAPTER FOURTEEN

Outline

A. Luke told about some things that happened when Jesus went into the house of a ruler of the Pharisees to eat (1-24).
   1. The miracle He performed (1-6).
      a) The circumstances.
         (1) It was in the house of the Pharisee.
         (2) It was on the sabbath.
         (3) They were watching Jesus.
         (4) A man with dropsy was there.
      b) The miracle.
         (1) Jesus asked, "Is it lawful to heal on the sabbath or not?"
         (2) They refused to answer.
         (3) Jesus healed the sick man and let him go.
      c) The victory: After He had healed the man, He followed up His victory by thoroughly discrediting those who had hoped to embarrass Him.
         (1) He said, "Which of you who has an ass or ox fall into a well, will not pull him out on the sabbath?"
         (2) They couldn't answer these questions.
   2. The lesson on humility (7-14).
      a) The lesson for guests (7-11).
         (1) They had been choosing the chief seats at the table.
         (2) He illustrated His lesson by referring to the wedding feast, suggesting that guests should take the lowest place until invited to a place of greater honor.
         (3) His point: "Every one that exalts himself shall be humbled and every one that humbles himself shall be exalted."
      b) The lesson for the host (12-14).
         (1) Don't invite those who can repay you; invite the poor, the maimed and the lame.
         (2) In doing so you will be rewarded in the resurrection of the just.

240

3. The parable of the Great Supper (15-24).
   a) The occasion: One of the guests had spoken of eating in the kingdom of God—heaven.
   b) The points of the parable.
      (1) Invited guests offered weak excuses for not attending.
      (2) The angry master of the house sent a second invitation to the poor.
      (3) Because there was still room, He sent a third invitation that His house might be filled.
      (4) None of those invited the first time were to taste his supper.

B. Luke told about Jesus' challenging message to the crowd (25-35).
  1. The cost of discipleship (25-32).
   a) Jesus told them what was involved.
      (1) Hating members of one's own family.
      (2) Taking up the cross and following Him.
   b) Jesus illustrated the lesson.
      (1) Counting the cost to build a tower.
      (2) Considering the number of troops necessary to meet the enemy.
  2. The necessity of complete surrender (33-35).
   a) He said, "The one who does not renounce all cannot be by disciple."
   b) He illustrated His meaning with the parable of Salt.
      (1) Salt is good, but if it loses its saltiness what then?
      (2) The answer: Good for nothing but to be thrown out.
   c) The solemnity of His words: "He who has ears, let him hear."

Jesus Healed a Man With Dropsy

Scripture

14:1-6 And it came to pass, when he went into the house of one of the rulers of the Pharisees on a sabbath to eat bread, that they were watching him. 2 And behold, there was before him a certain man that had the dropsy. 3 And Jesus answering spake unto the lawyers and Pharisees, saying, Is it lawful to heal on the sabbath,

241

or not? 4 But they held their peace. And he took him, and healed him, and let him go. 5 And he said unto them, Which of you shall have an ass or an ox fallen into a well, and will not straight-way draw him up on a sabbath day? 6 And they could not answer again unto these things.

Comments

when he went into the house.—He had gone into the house of a ruler of the Pharisees on the sabbath to have a meal. The Pharisee could have been a ruler of the synagogue or he could have held some other position of authority among the Jews.

there was before him a certain man.—This sick man was in the immediate presence of Jesus. Had he been invited or was he—as in the case of the woman of the city (8:37-38)—one of the poor who had come in uninvited? The fact that Jesus sent him away after the miracle may suggest that he had come in of his own accord. On the other hand, it is possible that he had been invited for the very purpose of baiting a trap for Jesus. The Pharisees were looking for an excuse to destroy Him. Had they heard how He had discredited the Pharisees and lawyers on other occasions (6:7-11)? Were they aware that Jesus had put His adversaries to shame when He healed the woman with a spirit of infirmity?

Luke says they were watching Him closely. See also Mark 3:2. Other had tried and failed; perhaps they were hoping that they would succeed in embarrassing Him before their own group.

And Jesus answering.—A question was implied by the presence of the sick man. In the minds of those watching, the question was this: "What will He do?" Jesus spoke in answer to the implied question.

Is it lawful to heal on the sabbath, or not?—The lawyers, no doubt, who were present had debated the question on many occasions. They should have known the answer. But they were unwilling to risk an answer at this time, so they entered a state of silence and left the issue up to Jesus.

And he took him and healed him.—This is evidently what they were hoping He would do. But before they could launch their attack, He fired a question at them that they could not or would not answer.

Which of you shall have an ox or ass fall.—When you have an ox or an ass fall into a well, what do you do, even if it is on the sab-bath? The answer was clear; they would pull it out. A human being was in distress; Jesus had extended a helping hand, even though it was on the sabbath.

Some texts add the word "son" to the list, but there is some question as to the correctness of the text in this matter. The comparison is stronger when it is between the man with dropsy and animals. *And they could not answer.*—He had easily answered the question implied by the presence of the sick man, but they could not refute His logic when He drew the comparison between man and animal. They had to admit that He was right or keep still.

A Lesson on Humility

Scripture

14:7-14 And he spake a parable unto those that were bidden, when he marked how they chose out the chief seats; saying unto them, 8 When thou art bidden of any man to a marriage feast, sit not down in the chief seat; lest haply a more honorable man than thou be bidden of him, 9 and he that bade thee and him shall come and say to thee, Give this man place; and then thou shalt begin with shame to take the lowest place. 10 But when thou art bidden, go and sit down in the lowest place; and when he that hath bidden thee cometh, he may say to thee, Friend, go up higher: then shalt thou have glory in the .presence of all that sit at meat with thee. 11 For every one that exalteth himself shall be humbled; and he that humbleth himself shall be exalted.

12 And he said to him also that had bidden him, When thou makest a dinner or a supper, call not thy friends, nor thy brethren, nor thy kinsmen, nor rich neighbors; lest haply they also bid thee again, and a recompense be made thee. 13 But when thou makest a feast, bid the poor, the maimed, the lame, the blind: 14 and thou shalt be blessed; because they have not *wherewith* to recompense thee: for thou shalt be recompensed in the resurrection of the just.

Comments

And he spake a parable.—There was an implied question in the presence of the sick man. Jesus called attention to a situation which all were able to observe and pointed out a lesson which it also implied. It was the right of the host to seat the guests in places of honor, but these rude people so lacking in humility were occupying the places of honor without waiting to be assigned to them by the host.

sit not down in the chief seats.—That is, do not recline on the couch reserved for the honored guest until invited to do so. To avoid the ambarrassment of being asked to move to a place of lower distinction, Jesus advised that they occupy the lower place first and wait until they were invited to occupy a place of greater honor. When the host says, "Friend, move up to a place of higher honor, you will be approved in the presence of all who are reclining at the feast with you."

It is evident that Jesus had not been invited to the place of honor that was rightly His, since He is the Son of God. A good question: To what place do we invite the Lord when we have banquets? *For everyone that exalteth himself.*—See Mark 10:42-45 for a similar lesson which Jesus taught the disciples. Peter says, "Humble yourselves therefore under the mighty hand of God, that he may exalt you in due time" (I Pet. 5:6). Humility is a virtue that should have been observed in the banquet which Jesus was attending. It is essential for those who hope to attend the heavenly banquet about which Jesus had been teaching. See Micah 6:8.

to him also that had bidden him.—The lesson on humility applied not only to guests but also to the host. It is evident that the motive of the one who invited Jesus was not what it should have been. He may have been seeking to take advantage of Jesus' own popularity. One poor man had been permitted to come into the house, but the guests for the most part were his rich neighbors and friends.

When thou makest a dinner or supper.—Or as we would say, a luncheon or dinner, for Jesus referred to a noon meal and an evening meal. The "feast" was a banquet.

lest haply they also bid thee again.—This was not to say that the rich man could not have his neighbors and friends as guests in his home; but this could be done from the wrong motive, for some expected to be invited into the homes of their guests.

The gospel invitation, as the parable of the Great Supper shows, is to the poor, the maimed, the lame, and the blind—that is, sinners who need the cleansing power of the Lord.

and thou shalt be blessed.—In the Book of Acts, Luke quotes these words of Paul, "Ye ought to help the weak, and to remember the words of the Lord Jesus, that he himself said, It is more blessed to give than to receive" (Acts 20:35). There is a blessing in helping the needy. All of us need to help others, for in doing so we help ourselves in a way that nothing else can.

recompensed in the resurrection of the just.—There will be a time when you will be paid back for what you have done for the poor. That will be in the resurrection of the just.

The resurrection, of course, is not limited to the just, but they are the ones who will be blessed in the resurrection. Paul spoke of the resurrection of the just and the unjust (Acts 24:15). Jesus said, "The hour cometh, in which all that are in the tombs shall hear his voice, and shall come forth; they that have done good, unto the resurrection of life; and they that have done evil, unto the resurrection of judgment" (John 5:28-29). There is one resurrection at which time both the just and unjust will be raised.

The Great Supper
Scripture

14:15-24 And when one of them that sat at meat with him heard these things, he said unto him, Blessed is he that shall eat bread in the kingdom of God. 16 But he said unto him, A certain man made a great supper; and he bade many: 17 and he sent forth his servant at supper time to say to them that were bidden, Come; for all things are now ready. 18 And they all with one consent began to make excuse. The first said unto him, I have bought a field, and I must needs go out and see it; I pray thee have me excused. 19 And another said, I have bought five yoke of oxen, and I go to prove them; I pray thee have me excused. 20 And another said, I have married a wife, and therefore I cannot come. 21 And the servant came, and told his lord these things. Then the master of the house being angry said to his servant, Go out quickly into the streets and lanes of the city, and bring in hither the poor and maimed and blind and lame. 22 And the servant said, Lord, what thou didst command is done, and yet there is room. 23 And the lord said unto the servant, Go out into the highways and hedges, and constrain them to come in, that my house may be filled. 24 For I say unto you, that none of those men that were bidden shall taste of my supper.

Comments

Blessed is he that shall eat bread in the kingdom of God.—Heaven is thus represented as a great feast. The idea seems to have been suggested by the remarks Jesus had made about inviting the poor to lunch or dinner. How fortunate it will be for those who shall have the privilege of being present at that heavenly banquet. Jesus used the occasion for two things: (1) to point out the general disregard for God and His Son whom He sent to tell those who had been invited to come to the feast, and (2) to indicate that although these had slighted the invitation, others would be invited and the places at the heavenly banquet would be filled.

A certain man made a great supper.—Jesus vividly set forth God's concern for the Jewish people and their disregard for all His efforts to get them to respond to His directions for their lives as His chosen people. They had known since God constituted them a nation at Sinai that they were invited to the heavenly banquet.

he sent forth his servant.—This seems to be a reference to the ministry of Jesus, a last effort to get the nation of Israel to respond to God.

And they all with one consent began to make excuse.—"They that were his own received him not" (John 1:11) is John's way of saying that the Jews in general—not just the Pharisees—had rejected the appeal of Jesus. On another occasion Jesus told the parable of The Wedding of the King's Son (Matt. 22:1-14). It teaches the same general lesson about the rejected invitation.

The Jews were God's chosen people, but, by the time Jesus came to the lost sheep of the house of Israel, they had assumed an attitude of utter indifference to God that exactly fits the description of the excuse-makers of this parable. Their excuses were insulting to the one who had invited them and wholly without justification. They were not the kind to buy a piece of land or a team of oxen without knowing something about them. The excuses were ridiculous. The one who said he couldn't come because he had just married a wife was disregarding the Law of Moses (Deut. 24:5). During the first year of marriage a man was excused from military duty so that he might have time for just such occasions as described in the parables.

While the Jews in general rejected Christ, the publicans and sinners did turn to Him for forgiveness and help. This is the second invitation which was extended by Jesus.

and yet there is room.—There is room in the heavenly banquet for others than the outcasts of the ancient Jewish society. So a third invitation was sent to those that might be found by the roads that let away from the crowded cities. This may suggest that the poor had found shelter along the hedges that grew by the roadside. These were compelled to come in. Jesus is still emphasizing the fact that the invitation is extended to the humble.

The great commission is suggested by the third invitation. See Mark. 16:15-16; Matt. 28:18-20. This third invitation is not limited to Gentiles, for the gospel invitation includes Jews as well as Gentiles. "Whosover will, may come."

Jesus told the Jews who failed to produce the fruit of the kingdom that the kingdom would be taken from them and given to another nation that would produce the fruits of it (Matt. 21:43). That nation is composed of believers in Christ, whether Jews or Gentiles (Rom. 1:16-17; Gal. 3:28). The book of Romans proves that there is no distinction between Jews who are sinners and Gentiles who sin, for all sinners are objects of God's mercy and are in need of His grace. All are to come on the basis of faith expressed in obedience, since that is all that any sinner can offer (Rom. 3-21-25; 1:5; 6:1-4; 12:1-2).

and constrain them to come in.—By what means was the servant to constrain them to come in? Certainly not physical force. In all probability, the simple appeal of good food was enough to compel the hungry to come. But many are not hungering and thirsting after righteousness. Many are like the Rich Fool who was satisfied with material things and thought nothing of food for the soul.

Since the third invitation represents the gospel invitation, we may ask what force compels one to respond to it? The gospel is the power of God to save the believer. The force of the facts of the gospel— the evidence of the resurrection of Christ who died to save the lost— is sufficient to compel the earnest enquirer to believe that Jesus is the Christ (John 20:30-31). The gospel of God's love is a motivating force sufficient to lead one to repentance (Rom. 2:4). But even this force cannot reach those callous hearts that are past feeling because of long indulgence in sinful practices (Eph. 4:17-20). The gospel message about the power of the blood of Christ to wash away sin is a compelling force to the weary sinner (Heb. 9: 14-15; I Pet. 1: 19). The sinner that recognizes his need for a clean conscience will be compelled to come to the Lord for cleansing (Heb. 10:22; I Pet. 3:21).

Sinners were drawn to Christ for they saw in Him the embodiment of the message He proclaimed. Nothing less will be effective in the efforts of His followers who seek to compel others to come to Him.

that my house may be filled.—This is the answer to the question about few being saved.

none of those men that were bidden. —Jesus again and again pointed out the fate of those who were rejecting Him. They will not taste of His supper; they will be on the outside watching those who come from the four corners of the earth to sit with Abraham, Isaac, and Jacob in the kingdom of heaven.

Counting the Cost

Scripture

14:25-35 Now there went with him great multitudes: and he turned, and said unto them, 26 If any man cometh unto me, and hateth not his own father, and mother, and wife, and children, and brethren, and sisters, yea, and his own life also, he cannot be my disciple. 27 Whosoever doth not bear his own cross, and come after me, cannot be my disciple. 28 For which of you, desiring to build a tower, doth not first sit down and count the cost, whether he have wherewith to complete it? 29 Lest haply, when he hath laid a foundation, and is not able to finish, all that behold begin to mock him, 30 saying, This man began to build, and was not able to finish. 31 Or what king, as he goeth to encounter another king in war, will not sit down first and take counsel whether he is able with ten thousand to meet him that cometh against him with twenty thousand? 32 Or else, while the other is yet a great way off, he sendeth an ambassage, and asketh conditions of peace. 33 So therefore whosoever he be of you that renounceth not all that he hath, he cannot be my disciple. 34 Salt therefore is good: but if even the salt have lost its savor, wherewith shall it be seasoned? 35 It is fit neither for the land nor for the dunghill; men cast it out. He that hath ears to hear, let him hear.

Comments

and hateth not his own father, and mother.—On another occasion Jesus stated this same lesson in a positive form: "He that loveth father or mother more than me is not worthy of me" (Matt. 10:37). Therefore we are forced to understand the expression "hate" in the light of this positive statement. It simply means that when it comes

248

to a matter of devotion to Christ or parents, Christ must be first in the absolute sense; parents, by contrast, are to be hated, for they cannot be put before Him.

But Jesus upheld the Old Testament law that required children to honor their parents (Ex. 29:2; Deut. 5:6; Eph. 6:2-4). He severely condemned the hypocracy of the Pharisees who made the Word of God an empty thing by their tradition that said if a man gave to God what he might spend to care for his parents he was not required to care for them (Matt. 15:3-6). Evidently, they were merely saying that they were giving to God, but in reality neither giving to God nor caring for their parents. Actually, caring for aged parents in obedience to God's command would have been giving to God.

Except for those cases in which parents bitterly opposed Christ, there would be no conflict in loving Him and parents also. See 12: 49-53.

and his own life.—This shows that Jesus did not intend for a man to hate his parents in the ordinary sense of the term. But nothing— not even the dearest members of one's own family or life itself—can be exalted above Christ, if one is to be His disciple.

bear his own cross.—Jesus demands absolute priority in the thinking and love of His disciples. Selfish ambition has no place in the life of His followers. He had explained this to the disciples before (9:23). Now the multitudes are to learn the same lesson. Jesus was not willing to accept any disciple who was not willing to meet the demands of discipleship. See 9:57-62. If He had been interested in merely becoming the popular leader of an irresponsible crowd—a charge made at the time of His trial (23:2)—He would have made no such demands.

For which of you desiring to build a tower.—The high standard of discipleship made it necessary for those who would be His followers to count the cost before entering the service of the Lord. In our eagerness to see people become Christians, do we sometimes fail to observe Jesus' warning about counting the cost? Jesus' reference to building a tower and to the number of troops necessary to meet the enemy illustrates the lesson. Count the cost before beginning such projects, if you are to avoid the embarrassment of possible failure. Not just those who enlist, but those who fight the good fight, finish the course, and keep the faith are to receive the crown of righteousness (II Tim. 4:7-8; Rev. 2:10).

that renounseth not all that he hath.—Paul is an excellent example of one who renounced all for the sake of Christ (Phil. 3:8-11). But no less is required of all other followers of Christ. Jesus had already illustrated this in the parables of the Hidden Treasure and the Pearl of Great Price (Matt. 13:44-45). All these remarks explain the meaning of true self-denial. See also Paul's challenge to Timothy as a good soldier of Jesus Christ (II Tim. 2:3-4).

he cannot be my disciple.—This is absolute! There is no place for half-hearted discipleship in the service of the Lord. See Jesus' warning to the lukewarm Laodicean church (Rev. 3:14-22).

Salt therefore is good.—This is still another illustration of the necessity of weighing the issues involved and remaining faithful to the end. Salt in this context is a symbol of dedication to Christ. Without dedication, a disciple is ineffective in his efforts to influence others for Christ; he is certainly to be rejected in the end.

Jesus used this same expression in another context (Mark 9:49-50). He had been discussing the destruction of the wicked in hell and added, "For everyone shall be salted with fire." He was referring to His teaching about hell which would act as a deterent to wickedness. He said, "Have salt in yourselves"—that is, have this knowledge about the fate of the wicked in your minds that it might keep you from such destruction.

On still another occasion, Jesus spoke of His disciples as the salt of the earth (Matt. 5:13). In all probability, this means that the disciples by Christlike character and conduct and by teaching the truth of His Word are to preserve others from destruction.

but if the salt have lost its savor.—If the salt loses its salty taste, what then? It is fit for nothing but to be cast out. A disciple who loses the necessary dedication and consecration to Christ as suggested by cross-bearing and self-denial will be rejected; such a person cannot be His disciple.

He that hath ears to hear.—Thus Jesus emphasizes the lesson He has just taught. His hearers should heed His challenge and His warning.

Summary

Opposition to Jesus became more intense as He came closer to the day when He would lay down His life for His people. His great popularity with the common people was a real challenge to the leaders who were determined to destroy Him, one way or another.

Another Pharisee invited Him to his house to eat. But a man with dropsy was there and they were watching Jesus to see what He would do, for it was the sabbath. He accepted the challenge; He healed the man; He embarrassed those who hoped to embarrass Him, for they were not able to answer the logic of His questions about their own acts on the sabbath.

Jesus was also watching the guests on that occasion. He saw them choosing the chief seats without waiting to be asked by the host to take the place of honor. He taught the powerful lesson, "Everyone that exalts himself be humbled and every one that humbles himself shall be exalted." And He was aware that the host had invited his rich friends who would in turn invite him to their homes. Jesus said to him, "Invite the poor, and you will be rewarded in the resurrection of the just."

One of the guests began to speak about the fortunate state of those who would be at the heavenly banquet. Jesus responded with the story of the Great Supper. God had invited His chosen people to come to the feast, but they made lame excuses for their insulting disregard for Him. Then Jesus indicated that the gospel invitation would be given to the sinners of all classes and that the heavenly banquet table would be filled, but those who had been invited would not get to taste the supper.

It is a serious matter to be a disciple of Jesus. He demands first place in the hearts of all who would be His followers. Not even father or mother may be put before Him. Before undertaking discipleship, count the cost. Complete dedication to Him is the price. Salt that loses its saltiness is good for nothing. A disciple who loses his devotion to Christ is worthless. Jesus closed His remarks with the solemn warning, "He who has ears, let him hear."

Questions

1. Why did the Pharisees invite Jesus to eat with them?
2. How account for the presence of the sick man on that occasion?
3. Why does Luke say that they were watching Him closely?
4. What day of the week was it?
5. What question did Jesus put to the lawyers? Why?
6. Why didn't they answer Him?
7. How did Jesus defend His action of healing the man on the sabbath?

8. What contrast did His remarks make between what He had done and what they were accustomed to do?
9. What were the guests doing that led to Jesus' lesson on humility?
10. What did He suggest that they do?
11. What happens to the one who exalts himself?
12. What did Peter say about humility?
13. What did Jesus say to His host about the guests he had invited?
14. Where should he have been looking for his reward?
15. What do the Scriptures teach about the resurrection of the just and unjust?
16. What was the occasion for the parable of the Great Supper?
17. What did Jesus show about the attitude in general toward God's invitation to the Great Supper?
18. What excuses had the Jews made for not responding?
19. To what class was the second invitation given?
20. How was this fulfilled during the ministry of Jesus?
21. Why was a third invitation given?
22. What does the third invitation represent?
23. To whom is the third invitation sent?
24. How can people be compelled to respond to the invitation?
25. How did Jesus illustrate the necessity of counting the cost of discipleship?
26. What did Jesus demand of those who were to be His disciples?
27. What is the significance of His remarks about salt in this context?
28. How are we to understand His remarks about one's parents?
29. What was the Old Testament law about caring for parents?
30. What had the Pharisees done that had nullified this law?
31. How does Jesus illustrate the meaning of cross-bearing and self-denial in this context?
32. Why did Jesus make such demands on His disciples?
33. Is the demand any less now?
34. What did Jesus mean when He said that everyone shall be salted with fire?
35. In what sense are His disciples the salt of the earth?
36. What did He mean by the reference to salt that has lost its taste?

37. What is to be done with the disciple that is like salt that loses its saltiness?
38. Why did He say, "He that hath ears to hear, let him hear"?

CHAPTER FIFTEEN

Outline

A. Luke told about another complaint of the Pharisees and scribes (1-2).
   1. The complaint was made when publicans and sinners were being attracted to Jesus in large numbers (1).
   2. The Pharisees and scribes muttered their grumbling complaint: "This one is welcoming sinners and is eating with them" (2).
B. He told how Jesus answered their complaint with three parables about the lost (3-32).
   1. The parable of the Lost Sheep (3-7).
      a) Jesus' question in answer to their complaint: What man who has a hundred sheep, if one of them gets lost, would not leave the ninety-nine and go after the lost one until he finds it?
      b) What would he do when he finds the sheep? He would call his friends to rejoice with him, saying, "I have found my sheep that was lost."
      c) The lesson applied: There will be more joy in heaven over one sinner that repents than over the ninety-nine
   2. The parable of the Lost Coin (8-10).
      a) Jesus' question: What woman who has ten pieces of silver wouldn't, if she loses one, search the house until she finds it?
      b) What would she do when she finds it? She would call her neighbors and say, "Rejoice with me, for I have found the piece that was lost."
      c) The lesson applied again: There will be more joy in heaven over one sinner that repents than over ninety-nine persons who need no repentance.
   3. The parable of the Lost Son (11-32). In this parable Jesus gave detailed answers to all the problems involved in the complaint that He was receiving and associating with sinners.
      a) The story of the prodigal son (11-20a).
         (1) A man had two sons; the younger demanded his inheritance which the father gave to him.
         (2) Soon the young man took all he had and went into a far country and wasted it in riotous living.

(3) After he had spent all his fortune, a famine occurred in the land; so he took a job herding swine.

(4) He became so destitute that he actually ate what
the swine ate, but no man gave him a thing!

(5) When he came to his senses, he said, "How many
servants in my father's house have food in abundance, and I am pershing in hunger!"

(6) He resolved to go back to his father and say,
"Father, I have sinned against heaven in your
sight; I am not worthy to be called your son;
make me as one of your hired servants."

(7) The lost son followed out his resolution and went
to his father.

b) The wonderful welcome the lost son received from his
father (20b-24).

(1) The father saw him coming from afar; he was
deeply moved and, running to meet him, embraced
him and kissed him.

(2) The son acknowledged his sin before his father;
he said, "Father, I have sinned against heaven in
your sight; I am not worthy to be called your
son."

(3) But Jesus said that the father ordered the servants
to bring a robe and put it on him and a ring and
put it on his finger and put shoes on his feet. He
ordered them to kill the fatted calf and prepare a
feast so that all of them might eat and make
merry.

(4) He also told how the father revealed his very
heart when he said, "This my son was dead and is
alive; he was lost and is found."

(5) They began to make merry!

c) The murmuring complaint of the older brother (25-32).

(1) As he neared the house, he heard music and dancing and asked, "What's the meaning of this?"

(2) They told him that his lost brother had returned,
and that his father had welcomed him with the
feast because he had received him safe and sound.

(3) The older brother got angry and wouldn't come
into the house even though the father urged him
to do so.

(4) His bitter complaint:
    (a) I served you all these years and never disobeyed a command of yours.
    (b) You never gave me anything that I might make merry with my friends.
    (c) But when this son of yours who devoured your living with harlots comes home, you kill the fatted calf for him!

(5) The father's answer. This is Jesus' answer to the the complaint of the Pharisees that he was receiving sinners.
    (a) "Son, you have been with me always, and all that is mine is yours too."
    (b) "But it is right to make merry and be glad, for this your brother was dead and is alive; he was lost and is found!"

Christ Receives Sinful Men

Scripture

15:1-2   Now all the publicans and sinners were drawing near unto him to hear him. 2 And both the Pharisees and the scribes murmured, saying, This man receiveth sinners, and eateth with them.

Comments

all the publicans and sinners.—Jesus had just been talking about the cost of discipleship and the demands which He was making on those who would be His followers. But the crowds of publicans and sinners—social outcasts who were looked upon with contempt by the Pharisees—continued to draw near to hear Him teach. It seems that the high standard of discipleship served to attract those who really knew what it meant to need the Savior. The challenge of the cross will draw men to Christ where a diluted "gospel" of ease will fail.

The Pharisees were always ready to seize upon these occasions to condemn Jesus. They were eager to make it appear that He was a "friend of sinners" when, as a matter of fact, He is *the* Friend of sinners.

Tax-collectors were generally looked upon as guilty of abusing their office and, of course, were classed as sinners.

murmured.—Jesus had on a few occasions been invited to have dinner with Pharisees, but when He ate with publicans and sinners these same Pharisees were quick to condemn Him. They tried to make it appear that He was a sinner too—guilt by association.

This same Satanic scheme is seen in various places in the ministry of Christ and His apostles. The Pharisees had tried to discredit Jesus in the eyes of the people by saying that He was casting out demons by the power of Beelzebub. Paul and Silas faced the possibility of having their work ruined because of the demon-possessed person who followed them at Philippi (Acts 16:16-18).

receives sinners.—Jesus had made it clear that He had come to seek and save sinners—not any kind of sinners, but those who repented. He required His followers to renounce all and take up their cross and follow Him daily. Pharisees, of course, felt that they needed no repentance.

In answering the charge of the Pharisees, Jesus takes them at their own estimate of themselves and still shows that they were wrong in condemning Him for His attitude toward sinners. In the three parables that follow, He more than justifies His position.

Parable of the Lost Sheep

Scripture

15:3-7   And he spake unto them this parable, saying, 4 What man of you, having a hundred sheep, and having lost one of them, doth not leave the ninety and nine in the wilderness, and go after that which is lost, until he find it? 5 And when he hath found it, he layeth it on his shoulders, rejoicing. 6 And when he cometh home, he calleth together his friends and his neighbors, saying unto them, Rejoice with me, for I have found my sheep which was lost. 7 I say unto you, that even so there shall be joy in heaven over one sinner that repenteth, more than over ninety and nine righteous persons, who need no repentance.

Comments

this parable.—Jesus used three parables or illustrations to answer the complaint of the Pharisees. They were three devastating blows at their false position. In them, Jesus more than justified His action in receiving sinners and eating with them, for His mission was to seek and save the lost.

257

The church, as the body of Christ, has the same mission. Evangelism is the first business of the church. But one wonders if the church has lost sight of its purpose in the world. Social reform—and there is need for so much work in this area—is not the first business of the church. Only the gospel can transform the hearts of men (Rom. 12:1-2). When that happens, he can transform the society in which he lives. The leaven of the gospel must be hidden in the heart before an effective transformation of society can be expected. It is the gospel that saves from sin, and it is sin that is causing all the trouble in the world today.

It is not the task of the church to take over the responsibility of the home and relieve parents of their duty to train the child in the nurture and admonition of the Lord. But many parents expect some faithful Bible school teacher to give their children all the religious training they will ever get; they seldom stop to thank the teacher for this work of love.

Much that is done in youth programs today merely serves to relive parents from a responsibility that is theirs. Many parents never open their homes for youth meetings or provide transportation for groups of young people or funds for the necessary expense of the work. Yet these same people are quick to complain if "the church" fails to meet the problems of youth. Of course, parents who are active workers in the church will find that the association with other Christian parents helps immensely in the task of guiding young people in this evil day.

In many instances, the church faces the real danger of leaving its first love—love for Christ—by failing to do its first work which is the work of preaching the gospel to save sinners.

It is the responsibility of the church to uphold the standards of conduct that meet the approval of God. In no place is this more true than in upholding the Biblical standard for the Christian home. *one of them lost.*—This is the point of the parable. Jesus was justifying His effort to save the lost sinner. No one could argue that it was wrong to look for the sheep that was lost, and it took only little effort to apply this principle to the sinner who was certainly lost.

The sheep that got lost may have wandered off from the rest of the flock; perhaps it was still young and had not learned the dangers that beset its path. The case is different with men. Some are lost because they do not have the kind of home that God intended all children to have. Children from broken homes or from homes where Christ and His Word are not honored have little chance to escape from the alluring appeals of sin today.

the ninety and nine.—The ninety-nine represent the Pharisees who felt that they were righteous and needed no repentance. The nine coins that were not lost and the elder brother who "never disobeyed a command" of his father also represent what the Pharisees thought they were. Jesus didn't argue this point with them. He was justifying His effort on behalf of those who knew they were sinners and needed His help.

Rejoice with me.—If the Pharisees had really needed no repentance they would have rejoiced when the sinner was saved. Heaven did; why didn't they?

need no repentance.—Repentance is the decision to forsake sin and live the kind of life that is acceptable in the sight of God. Both John and Jesus preached the gospel of the kingdom that called on sinners to repent and produce the fruit of righteousness. Jesus came to call sinners to repentance. Of course, the Pharisees needed repentance just as much as any other sinner, but they were unaware of it. The case of the elder brother shows this to be true.

Parable of the Lost Coin

Scripture

15:8-10 Or what woman having ten pieces of silver, if she lose one piece, doth not light a lamp, and sweep the house, and seek diligently until she find it? 9 And when she hath found it, she calleth together her friends and neighbors, saying, Rejoice with me, for I have found the piece which I had lost. 10 Even so, I say unto you, there is joy in the presence of the angels of God over one sinner that repenteth.

Comments

ten pieces of silver.—Much has been said about what these represent. The tendency to treat the illustration as an allegory may cause one to lose sight of the real lesson. The parable simply says that the woman had ten pieces and lost one. What woman would not search diligently until she found the lost coin? So Jesus again justified His effort to find the lost sinner.

There is nothing to suggest that this parable teaches anything different from that which is taught by the parable of the Lost Sheep, for the lost sheep and the lost coin represent the lost sinner.

Without reading too much into the stories, it is possible to see that the sheep got itself lost while the woman lost the coin. Was it through carelessness, or neglect, or irresponsibility? These parables are not about sheep and coins, but people! People are lost sometimes by neglect or indifference or carelessness on the part of others who should show some concern for their fellowmen. Who cares about the drop-out? In some Bible classes, one has to attend three times to become "a member." But he can be absent indefinitely without having anyone bother to find out why. Who speaks to the lonely stranger at church? Are some lost because no one has time to show them that the Savior cares?

joy in the presence of the angels of God.—If angels rejoice over the sinners who repent, why condemn Jesus for His effort to save them? The contrast is so great that we wonder if the Pharisees were beginning to regret the unfortunate position they had taken?

The Parable of the Lost Son

Scripture

15:11-32   And he said, A certain man had two sons: 12 and the younger of them said to his father, Father, give me the portion of thy substance that falleth to me. And he divided unto them his living. 13 And not many days after, the younger son gathered all together and took his journey into a far country; and there he wasted his substance with riotous living. 14 And when he had spent all, there arose a mighty famine in that country; and he began to be in want. 15 And he went and joined himself to one of the citizens of that country; and he sent him into his fields to feed swine. 16 And he would fain have filled his belly with the husks that the swine did eat: and no man gave unto him. 17 But when he came to himself he said, How many hired servants of my father's have bread enough and to spare, and I perish here with hunger! 18 I will arise and go to my father, and will say unto him, Father, I have sinned against heaven, and in thy sight: 19 I am no more worthy to be called thy son: make me as one of thy hired servants. 20 And he arose, and came to his father. But while he was yet afar off, his father saw him, and was moved with compassion, and ran, and fell on his neck, and kissed him. 21 And the son said unto him, Father, I have sinned against heaven, and in thy sight: I am no more worthy to be called thy son. 22 But the father said to his servants, Bring forth quickly the best robe, and put it on him; and put a ring on his hand, and shoes on his feet: 23 and bring the fatted calf, and kill it, and let us eat, and make merry: 24 for this my son was dead, and is alive again; he was lost, and is found. And they began to be merry. 25 Now his elder son was in the field: and as he came and drew nigh to the house, he heard music and dancing. 26 And he called to him one of the servants, and inquired what these things might be. 27 And he said unto him, Thy brother is come; and thy father hath killed the fatted calf, because he hath received him safe and sound. 28 But he was angry, and would not go in: and his father came out, and entreated him. 29 But he answered and said to his father, Lo, these many years do I serve thee, and I never transgressed a commandment of thine; and yet thou never gavest me a kid, that I might make merry with my friends: 30 but when this thy son came, who hath devoured thy living with harlots, thou killedst for him the fatted calf. 31 And he said unto him, Son, thou art ever with me, and all that is mine is thine. 32 But it was meet to make merry and be glad: for this thy brother was dead, and is alive again; and was lost, and is found.

Comments

A certain man had two sons.—Note the progress of thought in the three parables: a lost sheep, a lost coin, a lost son. The sheep got lost; someone lost the coin; but the son was an intelligent human being created in the image of God with the ability to think and decide his course of action. He deliberately left his father's house and wasted his life in riotous living.

to feed swine.—The wastefulness of sin led to degradation in sin. Jews were proud shepherds of sheep. They loved David, their shepherd king. Jesus called Himself the Good Shepherd. But for a Jew to become a swineherd was to sink to the lowest possible state of disgrace. Swine, according to the Law of Moses, were unclean. But this destitute son who was really lost actually ate with the swine.

no man gave to him.—He had friends while his money lasted, but none when it was gone. Those who lead others to sin usually abandon them when they are of no further use to them. This should be

261

a strong warning to those who run with the crowd that cares nothing for God or Christ or the Bible.

But when he came to himself.—When he realized that he was needlessly wasting his life, he resolved to do something about it. Repentance is mentioned in each of the parables, but in this one Jesus shows what it means to repent. It arose out of the awareness of the sinful, lost, and utterly hopeless state of the son who had wasted his life. It is the resolution to do something about the situation. It is inspired by the memory of home and all that it meant to be a son. It is accompanied by a sense of genuine humility that recognized that the right to be called "son" had been forfeited. It was a sense of appreciation of the privilege of becoming a servant in the father's household. It is the decision of the lost son who said, "I will arise and go to my father."

Sinners do have a responsibility for their condition and can do something about it; they can follow the instruction of the Word of God and go back to the Heavenly Father through the grace of the Lord Jesus Christ who died that their sins might be blotted out. Repentance is accompanied by confession to the father of the sin committed against heaven in the father's sight. Few people have the courage to make such an acknowledgement before God. Too many are like the Pharisee who "needed no repentance." Such are not saved from their sins; they merely "join" the church! They are not really hungry for the "bread in the father's house." They act as if they were doing God a favor by casting their influence with His church. Phariseeism is present in so many places today!

And he arose and came to his father.—The prodigal had left his father's house by his own free choice; he was returning as a result of the decision he had made to go to his father and home. Those who teach that we are born with a tendency to sin fail to see that it was absolutely unnecessary for him to have left in the first place. Neither was it necessary to waste his inheritance. James plainly says that "each man is tempted when he is drawn away by his own lust and enticed" (James 1:14). His own lust is his desire for that which is evil. God did make man with the ability to choose between the heavenly home and the alluring thing that Satan offers, but He did not make man incapable of resisting the devil. James says, "resist the devil and he will flee from you" (James 4:7). Being made in the image of God, man is capable of deciding whether he will please God or Satan—it is just that simple. The prodigal went into sin by

262

his own deliberate act; he returned to the father by his own deliberate choice, because he wanted to escape the intolerable state of sin.

But while he was yet afar off.—The father didn't wait until he came knocking at the door; he saw him afar off and ran to meet him.

God was in Christ reconciling the world unto himself (II Cor. 5:19). He came from heaven to Calvary to meet the sinner who had the courage to start toward heaven. The starting point was the decision to get up and go to the father.

moved with compassion.—God's love and pity for a lost son is shown in the father's attitude toward his son who had the courage to want to get out of his sad state. This is Jesus' answer to those who were criticizing Him for receiving sinners.

And the son said unto him, Father.—Only part of the words of verses 18-19 are restated here. According to the footnote, the son repeated the confession as he planned it. Some may ask, "Did the father interrupt the son's confession?" It is impossible to tell from the text. The son planned the confession. For the son's sake, the father probably heard him out. After all, it was brief, but very necessary. "If we confess our sins, he is faithful and righteous to forgive our sins, and to cleanse us from all unrighteousness" (I John 1:9). One of the hardest things we may be called on to do is to admit that we have sinned, but the prodigal said to his father, "I have sinned." The Pharisee, of course, according to his own opinion of himself, didn't need to make such a confession. He was one of the ninety-nine that didn't need to repent. But John says that if we say that we have not sinned, we make God a liar and His word is not in us (I John 1:10).

Bring forth the robe.—There is nothing in the father's action that indicates that anything less than full restoration of the lost son had ever entered his mind. It reveals the true story of the grace and mercy of the Heavenly Father. The sinner who repents and gets himself baptized into Christ, washing away his sins in the blood of the Lamb, becomes a member of the family of God with all the rights and privileges of a child of God.

"As far as the east is from the west, so far has he removed our transgressions from us" (Psa. 103:12). He has said through the inspired apostle, "Repent and turn again that your sins may be blotted out" (Acts 3:19). He has promised in the Word, "Their sins and iniquities I will remember no more forever" (Heb. 8:12). How wonderful is the grace of our Heavenly Father!

263

To be effective in the proclamation of the gospel, the church must return to the high standard of Christian living that meets God's approval (Rom. 12:1-2). Too many try to live half in Egypt and half in the Promised Land. The Father has not required the impossible, for He has provided the armor with which to withstand the devil. With the shield of faith, the Christian can quench all the fiery darts of the evil one (Eph. 6:16).

let us eat and make merry.—The feasting and joy in the father's house is contrasted with the famine and sorrow of the life of sin.

for this my son was dead and is alive again.—Sin brings death (Rom. 6:23). Did the critical Pharisee now see why Jesus was receiving sinners? He had reached the climax of His argument; with the finding of the lost son there was cause for real rejoicing by all.

Now his elder son.—The elder son presents a clear picture of the Pharisee's estimate of himself; he was like one of the ninety-nine that didn't need to repent. But he was angry that the father had received his lost son back into the family.

I never transgressed a commandment of thine.—If there had been any doubt that Jesus had the Pharisees in mind when He spoke of the ninety-nine, the nine, and the elder brother, this should remove it. The elder brother reacted exactly as the Pharisees had done.

The claim of the elder brother is remarkable to say the least. But the father didn't stop to argue the point with him; he accepted it at face value, but argued that it was appropriate to welcome his lost son who had returned.

this thy brother was dead.—The elder son in his anger had disowned his younger brother, just as the Pharisees had disowned the publican and sinner. With contempt, he said to his father, "This son of yours" devoured your living. He spoke as if he were in no way related to him. But the father, correcting this attitude, said, "This brother of yours was dead and is alive again; he was lost and is found."

A more devastating answer to the position of the Pharisee could hardly be imagined. Only hearts that were completely hardened could fail to respond to the logic and love of Jesus' defense of His mission of seeking and saving the lost.

Sinners are dead through their trespasses and sins (Eph. 2:1). Christ shed His blood that their sins might be blotted out and that they might be made alive together with Him and sit with Him in the heavenly places (Eph. 2:4-10).

264

Summary

Perhaps there is no place in the whole Bible where the saving grace of God is more clearly presented than in this chapter devoted to the three parables of grace. Christ defended His mission against the hypocritical charge of the Pharisees with a logic and love that could not be answered by His critics. It is true that they were not converted, but sinners of all ages since then have been grateful for His clear explanation of God's grace which He made available by His death on the cross.

Sinners are lost as the lost sheep, the lost coin, and the lost son clearly show. The story of the lost son shows what it means to repent, for he decided to get up and go to his father. The once arrogant lad came back in genuine humility; he only asked to be made as one of his father's hired servants.

A welcome awaits the lost when they return to the Heavenly Father's house. Heaven rejoices over one sinner who repents. The rejoicing over finding the lost sheep and the lost coin indicate it, but the feast of joy in the father's house when his son returned shows what it means to God. It was certainly appropriate to rejoice and make merry for the brother was dead, but was alive; he was lost, but found!

Questions

1. What was the occasion for the Pharisees' complaint against Jesus?
2. What was their object in making the complaint?
3. How did Jesus answer the complaint?
4. In the parable of the Lost Sheep, who were represented by the ninety-nine?
5. Did the Pharisees need to repent?
6. Why didn't Jesus attack their sinful lives at this time?
7. Why did He tell about the shepherd who went to find the lost sheep?
8. Why did He tell about the rejoicing when the sheep was found?
9. Over what sinners does heaven rejoice?
10. What kind of sinners does Jesus receive? Where did this leave the Pharisees, in reality?
11. In considering the whole chapter, why can we say that the

"ninety and nine who need no repentance" represent the Pharisees?

12. What does the story of the lost sheep show about people who are lost?
13. What is the purpose of the parable of the Lost Coin?
14. What do these parables suggest about the first business of the church?
15. What is the relation of preaching to social reform?
16. Should the church take over the responsibility for teaching children? What about parental responsibility?
17. What responsibility does the church have in regard to standards for the home?
18. What is a possible distinction between the fact that a sheep was lost and a coin was lost?
19. What should be the concern of church leaders for those who drop out of Bible school or church?
20. What attitudes of church people may cause others to be lost?
21. Why mention the rejoicing among the angels?
22. What makes the case of the lost son different from that of the lost sheep or lost coin?
23. How did Jesus picture the degradation and waste of sin?
24. What was the attitude of Jews toward swine? What bearing on the job the prodigal took?
25. What became of the prodigal's friends when his money was gone?
26. What caused him to think of his father's house?
27. How does his story illustrate the meaning of repentance?
28. What does James say about the cause of sin?
29. What does the father's attitude toward the returning son teach about God's attitude toward sinners who repent?
30. How far did the Heavenly Father go in order to meet the sinner?
31. What does the parable of the Lost Son show about the necessity of confessing sins to the Father?
32. What did the father do for his son upon his return to the home?
33. What does this teach about God's treatment of sinners who repent?
34. What do the Scriptures say about the removal of our sins?
35. What kind of standard must the church uphold in the matter

of living if it is to be effective in proclaiming the gospel to the lost?

36. How did the father describe the fact that the son had returned?
37. Who is represented by the elder brother?
38. What about his claim that he had never transgressed a commandment of his father's?
39. Why didn't the father argue the point with him?
40. What did he call the lost brother?
41. How did the father correct this view?
42. How did he appeal to the elder son to accept his own brother?

CHAPTER SIXTEEN

Outline

A. Luke told about Jesus' lesson on the need of preparation for life after death: The parable of the unrighteous steward (1-18).
   1. The facts of the parable (1-8).
      a) The unrighteous steward had been wasting his master's goods and was called on to give account, since he was to be discharged.
      b) The steward, facing the situation, decided on a course of action.
         (1) He was not strong enough to work, and was ashamed to beg.
         (2) He hit on a plan that would cause people to take him into their homes when he lost his position.
            (a) He said to one of his master's debtors who owed a hundred measure of oil, "Change it to fifty."
            (b) To another who owed a hundred measures of wheat, he said, "Write eighty."
      c) The master commended him for his intelligence in providing for his future.
   2. The need of preparation for life after death (9-18).
      a) Application of the principle: "Make friends for yourselves by means of the mannom of unrighteousness that when it fails they may receive you into the eternal tabernacles."
      b) The need of faithfulness in the discharge of responsibility (10-13).
         (1) The principle: Faithfulness in little leads to faithfulness in much; dishonesty in little leads to dishonesty in much.
         (2) The question of unrighteous mammon contrasted with true riches:
            (a) If you have been unfaithful in the use of unrighteous mammon, who will trust you with true riches?
            (b) If you have not been faithful in what belongs to another, who will give you what belongs to you?

(3) The application.
    (a) No servant can serve two masters; he will hate one and love the other, or hold to one and despise the other.
    (b) You cannot serve God and mammon!
c) The lesson applied to the Pharisees (14-18).
  (1) They were lovers of money and scoffed at Jesus' views on the subject (14-15).
    (a) Jesus said, "You justify yourselves before men, but God knows your hearts.
    (b) He also said, "What is exalted among men is an abomination in the sight of God."
  (2) They were out of harmony with the law (16-18).
    (a) The law and the prophets were preached until John; since then, the gospel of the kingdom is preached.
    (b) Everyone is trying to enter the kingdom by force. ,
    (c) But it is easier for heaven and earth to pass away than for the law to fail in the least point.
    (d) As an example of the unshakable nature of the law, Jesus added, "Every one who divorces his wife and marries another commits adultry, and the one who marries her when she is divorced from her husband commits adultery."
B. Luke told about Jesus' lesson on the failure to prepare for life after death: The rich man and Lazarus (19-31).
  1. The contrast between the two in their lifetime (19-21).
    a) The rich man was clothed in splendor and enjoyed himself every day.
    b) Lazarus, a poor beggar, desired to eat what fell from the rich man's table; dogs licked his many sores.
  2. The contrast between the two in death (22).
    a) When the poor man died, angels carried him to Abraham's bosom.
    b) The rich man died and was buried.
  3. The contrast between the two after death (23-26).
    a) The rich man in torment in Hades looked up and saw Lazarus in Abraham's bosom.

b) He called out, "Father Abraham, have mercy on me and send Lazarus to dip the tip of his finger in water to cool my tongue, for I am in anguish in this flame."

c) But Abraham said, "Son, remember that in your lifetime you received your good things and Lazarus evil things; now he is comforted and you are in anguish."

d) Then Abraham added, "Besides all this, between us and you, a great chasm is fixed that prevents crossing from one side to the other."

4. The rich man's plea for his brothers (27-31).

a) He asked to have someone go to his five brothers to warn them not to come to that place of torment.

b) Abraham said, "They have Moses and the prophets; let them hear them."

c) The rich man protested, "No, father Abraham; but if one go to them from the dead, they will repent."

d) Abraham said, "If they do not hear Moses and the prophets, they will not be persuaded if one arise from the dead."

The Parable of the Unrighteous Steward

Scripture

16:1-18 And he said unto the disciples, There was a certain rich man, who had a steward; and the same was accused unto him that he was wasting his goods. 2 And he called him, and said unto him, What is this that I hear of thee? render the account of thy stewardship; for thou canst be no longer steward. 3 And the steward said within himself, What shall I do, seeing that my lord taketh away the stewardship from me? I have not strength to dig; to beg I am ashamed. 4 I am resolved what to do, that, when I am put out of the stewardship, they may receive me into heir houses. 5 And calling to him each one of his lord's debtors, he said to the first, How much owest thou unto my lord? 6 And he said, A hundred measures of oil. And he said unto him, Take thy bond, and sit down quickly and write fifty. 7 Then said he to another, And how much owest thou? And he said, A hundred measures of wheat. He saith unto him, Take thy bond, and write fourscore. 8 And his lord commended the unrighteous steward because he had done wisely: for the sons of this world are for their own generation wiser than the sons of the light. 9 And I say unto you, Make to yourselves friends by means of the mammon of unrighteousness; that, when it shall fail, they may receive you into the eternal tabernacles. 10 He that is faithful in a very little is faithful also in much: and he that is unrighteous in a very little is unrighteous also in much. 11 If therefore ye have not been faithful in the unrighteous mammon, who will commit to your trust the true riches? 12 And if ye have not been faithful in that which is another's, who will give you that which is your own? 13 No servant can serve two masters: for either he will hate the one, and love the other; or else he will hold to one, and despise the other. Ye cannot serve God and mammon.

14 And the Pharisees, who were lovers of money, heard all these things; and they scoffed at him. 15 And he said unto them, Ye are they that justify yourselves in the sight of men; but God knoweth your hearts: for that which is exalted among men is an abomination in the sight of God. 16 The law and the prophets *were* until John: from that time the gospel of the kingdom of God is preached, and every man entereth violently into it. 17 But it is easier for heaven and earth to pass away, than for one tittle of the law to fall.

18 Every one that putteth away his wife, and marrieth another, committeth adultery: and he that marrieth one that is put away from a husband committeth adultery.

Comments

And he said unto the disciples.—There is an apparent connection between this chapter and the preceding one in which Jesus completely discredited the Pharisees who had complained that He was receiving sinners. He proved that He was receiving only such sinners as were willing to repent of their sins and conduct themselves in a manner that glorified the Lord. The lessons of chapter sixteen are primarily to the disciples, although He had some things to say directly to the Pharisees.

The two parables of this chapter, while dealing incidentally with the subject of riches, stress the importance of doing something about entrance into the eternal happiness of those who use the opportunities of this life to prepare for life after death. For example, in the parable of the Unjust Steward, Jesus shows that the man was commended for making preparation for the time when he

271

would no longer have an income. But the real lesson points to the necessity of preparing for the eternal home.

In the parable of the Rich Man and Lazarus (assuming that it is a parable) Jesus contrasts the rich man and the beggar in this life, but elaborates on their states after death. It would seem, therefore, that riches, about which Jesus said some important things, was not the primary lesson to be learned from the story of the rich man and Lazarus. Eternal life, a subject that seemed to be taken lightly by the Pharisees, was not to be taken for granted by the disciples. "Joy in heaven" is stressed in the parables of grace, and the thought continues in the parables of chapter sixteen. What Jesus said about riches in this chapter is not, of course, to be minimized. *There was a certain rich man.*—The dishonest steward is the central character in this story; he was not commended for his dishonesty, but for his wisdom in preparing for the future. Dishonesty was the occasion for his losing his position. The fact that he was about to lose his income made it necessary for him to do something about his future. Everyone faces the necessity of doing something about life after death, for "it is appointed unto man once to die, and after that cometh the judgment." The vital question is: Where will you spend eternity? The second parable of the chapter indicates that there are but two places in which to spend it.

the same was accused unto him.—Someone had reported to his master that he was wasting his master's goods. There must have been truth to it, for the steward immediately took steps to provide for himself when he was no longer privileged to serve his master.

render the account of thy stewardship.—The master demanded a statement of his accounts. He was to turn in a report of his stewardship since he was no longer to be steward.

Since the lesson deals with eternal life, it is well to think of it as having to do with one's relationship to God. It does not suggest that all men are dishonest in life's work; but all "must render account of the things done in the body, whether they are good or bad" (II Cor. 5:10).

I am resolved what to do.—The steward said to himself, "I do not have the strength to do hard physical labor and I am ashamed to beg. What shall I do?" Suddenly the idea struck him! "I know," he said, "I'll arrange it so they will take me in when I lose the stewardship." "They" were the ones who owed his master. This is the central idea of the parable: providing for the future.

And calling to him each of his lord's debtors.—The example of what he said to two of them is sufficient to indicate his action with reference to the rest. To the one who owed a hundred measures of oil, he said, "Take your bill and write fifty." To another who owed a hundred measures of wheat, he said, "Make it eighty." The debtors apparently entered into the dishonest deal without protest. We need not be concerned about the two words for "measure"; one of them refers to liquid and the other to dry measure. It would be difficult to determine exactly—even if there were a point in doing so—how much they represent in our measures. Neither do we know why he discounted one 50% and the other 20%. It has nothing to do with the lesson of the parable. What the steward did was enough to gain his point, making friends who would later take him into their homes. *and his lord commended the unrighteous steward.*—The master of the steward who added dishonesty to his wastefulness commended the servant because he had acted intelligently in providing for the future. It was certainly not for dishonesty that he was commended, and he had already been discharged for wastefulness.

for the sons of the world are for their own generation wiser.—These words are added as Jesus' own comment on the situation. People of this age—this life as compared to the spiritual life that extends into heaven—are wiser toward those of their generation than "the sons of light." How often the "sons of light" act unwisely! They let the things of this material world keep them from preparing for the heavenly experience. In the parable of The Sower, Jesus spoke of those who allow the cares of the world and the deceitfulness of riches to choke out the implanted Word of God. The "sons of light" should know how to please the Heavenly Father; they should know the importance of doing His will; they should be aware of the necessity of preparing for the life after death.

Make to yourselves friends by means of the mammon of unrighteousness.—"Mammon" refers to material riches. It is called "mammon of unrighteousness" because it is so often used in unrighteous ways. There is no suggestion in this expression that material wealth is in itself unrighteous. Neither is there, for that matter, any virtue in poverty in itself. It is the use to which wealth is put that determines its value.

Those women who accompanied Jesus and the apostles were, no doubt, people of some financial standing. Joseph, the man who buried the body of Our Lord, was rich. Abraham, for his day, was certainly a rich man, but he was a man of faith and looked for the city that hath foundations whose builder and maker is God.

With whom, then, are you to make friends by the proper use of wealth? Jesus indicates that it is with those who can receive you into the eternal tabernacles, heaven itself. Who are they who will receive you? The Father and the Lord Jesus Christ.

How can one use wealth to gain such an end? There are several ways in which money can be used to the glory of the Lord: (1) don't worship riches; (2) use wealth to promote the welfare of the needy (Matt. 25:40); (3) use it to promote the kingdom of God on earth (Phil. 4:41-6).

Of course, the Bible indicates that there is more to the matter of entering the heavenly tabernacles than the right attitude toward wealth. It is this plus complying with the terms of salvation under the New Covenant as set forth in the nine cases of conversion in the book of Acts. It is this plus a life that actually produces the fruit of repentance. See Gal. 5:16-24; Eph. 4:; 7:32; Col. 3:1-17; II Pet. 1:5-11. These are but a few of the many statements of Scripture on the necessity of living the Christian life. The person who does have the Scriptural view of money will, in all probability, take the other issues into consideration also.

He that is faithful in a little—The principle that is involved in this statement holds good whether one has little or much. If you have not been faithful in handling the wealth of this life, who will commit true riches to your trust? Jesus restated the principle in another form, "If you have not been faithful in that which belongs to another, who will give you what belongs to you?" This was the problem of the unrighteous steward; he was not faithful in managing his masters possession and could not expect him to give him a home after he was discharged. Is Jesus suggesting that the things of the world really do not belong to us? It seems so. Then the possession of heaven really does belong to the saints, for they are heirs of God and joint-heirs of Jesus Christ.

Ye cannot serve God and mammon.—This removes any doubt about what was commended in the steward's conduct. It was not dishonesty, but the wisdom of the dishonest servant who had the foresight to prepare for the day when riches would fail. The really wise person will see that this calls for preparation for life after death.

As a servant cannot serve two masters, Jesus said that you cannot serve God and mammon. Why try the impossible? Apparently Judas tried it, but he failed.

And the Pharisees.—Jesus had been instructing His disciples, but the Pharisees who were lovers of money heard what He said and began to scoff at His views on wealth. Literally, they turned up their noses at the idea He presented. Their disgust must have shown in some manner on their faces.

were lovers of money.—Evidently they were loving money and trying to make it appear that they also loved God at the same time. But this was impossible, for Jesus said, "You cannot serve God and mammon." They were so sure that the favor of God rested on them that the words of Jesus seemed ridiculous to them.

that which is exalted among men is an abomination in the sight of God.—The Pharisees were exalting material riches; but this was an abomination in the sight of God who knew their hearts.

The law and the prophets.—Why did Jesus mention the law and the prophets? Evidently because the Pharisees prided themselves on keeping them, but Jesus had showed how they were failing to do so. They were pretending to obey the Law of God, but, in reality, were serving material wealth.

There are several problems of interpretation in this verse. Take for example the first clause as it reads in Greek: "The law and the prophets until John." There is no verb in this clause because it is implied in the verb of the main clause. We must understand it to read, "The law and the prophets *were preached* until John; after that the gospel of the kingdom is preached." This avoids the error that assumes that the jurisdiction of the law and prophets extended only to the time of John. The facts are that it extended to Pentecost, the beginning of the jurisdiction of the New Covenant. What Jesus said, then, is that the gospel of the rule of God in the hearts of men which John preached and which He also preached held exactly the same view toward exalting material riches as the Law of Moses which forbade having any other god before the God of Israel.

What is meant by saying "Every man entereth violently into it"? This is to say that every man was attempting by force to enter the kingdom in his own way. In reality, it is impossible to force one's way into the kingdom. "No man comes to the Father but by me," said Jesus. Were the Pharisees, by setting up their own standards, trying to take over the kingdom by force? The context seems to suggest that they were. Others were also trying it. After the feeding of the five thousand, the people came to take Jesus by force and make Him their king. He prevented it by withdrawing into the mountain to pray (John 6:15). Even Peter and James and John had their own ideas of what Jesus' kingdom should be, but they couldn't persuade Him to adopt them.

A similar statement is given in Matt. 11:12, "From the days of John the Baptist until now the kingdom of heaven suffereth violence, and men of violence take it by force," that is, they were trying to do so.

But it is easier for heaven.—What God had said in His law about riches stands. Jesus lived and taught under the jurisdiction of the Law, but this principle is not changed under the New Covenant. See James 5:1-6.

Every one that putteth away his wife.—Apparently, this is another one of those things which men were advocating that was an abomination before God. Jesus said that every one who divorces his wife and marries another commits adultery, and he that marries the divorced woman commits adultery. Divorce did not end the marriage contract. The Pharisees had been scoffing at Jesus—and there are many who scoff at His teaching on divorce today—but He did not hesitate to let them know exactly what the Law of God said on the matter.

What is said on the subject of divorce in Matt. 19:3-12—if we are to assume that there is any difference between that account and this one in Luke—does not affect the teaching of the New Covenant on the issue of marriage. According to Romans 7:2 and I Corinthians 7:7. "A wife is bound for so long time as her husband liveth." Only death severs the marriage bond. Jesus made it plain that from the beginning divorce and remarriage was not a part of the plan of God. Divorce was permitted by Moses because of the "hardness of their hearts," but it was not so from the beginning. There is a serious question on which there is no uniform opinion as to whether or not remarriage was permitted by the regulation of Moses. See STUDIES IN FIRST CORINTHIANS, chapter seven, for further discussion of the problem.

Divorce is having a serious effect on the home in our time. Civil authorities are beginning to see the evil effect of it and are suggesting ways of coping with it. But the church has the answer in the Bible. It is the duty of Christian people to teach and practice what is written in the Word. It is the only way to restore the home to the original standard of God. The future of the nation and of the church demands a return to the divine regulation for the home where children may be brought up in the nurture and admonition of the Lord (Eph. 6:1-4). Divorce is not the only problem, but it is a major one.

The Rich Man and Lazarus

Scripture

16:19-31 Now there was a certain rich man, and he was clothed in purple and fine linen, faring sumptuously every day: 20 and a certain beggar named Lazarus was laid at his gate, full of sores, 21 and desiring to be fed with the crumbs that fell from the rich man's table; yea, even the dogs came and licked his sores. 22 And it came to pass, that the beggar died, and that he was carried away by the angels into Abraham's bosom: and the rich man also died, and was buried. 23 And in Hades he lifted up his eyes, being in torments, and seeth Abraham afar off, and Lazarus in his bosom. 24 And he cried and said, Father Abraham, have mercy on me, and send Lazarus, that he may dip the tip of his finger in water, and cool my tongue; for I am in anguish in this flame. 25 But Abraham said, Son, remember that thou in thy lifetime receivedst thy good things, and Lazarus in like manner evil things: but now here he is comforted, and thou art in anguish. 26 And besides all this, between us and you there is a great gulf fixed, that they that would pass from hence to you may not be able, and that none may cross over from thence to us. 27 And he said, I pray thee therefore, father, that thou wouldest send him to my father's house; 28 for I have five brethren; that he may testify unto them, lest they also come into this place of torment. 29 But Abraham saith, They have Moses and the prophets; let them hear them. 30 And he said, Nay, father Abraham: but if one go to them from the dead, they will repent. 31 And he said unto him, If they hear not Moses and the prophets, neither will they be persuaded, if one rise from the dead.

Comments

Now there was a certain rich man.—Some raise the question whether or not this is a parable in the true sense. Luke does not say that it is a parable, but it has the general characteristics of a parable and may be treated as one. This does not weaken the truth taught by

277

it nor permit us to indulge in fanciful interpretation. The flames in which the rich man found himself and the torment which he was experiencing cannot be explained away by saying that this is just a parable. In this illustration, Jesus contrasted the lives of the two men in this life and in death and after death.

and a certain beggar.—Jesus had just been warning the Pharisees about their practice of exalting the love of money above their love for God. The rich man in the parable had been doing just that. But a poor man can be guilty of doing the same thing, although it is clear that Lazarus was not.

laid at his gate.—The language does not suggest that he was gently laid at the rich man's gate; rather, it appears that he was "dropped off" in a rough manner and left to take care of himself. His condition was unbearable; his body was full of sores and his suffering was made worse by the fact that unclean dogs of the street came and licked his sores. There is no indication that his desire to eat what fell from the rich man's table was granted.

the beggar died.—Nothing is said about his funeral, but angels carried him to Abraham's bosom. This was the place of highest honor in the kingdom of heaven.

Angels are "ministering spirits sent forth to do service for the sake of those who shall inherit salvation" (Heb. 1:14). To be absent from the body is to be at home with the Lord (II Cro. 5:8). In the resurrection, the disease-ridden body of the beggar will be fashioned anew to conform to the glorious body of the Lord (Phil. 3:20).

the rich man also died, and was buried.—The contrast is striking; and after death it is even greater. Jesus said, "In Hades he lifted up his eyes, being in torments, and seeth Abraham afar off, and Lazarus in his bosom." Hades is the abode of the dead, the intermediate state between life and heaven or hell. Hades is not hell, although the wicked who are in Hades are in torment. But the righteous are in Paradise (Luke 23:43), a term equivalent to Abraham's bosom.

Peter says that Jesus was not left in Hades (Acts 2:22-36), a fact that shows that the righteous dead are in Hades but certainly not in torment.

Son remember.—There are some pertinent facts about the state of the wicked in these words of Jesus: (1) the rich man was conscious; (2) he was able to recognize Abraham and Lazarus; (3) he was in

278

torment and anguish; (4) he was able to remember his own life and that of his five brothers.

a great gulf fixed.—The chasm was fixed so that those who would cross from one side to the other could not. After death, there is no opportunity to prepare for heaven. It is true that sin separates sinner and saint in this life, but there is a way to cross it, the way of the cross of Christ. It calls for faith in Christ, repentance of sins, and baptism for the remission of sins (Acts 2:38). Those who cross from a state of sin to a state of forgiveness and remain faithful unto death will receive the crown of life (Rev. 2:10). Those who fail to continue steadfastly will be with the wicked in Hades (Acts 2:42; II Thes. 1:7-10; Heb. 3:7-4:11; II Pet. 2:20-22).

I have five brethren.—The time to have helped them was while he was living. He wanted Lazarus to go from the dead to warn them not to come where he was in that place of torment. But Abraham said, "They have Moses and the prophets; let them hear them." The Word of God gives all the necessary direction, motivation, and help that a sinner could possibly use to help him to escape the bondage of sin in this life. "The word of the cross is to them that perish foolishness, but to us who are being saved it is the power of God." If a sinner will not hear the Word, he will not be persuaded though one arise from the dead to urge him to do so. Jesus was soon to prove the point by His own resurrection.

Hardship, persecution, tragedy—these seldom produce repentance (Rev. 9:20-21; 16: 10-11). Let those who imagine that persecution such as existed in the days of the martyrs would lead to repentance ponder these Scriptures. It is the preaching of the Word that leads to repentance as men learn of the goodness of God and find their way out of the sorrow of sin, (Rom. 2:4; II Cor. 7:10).

For the teaching of the Scriptures on the second coming of Christ and the resurrection and the judgment see Heb. 9:27; John 5: 28-29; I Cor. 15:50-58; Matt. 25:31-46; Rev. 20:11-15. Death and Hades will be abolished; heaven and hell follow. See Rev. 21:1-8; 21:26-27; 22:1-5, 14-15.

Summary

The two parables of this chapter complete a series of five which begins with the three parables of grace given in chapter fifteen. The series has a common topic since the parables of grace have to do with saving the lost sinner while the parables of this chapter are about the necessity of preparing for life after death.

The parable of The Unrighteous Steward teaches the lesson of wisdom in preparing for the future. The unrighteous steward was commended by his master, not because of his dishonesty, but because he had the wisdom to prepare for the future. Jesus indicated that it is necessary to make friends by means of the mammon of unrighteousness that when it fails these friends, the heavenly Father and the Lord Jesus Christ, may receive you into the eternal home.

Jesus said, "You cannot worship God and mammon." Wisdom indictes the necessity of worshipping God in this life in order to have that eternal home in heaven.

The Pharisees who were lovers of money were listening and began to scoff at Jesus' views of wealth. He said, "The thing that is exalted by men is an abomination in the sight of God." The Pharisees were proud of their claim to be keeping the Law of Moses. Jesus reminded them that no part of it was to fall and indicated that their views on the subject of divorce contradicted what God had said on the matter.

The story of the Rich Man and Lazarus enforces the same lesson by showing what happens after death. The state of the two was not determined by riches or poverty, but by the use to which the rich man put his wealth and the manner in which Lazarus conducted himself in poverty and sickness. In Hades, the abode of the dead, the rich man lifted up his eyes and saw Lazarus in Abraham's bosom—the place of highest honor for a Jew. But the rich man was in torment, and begged that Lazarus might be sent to relieve his suffering. Abraham reminded him that in his lifetime he had enjoyed good things, but Lazarus had evil things. Besides, the chasm that separated them made it impossible to grant his request.

Then the rich man remembered his brothers and begged that someone be sent to warn them not to come to the place where he was. But Abraham said, "They have Moses and the prophets; let them hear them, for if they do not neither will they hear one from the dead."

The time to prepare for life after death is now!

Questions

1. What is there to suggest the connection between the subject of this chapter and that of the preceding one?

2. What is the subject of this series of parables?
3. Why did Jesus use the story of the dishonest steward to illustrate the necessity of preparing for life after death?
4. For what did his master commend him?
5. What do the Scriptures teach about every one giving account of his life?
6. What did the steward do when he learned that he was to lose his position?
7. Why did he have the debtors change the records?
8. In what way are the "sons of the world" wiser than the "sons of light"?
9. What does "mammon" mean? Why called "unrighteous"?
10. Can men of wealth also be men of faith?
11. How can one use wealth so as to have God's approval?
12. What did Jesus say about faithfulness in much or in little?
13. Why did He say that no man can serve two masters?
14. How did Jesus' statements about money apply to the Pharisees?
15. What were men doing that was an abomination in the sight of God?
16. Why did Jesus mention the Law and the prophets in this connection?
17. What does "the law and prophets *were* until John" mean?
18. In what way was the kingdom suffering violence?
19. What does this mean? How can one enter the kingdom?
20. How did Jesus show that the Law could not be set aside?
21. What did this have to do with the Pharisees views on divorce?
22. What does the New Covenant say about the duration of marriage?
23. What can the church do to uphold the dignity and sanctity of the home?
24. What may be said about treating the story of the Rich Man and Lazarus as a parable?
25. What similarity between the rich man and the Pharisees?
26. How did Jesus describe the condition of the beggar?
27. What happened to him when he died?
28. What service do angels render those who inherit salvation?
29. What change in the beggar's body will there be in the resurrection?
30. What does "Hades" mean?

31. What was the state of the rich man in Hades?
32. What does this story teach about recognition after death?
33. What does it teach about consciousness after death?
34. What is said about the impossibility of changing one's state after death?
35. How and where may a change of state be made?
36. What was the rich man's concern for his brothers?
37. Why was his request refused? Of what significance is this to the Christian?
38. What leads to repentance?
39. When will Hades be abolished?
40. What is to follow after that happens?

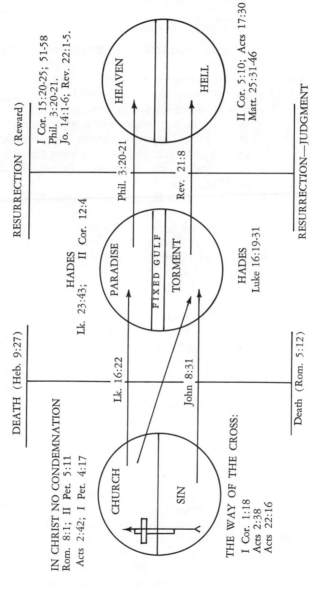

THE   FIXED   GULF

RESURRECTION (Reward)

I Cor. 15:20-25; 51-58
Phil. 3:20-21.
Jo. 14:1-6; Rev. 22:1-5.

II Cor. 5:10; Acts 17:30
Matt. 25:31-46

RESURRECTION—JUDGMENT

HEAVEN

HELL

Phil. 3:20-21

Rev. 21:8

PARADISE

FIXED GULF

TORMENT

HADES
Lk. 23:43;   II Cor. 12:4

HADES
Luke 16:19-31

DEATH (Heb. 9:27)

Lk. 16:22

John 8:31

IN CHRIST NO CONDEMNATION
Rom. 8:1; II Pet. 5:11
Acts 2:42; I Pet. 4:17

Death (Rom. 5:12)

CHURCH

SIN

THE WAY OF THE CROSS:
I Cor. 1:18
Acts 2:38
Acts 22:16

283

CHAPTER SEVENTEEN

Outline

A. Luke told about Jesus' instruction on the subject of forgiveness (1-10).
   1. The duty of His disciples to forgive (1-4).
      a) Occasions of stumbling are inevitable.
      b) Warning to the disciples in view of this.
         (1) Woe to him through whom they come.
         (2) It would be better for him to have a millstone put around his neck and be cast into the sea than to cause one of the little ones (young in faith) to stumble.
      c) What they were to do if a brother should sin.
         (1) Watch themselves.
         (2) Rebuke the brother who sins.
         (3) Forgive the brother who repents.
         (4) Forgive him even if it should happen seven times a day, if he says "I repent."
   2. The inference of His disciples that it was too much for them to obey such an order (5-10).
      a) It is implied in their request for increased faith.
      b) It is answered in Jesus' remarks:
         (1) About "faith as a grain of mustard seed."
            (a) He assumed that they had such faith.
            (b) By exercising it, they could command the tree to be unrooted and planted in the sea and it would obey them.
         (2) About the unprofitable servant.
            (a) The servant who after working all day in the field came in and served his master was not thanked because he had done what he was commanded to do.
            (b) In the same way, the disciples should treat the command to forgive; they were unprofitable servants; this was their duty.
B. Luke told about the incident of healing the ten lepers (11-19).
   1. The marvel of their being healed (11-14).
      a) It happened on their way to Jerusalem in a village in the area between Samaria and Galilee.

     b) The lepers from afar begged Jesus for mercy.

     c) He told them to go and show themselves to the priests.

     d) As they went they were cleansed.

  2. There was one, a foreigner, who returned to thank the Lord for what He had done (15-19).

     a) When he saw that he was healed, he turned back and with a loud voice glorified God and fell at Jesus feet and thanked Him.

     b) He was a Samaritan.

     c) Jesus said, "The ten were cleansed, were they not? The nine, where are they? Were there none who returned to give glory to God except this stranger?"

     d) Jesus said to him, "Arise, go your way; your faith has saved you," that is, from the plague of leprosy.

C. He told about Jesus' lesson concerning the coming of the kingdom (20-37).

  1. What He said to the Pharisees (20-21).

     a) The kingdom was not to come with observation; it could not be pointed to as being "here" or "there."

     b) "The kingdom of God is within you."

  2. What He said to His disciples (22-37).

     a) He warned about deceptive claims that would be made about His second coming (22-25).

       (1) The warning was necessary for the disciples would desire to see one of the days of the Son of Man.

       (2) They were not to follow those who would say, say, "Lo, here! Lo, there!"

       (3) They were to remember that His coming would be as clear as lightning from heaven; there would be no need to follow false reports.

       (4) He said that He must first suffer and be rejected by that generation.

     b) He told of conditions that would prevail at the time of of His coming (26-37).

       (1) It would be like the days of Noah when life went on normally until the day he entered the ark.

       (2) It would be like the days of Lot when life went on normally until God rained fire and brimstone from heaven and destroyed Sodom.

(3) It would be too late to prepare—Remember Lots' wife.

(4) It would be a time of separation.

(5) It would be where the condition existed that merited it: they asked, Where, Lord?" He answered, "Where the body is, there the eagles will be gathered together."

The Duty to Forgive

Scripture

17:1-10 And he said unto his disciples, It is impossible but that that occasions of stumbling should come; but woe unto him, through whom they come! 2 It were well for him if a millstone were hanged about his neck, and he were thrown into the sea, rather than that he should cause one of these little ones to stumble. 3 Take heed to yourselves: if thy brother sin, rebuke him; and if he repent, forgive him. 4 And if he sin against thee seven times in the day, and seven times turn again to thee, saying, I repent; thou shalt forgive him.

5 And the apostles said unto the Lord, Increase our faith. 6 And the Lord said, If ye had faith as a grain of mustard seed, ye would say unto this sycamine tree, Be thou rooted up, and be thou planted in the sea; and it would obey you. 7 But who is there of you, having a servant plowing or keeping sheep, that will say unto him, when he is come in from the field, Come straightway and sit down to meat; 8 and will not rather say unto him, Make ready wherewith I may sup, and gird thyself, and serve me, till I have eaten and drunken; and afterward thou shalt eat and drink? 9 Doth he thank the servant because he did the things that were commanded? 10 Even so ye also, when ye shall have done all the things that are commanded you, say, We are unprofitable servants: we have done that which it was our duty to do.

Comments

And he said unto his disciples.—Some assume that there is no connection between the three thoughts that follow: (1) offenses; (2) the request for increased faith; (3) the story of the unprofitable servant. It does make sense, however, to take them as a unit. Offenses are impossible to avoid, but one must forgive a brother who sins and repents even if it is seven times a day. Such an order was so astounding that the disciples said, "Lord, increase our faith." But it was not increased faith that they needed; all they needed was to obey His command to forgive. The story of the unprofitable servant illustrated this very point.

It is impossible but that occasions of stumbling should come.—Since it is impossible to avoid occasion that lead to giving offense, one must be ready always to forgive when the offender says, "I repent." To be guilty of causing another to sin is a serious offense. It would be better if one were drowned in the sea rather than suffer the consequences of causing one who is immature in the faith to sin. Sin can lead to eternal death. What awful danger and responsibility are involved in "occasions of stumbling!"

If your brother sin.—Watch out! This is a very real possibility. What are you to do to avoid the consequences of it? Two things are suggested: (1) rebuke him, and (2) forgive him.

It is wrong to let a brother go on in sin without trying to lead him to repent. James has a word to say about this: "My brethren, if any among you err from the truth, and one convert him; let him know that he who converteth a sinner from the error of his way shall save a soul from death, and shall cover a multitude of sins" (James 5:19-20).

And if he sin against thee seven times a day.—This means that there is no limit to forgivness "if he repent." The one who sins has an obligation in the matter also. If he sins, he should repent and seek forgiveness. But an unforgiving attitude on the part of the offended party could cause the sinner to be lost eternally. See II Cor. 2:5-11; Matt. 5:23-24; 18:35; Eph. 4:31-32; Col. 3:13.

Increase our faith.—The response of Jesus' disciples seems to suggest that they felt that His command was too much for them to obey. But what did they mean by the request to increase their faith? Were they suggesting that it would take a miracle to carry it out? One thing is certain: Jesus' reply indicates that all they needed was to obey His order.

If you had faith as a grain of mustard seed.—See also Matt. 17:21 where this expression is found in connection with the miracle of casting out the demon from the epileptic boy. See also Luke 9:37-45 for meaning of "faith as grain of mustard seed." The least of this faith would cause the sycamine tree to obey them. No increase in faith in connection with power to perform miracles was necessary; all they needed was simply to believe Him and show that they did

287

by obeying what He said about forgivness. This faith involves a total commitment to Christ that is intellectual, volitional, and emotional. This is the faith that takes the Lord at His word and does what He says. See it illustrated in the lives of the great men of faith as reported in Hebrews 11:1-12:2.

The reference to faith in Mark's account of healing of the epileptic boy helps us to see the difference between faith in connection with miracles and faith that is trust in the Lord. See Mark 9: 22-24. The disciples had failed to help the grief-stricken father. When Jesus arrived, he said, "If you can do anything, help us; have pity on us." Our text seems to suggest that Jesus rebuked him for saying "If you can." It is quite possible, however, that Jesus' response should be translated: "As to your suggesion, 'If you can,' why, all things are possible to the one who believes." Then the father said, "I do believe; help my unbelief." His unbelief had to do with his questioning Jesus' ability to perform the miracle. This is not the "little faith" of the disciples, for that concerned the ability on their part to perform the miracle.

Our own unbelief may need to be overcome on many occasions. It can be done by knowing what He would have us do and by a willingness to trust Him even though we may not always see the immediate outcome. Knowing what He would have us do depends on studying His revealed will, the Bible. The examples of those who have acted by faith can help to encourage us to trust the Lord. As we see in our own experience what it means to trust Him we are strengthened in our desire and determination to live the life of faith. *But who is there of you, having a servant plowing.*—This illustration shows that the disciples were under obligation to obey the command to forgive. The servant does not tell the master what he will do. Even when he has worked hard all day, he may have additional services to perform in the evening. But not even for that is he thanked, for it is his duty to do whatever his master commands. It was the duty of Jesus' disciples to do whatever He commanded them—forgive even seven times in a day—even though it might seem difficult. *Even so ye also.*—There could be no mistake about the purpose of the story: Jesus meant for them to obey His command to forgive. This was their duty, for they were like unprofitable servants. The reason which lies back of this is seen in the story of forgivness which is presented in Matt. 18:21-35. When God forgives those who sin against Him, He does so not because of duty but of grace. That puts the forgiven sinner under obligation to forgive his fellowman from the heart.

Healing the Ten Lepers

Scripture

17:11-19   And it came to pass as they were on the way to Jerusalem, that he was passing along the borders of Samaria and Galilee. 12 And as he entered into a certain village, there met him ten men that were lepers, who stood afar off: 13 and they lifted up their voices, saying, Jesus, Master, have mercy on us. 14. And when he saw them, he said unto them, Go and show yourselves unto the priests. And it came to pass, as they went, they were cleansed. 15 And one of them, when he saw that he was healed, turned back, with a loud voice glorifying God; 16 and he fell upon his face at his feet, giving him thanks: and he was a Samaritan. 17 And Jesus answering said, Were not the ten cleansed? but where are the nine? 18 Were there none found that returned to give glory to God, save this stranger? 19 And he said unto him, Arise, and go thy way: thy faith hath made thee whole.

Comments

along the borders of Samaria and Galilee.—The route He was following lay along the line that separated Samaria from Galilee. To say "through the midst" would be to suggest that He was actually going through these two provinces.

there met him ten men who were lepers.—For the subject of leprosy, see comment on the healing of the leper in 5:12-16. These men followed the law of the leper, standing afar off and calling out to Jesus for mercy.

Go show yourselves unto the priests.—This also was a part of the law of the leper. The priest was appointed to pronounce on the cure. The remarkable thing about it is that Jesus ordered them to go show themselves before they were healed. He knew, of course, that they would be cleansed as they went.

And one of them.—All ten were cleansed, but only one thought to return to give glory to God. He was a Samaritan, but he fell on his face before Jesus and thanked Him for what He had done.

Were not the ten cleansed?—The thing that puzzled Our Lord was the fact that only the Samaritan had returned to praise God and thank Him for the miraculous healing.

thy faith hath made thee whole.—Jesus said this same thing on many occasions to those whom He had healed. He believed that Christ could save him from the awful plague of leprosy; he expressed that belief by going on his way to the priest, and as he went the miracle took place.

The Coming of the Kingdom

Scripture

17:20-30   And being asked by the Pharisees, when the kingdom of God cometh, he answered them and said, The kingdom of God cometh not with observation: 21 neither shall they say, Lo, here! or, There! for lo, the kingdom of God is within you.

22 And he said unto the disciples, The days will come, when ye shall desire to see one of the days of the Son of man, and ye shall not see it. 23 And they shall say to you, Lo, there! Lo, here! go not away, nor follow after them: 24 for as the lightning, when it lighteneth out of the one part under the heaven, shineth unto the other part under heaven; so shall the Son of man be in his day. 25 But first must he suffer many things and be rejected of this generation. 26 And as it came to pass in the days of Noah, even so shall it be also in the days of the Son of man. 27 They ate, they drank,they married, they were given in marriage, until the day that Noah entered into the ark, and the flood came, and destroyed them all. 28 Likewise even as it came to pass in the days of Lot; they ate, they drank, they bought, they sold, they planted, they builded; 29 but in the day that Lot went out from Sodom it rained fire and brimstone from heaven, and destroyed them all: 30 after the same manner shall it be in the day that the Son of man is revealed.

31 In that day, he that shall be on the housetop, and his goods in the house, let him not go down to take them away: and let him that is in the field likewise not return back. 32 Remember Lot's wife. 33 Whosoever shall seek to gain his life shall lose it: but whosoever shall lose *his life* shall preserve it. 34 I say unto you, In that night there shall be two men on one bed; the one shall be taken, and the other shall be left. 35 There shall be two women grinding together; the one shall be taken, and the other shall be left. 37 And they

answering say unto him, Where, Lord? And he said unto them, Where the body *is*, thither will the eagles also be gathered together.

Comments

when the kingdom of God cometh.—It was the Pharisees who asked Him when the kingdom of God was coming. Were they sincere or were they taunting Him about a favorite subject on which He had been teaching for nearly three years? Of course, not all of the Pharisees were opposed to Him, but most of them were. Nicodemus was sincere in his desire to learn about the kingdom—some would even question this.

If they were sincere, it is evident that they didn't understand the nature of His kingdom, for Jesus had to tell them that it could not be located "here" or "there." It was not an earthly kingdom.

the kingdom of God is within you.—Some assume that this meant that the kingdom was "in their midst" as represented by the presence of Christ the King. But more likely, it had to do with the spiritual kingdom or rule of God in the hearts of those who were willing to accept Christ as their King and obey His word. The spiritual kingdom, the church, did come on the Day of Pentecost. The citizens of that kingdom do acknowledge Him as King and Savior so that He does rule in their hearts.

And he said unto his disciples.—Having answered the question of the Pharisees, Jesus turned to the disciples to instruct them on another phase of the kingdom, that is, the eternal kingdom of Our Lord and Savior Jesus Christ into which the saints will enter when He comes again. See II Pet. 1:11.

one of the days of the Son of man.—Not one of the days when He was on earth with them, but one of the days of His coming in His glorious kingdom. Just as He was to suffer before that day was to come, so they were to face persecution and even death. As this happened, they would long for the triumph of the gospel and the day of His coming; but it would not be in their day. Paul is a good example of this. See Phil. 1:23 and II Pet. 1:12-15.

And they shall say to you, Lo, there! Lo, here.—This is what false prophets and false Christs would say in order to deceive even the elect at the time of the destruction of Jerusalem. See Mat. 24: 23-24 and Luke 21:5-8.

for as the lightning.—Why shouldn't they follow those who would speak of His coming in the days of distress and longing to be with

291

Him? His answer is clear: they would not need to be deceived, for His coming will be as lightning from heaven—everybody will recognize Him when He comes. There will be no need for anyone to say, "He is there, or He is here."

He mentioned the nature of His second coming in connection with His prediction of the destruction of Jerusalem to let the disciples see the contrast between His coming and the deceptive claims of the false prophets.

must suffer many things and be rejected.—They had failed to grasp this point in His teaching because of their own mistaken notion about the nature of His kingdom. They thought of an earthly kingdom like that of David or Solomon. They dreamed of the time when the Jews would again be a nation respected and honored among the nations of the world. But His kingdom was not of this world. He refused the crown when men tried to force it upon Him, for He came to give His life a ransom for His people. He came to die on Calvary for the sins of the world. He came to conquer the devil who has power of death, and that required His death on the cross (Heb. 2:14). But death, and suffering, and pain will forever be banished from His eternal kingdom.

As it was in the days of Noah.—This refers to His second coming. It will be as sudden and unexpected as the closing of the door of the ark or the raining of fire and brimstone on Sodom.

They ate, they drank, they married, and were given in marriage.— This is often taken to mean that extreme wickedness will be a sign of His coming just as extreme wickedness prevailed before the Flood. But the point is this: Life will go on in its normal fashion right up to that day just as it had done in the days of Noah.

There is no reason to assume that eating means gluttony, or that drinking means drunkenness, or that marrying means immorality. No one denies that these sins are present today, or that they have been present in all ages of the past and probably will be when Christ comes again. But these are not signs of His coming, for that will be at an unknown time.

There were to be signs warning people of the approaching destruction of Jerusalem which came in 70 A.D. But the warning about Christ's second coming is given in His word and the word of His apostles. That warning indicates that it will be at an unknown time as life is going on in a normal fashion. That's why He said, "Watch and be ready," for no one knows when it will be.

In that day, he that shall be on the housetop.—He is still speaking of the day of His second coming. There will be no time to prepare when He comes. Now is the time to make preparation for that great event. This is clearly illustrated by the parable of The Virgins (Matt. 25: 1-13).

Remember Lot's wife.—The story is found in Gen. 19:26. Her heart was set on that wicked city even in the hour of its terrible destruction. The Christian is warned not to have his heart set on this world that will be destroyed by fire when He comes. Not even a longing glance at the world where sin did its corrupting work will be tolerated when the Lord comes. The one who seeks to preserve life as he is living it here will lose it, but the one who sets his hope on the Lord and life eternal will find it.

In that night there shall be two men in one bed.—Not only is the coming of Christ to be at an unexpected time, but it will also be at a time of separation (Matt. 25:32). Jesus dramatically pictures that time by saying, "Two men shall be sleeping in a bed; one shall be taken and the other left." "Two women shall be grinding together; one of them shall be taken and the other left." The same thought is suggested by the separating of the wheat from the tares (Matt. 13:40).

Where the body is, thither will the eagles be gathered together.—These words are also found in Matt. 24:40 where they may refer to the destruction of Jerusalem. The judgment on Jerusalem was like that of the Judgment Day, for both deal with the rejection of Christ. The words as Luke records them definitely refer to the final Judgment and the separation that will occur when He comes. The disciples had asked, "Where, Lord?" That is, "Where would this terrible thing take place?" Would it be on this earth? Would it be at the end of the age? The final separation is at the end of the age (Matt. 13:40). But of course, sin separates and brings judgment wherever it is practiced. Jesus' words seem to indicate that wherever a condition exists that merits judgment, there judgment will come.

Summary

Occasions of stumbling are inevitable, but there is a fearful penalty involved in causing the little ones who believe in Christ to fall. The brother who sins and repents is to be forgiven, even if it happens seven times a day.

This is a command that is to be obeyed. It took no miracle to do so. The disciples had been given power to perform miracles and the faith through which that power was made operative. They could even command a tree to be planted in the sea and it would obey them. They, then, as intelligent followers of Christ could obey His command to forgive. Jesus illustrated the point with the story of the servant whose duty it was to do all that his master told him to do.

As Jesus and His disciples were traveling along the route that lay along the border between Samaria and Galilee, they met ten men who were lepers. Jesus told them to go and show themselves to the priest. As they went they were healed. Only one, a Samaritan, returned to thank Him. Jesus said, "There were ten healed, were there not?" Why was it that only the Samaritan returned? Ingratitude? Jesus' language seems to indicate that it was. Their failure does emphasize the gratitude of the foreigner who came back to glorify God for what happened to him.

The Pharisees asked Jesus, "When is the kingdom coming?" They may have been taunting Him, or again they could have been sincere. He said, "It is within you." Evidently they were not submitting to God's rule or they would have known this.

This became an occasion for Jesus to teach His disciples about His second coming. As they faced persecution, they would long for the triumph of the gospel and the eternal kingdom of Our Lord and Savior, Jesus Christ. He warned them against those who would say that it is here or there, for when He comes all will know about it. But it will be at an unknown time and a time of separation. Judgment, of course, will come wherever there is a condition that merits it.

Questions

1. What is the connection between Jesus' command to forgive, the disciples request for increased faith, and the story of the unprofitable servant?
2. How often should one be forgiven?
3. On what condition is one to be forgiven?
4. What responsibility does the one who is sinned against have?
5. What does James say about the erring brother?
6. What did the disciples imply by their request for increased faith?
7. Why didn't they need to have their faith increased?
8. What did they need?

9. What may be done to help those who are weak in faith?
10. What is the lesson of the story of the unprofitable servant?
11. Why did the lepers stand afar off?
12. Why did Jesus tell them to show themselves to the priest?
13. When did their healing take place?
14. Who was the one who returned to glorify God?
15. What about the nine?
16. Explain the fact that the faith of the Samaritan made him whole.
17. Why did the Pharisees ask Jesus about the kingdom of God?
18. Why did He say that it was not "here or there"?
19. Where, then, is the kingdom?
20. Why didn't the Pharisees know this?
21. What phase of the kingdom did Jesus have in mind as He spoke to the disciples?
22. What did He mean by "one of the days of the Son of man"?
23. What would happen before that time?
24. Why were they to pay no attention to those who would say that it is "here or there"?
25. What does the reference to lightning from heaven indicate about the coming of Christ?
26. What does the reference to Noah teach about His coming?
27. What marks the difference between the destruction of Jerusalem in 70 A.D. and the second coming of Christ?
28. How did Jesus show that there will be no time to prepare when He comes?
29. Why did He say, "Remember Lot's wife"?
30. How did He show that His coming will be at a time of separation"?
31. What is meant by, "Where the body is, there will the eagles be gathered together"?

Outline

A. Luke recorded two more of Jesus' parables on prayer (1-14).
  1. The Widow and the Judge (1-8).
    a) The facts of the parable (1-5).
      (1) Its purpose: To show the disciples that they ought always to pray and not lose heart (1).
      (2) The unrighteous judge: He claimed that he neither feared God nor regarded man.
      (3) The widow: She kept coming asking that her case be heard.
      (4) The decision: Because the judge was being worn out by her persistence, he finally heard the case.
    b) The lessons of the parable (6-8).
      (1) God answers speedily: In contrast to the unrighteous judge, God will speedily avenge those who call on Him.
      (2) What about that kind of faith? "When the Son of Man comes, will He find that kind of faith on earth?"
  2. The Pharisee and the Publican (9-14).
    a) The facts of the parable (9-13).
      (1) It concerned those who were confident that they were righteous, but discredited everyone else.
      (2) The Pharisee and the publican went to the temple to pray.
        (a) The Pharisee's prayer.
          i) He stood and prayed to God.
          ii) He thanked God that he was not like the rest—extortioners, unjust, adulterers, or even as this publican.
          iii) He told God about his works: I fast twice a week; I give tithes of all I get.
        (b) The publican's prayer.
          i) He stood afar off and wouldn't lift his eyes to heaven, but beat his breast as he prayed.
          ii) Humbly, he said, "God be merciful to me the sinner."

    b) The lessons of the parable. (14)

        (1) Jesus said the publican went down to his house justified rather than the Pharisee.

        (2) He added, "Everyone who exalts himself shall be humbled, but he who humbles himself shall be exalted."

B. Luke told about parents who brought little children to Jesus (15-17).

  1. The attitude of the disciples: The disciples rebuked the parents who wanted Jesus to touch their children (15).

  2. The attitude of Jesus:

    a) He said, "Let the little children come to me and do not forbid them, for to such belongs the kingdom of heaven."

    b) Then He added, "Whoever does not receive the kingdom of God as a little child shall not enter into it."

C. Luke told about the Rich Young Ruler (18-30).

  1. His conversation with Jesus (18-23).

    a) His question: "Good teacher, what shall I do to inherit eternal life?" (18).

    b) Jesus' answer: "Why call me good; one is good—God." "You know the commandments"

        (1) Do not commit adultery.

        (2) Do not kill.

        (3) Do not steal.

        (4) Do not bear false witness.

        (5) Honor your father and mother.

    c) His response: "All these things I have observed from my youth."

    d) Jesus' challenge: "You lack one thing: sell all you have and give to the poor and you will have treasures in heaven, and come, follow me."

    e) His rejection: When he heard this, he was very sorrowful, for he was very rich.

  2. Jesus' lesson that grew out of this incident (24-30).

    a) Salvation and riches (24-27).

        (1) A difficult thing: "How hard it is for those who have riches to enter into the kingdom of God."

        (2) An impossible thing: "It is easier for a camel to go through a needle's eye than for a rich man—

      —one who makes riches his god—to enter into the kingdom of God."

      (3) All things are possible with God: "Who can be saved?" Jesus said that things that are impossible with men are possible with God.

  b) Eternal life (28-30).

      (1) The condition: Peter said, "We have left all our things and followed you."

      (2) The reward: Jesus said, "There is no man who has left house or wife or brothers or parents or children for the sake of the kingdom of God who shall not receive manifold more in this time and in the age to come, eternal life."

D. Luke told of Jesus' effort to get the twelve to become aware of what awaited Him at Jerusalem (31-34).

  1. He told them that all things the prophets had written about the Son of Man would be accomplished (31).

  2. He mentioned these things in detail (32-33).

    a) He would be delivered up to the Gentiles.

    b) He would be mocked, shamefully treated, and spit upon.

    c) He would be scourged and killed.

    d) The third day, He would arise again.

  3. The disciples understood none of what He said (34).

E. Luke told about healing the blind beggar at Jericho (35-43).

  1. The blind man's pitiful request (35-39).

    a) He heard the crowds going by and asked what it meant.

    b) He was told that it was Jesus of Nazareth.

    c) He called for mercy.

      (1) He said, "Jesus, thou son of David, have mercy on me."

      (2) The crowds told him to be quiet.

      (3) But he cried out the more and said, "Thou son of David, have mercy on me."

  2. Jesus' merciful answer (40-42).

    a) Jesus had the blind man brought to Him and asked, "What will you have me do for you?"

    b) He said, "Lord, that I may receive my sight."

    c) Jesus answered, "Receive your sight! Your faith has saved you."

3. The effect of the miracle (43).
   a) Immediately he received his sight.
   b) He followed Jesus, glorifying God.
   c) When the people saw it, they gave glory to God.

The Parable of the Widow and the Judge

Scripture

18:1-8 And he spake a parable unto them to the end that they
ought always to pray, and not to faint; 2 saying, There was in a
city a judge, who feared not God, and regarded not man: 3 and
there was a widow in that city; and she came oft unto him, saying,
Avenge me of mine adversary. 4 And he would not for a while: but
afterward he said within himself, Though I fear not God, nor regard
man; 5 yet because this widow troubleth me, I will avenge her,
lest she wear me out by her continual coming. 6 And the Lord
said, Hear what the unrighteous judge saith. 7 And shall not God
avenge his elect, that cry to him day and night, and yet he is longsuffering over them? 8 I say unto you, that he will avenge them
speedily. Nevertheless, when the Son of man cometh, shall he find
faith on the earth?

Comments

to the end that they ought always to pray.—A lesson on persistence
in prayer is the purpose of the parable. There is no reason to lose
heart simply because prayer may not be answered as soon as we
expect. There will be trials and hardships before the Lord comes
again, but that is all the more reason to keep on praying.

Some have assumed that the Lord has delayed His coming because
there has not been enough praying. Peter, however, makes it clear
that His coming is delayed because of God's long suffering; He
wants all men to come to repentance. See II Peter 3:9.

This parable does not teach the same lesson as the parable of
the Friend at Midnight (11:5-13). There the thought was: Don't
be ashamed to ask God. Here it is: Keep on praying. Both emphasize
this: God does answer prayer.

There was in the city a judge.—The wicked judge is contrasted with
the gracious heavenly Father. We miss the point of the parable if
we fail to see this contrast. The judge was about as indifferent to
the needs of others as a man could possibly be, but the Father is

299

kind and eager to help those who call on Him. The judge delayed action until he was forced to do something; the Father, as Jesus put it, will "speedily avenge" those who call on Him.

and she came oft unto him.—Again the contrast must be noted: the widow kept coming, apparently with the same request. But the heavenly Father is ready to hear the prayers of His children at all times. The only reason the wicked judge paid any attention to the widow's request was a selfish desire to be rid of her. The heavenly Father demonstrated His eagerness to help His people when He sent the Christ into the world to give help to the seed of Abraham—that is, to the men of faith (Heb. 2:16). The Lord said, "Hear what the wicked judge said"—that is, about being troubled and worn out by the widow's continual coming.

And shall not God avenge His elect.—If the unrighteous judge was willing at last to render justice in the case of the widow, certainly God will see that justice is done in the case of His chosen. The elect are the ones who choose to be members of the family of God by dedicating themselves to the Lord Jesus Christ through faith and obedience to His Word. The chosen are those who choose to accept Jesus as the Christ. All who will may make this choice for themselves (Rev. 22:17; John 3:16).

he is longsuffering over them?—God will see that His chosen ones are given just treatment before Him; He does not grow weary with their coming to Him day and night. This is the point of the parable. God is not a wicked judge nor a pevish parent that grows weary listening to the cries of His children.

he will avenge them speedily.—Some assume that Jesus was saying that His coming and judgment on the wicked were to come speedily. The lesson, however, is on prayer. Jesus was urging the disciples to pray always and not grow weary in doing so. The Father would hear them and answer their cry without waiting until the Judgment Day to do it. Christ, our high priest, is able to save completely because He lives to make intercession for us (Heb. 7:25).

Nevertheless, when the Son of man cometh.—Although God will answer their cries without delay, Jesus asks, "Will there be that kind of faith on earth when the Son of Man comes?" That is, will the elect show that kind of faith that will keep them praying without ceasing until He comes? It is a question that every disciple of Christ must ask and answer for himself.

The Pharisee and the Publican

Scripture

18:9-14 And he spake also this parable unto certain who trusted in themselves that they were righteous, and set all others at nought: 10 Two men went up into the temple to pray; the one a Pharisee, and the other a publican. 11 The Pharisee stood and prayed thus with himself, God, I thank thee, that I am not as the rest of men, extortioners, unjust, adulterers, or even as this publican. 12 I fast twice in the week; I give tithes of all that I get. 13 But the publican, standing afar off, would not lift up so much as his eyes unto heaven, but smote his breast, saying, God, be thou merciful to me a sinner. 14 I say unto you, This man went down to his house justified rather than the other: for every one that exalteth himself shall be humbled; but he that humbleth himself shall be exalted.

Comments

that they were righteous and set all others at naught.—There is no mistaking the purpose of this parable. Jesus directed it toward the self-righteous Pharisees in contrast to the humble people of His day. He was answering the claims of the Pharisees that they were the only righteous ones: they "never transgressed a commandment" of the Father. But Jesus did not hesitate to point out their sins. A pharisaical attitude is so easy to acquire. It should be shunned, however, for it is sinful. Could there be any worse place to display it than in prayer?

The Pharisee stood and prayed.—His prayer was about himself. There are two topics in the prayer: (1) his moral integrity, and (2) his religious activity. As to his morality, he thanked God that he was not like others who were extortioners, unjust, adulterers, or even like that publican who was also in the temple, praying. As to his religious devotion, he reminded God that he did fast twice a week and that he gave tithes of all he got. He was evidently satisfied with himself, a perfect example of self-righteousness.

But the publican.—What a contrast he presented! He stood afar off and would not lift up so much as his eyes to heaven. He presented a perfect example of humility: he knew that he was a sinner. He also knew, as he beat his breast and prayed, "God be merciful to me *the* sinner," that the Pharisee was talking about him. While it may be quite easy for one to assume a parisaical attitude,

301

it is never easy to say, "I am a sinner." The Bible record mentions a few who did: Saul, David, Peter, Judas, and Paul. Too often, real humility is absent when we ask God for mercy.

be thou merciful to me.—God's mercy that pardons the guilty is available through Jesus Christ who died for all. The publican's spirit of humility is necessary on the part of all who would receive that mercy. Jesus said that he went down to his house pardoned rather than the other one. Then He added, "Everyone that exalteth himself shall be humbled; but he that humbleth himself shall be exalted."

Bringing Babes to Jesus

Scripture

18:15-17　　And they were bringing unto him also their babes, that he should touch them: but when the disicples saw it, they rebuked them. 16 But Jesus called them unto him, saying, Suffer the little children to come unto me, and forbid them not: for to such belongeth the kingdom of God. 17 Verily I say unto you, Whosoever shall not receive the kingdom of God as a little child, he shall in no wise enter therein.

Comments

bringing unto him also their babes.—There is nothing in this incident that supports the practice of infant baptism or the substitute for it, infant dedication. It does show that parents were concerned about their children and wanted Jesus to touch them. The desire to have Him pray for them was perfectly natural. See Matt. 9:13-15. They had seen the effect of His healing hand on the blind, the lame, and the sick. They wanted His blessing to be on their children—a thing that any parent who knows Him would want.

Parents are instructed to bring up their children in the "nurture and admonition of the Lord" (Eph. 6:4). Responsibility rests on them to see that their children have the opportunity to learn about the Lord Jesus and the blessing He has for all who walk in the light of His Word. This calls for parents to dedicate themselves to the Lord and to follow His instruction for child-training, including the example they should set in Christian living.

they rebuked them.—It is strange that the disciples should think that Jesus was not interested in children or that He did not have time for them. The Old Testament speaks of the importance of training the child in the way of the Lord (Deut. 6:6-7; Prov. 22:6). Timothy is a good example of the effectiveness of such training (II Tim. 1:5; 3:14). Taking children to Sunday school is a poor substitute for parental responsibility in religious training of children. The Sunday school performs a much needed task, but is not designed to relieve parents of their responsibility. Too often what little religious instruction there is in the home is left to the mother, while it should be the responsibility of both parents. The home with the help of the church should be able to give every child a good foundation in Bible knowledge. Children who have the advantage of such instruction will probably love the Lord just as much as they did in the day when He laid His hands on the little children.

Suffer the little children to come unto me.—Jesus turned the rebuke upon the disciples and told them to let the children come to Him. He said, "Do not forbid them for to such belongs the kingdom of God."

Whosoever shall not receive the kingdom as a little child.—This implies the necessity of purity and trust on the part of those who would enter the kingdom. This is true of the heavenly kingdom, and it is true of the earthly phase of Christ's kingdom, the church. That's why sinners are commanded to repent and be baptized for the remission of their sins in order to enter the body of Christ, the church.

The Rich Young Ruler

Scripture

18:18-30 And a certain ruler asked him, saying, Good Teacher, what shall I do to inherit eternal life? 19 And Jesus said unto him, Why callest thou me good? none is good, save one, even God. 20 Thou knowest the commandments, Do not commit adultery, Do not kill, Do not steal, Do not bear false witness, Honor thy father and mother. 21 And he said, All these things have I observed from my youth up. 22 And when Jesus heard it, he said unto him, One thing thou lackest yet: sell all that thou hast, and distribute unto the poor, and thou shalt have treasure in heaven: and come, follow me. 23 But when he heard these things, he became exceeding sorrowful; for he was very rich. 24 And Jesus seeing him said, How hardly shall they that have riches enter into the kingdom of God! 25 For it is easier for a camel to enter in through a needle's eye, than for a rich man to enter the kingdom of God. 26 And they that heard it said, Then who can be saved? 27 But he said, The things which are impossible with men are possible with God. 28 And Peter said, Lo, we have left our own, and followed thee. 29 And he said unto them, Verily I say unto you, There is no man that hath left house, or wife, or brethren, or parents, or children, for the kingdom of God's sake, 30 who shall not receive manifold more in this time, and in the world to come eternal life.

Comments

And a certain ruler.—The account of the Rich Young Ruler is given in all three synoptic gospels. Matthew calls him a young man, probably in his thirties. As a ruler he would have responsibilities that called for some maturity. References to age are usually relative and should be understood in their context.

There can be no question about the sincerity of this young man, for Mark says that he ran to Jesus and knelt before Him and asked Him, "Good Teacher, what shall I do that I may inherit eternal life?" See Mark 10:17.

Why callest thou me good?—Jesus' question pointed to the only source of eternal life. He added, "No one is good except One, even God." The answer to the question of eternal life cannot be separated from God. Jesus, who answered the question, is clearly identified with Him. It is doubtful if the ruler was able to see through this. But it becomes clear as the conversation progresses.

Thou knowest the commandments.—Eternal life, since they were under the Old Covenant, depended on keeping the commandments (Lev. 18:5; Gal. 3:12; Rom. 10:5). For the answer to the question under the New Covenant, see Acts 2:26-42 and the other cases of conversion recorded in the Book of Acts.

Then Jesus recited the commandments, mentioning five of the six that have to do with man's duties to man and significantly leaving out those that had to do with duties to God. The young man said, "I have done all these since I was a boy." Except for his own word, we have no way of knowing whether he had or not. But Jesus did not question his statement; He seems to to have accepted it at face value. It was not impossible for him to do what God commanded, even though theologians through the centuries have said that man is incapable of doing such a thing.

304

One thing thou lackest.—There were two tables of the law. The first said, "Thou shalt have no other gods before me." It is quite evident that the ruler had neglected to observe this first table of the Law. What was the god he was worshipping instead of the Lord God under whose covenant he was living?

Jesus said, "Sell everything you have; distribute it to the poor, and you will have treasures in heaven, and come follow me." He made the issue clear: the young ruler was worshipping gold rather than God. He had to remove the false god and follow the Lord Jesus. Now we see why Jesus asked, "Why do you call me good? Only God is good."

When he heard these things.—A storm cloud swept over his face like the dark clouds that blot out the light of the sun. The price was too great, for he was very rich. Although Jesus loved him for his clean life, He could not offer eternal life at a discount (Mark 10:21).

And Jesus seeing him.—The struggle that went on in the young man's soul was plain for Jesus to see. He said, "With what difficulty those who have riches enter into the kingdom of God!" His problem was in putting God first in his life. He made the fatal decision to let gold be first.

It is easier for a camel.—Jesus was speaking of a literal camel and a literal needle's eye; to assume otherwise is to ruin the lesson Jesus taught. The ruler was making gold his god; that made it impossible for him to enter the kingdom of God.

Who then can be saved?—Man cannot save himself, not even with all his gold. But God can save the one who turns to Him by obeying His commands.

Lo, we have left our own, and followed thee.—Peter was quick to respond in face of the refusal of the rich ruler to comply with Jesus' demands. He said, "We have left our things, and have followed you." According to Matthew, he added, "What then shall we have?" They were far from being unselfish in following Jesus. Their dream of an earthly kingdom had much to do with it.

for the kingdom of God's sake.—Jesus said that anyone—not just the Rich Ruler—who has left possessions or family for the sake of the kingdom of God will receive many times more in this life, and in the age to come eternal life.

Matthew also adds these words of Jesus: "But many shall be last that are first and first that are last." See Matt. 19:30. Jesus illustrated

His meaning with the parable of the Laborers in the Vineyard. At the end of the day, all received exactly the same amount—not as wages but as the gift of the master. As He closed the parable, Jesus repeated the words, "So the last shall be first, and the first last" (Matt. 20:16). This suggests that the story of the Rich Ruler, Peter's question about the reward of the apostles, and the parable of the Vineyard constitute three phases of Jesus' lesson on eternal life. It is not a question of rich or poor, apostle or other worker, for all who follow Christ and serve Him faithfully will have the same gift, eternal life.

The work of the apostles in the kingdom was different, for they were to sit on twelve thrones judging the twelve tribes of Israel, but the reward was no greater than for the least in the kingdom. See Luke 22:30 for further discussion of meaning of judging the twelve tribes of Israel.

What Awaited Jesus at Jerusalem

Scripture

18:31-34   And he took unto him the twelve, and said unto them, Behold, we go up to Jerusalem, and all the things that are written through the prophets shall be accomplished unto the Son of man. 32 For he shall be delivered up unto the Gentiles, and shall be mocked, and shamefully treated, and spit upon: 33 and they shall scourge and kill him: and the third day he shall rise again. 34 And they understood none of these things; and this saying was hid from them, and they perceived not the things that were said.

Comments

Behold we go up to Jerusalem.—Jesus had already warned the apostles that He had to die at Jerusalem, but they were unable to fit the cross into their own views of His kingdom. As they neared the city, He again attempted to get them to understand what awaited Him there.

all the things that are written through the prophets.—He was (1) to be delivered to the Gentiles, (2) mocked, (3) shamefully treated, (4) spit upon, (5) scourged, and (6) killed. On the third day, He would rise again.

they understood none of these things.—They didn't understand because their view of the kingdom required Him to be on an earthly throne. Actually, it was not until the Day of Pentecost that they understood His death and resurrection. When they knew that He had sat down at the right hand of the throne of God, they understood what He had tried to tell them about His kingdom.

Healing the Blind Beggar

Scripture

18:35-43 And it came to pass, as he drew nigh unto Jericho, a certain blind man sat by the way side begging: 36 and hearing a multitude going by, he inquired what this meant. 37 And they told him, that Jesus of Nazareth passeth by. 38 And he cried, saying, Jesus, thou son of David, have mercy on me. 39 And they that went before rebuked him, that he should hold his peace: but he cried out the more a great deal, Thou son of David, have mercy on me. 40 And Jesus stood, and commanded him to be brought unto him: and when he was come near, he asked him, 41 What wilt thou that I should do unto thee? And he said, Lord, that I may receive my sight. 42 And Jesus said unto him, Receive thy sight: thy faith hath made thee whole. 43 And immediately he received his sight, and followed him, glorifying God: and all the people, when they saw it, gave praise unto God.

Comments

a certain blind man.—This incident is also reported in Matt. 20:29-43 and Mark 10:64-52. According to Matthew, there were two blind men sitting by the wayside; Mark and Luke mention only one of them. Mark gives his name, Bartimaeus. Mark begins his account "as they come to Jericho," indicates that the miracle occurred as "He went out from Jericho." Matthew tells only what happened as they went out from Jericho. Luke did not see fit to explain at what point the miracle actually took place. He begins his next story, the one about Zacchaeus the Publican, by saying that "He entered in and was passing through Jericho." The exact place where He met Zacchaeus or where He healed Bartimaeus does not seem to be important to him. The miracle that opened the eyes of one man and the message of salvation that changed the life of another are the things of real importance.

A number of solutions to the problem of harmony between the accounts have been suggested. They show that while the data are limited there is no need to assume that a contradiction exists. The answer to the problem may lie in the history of Jericho. Archaeology sheds some light on that history. What appears to be a problem to us may have been no problem whatever to the writers of the Gospels.

hearing the multitude.—The crowds informed Bartimaeus that Jesus was passing by. He must have known about Him, for he cried out, "Son of David, have mercy on me." "Son of David" is equivalent to "Messiah," for all knew that the Christ was to be the son of David. His confession was about the same as that of Peter or Nathaniel. See Matt. 16:16; John 1:49.

And they that went before him rebuked him.—This harsh attitude of the crowds is in sharp contrast with the mercy of Jesus. Jesus was ready to listen to his amazing request: "Lord, that I may receive my sight." That, of course, was asking for a miracle. He evidently believed that Jesus could do this for him. Jesus said, "Receive your sight." In these brief words, the miracle of opening the eyes of a blind man is described by the gospel writers. Jesus added, "Your faith has saved you"—that is, from blindness. Distressed people have believed the claims of quacks, but no miracle results from their belief no matter how sincere it may be. The power to perform the mircale was exercised by Jesus to prove His right to be called, "Son of David," that is "Messiah." See John 20:30-31.

And immediately.—This is the sign of a genuine miracle. He received his sight, followed Jesus, and glorified God. The crowds that had told him to be quiet were now ready to praise God also.

Summary

Luke's emphasis on the prayer life of Jesus is seen in two more parables which are given in this chapter. The parable of the Widow and the Judge was given to teach the disciples that they ought always to pray and never lose heart. Will the Son of Man find that kind of faith on earth when He comes again?

The parable of the Pharisee and the Publican reveals the necessity of humility on the part of these who pray to God for mercy.

In the busy ministry of Jesus, the disciples tried to keep parents from bringing their children to Jesus that He might touch them and bless them. But Jesus took this as an occasion to teach the important lesson that it is necessary to receive the kingdom of God in the spirit of the little child. Without that purity and trust, no one could enter the kingdom.

The story of the Rich Young Ruler presents another lesson on the theme of Eternal Life. The young man ran to Jesus and knelt before Him and asked, "Good Teacher, what shall I do to have eternal life?" When Jesus told him to keep the commandments, quoting those that had to do with man's duties to man, he said, "I have done this since I was a boy." But there was one thing that he lacked, his duty to God. He was a man of great wealth; gold was evidently his god. Jesus told him to sell all and he would have treasures in heaven. Then He added, "Come, follow me." What he needed was to worship Jesus as Lord, not gold. There is no other possible way for man to have eternal life. The apostles had left all to follow Him. Jesus said that in this life they would have manifold more and in the age to come they would have eternal life.

Luke significantly followed the lesson on eternal life with Jesus' effort to get His disciples to become aware of what was to happen to Him in Jerusalem. All that the prophets had written about Him was to be accomplished. He was to be put to death and on the third day rise again in order that those who believe on Him might have eternal life.

The chapter closes with the miracle of opening the eyes of the blind beggar. The scene was at Jericho. Crowds were following the Lord. The blind man heard them passing by and asked who it was. When he learned that it was Jesus, he called out for Him to have mercy on him. When his sight was restored, he followed Jesus and glorified God.

Questions

1. What suggestion is there that this chapter continues the thought of the preceding one.
2. What is the purpose of the parable of the Widow and the Judge?
3. How does it differ from the lesson taught by the parable of the Friend at Midnight?
4. Why is the Coming of Christ delayed?
5. What contrast is there between the wicked judge and the heavenly Father?
6. What lesson is taught by the fact that the widow kept coming to the judge with her plea?

7. What caused the judge to finally hear her?
8. What has this to do with prayer?.
9. Who are the elect? How do they become the chosen of God?
10. What did Jesus say about the longsuffering of God?
11. What did He say about the manner in which He responds to the pleas of His chosen ones?
12. What do the Scriptures teach about Jesus' work as high priest?
13. How are we to understand Jesus' question, "When the Son of man cometh, shall he find faith on the earth?"
14. How is the question to be answered?
15. What is the lesson taught by the parable of the Pharisee and the Publican?
16. To what class of people did Jesus direct this parable?
17. What did the Pharisee think of himself? What bearing does this have on the references to the Pharisees in chapter fifteen?
18. What contrast did Jesus make between the Pharisee and the publican?
19. What is there that shows that the publican was aware of the attitude of the Pharisee toward him?
20. How is his humility shown?
21. What does the Bible say of those whose confessions of sin are recorded in it?
22. Why was the publican pardoned?
23. What lesson did Jesus teach from this parable?
24. Why did the parents bring their babes to Jesus?
25. Why did the disciples rebuke them for doing so?
26. What is the responsibility of parents in the matter of religious training? of the church?
27. According to the Old Testament, who was responsible for teaching the Law of God to the children?
28. From whom did Timothy learn about the sacred writings?
29. What should be the relation between the home and the church in child training?
30. What did Jesus mean by saying that "to such belongs the kingdom of God"?
31. Why are sinners told to repent and be baptized to enter the body of Christ, the church?
32. What do the three accounts reveal about the story of the Rich Young Ruler?
33. What may be said about his age?
34. What did he call Jesus?

35. Why did Jesus challenge this remark?
36. What did Jesus mean by saying, "No one is good except One."
37. Why did Jesus quote only the commandments that had to do with man's duties to man?
38. What did the young ruler lack?
39. What did he have to do to overcome it?
40. What did Jesus mean by the reference to a camel and a needle's eye?
41. What did Peter say when he heard Jesus' remarks about the rich?
42. What is the meaning of Jesus' words, "Many shall be last that are first and first that are last"?
43. Why did Jesus call attention to the things that were to happen to Him at Jerusalem?
44. Why didn't the disciples understand?
45. What are the facts about the miracle of healing the blind beggar as given in all three synoptic gospels?
46. Why didn't Luke state exactly where it took place?
47. Why did the beggar call Jesus "Son of David"?
48. What was the attitude of the crowd toward the beggar?
49. What was implied in his request that he might receive his sight?
50. What did his faith have to do with the miracle?

CHAPTER NINETEEN

Outline

A. Luke recorded the story of Zacchaeus the Publican (1-10).
  1. His desire to see Jesus (1-4).
      a) Jesus was passing through Jericho.
      b) Zacchaeus was a chief publican, and rich.
      c) Being small of stature, he ran ahead of the crowd and climbed up into a sycamore tree.
  2. Jesus in the house of Zacchaeus (5-7).
      a) When Jesus saw him, He said, "Hurry and come down, for I must stay at your house today."
      b) Zacchaeus welcomed him with joy.
      c) The people criticized Him, saying, "He has gone in to lodge with a man who is a sinner."
  3. The effect of Jesus presence in the home of Zacchaeus (8-10).
      a) Zacchaeus said, "Behold, Lord, half of my goods I give to the poor; and if I have defrauded anyone, I restore it fourfold."
      b) Jesus said, "Today is salvation come to this house, since he is also a son of Abraham."
      c) Then He added, "For the Son of man came to seek and to save that which was lost."

B. Luke recorded the Parable of the Pounds (11-27).
  1. The occasion: He was near Jerusalem, and some supposed that the kingdom of God was to appear immediately (11).
  2. The nobleman who was to receive a kingdom (12-14).
      a) He went to a far country to receive a kingdom and to return.
      b) He gave his servants ten pounds and said, "Trade with these until I come."
      c) His citizens hated him and sent a delegation to say, "We won't have this man reigning over us."
  3. What happened when the nobleman returned (15-27).
      a) The accounting by the servants (15-26).
          (1) One had gained ten pounds and was given authority over ten cities.

      (2) Another gained five pounds and was put over five cities.

      (3) One gained nothing:

          (a) He made the excuse that he was afraid and uttered false charges against his master.

          (b) But the king showed how he could have at least returned the money with interest.

          (c) His pound was given to the one who had ten.

      (4) The principle involved: "To every one who has gained, there shall be given more; but from the one who has no increase, even what he has shall be taken away."

  b) The death sentence for those who refused to have him as their king (27).

C. Luke gave the account of the Triumphal Entry (28-40).

  1. The preparation (28-35).

    a) Time: After He had spoken the parable of the Pounds, as He was going on to Jerusalem (28).

    b) Place: Near Bethphage and Bethany (29).

    c) Action: The disciples bring a colt for Him to ride on (30-35).

      (1) They told the owner that the Lord had need of the colt.

      (2) They threw their garment on the colt, and Jesus sat on him.

  2. The welcome (36-38).

    a) They spread their garments on the way.

    b) At the descent of the mount of Olives, the crowd praised God saying, "Blessed is the King that cometh in the name of the Lord; peace in heaven and glory in the highest."

  3. The complaint (39-40).

    a) The Pharisees said, "Teacher, rebuke your disciples."

    b) He said, "I tell you, if they become silent the stones will cry out."

D. Luke told about Jesus' lament over Jerusalem (41-44).

  1. When He saw the city, He wept over it (41).

  2. He said, "If you had known the things that make for peace! But now they are hid from your eyes."

  3. What would happen to the city (43-44).

         a) It would be besieged by the enemy.
         b) Its people would be dashed to the ground.
         c) Its building would be destroyed.
     4. All this, because they did not know the time of their visitation (44).
E. Luke told about the cleansing of the Temple (45-48).
     1. The temple cleansed (45-46).
         a) He drove the merchants out.
         b) He said, "It is written, My house shall be a house of prayer, but you have made it a den of robbers."
     2. The Teacher threatened (47-48).
         a) He was teaching daily in the temple.
         b) The chief priests, the scribes, and the principal men of the people sought a way to destroy Him.
         c) They were unable to do so for all the people were hanging on His words listening to Him.

Zacchaeus the Publican

Scripture

19:1-10   And he entered and was passing through Jericho. 2 And behold, a man called by name Zacchaeus; and he was a chief publican, and he was rich. 3 And he sought to see Jesus who he was; and could not for the crowd, because he was little of stature. 4 And he ran on before, and climbed up into a sycomore tree to see him: for he was to pass that way. 5 And when Jesus came to the place, he looked up, and said unto him, Zacchaeus, make haste, and come down; for to-day I must abide at thy house. 6 And he made haste, and came down, and received him joyfully. 7 And when they saw it, they all murmured, saying, He is gone in to lodge with a man that is a sinner. 8 And Zacchaeus stood, and said unto the Lord, Behold, Lord, the half of my goods I give to the poor; and if I have wrongfully exacted aught of any man, I restore fourfold. 9 And Jesus said unto him, To-day is salvation come to this house, forasmuch as he also is a son of Abraham. 10 For the Son of man came to seek and to save that which was lost.

Comments

Jericho.—The place of the healing of the blind man (18:35) and location of the story of the Good Samaritan (10:30). For its Old

Testament history, see Joshua 2:1; 6:1-2, 26-27; I Kings 16:34. For its later history, see Bible Dictionaries and works on Archaeology.

Zacchaeus, and he was a chief publican.—Luke made his story of the Life of Christ live by giving names of people and places and by showing the Lord in action as He dealt with all kinds of people.

Zacchaeus was a chief publican, and rich. He probably had other tax collectors working under him. Tax collectors were generally thought to have gotten their wealth by abuse of their office.

he sought to see Jesus.—We do not know why; perhaps he had heard of Jesus' attitude toward publicans. Being a little man, he was unable to catch a glimpse of Jesus because of the crowds. He didn't let his handicap keep him for realizing his desire; he made up for it by extra effort. He ran on before the crowd and climbed up into a sycamore tree in order to see Jesus as He passed by. There is no indication that he even thought of Jesus looking up and seeing him.

today I must abide at thy house.—Did Luke abbreviate the story, or did Jesus speak abruptly as the record shows? He was very busy, but was never discourteous or offensive in His approach to people. See 14:7-14. It may be that Zacchaeus' own interest was so evident that nothing more needed to be said. Jesus went directly to the point and told him that He was to stay in his house that day. Zacchaeus was delighted, but the crowds were critical because He was going in to lodge in the house of a publican. But Jesus openly and boldly identified Himself with this one in need of salvation, this one whom the crowds designated a sinner.

Lord, behold, Lord.—Many other words may have been spoken by Jesus and Zacchaeus, but Luke reported the essentials of the story. The words of Zacchaeus are significant; they acknowledge Jesus as Lord, meaning far more than words of polite address. The gift of his goods to the poor was indicative of a change that had taken place because of the presence of Jesus, not only in his house, but also in his heart.

if I have wrongfully exacted aught.—"If" does not suggest that there was any doubt about it. He knew that he had cheated and used pressure because of his office to get his wealth. Now he must make restitution, a sure sign of repentance.

To-day is salvation come to this house.—The Savior had sought and found another lost sinner. Salvation had come to Zacchaeus for he was a son of Abraham—a Jew, yes, but more than that, he was a believer in the Lord Jesus Christ. See John 8:31-44 for Jesus' comment about those who are truly Abraham's children.

For the Son of man came to seek and save that which was lost.— Jesus had already successfully defended His ministry against the false charges of the Pharisees that He was receiving sinners (15: 1-32). Now He is proving the correctness of His position by actually rescuing this publican, "a man that is a sinner," from his lost estate.

Today is still "the day of salvation." The church which is the body of Christ should be following the example of Christ in seeking and saving the lost sinner. This is its first business in the world until Christ comes again.

The Parable of the Pounds

Scripture

19:11-27   And as they heard these things, he added and spake a parable, because he was nigh to Jerusalem, and because they supposed that the kingdom of God was immediately to appear. 12 He said therefore, A certain nobleman went into a far country, to receive for himself a kingdom, and to return. 13 And he called ten servants of his, and gave them ten pounds, and said unto them, Trade ye herewith till I come. 14 But his citizens hated him, and sent an ambassage after him, saying, We will not that this man reign over us. 15 And it came to pass, when he was come back again, having received the kingdom, that he commanded these servants, unto whom he had given the money, to be called to him, that he might know what they had gained by trading. 16 And the first came before him, saying, Lord, thy pound hath made ten pounds more. 17 And he said unto him, Well done, thou good servant: because thou wast found faithful in a very little, have thou authority over ten cities. 18 And the second came, saying, Thy pound, Lord, hath made five pounds. 19 And he said unto him also, Be thou also over five cities. 20 And another came, saying, Lord, behold, here is thy pound, which I kept laid up in a napkin: 21 for I feared thee, because thou art an austere man: thou takest up that which thou layedst not down, and reapest that which thou didst not sow. 22 He saith unto him, Out of thine own mouth will I judge thee, thou wicked servant. Thou knewest that I am an austere man, taking up that which I laid not down, and reaping that which I did not sow; 23 then wherefore gavest thou not my money into the bank, and I at my coming should have required it with interest? 24 And he said unto them that stood by, Take away from him the pound, and give it unto him that hath the ten pounds. 25 And they said unto him, Lord, he hath ten pounds. 26 I say unto you, that unto every one that hath shall be given; but from him that hath not, even that which he hath shall be taken away from him. 27 But these mine enemies, that would not that I should reign over them, bring hither, and slay them before me.

Comments

And as they heard these things.—The crowds that saw Jesus go into the house of Zacchaeus heard what He said about seeking and saving the lost. This was the occasion for further instruction about the kingdom of God and the work that the King expected His servants to be doing until He comes again.

The two reasons for the parable are: (1) The fact that He was near Jerusalem; and (2) the supposition of the people that the kingdom of God was to appear immediately. The anticipation of the people must have increased to the point of excitement as Jesus neared the city. He had made it clear for several months that His goal was Jerusalem. The climax of His ministry was soon to occur. When John the Baptist began his ministry, the people were expecting some momentous thing to happen. The impact of three years of Jesus' teaching about the kingdom must have raised their hopes to the point that they supposed that it was soon to appear. Perhaps they were asking themselves, "Is this the time when He will restore the kingdom to Israel?

It is strange that they didn't understand what He had repeatedly taught: He was going to die at Jerusalem, giving His life as a ransom for the many (Mark 10:45). But not even the disciples who were closest to Him understood it (Acts 1:6).

to the many mistaken notions which the people had about the
He said therefore.—The Parable of the Pounds was Jesus' answer
nature of the kingdom of God.
A certain nobleman went into a far country.—As Jesus began the parable, He made it clear that He, like the nobleman, must go into a far country to receive His kingly authority and return. This, we know from the events that followed, meant that He was about to be put to death at Jerusalem, arise from the dead, and ascend to the

317

right hand of the throne of God. For the history of this beginning of His kingdom see Acts 1:6-11; 2:29-36, 38-42.

On the Day of Pentecost, the apostles under the control of the Holy Spirit announced to the crowds that "God had made him both Lord and Christ," fulfilling the promise to David that He would set one on his throne forever.

Many who followed Him to Jerusalem were disappointed that their views of the kingdom were not realized, but three thousand people on the Day of Pentecost did accept His rule in their hearts. They got themselves baptized for the remission of their sins and continued steadfastly in the apostles' teaching and fellowship, in breaking of bread and prayers.

And he called ten servants.—While the nobleman was away his servants were to be busy performing the tasks he had assigned them.

As the nobleman clearly represents Christ the King, so the servants .represent all of those who accept His authority and are busy doing His will. They have a task to perform while He is away. Just before He left, He told His followers to take the gospel into all the world, make disciples and baptize them, and teach them to observe all that He had commanded. See Acts 1:8; Mark 16:15-16; Matt. 28:18-20.

The task is two-fold: (1) Evangelize and (2) educate. Evangelize means that they are to seek and save the lost; educate means that they are to teach new converts to observe all that Christ has commanded. This program is to be carried on by each succeeding generation of His followers until He comes again. See II Tim. 2:1-2. He has sent no other orders.

But his citizens hated him.—The citizens are not the same as the servants who were told to trade with the ten pounds while he was away. Jesus identified them as enemies (27). They sent a delegation to say that they wouldn't have Him as their king. They were the citizens of the kingdom that had failed in its mission. They were the enemies who crucified the Son of God. See Psa. 89:3-4; Lk 1:32; Acts 2:22-36.

While this is a direct reference to the Jews who crucified Jesus, there is no difference between them and any others who are guilty of rejecting Him as Lord; their punishment will be the same (II Thes. 1:8-10; I Cor. 15:25-26).

And it came to pass, when he came back.—This points to the second coming, for Christ is coming again! Heb. 9:27-28; I Thes. 4:14-15; Acts 1:10-11.

He had already indicated that His coming would be at a time of judgment (17:22-23). The Parable of the Pounds and the Parable of the Talents (Matt. 25:14-30), which is similar to it in many ways, give interesting details about the judgment which will take place when He comes again.

having received the kingdom.—He received the kingdom while he was away, not after he returned. This is true of Christ: When He went away He sat down at the right hand of the throne of God where He reigns as King; when He comes again He will sit on the throne of His glory as Judge, separating the "sheep from the goats." It will be too late to accept Him as King when He returns as Judge. Now is time to confess Him before men as Lord and Christ.

And the first came before him.—The reward of the king was for the faithful who had discharged their duties while awaiting his return. The one who gained ten pounds was given authority over ten cities. This clearly represents what Christ will do when He returns, for "each one will receive the things done in the body, according to what he hath done, whether it be good or bad" (II Cor. 5:10).

Lord, here is thy pound.—The unfaithful one was also unreasonable; he could have put the money in the bank that it might, with interest, be presented to the king when he returned. Evidently, Christ will accept no excuse for not doing what He has told us to do, whether our ability be great or small.

Out of thine own mouth will I judge thee.—What the wicked servant said against his master was not true; neither did it justify his failure to make the very best use of the talent that had been given to him. Condemning Christ does not excuse the church for failure to perform the task which He left for it to do.

unto every one who has.—To every one who has gained by using his talent, more will be given; but for the one who has no increase to show, even what he had—the opportunity to serve—will be taken away when the Lord comes again.

But these mine enemies.—They were to be slain because they had refused to have him as king. The Jews rejected their King; Jerusalem suffered unbelievable destruction because of it, and in the Judgment all who reject Him as King by refusing to have Him rule in their hearts will suffer even greater punishment.

slay them before me.—Some assume that the gentle Jesus and the loving heavenly Father would never do such a thing, but Jesus said it will happen. Our God is a consuming fire to those who refuse to

319

obey Him (Heb. 12:29). Satan and all those who insist on serving him will be destroyed (Rev. 20:10, 15).

The Triumphal Entry

Scripture

19:28-40   And when he had thus spoken, he went on before, going up to Jerusalem.

29 And it came to pass, when he drew nigh unto Bethphage and Bethany, at the mount that is called Olivet, he sent two of the disciples, 30 saying, Go your way into the village over against you; in which as ye enter ye shall find a colt tied, whereon no man ever yet sat: loose him, and bring him. 31 And if any one ask you, Why do ye loose him? thus shall ye say, The Lord hath need of him. 32 And they that were sent went away, and found even as he had said unto them. 33 And as they were loosing the colt, the owners thereof said unto them Why loose ye the colt? 34 And they said, The Lord hath need of him. 35 And they brought him to Jesus: and they drew their garments upon the colt, and set Jesus thereon. 36 And as he went, they spread their garments in the way. 37 And as he was now drawing nigh, even at the descent of the mount of Olives, the whole multitude of the disciples began to rejoice and praise God with a loud voice for all the mighty works which they had seen; 38 saying, Blessed is the King that cometh in the name of the Lord: peace in heaven, and glory in the highest. 39 And some of the Pharisees from the multitude said unto him, Teacher, rebuke thy disciples. 40 And he answered and said, I tell you that, if these shall hold their peace, the stones will cry out.

Comments

going up to Jerusalem.—Jesus frequently reminded the disciples that He was going to Jerusalem where He would bring His earthly ministry to its climax.

when he drew nigh to Bethphage and Bethany.—Little is known about Bethphage except that the word means "house of figs," and that it was near Bethany.

Bethany———"house of affliction" or, according to some, "house of dates"—is well known as the home of Mary and Martha, sisters of Lazarus. Jesus stayed at their home when He was in that area (10:

38-42; John 12:1). It was located on the southeast slope of the mount of Olives a short distance from Jerusalem.

John indicates that the triumphal entry occurred on the day after Jesus' arrival at Bethany which was six days before the passover. See John 12:1, 12.

Go your way into the village.—One of the two just mentioned, or possible another that was near.

Jesus gave detailed instruction about the colt which the disciples were to bring for Him to ride on. No man had ever ridden the colt. Why Jesus selected it is not stated. Prophecy, of course, indicated that He was to enter the city riding on the colt.

The Lord hath need of him.—There has been much speculation as to whether or not Jesus used supernatural knowledge in giving this detailed instruction to His disciples. An example of His use of such power is given in Matt. 17:27. But it isn't necessary to assume that he made use of it in this case. Previous arrangements could have been made by Him with the owners. All the disciples had to say was: "The Lord has need of him."

Jesus' miraculous powers were used to demonstrate God's approval of His teaching and work. He never used it merely to amaze people. See 23:8-12.

and set Jesus thereon.—The disciples threw their garments on the colt and set Jesus on him. Both Matthew and John mention the prophecy of Zech. 9:9 which was fulfilled as the victorious King came triumphantly, even though humbly, riding into Jerusalem.

at the descent of the mount of Olives.—Jesus and the disciples had gone to the top of the mount of Olives and were ready to go down the western slope that led to the city of Jerusalem when the multitudes met Him and began praising God for the works they had seen done.

John suggests that the resurrection of Lazarus had greatly influenced the people at this time (John 12:9-13).

Blessed is the King that cometh in the name of the Lord.—Suggested by Psa. 118:26 and Isa. 62:11. See comment on 13:35.

They had been wondering when the kingdom was to appear; now they were acclaiming Jesus as King.

And some of the Pharisees.—The Pharisees kept a close watch on all of Jesus' activities. When they heard the crowd praising Him, they said, "Teacher, rebuke your disciples." In their opinion, this was blasphemy. They wanted Him to stop the praise that came spontaneously from the hearts of the people.

if they shall hold their peace.—Jesus' answer made it clear to the Pharisees that He did approve what the people were doing and that He had no intention of restraining them. Nothing could prevent their expression of gratitude to God for what He had done for them through Jesus. "If the people become silent," He said, "the stones will cry out."

Jesus' Lament Over Jerusalem

Scripture

19:41-44   And when he drew nigh, he saw the city and wept over it, 42 saying, If thou hadst known in this day, even thou, the things which belong unto peace! but now they are hid from thine eyes. 43 For the days shall come upon thee, when thine enemies shall cast up a bank about thee, and compass thee round, and keep thee in on every side, 44 and shall dash thee to the ground, and thy children within thee; and they shall not leave in thee one stone upon another; because thou knewest not the time of thy visitation.

Comments

he saw the city and wept over it.—What should have been a joyous occasion, for the people were praising Him as King, was a sad one to Jesus. Not the momentary acclaim of the crowds, but the fact that many of these same people who soon would be crying out, "Crucify him, crucify him," was in the mind of the Lord. The deep sorrow that disturbed him as He thought of what was going to happen to the "City of the Great King" caused Him to break forth in sobs that shooks His body. Once before His sorrow had caused Him to break into tears. That was just before He raised Lazarus from the dead (John 11:35). Luke does not mention tears at this time; he told about the agonizing sobs that expressed the Savior's grief.

If thou hadst known.—Jesus spoke to the city, meaning, of course, the people of the city. If they had known the things of peace which even then were hid from their eyes, they would have escaped the awful destruction that was coming upon them. If they had listened to the message of the angels' song at the time of His birth or to His teaching about the peacemakers or to His pleas for sinners to repent before it was too late, they would have escaped the most terrible punishment ever visited on any city (Matt. 24:21).

This may well indicate the remorse of those who will stand in the Judgment without having made peace through the blood of His cross.

but now they are hid from your eyes.—The things of peace were hid from their eyes, for they saw Jesus only as a man who was perverting their nation (23:2).

For the days shall come upon thee.—Jesus foretold in detail what was coming upon the city. He mentions it briefly here but in detail in Matt. 24:1-34 and Luke 21:5-32. Escape would be cut off; the people would be crushed to the ground; the city would be completely destroyed. It all happened in 70 A. D. when the Romans destroyed Jerusalem.

because thou knewest not the time of thy visitation.—What is meant by "visitation"? There are two possible interpretations of this passage. In Isa. 10:3, the Hebrew word which is translated in the LXX by the Greek word that Luke uses here means a visitation that results in punishment. This illustrates the fact that the word can be used of the coming of the Judge who rewards the faithful and punishes the wicked. See I Peter 2:12 where this might apply. But in Luke 1:68, it is stated that God "visited" His people and wrought redemption for them. This was in the person of the Lord Jesus Christ.

The concensus of commentators is that "visitation" in Luke 19:44 refers to the redemption which Jerusalem did not accept, just as she did not know the things of peace. But Jesus might have been speaking of the destruction that He was to bring on the city that rejected Him, when He mentioned "the time of their visitation."

Cleansing the Temple

Scripture

19:45-48   And he entered into the temple, and began to cast out them that sold, 46 saying unto them, It is written, And my house shall be a house of prayer: but ye have made it a den of robbers.

47 And he was teaching daily in the temple. But the chief priests and the scribes and the principal men of the people sought to destroy him: 48 and they could not find what they might do; for the people all hung upon him, listening.

Comments

began to cast out them that sold.—All three of the synoptic writers record this incident (Matt. 21:12-14; Mark 11:15-18; Luke 19:45-48). But John gives the account of the cleansing of the temple that occurred at the beginning of Jesus' ministry (John 2:13-22). There is no good reason for assuming that such an incident could not have occurred at the beginning of His ministry and again at its close. The fact that they are similar does not rule out the possibility of two separate cleansings. It takes a very short time for people to revert to their old ways. Selling sacrificial animals was undoubtedly a very good business, and the merchants did not give it up for long.

It is written.—Jesus' appeal to what was written shows His approval of the Old Testament Scriptures. Jews pretended to approve them, but their conduct proved otherwise.

The temple was not built as a place of business, but as a house of prayer. It was a place for worshippers to offer their gifts and sacrifices to the Lord. It was a place where they were to receive His gracious blessings.

They had so perverted this purpose that Jesus said, "You have made it a den of robbers."

The church is the temple of God. In the light of what happened to the temple in Jerusalem, Christian people might well examine their relation to this spiritual temple to see if it too has been put to other uses than the divinely appointed one. See I Pet. 2:1-10. In the light of what is "written," what will the answer be?

And he was teaching daily in the temple.—From beginning to end, Jesus' ministry was one of teaching as He proclaimed good news to the people. A return to a teaching ministry in the church is long overdue.

sought to destroy him.—There was no denying what their real intent was; they were bent on destroying this One who was taking their place in the hearts of the people. The conspiracy included the chief priests and scribes and the prominent men of the nation.

There was only one thing holding them back: How could they do it without violent reaction from the people? The people were clinging to His words as they listened to Him. What a thrilling experience it must have been to hear the Teacher sent from God tell the story of eternal life!

324

Summary

As Luke neared the close of his account of the Life of Christ, he crowded as many incidents into it as possible. Five are given in this chapter, some of which are mentioned only briefly.

The story of Zacchaeus presents another practical defense of Jesus' ministry in behalf of the lost sinner. He was criticized, of course, for going into the house of this chief publican, but He answered, "The Son of man came to seek and save that which was lost."

The Parable of the Pounds answers many questions about the nature of the kingdom of God. The story of the nobleman who went into a far country to receive a kingdom and return shows that Jesus was soon to return to the Father where He would be seated at the right hand of the throne of God and reign as King until the end of the age. Then He will return to call upon His servants to render account of their stewardship. Those who have been faithful will be rewarded accordingly, but no excuse will be accepted for failing to carry out His orders. Even the opportunity to serve will be taken away from the one who does not use it in this life. Those who reject Him as King will be destroyed when He comes again.

The story of the Triumphal Entry presents Jesus riding into Jerusalem on a colt as the prophet had said. As He came to the descent of the mount of Olives, He was met by a crowd that spontaneously cried out, "Blessed is the King that comes in the name of the Lord." The ubiquitous Pharisees heard it and said, "Teacher, rebuke your disciples." He said, "I tell you if they become silent, the stones will cry out." But soon the enemy would stir them up and they would be yelling, "Let him be crucified."

As Jesus looked at the city He wept over it. "If you had known the things that belong to peace, but now they are hid from your eyes." The time would come when their city would be besieged, its people dashed to the ground, and its buildings utterly destroyed. All this was because they did not know the One sent from God with the message of peace.

He went into the city and once again found the temple being used as a place of merchandise. He drove out the merchants as He had done at the beginning of His ministry and said again, "It is written, My house shall be called a house of prayer. You have made it a den of robbers."

As He was teaching in the temple, the chief priests and scribes and prominent men were seeking a way to destroy Him. How to do it without arousing the people, was their only concern, for all the people were hanging on His words, listening to the story of eternal life.

Questions

1. What is known about the history of Jericho?
2. Why was Zacchaeus called a chief publican?
3. Why did he want to see Jesus?
4. How did he overcome his handicap?
5. Why did Jesus say, "I must abide in your house today"?
6. What did the crowds say about this?
7. What did Zacchaeus propose to do about his life?
8. What is the significance of the remark: "If I have wrongfully exacted aught"?
9. Why did Jesus say that salvation had come to his house?
10. What did his being a son of Abraham have to do with it?
11. What was the purpose of Jesus' ministry as seen in His remark at the close of the story of Zacchaeus?
12. What was the occasion for telling the Parable of the Pounds?
13. What is the parable about?
14. Why didn't the people understand Jesus' purpose in going to Jerusalem?
15. Who is represented by the nobleman in the parable?
16. What does the parable teach about the kingdom of God and the office of Christ as King?
17. When did He receive the kingdom?
18. What will He do when He comes again?
19. What are His servants to do while He is away?
20. Who are represented by the citizens who refused to have Him as their King?
21. On what basis were the servants rewarded?
22. What lesson is taught by the one who didn't use his talent?
23. When will the opportunity to serve be taken away?
24. What will happen to those who reject Christ as King?
25. What does Bethphage mean? Bethany?
26. Where were these villages located?
27. How explain the owners willingness to let the disciples take the colt?

326

28. What is suggested by the fact that Jesus rode the colt into Jerusalem?
29. What did the people say when they saw Him coming?
30. What was the objection of the Pharisees?
31. How explain Jesus' answer?
32. What did Jesus do when He saw the city? Why?
33. What is meant by "the time of visitation"?
34. What was to happen to the city? When?
35. What evidence is there to support the view that Jesus cleansed the temple at the beginning of His ministry and again at its close?
36. What is the significance of Jesus' statement, "It is written"?
37. What method did Jesus use in His ministry and what does it suggest for the present age?
38. Who were involved in the conspiracy to destroy Jesus?
39. What was restraining them?
40. How does Luke describe the attitude of the people toward Jesus' ministry of teaching?

Outline

A. Luke told how the Jews challenged Jesus' authority (1-8).
   1. The challenge (1-3).
      a) The time: One of the days when He was teaching in the temple and preaching the gospel.
      b) The challengers: The chief priests, scribes and elders.
      c) The questions: By what authority do you do these things? Who gave you this authority?
   2. The answer: Jesus asked them a question to force them to answer their own question: "The baptism of John, was it from heaven or from men?" (3-4).
   3. The reaction to His question (5-7).
      a) Their first reaction: "If we say that it was from heaven, He will ask why we didn't believe him."
      b) Their second thought: "If we say it was from men, the people will stone us, for they were convinced that John was a prophet."
      c) Their conclusion: "Teacher, we don't know."
   4. The response of Jesus: "Neither will I tell you by what authority I do these things" (8).
B. Luke recorded Jesus' parable of The Husbandmen (9-18).
   1. The facts of the parable (9-15a).
      a) A man planted a vineyard, let it out to husbandmen, and went to a far country (9).
      b) The husbandmen mistreated those sent to receive the owner's share of the crop (10-12).
         (1) They sent the first away empty.
         (2) They beat and shamefully treated another, sending him away empty also.
         (3) They wounded a third and sent him away.
      c) The owner finally decided to send his son (13-15a).
         (1) He said, "They will respect him."
         (2) Since he was the heir, they decided to kill him and take over the vineyard.
   2. Jesus applied the lesson of the parable (15b-18).
      a) The owner's reaction.
         (1) Jesus asked, "What will he do?"

  (2) They said, "He will destroy them and give the vineyard to others." They said, "God forbid."

 b) The meaning of the Scripture.

  (1) "The stone which the builders rejected,
The same was made the head of the corner."

  (2) Jesus explained: "Everyone who falls on the stone will be broken in pieces, and on whomsoever it falls it will grind him to powder."

C. Luke told of the search for an excuse to hand Jesus over to the governor (19-47).

 1. Their reasons (19).

  a) They feared the people.

  b) They knew the parable referred to them.

 2. Their strategy (20-40).

  a) Spies sent to listen to Him (20).

  b) Their first thrust: The question of tribute to Caesar (21-26).

   (1) Their flattering approach.

   (2) The subtle question: "Is it lawful to give tribute to Caesar?"

   (3) Jesus' answer:

    (a) The denarius with Caesar's image on it.

    (b) "Render to Caesar the things that are Caesar's, and to God, the things that are God's."

   (4) Their defeat.

    (a) They couldn't use it against Him before the people.

    (b) They kept still.

  c) The Sadducees took up the battle (27-40).

   (1) Their question was about the resurrection and the Law of Moses.

   (2) Their hypothetical case: A woman married to seven brothers; whose wife will she be in the resurrection?

   (3) Jesus demolished their argument.

    (a) The marriage vow does not extend to the resurrection.

    (b) The case of the Burning Bush proves there is life after death.

    (c) God is not the God of the dead, but of the living.

> (4) The scribes admit their defeat, "Teacher, you have spoken well." They did not dare risk another question.
3. Jesus' counterattack (41-47).
>> a) His two-fold question about the Christ (41-44).
>>> (1) How can they say that He is David's son?
>>> (2) How can David call him Lord, since he is his son?
>> b) His warning to the disciples (45-47).
>>> (1) In the hearing of all the people, He warned against the scribes.
>>> (2) He lashed out against their hypocracy.
>>>> (a) They loved long robes, salutations in the market places, chief seats at feasts.
>>>> (b) For a pretence they made long prayers.
>>>> (c) They will receive greater condemnation.

The Authority of Jesus Challenged

Scripture

20:1-8 And it came to pass, on one of the days, as he was teaching the people in the temple, and preaching the gospel, there came upon him the chief priests and the scribes with the elders; 2 and they spake, saying unto him, Tell us: By what authority doest thou these things? or who is he that gave thee this authority? 3 And he answered and said unto them, I also will ask you a question; and tell me: 4 The baptism of John, was it from heaven, or from men? 5 And they reasoned with themselves, saying, If we shall say, From heaven; he will say, Why did ye not believe him? 6 But if we shall say, From men; all the people will stone us: for they are persuaded that John was a prophet. 7 And they answered, that they knew not whence it was. 8 And Jesus said unto them, Neither tell I you by what authority I do these things.

Comments

as He was teaching the people.—Jesus' authority was challenged on one of those days when He was teaching in the temple. His whole ministry consisted in teaching, preaching, and performing signs to prove that He spoke the message of the heavenly Father. Jesus taught the people. It is one thing to teach a lesson where the concern is primarily with the content, but another thing to teach a lesson to people. People were always in the mind of the Master as He taught them the lessons about repentance and righteous living. He taught them how to escape from Satan's clutches and how to serve God—lessons that also need to be taught today.

and preaching the gospel.—It is probably wrong to make too great a distinction between teaching and preaching. Jesus was a Preacher who taught the people. He taught crowds and He taught small groups; when He had the opportunity, He took time to teach one person. Teaching was the process by which He sought to get people to turn back to God.

The expression "preaching the gospel"—one word in Greek—gives us our word "Evangelize." It was the process of making people aware of the good news of salvation through Christ. It takes the whole story of the Bible to do this, not just a part of it.

The term "proclaim" or "preach" is used many times in the New Testament. It had to do with the spreading of the good news (Lk. 4:18). It does not suggest a difference in content, but the manner in which the good news was heralded by the gospel preacher.

All of these terms are brought together in one verse (Matt. 9: 35) which tells of Jesus teaching in the synagogues and preaching the gospel of the kingdom and healing all manner of disease.

there came unto him the chief priests.—The enemy was always present, seeking to find an excuse to condemn Jesus. Priests, scribes, elders—all these should have been helping Jesus in His mission of teaching the people—were doing everything within their power to destroy Him.

By what authority.—They had two questions: (1) By what right are you doing these things and (2) Who gave you this right? Matthew says that He had just been cleansing the temple and healing a blind man (Matt. 21:4). It was difficult to condemn Him before the people for such work as that. Once before they had tried to discredit His miracles by saying that He performed them by the power of Beelzebub, but their effort was a miserable failure. Now they ask about "these things," vaguely suggesting that He had done something wrong. They couldn't bring themselves to join the people who praised God for the glorious things He was doing for them.

I also will ask you a question.—They had expected Him to answer as He had done on many occasions that God had given Him the right to perform miracles and teach the people. They could have twisted such an answer and brought the charge of blasphemy as they had so often done (John 5:17-18). But He saw through their hypocracy. He asked them a question that forced them to answer their own.

The baptism of John.—Was John's authority to baptize from heaven or from men? They discussed it and saw that if they should say from heaven, He would say, "Why, then, didn't you believe him?" John had declared that Jesus was the Lamb of God; that He was the Son of God; and that He was the one to baptize in the Holy Spirit (John 1:19-34). Why didn't they believe him? For a possible answer, see John 11:48.

On the other hand, if they should say that John baptized on human authority, they would have to answer to the people who believed that John was a prophet. They were not willing to risk being stoned by the people. "No, they couldn't say about John's authority."

And Jesus said to them.—Neither am I telling you by what right I am doing these things." There was no need to, for they had been forced by their own reasoning to admit that His authority was from God, just as John's was.

The Parable of the Husbandmen

Scripture

20:9-18   And he began to speak unto the people this parable: A man planted a vineyard, and let it out to husbandmen, and went into another country for a long time. 10 And at the season he sent unto the husbandmen a servant, that they should give him of the fruit of the vineyard: but the husbandmen beat him, and sent him away empty. 11 And he sent yet another servant: and him also they beat, and handled him shamefully, and sent him away empty. 12 And he sent yet a third: and him also they wounded, and cast him forth. 13 And the lord of the vineyard said, What shall I do? I will send my beloved son; it may be they will reverence him. 14 But when the husbandmen saw him, they reasoned one with another, saying, This is the heir; let us kill him, that the inheritance may be ours. 15 And they cast him forth out of the vineyard, and killed him. What therefore will the lord of the vineyard do unto them? 16 He will come and destroy these husbandmen, and will give the vineyard unto others. And when they heard it, they said, God forbid. 17 But he looked upon them, and said, What then is this that is written,

The stone which the builders rejected,

The same was made the head of the corner?
18 Every one that falleth on that stone shall be broken to pieces; but on whomsoever it shall fall, it will scatter him as dust.

Comments

And he began to speak unto the people.—He was teaching the people when the priests and elders interrupted Him with their question about His "right to do these things." He silenced them by the question He asked and, according to Matthew, followed up His victory with the parable of the Two Sons (Matt. 21:28-32). Then, according to Matthew, He introduced the parable of The Husbandmen by saying, "Hear another parable (Matt. 21:33). The parable was spoken to the people, but the scribes and priests also heard it and were aware of the fact that He was talking about them.
vineyard . . . husbandmen.—The vineyard represents God's people, Israel. The husbandmen are the leaders—elders, priests, scribes. They were responsible for the harvest—fruit of righteousness in the lives of the people.
And at the season he sent unto the husbandmen a servant.—The first was sent away empty; a second was beaten and shamefully treated and sent away empty also; a third was wounded and thrown out of the vineyard.
All this represents God's efforts throughout the years from the beginning of the kingdom at Sinai to the days of Jesus to get the leaders of the Jews to direct the people of the nation in the ways of righteousness.
I will send my beloved son.—This is such a clear reference to Jesus the Son of God that comment is unnecessary. Isaiah, Jeremiah, Amos and many others had tried to get the nation to "do justice, and love kindness, and to walk humbly with God" (Micah 6:8). John the Baptist had warned them of the necessity of producing the fruits of repentance. Then the Father sent His Son into the world, but "they that were his own received him not" (John 1:11; 20:21; Gal. 4:4).
This is the heir; let us kill him.—Jesus was aware of their murderous plot, and they knew it. But that didn't stop them for they were determined to destroy Him and take over completely. They were acting as if the vineyard was theirs and that Jesus was an intruder who was threatening their position and nation (John 11:48).
Jesus had foretold His death at the hands of the leaders of the

333

Jews on several occasions. In this parable, He represents it as an accomplished fact. His question was, "What therefore will the Lord of the vineyard do unto them?"

He will come and destroy these husbandmen.—The answer came from the people, since it is unlikely that the priests and scribes would give such an answer. According to Matthew, Jesus said, "Therefore I tell you, the kingdom of God will be taken away from you and given to a nation producing the fruits of it" (Matt. 21: 43). So the vineyard represents the kingdom of God, the nation of Israel. Some assume that the nation to which it is to be given will be made up of Gentiles. But it will be composed of believers in Christ whether Jews or Gentiles (Eph. 2:16; Gal. 3:26-28; Col. 3:10-11). That nation is the spiritual kingdom of Christ, the church (Col. 1:13).

Are we producing the fruits of it? See Col. 1:6-12.

And when they heard it, they said, God forbid.—Perhaps this was the reaction of the people to the whole story: "God forbid that the beloved Son should be killed and that the deed lead to the destruction of the husbandmen." The whole senseless plot of the priests and scribes was abhorrent to the people. How strange that in a short time they could be led to cry out, "Let Him be crucified," and become parties to this awful deed (Acts 2:23)!

What then is this that is written.—The quotation is from Psa. 118: 22-23. To those who were saying that this thing was too awful to be true, Jesus asked, "What then is the meaning of this which is written in the Psalms?" The builders rejected the stone that is made the head of the corner. See also Isa. 28:16; Acts 4:11 and I Pet. 2:7.

Everyone that falleth on that stone.—Christ is that stone. To those who oppose Him, He is a stone in their pathway over which they stumble. When that Stone falls on them they will be pulverized and blown away like dust.

The Search For An Excuse

Scripture

20:19-47   And the scribes and the chief priests sought to lay hands on him in that very hour; and they feared the people: for they perceived that he spake this parable against them. 20 And they watched him, and sent forth spies, who feigned themselves to be righteous, that they might take hold of his speech, so as to deliver him up to the rule and to the authority of the governor. 21 And they asked him, saying, Teacher, we know that thou sayest and teachest rightly, and acceptest not the person of any, but of a truth teachest the way of God: 22 Is it lawful for us to give tribute unto Caesar, or not? 23 But he perceived their craftiness, and said unto them, 24 Show me a denarius. Whose image and superscription hath it? And they said, Caesar's. 25 And he said unto them, Then render unto Caesar the things that are Caesar's, and unto God the things that are God's. 26 And they were not able to take hold of the saying before the people: and they marvelled at his answer, and held their peace.

27 And there came to him certain of the Sadducees, they that say that there is no resurrection; 28 and they asked him, saying, Teacher, Moses wrote unto us, that if a man's brother die, having a wife, and he be childless, his brother should take the wife, and raise up seed unto his brother. 29 There were therefore seven brethren: and the first took a wife, and died childless; 30 and the second: 31 and the third took her; and likewise the seven also left no children, and died. 32 Afterward the woman also died. 33 In the resurrection therefore whose wife of them shall she be? for the seven had her to wife. 34 And Jesus said unto them, The sons of this world marry, and are given in marriage: 35 but they that are accounted worthy to attain to that world, and the resurrection from the dead, neither marry, nor are given in marriage: 36 for neither can they die any more: for they are equal unto the angels; and are sons of God, being sons of the resurrection. 37 But that the dead are raised, even Moses showed, in the place concerning the Bush, when he calleth the Lord the God of Abraham, and the God of Isaac, and the God of Jacob. 38 Now he is not the God of the dead, but of the living: for all live unto him. 39 And certain of the scribes answering said, Teacher, thou hast well said. 40 For they durst not any more ask him any question.

41 And he said unto them, How say they that the Christ is David's son? 42 For David himself saith in the books of Psalms,

The Lord said unto my Lord,

Sit thou on my right hand,

43 Till I make thine enemies the footstool of thy feet.

44 David therefore calleth him Lord, and how is he his son?

45 And in the hearing of all the people he said unto his disciples, 46 Beware of the scribes, who desire to walk in long robes, and love

saluations in the marketplaces, and chief seats in the synagogues, and chief places at feasts; 47 who devour widows' houses, and for a pretence make long prayers: these shall receive greater condemnation.

Comments

sought to lay hands on him.—The scribes and priests knew that Jesus had been speaking of them in the parable of The Husbandmen, but they completely rejected His warning. They were ready at that very hour to arrest Him. All that kept them from it was their fear of the people who were still glorifying God for all that He had done for them. But they kept close watch on Him and sent spies to listen to Him as He taught the people, hoping that He might say something that would give them the excuse to turn Him over to the governor. They even attempted to flatter Him, hoping to throw Him off guard.

Teacher, we know.—According to Matthew, it was the Pharisees who sent the Herodians to set a trap for Jesus. The Herodians were a party of the Jews that supported the rule of the Herods whose power was derived from Rome. The Pharisees were, in their way, upholding the Law of Moses and submitting to the authority of Rome only because they had to. But these two opposing parties joined forces in an attempt to find an excuse to destroy Jesus.

What the Herodians said to Jesus was true: What He taught was right; He taught the way of God; He was impartial in dealing with men. They asked, "Is it lawful for us to give tribute to Caesar or not?" This could have been a real problem to conscientious Jews, but the hypocracy of the Herodians was poorly disguised.

But he perceived their craftiness.—They expected Him to answer "Yes" or "No." They were prepared to pounce on Him for whichever answer He would give. If He should say "yes," they were prepared to accuse Him of disloyalty to His people, the Jews. One of the favorite accusations against the early church was their supposed opposition to the Law of Moses (Acts 6:11; 26:22-23). If He should say "no," they were ready to report Him to the Roman authorities for disloyalty to the government under which He lived.

Show me a denarius.—It was a small coin with the image of Caesar on it. The superscription was Caesar's too. They had planned for two possible answers to their question, but there was only one possible answer to His question, "Whose image and superscription are on the denarius?" But He had two things to say to them that were unexpected: "Give to Caesar the things that are Caesar's, and to God the things that are God's."

They had intended to catch Him on one or the other of the two issues involved in their question. He, however, caught them on both issues involved in His answer. Had they paid their taxes honestly? Were they giving to God the lives they owed Him?

not able to take hold of the saying.—He was more than a match for them; they couldn't twist His answer so as to use it against Him. They knew that the people were with Him. They marvelled at His answer, but kept still.

And there came unto him certain Sadducees.—Jesus had so completely routed the enemy in the first encounter that one wonders how the Sadducees found the courage to try their favorite question on Him. But people who hold to views like theirs usually keep on trying them out on everyone who will listen. The Sadducees did not believe in the resurrection or in angels or spirits (Acts 23:8). While the Herodians had been silenced, these Sadducees seemed confident that their question could not be answered by anyone holding to the doctrine of the resurrection.

Teacher, Moses wrote unto us.—Jesus frequently appealed to the Scriptures as He taught. They must have felt that they were on safe ground when they referred to Moses. They did quote accurately from Deut. 25:5 which said that if a man's brother died leaving a childless wife, he was to take the wife and raise up children for his brother. Their hypothetical case: One woman was married to seven brothers before she died. All this was perfectly legal according to Moses! Then the question: "In the resurrection—supposing there is such a thing—whose wife will she be, for they all had her for a wife?"

As things like this usually go, it is not too much to suppose that the Sadducees broke out laughing at their clever question, being certain that He couldn't answer it. Undoubtedly, they had tried it on many a man, and no one had ever been able to give a satisfactory answer. They had the only solution: There simply couldn't be such a thing as a resurrection!

The sons of the world.—Jesus' answer begins with a contrast between this world and the heavenly state of righteousness. Those who belong to this world marry and are given in marriage, but those who attain to that world and the resurrection from the dead neither marry nor are they given in marriage. Marriage is for this age, but in the resurrection they are equal—in this respect—to the angels.

337

They are called sons of God because they have been raised from the dead.

they that are accounted worthy to attain unto that world.—Jesus does not imply that some will not be raised. He plainly stated that "all that are in the tombs shall hear his voice, and shall come forth; they that have done good, unto the resurrection of life; and they that have done evil, unto the resurrection of judgment" (John 5:28-29).

Paul also speaks of the "resurrection both of the just and unjust" (Acts 24:15; I Cor. 15:22).

But that the dead are raised.—Jesus then proceeded to show—and from the Scriptures, too—that there is a life beyond the grave. Moses spoke of God, when he told of His appearing in the burning Bush, as the God of Abraham, the God of Isaac, and the God of Jacob. But these men had long since been dead. Jesus explained: "He is not the God of the dead, but of the living, for all live unto Him." That is, Abraham, Isaac, and Jacob were living in the world beyond the grave where the eternal living God—the Lord—was their God.

Teacher, thou hast well said.—Some of the scribes were willing to admit that He had given the correct answer, a more gracious attitude than that of the Herodians who chose to remain silent. But there were no more questions of this kind for the Teacher!

And he said unto them.—It was His turn; they had asked Him two questions—according to Matthew, three—and now He had one for them: "How can they say that Christ is David's son?" The question seemed elementary, for all the Jews who knew anything about the Scriptures knew that Messiah was to be from the line of David. But the problem was greater than that. Jesus quoted Psalm 110:8, a Psalm of David, which said, "The Lord said unto my Lord, Sit thou on my right hand, Till I make thine enemies the footstool of thy feet." Then Jesus asked the hard one: "Since David calls him Lord, how is he his son?"

The answer is perfectly clear to those who know and believe the Word of God. Paul gives it in Rom. 1:3-4. Luke had already explained it to Theophilus in his account of the conception and birth of Jesus. Jesus was the son of David "according to flesh," but He was demonstrated to be the Son of God "according to the spirit of holiness"—a reference to the eternal One whom John calls "The Word"—by the resurrection from the dead.

And in the hearing of all the people.—They could have answered the question about David's son being Lord, but that would have compelled them to confess that Jesus was the Christ.

Now before all the people, He warned His disciples against these hypocrits. They walked in long robes and publically received the adulation of the people; they sought out the chief seats in the synagogues and at the feasts; they devoured widows' houses and for a pretense at being righteous, made long prayers. These were they who had sought to discredit the Lord Jesus Christ.

Summary

It seems strange that the One to whom all authority in heaven and on earth had been should be challenged by men. But the chief priests and the scribes with the elders had the audacity in Jesus' day to say, "By what authority do you do these things? Who gave you this authority?" Their vague reference to "these things" that He was doing included not only the cleansing of the temple but also the healing of a blind man. What authority, indeed?

But Jesus asked them a question that forced them to answer their own, although they were not big enough to admit that His authority was from God, just as John the Baptist's was.

The parable of The Husbandmen shows just what the attitude of the Jews toward Jesus was. They were waiting for their opportunity to kill Him and take over the kingdom of God. They did put Him to death, but the kingdom was given to those who produce the fruit of righteousness—the believers in Christ, whether Jews or Gentiles.

Those who rejected their Messiah have already suffered one devastating blow—the destruction of Jerusalem in 70 A. D. Another act of judgment awaits all who persist in rejecting Him as King. Like the stone that grinds to powder the one on whom it falls, the judgment of Christ will scatter those who oppose Him.

But the Jews persisted in their search for an excuse to destroy Him. They sent spies to listen in as He was teaching. They hoped to hear something on which to condemn Him; but He answered their questions and silenced them before the multitudes. They refused to answer His question about David's calling Christ "Lord" since He is David's son. Their hypocracy was so evident that Jesus took occasion to warn the disciples against them.

Questions

1. What was Jesus doing when His authority was challenged by the chief priests and scribes?

2. Why were they not more specific in their charge?
3. What, if any, is the difference between preaching and teaching?
4. How did Jesus force the priests to answer their own question about His authority?
5. Why didn't Jesus tell them that He had all authority in heaven and on earth?
6. Why did He tell the parable of The Husbandmen?
7. How did He show that He was aware of the thing the Jews were planning to do to Him?
8. What did the sending of the various servants suggest as to the treatment the Jews had given the prophets?
9. Who is represented by the son in the parable?
10. What did they intend to do after killing the son?
11. What is suggested by the fact that the Lord of the vineyard was to destroy those wicked men?
12. To whom was the kingdom to be given?
13. Is the church as the kingdom of Christ producing the fruits of it?
14. Why did Jesus quote the prophecy about the rejected stone?
15. What was to happen to those on whom the stone fell?
16. Why were the scribes and priests searching for an excuse to kill Jesus?
17. What question did the Herodians ask?
18. What answer did they evidently expect Him to give?
19. How did His answer prevent them from accusing Him of wrongdoing?
20. Who had joined the Herodians in this attempt to trap Jesus?
21. How did the Herodians react to His answer?
22. Why did the Sadducees take up the issue?
23. What was their peculiar belief and how did it differ from that of the Pharisees?
24. What was the foundation of the story they told?
25. Wherein had they erred in applying the Law of Moses to the issue of the resurrection?
26. How did Jesus show them their mistake?
27. How did He describe the state of those in the resurrection?
28. What did Jesus mean by saying that God is not the God of the dead, but the living?
29. What question did Jesus ask them about David's son?
30. Why couldn't they answer it?

CHAPTER TWENTY-ONE

Outline

A. Luke told about people putting gifts into the treasury (1-4).
    1. The people.
        a) Those who put in gifts out of their riches.
        b) A poor widow who put in just two small coins.
    2. The reaction of Jesus: "Truly, I say, this poor widow has put in more than all the rest, for out of their abundance they put something into the treasury, but she out of her poverty has put in all that she had to live on."

B. Luke recorded Jesus' prediction of the destruction of Jerusalem (5-32).
    1. The startling prediction (5-9).
        a) Occasion: Some spoke of the temple which was adorned with beautiful stones and offerings.
        b) Prediction: The days will come when there will not be a stone upon a stone that will not be thrown down.
        c) Reaction:
            (1) Question: Teacher, when will these things be, and what will be the sign when they are about to happen?
            (2) Answer:
                (a) Jesus warned against those who would come in His name.
                (b) He warned against being terrified by report of wars, for the end of Jerusalem was not to be immediately.
    2. Things that would occur before the destruction of Jerusalem (10-19).
        a) In the world about them:
            (1) Nation rising against nation.
            (2) Earthquakes.
            (3) Famine and pestilence.
            (4) Terrors and great signs in the heavens.
        b) In their own lives:
            (1) Arrest and persecution, in the synagogues.
            (2) Trials and persecutions, before governors.
            (3) Opportunities to testify: They would be supplied

both words and wisdom that could not be contradicted by their adversaries.

(4) Family strife and persecution; some even put to death.

(5) All men would hate them for His name's sake, but "not a hair of your head will perish."

(6) By patient endurance they would gain eternal life, even if some should suffer death.

3. The sign of the desolation and what to do when it appeared (20-21).

a) Jerusalem surrounded by armies.

b) Those in Judea were to flee to the mountains; those outside were not to enter the city.

4. The vengeance of those days (22-25).

a) All that had been written about it would be fulfilled.

b) The distress would be particularly hard on mothers and little children.

c) Many would fall by the sword; others would be carried away captive.

d) Jerusalem will be trodden down by the Gentiles until the times of the Gentile are fulfilled.

5. The signs that will plainly mark the Second Coming of Jesus (25-27). Note: Jesus presented this in contrast to the destruction of Jerusalem, because some would claim to be Christ at that time.

a) Accompanying signs:

(1) Signs in the sun, moon, and stars.

(2) Distress of nations and perplexity at the roaring of the sea.

(3) Men fainting for fear of what would be coming upon the world—inhabited earth.

(4) The powers of the heavens shaken.

b) THE SIGN OF THE SON OF MAN: His coming in a cloud with power and great glory.

6. Additional instruction about the destruction of Jerusalem (28-32).

a) When you (apostles) see these things (that have to do with the destruction of Jerusalem) take heart for your redemption is near.

b) The parable of the Fig Tree illustrates what He had said about Jerusalem.

c) They were to know that the kingdom of God was near.

d) That present generation would not pass away before the destruction of Jerusalem—"till all things be accomplished."

C. Luke reported what Jesus said about His coming at the end of the world (33-36).

  1. Time: "Heaven and heath will pass away, but my words will not pass away." Note: This answers a third question as reported by Matthew. See Matt. 24:3 "What shall be the sign of thy coming and of the end of the world?"

  2. Warning: Beware of careless living lest that day—of His coming—come on you suddenly as a snare.

  3. Place: It will come upon all who dwell on the face of all the earth.

  4. Exhortation: Watch at every season and pray that you may escape the things that will come to pass (trials of this life such as destruction of Jerusalem) and stand before the Son of Man (when He comes).

D. Luke told briefly about Jesus as He taught daily in the temple, but spent the nights in the mount called Olivet (37-38).

A Poor Widow's Two Small Coins

Scripture

21:1-4 And he looked up, and saw the rich men that were casting their gifts into the treasury. 2 And he saw a certain poor widow casting in thither two mites. 3 And he said, Of a truth I say unto you, This poor widow cast in more than they all: 4 for all these did of their superfluity cast in unto the gifts; but she of her want did cast in all the living that she had.

Comments

And he looked up.—Jesus had been teaching in the temple. He had just warned the people to beware of the hypocracy of the scribes whose long prayers failed to cover up the fact that they were devouring widows' houses. As He looked up, He saw the rich men putting their gifts into the treasury.

343

Earlier in His ministry, Jesus had spoken against the hypocracy of giving to be seen of men (Matt. 6:2-4). Nothing is said that would suggest that these rich men were guilty either of hypocracy or of acquiring wealth by defrauding the poor. Because some rich men make riches their god, there is no reason to assume that all do. The point of the lesson is the contrast between those who put in their gifts out of their riches and the poor widow who gave all she had to live on.

a certain poor widow casting in her two mites.—They were just two little copper coins. It didn't amount to much. It would scarcely be noticed in the total offering of that day, but Jesus saw it. Her act is memoralized in Luke's gospel for all ages to come.

Paul reminded the Corinthians that "If the readiness is there, it is acceptable as a man hath, not as he hath not" (II Cor. 8:12).

This poor widow cast in more than they all.—The Lord's work certainly requires large amounts from those who have riches as well as the seemingly insignificant amounts from those who are like the poor widow. But in the eyes of Jesus, the poor widow did more than all the others. The reason? She gave all she had to live on; the others gave out of their abundance.

Paul commended the churches of Macedonia for their liberality in face of their real poverty, "for they first gave their own selves to the Lord" (II Cor. 8:5). He also upheld the principle of proportionate giving (I Cor. 16:2).

Prediction of the Destruction of Jerusalem

Scripture

21:5-9　And as some spake of the temple, how it was adorned with goodly stones and offerings, he said, 6 As for these things which ye behold, the days will come, in which there shall not be left here one stone upon another, that shall not be thrown down. 7 And they asked him, saying, Teacher, when therefore shall these things be? and what shall be the sign when these things are about to come to pass? 8 And he said, Take heed that ye be not led astray: for many shall come in my name, saying, I am he; and, The time is at hand: go yet not after them. 9 And when ye shall hear of wars and tumults, be not terrified: for these things must needs come to pass first; but the end is not immediately.

344

Comments

And as some spake of the temple.—This discourse is also reported in Matt. 24:1-34 and Mark 13:1-30. All three records should be studied in order to understand as clearly as possible what Jesus said about the destruction of Jerusalem.

Jesus began with some remarks about the temple and the devastation that was to come upon the city of Jerusalem. What He said at this point about His second coming revealed the significant contrast between His coming, which will be at the end of the world, and the claims that were to be made by false prophets at the time of the destruction of Jerusalem. See Matt. 24:23-27. This was done to prevent confusion in the minds of the disciples as they saw the signs of the approaching destruction of Jerusalem.

Jesus continued the discussion of the principal theme of the discourse—the destruction of Jerusalem—by pointing out some things the disciples would see as that event drew near. See 21:28-32. When they saw these things, they were to know that their redemption—release from the distress of that time—was near. He illustrated the point with the parable of the Fig Tree. They were also to know that the kingdom of God—God's kingly authority visiting judgment upon the city that crucified His Son—was near. And more than that, all these things would take place within the lifetime of their own generation.

When Jesus had finished the discussion of the destruction of Jerusalem, He gave a brief answer to the question about the end of the world and His coming (33-36). The answer was brief, because He had already discussed it in connection with the destruction of Jerusalem (25-27). His coming will be at the end of the age. That He will come again, cannot be doubted by those who accept the testimony of the Scriptures. All thinking men should heed His warning about the necessity of being prepared for that day.

there shall not be left here one stone upon another.—Some of the people had just spoken to Him about the beauty and wealth of the temple. The thought of its being destroyed must have been shocking. They knew that its construction had already taken more than forty-six years; several more were to pass before it was to be completed. But utter destruction—not one stone left upon another—was awaiting not only that building but the whole city of Jerusalem (19:41-44).

And they asked Him.—Matthew says that it was the disciples who asked Him the question as He sat on the mount of Olives, but Mark is more specific and names them: "Peter and James and Andrew." *Teacher, when therefore shall these things be?*—that is, "When will the destruction of Jerusalem occur?" They also asked, "What shall be the sign that these things are about to take place?"

According to Matthew, they also asked a third question: "And what shall be the sign of your coming, and of the end of the world?" They evidently associated His coming with the end of the world, and correctly so. But their question suggests that they believed that nothing short of the end of the world could bring about the destruction of Jerusalem with its temple. To correct that notion, He told them about things they would see, both the things leading up to the destruction and the things that would signal its beginning. He drew a bold contrast between these things and the things that will happen when He comes again (21:25-27; Matt. 24:23-27). No one will be misled by false prophets when He comes again "in a cloud with power and great glory," for all will recognize Him then.

And he said, Take heed that ye be not let astray.—There would be many things happening at the time of the destruction of Jerusalem that might lead the disciples away such as false reports saying, "Here or there," that is, "Christ has come." To all these false reports, He said, "Don't follow them."

And ye shall hear of wars and tumults.—These rumors would be heard before the destruction of Jerusalem, but the disciples were not to be terrified by them, for they would not signify the end of Jerusalem. The history of the world is written in the story of "wars and rumors of wars," but a specific act of war—Jerusalem besieged by the Roman armies—would be the sign that the end of the city was at hand.

"Wars and rumors of wars," then, is not a sign of the coming of Christ, for His coming is to be at an unknown time at the end of the age.

Sufferings at the Destruction of Jerusalem

Scripture

21:10-19   Then said he unto them, Nation shall rise against nation, and kingdom against kingdom; 11 and there shall be great earthquakes, and in divers places famines and pestilences; and there shall be terrors and great signs from heaven. 12 But before all these things, they shall lay their hands on you, and shall persecute you, delivering you up to the synagogues and prisons, bringing you before kings and governors for my name's sake. 13 It shall turn out unto you for a testimony. 14 Settle it therefore in your hearts, not to meditate beforehand how to answer: 15 for I will give you a mouth and wisdom, which all your adversaries shall not be able to withstand or to gainsay. 16 But ye shall be delivered up even by parents, and brethren, and kinsfolk, and friends; and some of you shall they cause to be put to death. 17 And ye shall be hated of all men for my name's sake. 18 And not a hair of your head shall perish. 19 In your patience ye shall win your souls.

Comments

Nation shall rise against nation.—Wars, earthquakes, pestilence, terrors and great signs from heaven were to take place before the destruction of Jerusalem. These, of course, are things that occur continually in the history of the world. Just what Jesus meant by "terrors and great signs from heaven" may be difficult to know. But He included them in the list of catastrophic occurrences in the physical real. They do not seem to be the same as the "signs in the sun and moon and stars" which He associates with His coming (25-27). They may refer to falling meteors or other phenomena that cause men to be afraid. Storms and hurricanes often strike terror in the hearts of men as they think of the destruction that might befall them. But even these things did not indicate that the destruction of Jerusalem was to take place immediately.

But before all these things.—His followers were to expect persecution before the destruction of Jerusalem. They would be brought into the courts of both Jews and civil rulers. The Book of Acts gives the history of some of these persecutions. See Acts 4:1-21; 5:17-42; 7:54-8:3; 21:27-36.

It shall turn out unto you for a testimony.—They would have an opportunity to preach the gospel of Christ when subjected to these persecutions. Peter and John were arrested for preaching the resurrection of Jesus, but the Holy Spirit supplied the words of their defense (Acts 4:1-21). The amazing boldness of that defense caused their persecutors to take account of the fact that they had been with Jesus. Paul's defense before Aprippa is a defense of the gospel rather than of the apostle. The early church seized upon all these occasions as opportunities to tell about the Christ.

Settle it therefore in your hearts.—In those days of persecution, they

347

were not even to think beforehand what to say or how to say it. It would be given to them in the moment of need by the Holy Spirit. They, of course, had experienced the same thing when Jesus sent them on their first mission (Luke 12:11-12).

This ability to speak without previous meditation continued throughout the beginning days of the church, but when the completed revelation—the Bible—came, there was no further need for it. See *Studies in First Corinthians*, p. 243.

And not a hair of your head shall perish.—Despite the fact that some of them would be put to death during the perilous times before the destruction of Jerusalem, Jesus said that not a hair of their heads would perish. The words that follow explain what He meant. By their endurance of trials they were to save their souls, that is, they were to gain eternal life (Rev. 2:10).

The same thought is presented in Matt. 24:9-13. The disciples were to face persecution and hatred. False prophets would lead many astray, iniquity would be multiplied, and the love of many would grow cold. But Jesus said, "He that endureth to the end—the end of whatever persecution he might suffer, even death, during the period that led to the destruction of Jerusalem—will be saved."

Jerusalem Surrounded by Armies

Scripture

21:20-24   But when ye see Jerusalem compassed with armies, then know that her desolation is at hand. 21 Then let them that are in Judaea flee unto the mountains; and let them that are in the midst of her depart out; and let not them that are in the country enter therein. 22 For these are days of vengeance, that all things which are written may be fulfilled. 23 Woe unto them that are with child and to them that give suck in those days! for there shall be great distress upon the land, and wrath unto this people. 24 And they shall fall by the edge of the sword, and shall be led captive into all the nations: and Jerusalem shall be trodden down of the Gentiles, until the times of the Gentiles be fulfilled.

Comments

But when ye see Jerusalem surrounded with armies.—This was the sign that her destruction was at hand. And it did happen in 70 A. D. when the Roman legions surrounded the city, descrated its holy temple, and utterly destroyed the city with a devastation the like of which had not occurred from the beginning of the world nor would ever befall another city (Matt. 24:21). The next thing like it will be the destruction of the world at the end of the age.

Then let them that are in Judea.—Since this instruction was for those in Judea, it could not apply to the end of the world and the destruction that shall come upon all them that dwell on the face of all the earth (21:35).

For these are days of vengeance.—The wrath of the Lord came upon the nation that rejected its King. Jerusalem suffered because it would not let Christ save it from impending doom (13:34-35).

and Jerusalem shall be trodden down by the Gentiles.—As in the case of any occupied country, the people of Jerusalem must have hated the sound of marching feet as Roman soldiers moved everywhere through the streets of their city. They were eager to throw off the Roman yoke and might have been willing to follow Jesus if He had offered to lead them. We do not know the extent to which His refusal to let them make their king may have influenced them, but we do know that they turned away from Him and finally before the Roman judge cried out, "We have no king but Caesar." Because they crucified the Christ, their beloved city will be trodden down by the Gentiles until He comes again.

until the times of the Gentiles be fulfilled.—Some assume from Paul's reference to the "fulness of the Gentiles" (Rom. 11:25) that when the "full number" of Gentiles will have been converted to Christ, the Jews will come again into the favor of God. There seems to be no good reason for this view, for since the Day of Pentecost all whom God invites through the gospel message to come to Him, even those who are afar off whether Jews or Gentiles, may be saved. The priority of the Jew was forfeited at the cross, but the gospel, of course, is to be preached to all men, both Jews and Gentiles, until Christ comes again.

The history of Jerusalem to this day supports the view that the city will be under Gentile domination to the end of time.

Christ's Coming in Contrast to Destruction of Jerusalem

Scripture

21:25-27   And there shall be signs in sun and moon and stars; and upon the earth distress of nations, in perplexity for the roaring of the sea and the billows; 26 men fainting for fear, and for expectation of the things which are coming on the world: for the powers of the heavens shall be shaken. 27 And then shall they see the Son of man coming in a cloud with power and great glory.

Comments

And there shall be signs in sun and moon and stars.—The second coming of Christ will be marked by conclusions of the heavens and the earth. They are not the same as marked the approaching destruction of Jerusalem. Those signs gave the disciples time to prepare for what was about to happen by fleeing from the doomed city. His coming will be at an unknown time; the day of the Lord will come as a thief in the night. It will come when the longsuffering of God will have reached its end. At that time the heavens will pass away with a great noise; the earth and its works will be burned up. See II Pet. 3:9-10. The sight of it will cause men to faint with fear. Then they shall see the sign of the Son of Man: His coming in the clouds with power and great glory. See also Matt. 24:30.

Instruction About The Destruction of Jerusalem

Scripture

21:28-32　　But when these things begin to come to pass, look up, and lift up your heads; because your redemption draweth nigh.

29 And he spake to them a parable: Behold the fig tree, and all the trees: 30 when they now shoot forth, ye see it and know of your own selves that the summer is now nigh. 31 Even so ye also, when ye see these things coming to pass, know ye that the kingdom of God is nigh. 32 Verily I say unto you, This generation shall not pass away, till all things be accomplished.

Comments

But when these things begin to come to pass.—Verse 28 is usually treated as belonging to the paragraph about the coming of Christ. If, however, we make it the beginning of the new paragraph about the destruction of Jerusalem which ends at verse 32, it refers to the things the disciples were to see as that destruction drew near.

There are good reasons for treating it in this way: (1) It does not contradict the plain suggestion that the coming of Christ will be at an unknown time. (2) It makes Jesus' instruction to the disciples to look up and lift up their heads because their redemption was drawing near mean something to them, for some of them would be alive when the destruction of Jerusalem would occur. (3) It avoids the assumption that Jesus led the disciples to expect His coming in their lifetime.

your redemption draweth nigh.—Redemption means release. It may refer to the release from slavery to sin—the most common use of the term in the New Testament. It may refer to the release from the conditions imposed on creation because of the sin of man (Rom. 8:18-25). In this context, it refers to the disciples' release from the distress that led to the destruction of Jerusalem. Those who were in Judea who fled from the approaching doom, as Jesus told them to do, were able to save their lives (21:21).

And he spake to them a parable.—The parable of the Fig Tree is ordinarily interpreted as having to do with the second coming of Christ. In that case, the signs that Jesus had been telling His disciples about would indicate the approach of His coming, just as the new growth on the tree indicates the coming of summer. But if we make it a part of the paragraph that begins at verse 28—for the reasons given above—it refers to the approaching destruction of Jerusalem which did occur in 70 A. D. The point of the parable is: There are signs that indicate the nearness of something that is about to happen. The distress signals that Jesus pointed out enabled His disciples to see the approaching storm that fell with terrible devastation on the city that rejected her King.

know ye that the kingdom of God is nigh.—Consistency demands that this verse be interpreted in harmony with its context. If the whole context refers to the second coming of Christ, then "the kingdom of God" will naturally refer to the heavenly phase of the kingdom. But Luke used the expression "The kingdom of God is come high unto you" in a different sense in 10:9, 11. On their first mission, the disciples were to heal the sick and say to them, "The kingdom of God has come nigh unto you." God's rule as King had come to bless those who accepted His messengers. But those who rejected their message were also to be reminded that "the kingdom of God was nigh." That this that the judgment of God was about to come on them is seen in the fact that Jesus continued to say, "It shall be more tolerable in that day for Soddom than for that city." It seems logical, then, to think of the coming of the kingdom of God in connection with the destruction of Jerusalem as His judgment on that city.

In the parable of the King's Son, Jesus told about those who rejected the invitation of the king and said, "The king was wroth and sent his armies and destroyed those murderers, and burned their city." The kingdom of God—His kingly authority and rule—did come upon that city in judgment.

Another problem is presented by the text as Matthew gives it: "When you see all these things, know ye that he (or it) is nigh, even at the doors" (Matt. 24:33). The subject of the verb is not given in the Greek. It may be the neuter pronoun as in the King James or the masculine as in the American Standard and R. S. V. If we say, "he is near," we relate the whole context to the coming of Christ and are involved in the difficulties suggested by that interpretation. But if we say "it is near," we relate it to the destruction of Jerusalem, the theme of the discourse, and avoid these problems.

If we translate "It—meaning the destruction of Jerusalem—is near," We must interpret Luke's statement, "the kingdom of God is nigh" to mean that God's judgment was about to come on that wicked city.

This generation shall not pass away.—Some assume that this refers to the Jews as a race and that they are to continue as a people until the coming of Christ. It is well known that they have continued through the centuries since the destruction of Jerusalem without a central government—only a few of them are now in Israel—and without a common place of worship. They have undergone terrible persecutions. They are identifiable wherever they are found. But to use "generation" in this strained manner is to overlook the fact that Jesus was talking to His disciples about the generation to which they belonged. The destruction of Jerusalem was to occur within the lifetime of some of them.

Christ's Coming at the End of the World

Scripture

21:33-36 Heaven and earth shall pass away: but my words shall not pass away.

34 But take heed to yourselves, lest haply your hearts be overcharged with surfeiting, and drunkenness, and cares of this life, and that day come on you suddenly as a snare: 35 for so shall it come upon all them that dwell on the face of the earth. 36 But watch ye at every season, making supplication, that ye may prevail to escape all these things that shall come to pass, and to stand before the Son of man.

Comments

Heaven and earth shall pass away.—A new paragraph begins with this verse, and should so be indicated in the text. In Matthew 24, a new paragraph should begin with verse 35, although R. S. V. makes it begin with 36, while the American Standard begins the paragraph at 32 and runs through 44 without a break.

Jesus' remark, "Heaven and earth shall pass away" answers the disciples' question about the sign of His coming and the end of the world (Matt. 24:3). They had evidently assumed that the two would happen at the same time; the language seems to imply that they also believed that the destruction of Jerusalem would occur at the end of the world. Having explained in detail about Jerusalem, Jesus proceeded to tell about the end of the world. "Heaven and earth shall pass away"—of that they could be sure—but His "words shall not pass away."

Matthew records another statement which Jesus made in this connection. He said, "But of that day and hour knoweth no one, not even the angels of heaven, neither the Son, but the Father only" (Matt. 24:36). His coming will be at an unknown time. On the other hand, the signs of the destruction of Jerusalem enabled the disciples to anticipate the approaching doom of the city and escape before it was too late.

But take heed to yourselves.—The fact that His coming will be at an unknown time requires all His disciples at all times in all generations to be prepared for that great day.

and that day come on you suddenly as a snare.—If they are prepared at all times they will not be taken unawares. Paul reminded the Thessalonians that they knew that the day of the Lord comes as a thief in the night. But he also told them that they did not need to be taken unawares, for they were to live in the light of God's instruction and put on the armor of God so that they might obtain salvation through the Lord Jesus Christ. See I Thes. 5:2-11.

upon all them that dwell on the face of the earth.—The day of His coming will affect those living at that time and it also affects all those living before that time, for all must prepare to meet Him when He comes. That preparation must be made in this lifetime, for there will be no opportunity to do so after death. See Luke 16:26.

Watch at every season.—Everyone at all times must watch! Peter said, "Be sober, be watchful: your adversary the devil, as a roaring lion walketh about seeking whom he may devour, whom withstand in your faith" (I Pet. 5:8-9). Even though Peter had heard these words of Jesus, he let himself be caught off guard by the enemies of the Lord when He was on trial.

that ye may prevail.—Peter also reminds us to "give diligence to make your calling and election sure" (II Pet. 1:10). Those who fail to do so forget the cleansing from their old sins. Jesus urged His disciples to keep their eyes on His coming at all times.

and to stand before the Son of man.—that is, stand before Him like those of the Parable of the Pounds who used their opportunity to serve Him while waiting for His return. They could stand before the King without shame, for they were prepared for His coming.

Jesus Teaching in the Temple

Scripture

21:37-38   And every day he was teaching in the temple; and every night he went out, and lodged in the mount that is called Olivet. 38 And all the people came early in the morning to him in the temple, to hear him.

Comments

teaching in the temple.—At the age of twelve, He was in the temple amazing the Jewish leaders with His understanding and answers. A great deal of His teaching had been done in Galilee, in the synagogues or by the Sea of Galilee or in the villages of that district. On special occasions He came to Jerusalem and taught the people who came to the feasts. As the ministry of Jesus was drawing to a close, Luke reminded Theophilus that Jesus was daily in the temple teaching. But that temple was completely destroyed within a few short years from that time, never to be built again.

and lodged in the mount that is called Olivet.—He spent the night with His disciples in the mount of Olives. Luke does not inform us of the details. We may suppose that they camped out; after a busy day in the city, they went there to find rest and quiet.

the people came early in the morning.—Luke mentions the eagerness of the people when John began to preach, for they wondered if he could be the Christ. Undoubtedly, many of those who came early in the morning had heard Jesus teach before, but their eagerness was not dulled as they listened to the good news of salvation. How strange that they soon joined the mob that cried out for Him to be crucified.

Summary

This chapter deals with the subject of the destruction of Jerusalem. Two brief references to the second coming of Christ are made: one in connection with the things that were to happen at the time of the destruction of Jerusalem. It was given to show why the disciples need not be misled by false reports of His presence at that time. The sign of the destruction of Jerusalem would be the seige of the city of the armies of Rome, but the sign of the Son of Man will be His coming in the clouds with power and great glory. No one of them needed to be confused by rumors of false prophets. No one will be in doubt about it when they actually see Him when He comes at the end of the age. The other reference is given at the close of the discussion about Jerusalem. Heaven and earth will pass away, but His words will not pass away: He will come again as He said. The issue is: Be prepared for that day!

Questions

1. Why did Jesus comment on the widow's two small coins?
2. What had He said about hypocrisy in giving?
3. Is there anything to suggest that those who were putting into the treasury their gifts that came from their abundance were guilty of fraud or hypocracy?
4. Why was the widow's gift more than all the others?
5. What principles of giving did Paul teach?
6. Does the Lord's work really need the gifts of the rich?
7. In what chapters of the New Testament is the discourse on the destruction of Jerusalem found?
8. Why study all three accounts?
9. How did Jesus begin the lesson?
10. Why did He mention His coming in connection with the lesson He was teaching about the destruction of Jerusalem?
11. What would the disciples be able to see before the destruction of Jerusalem?
12. What did He mean by the reference to their redemption?
13. What did He mean by the reference to the kingdom of God in this connection?
14. What did He say about His coming at the close of the discourse on the destruction of Jerusalem?

15. How complete was the destruction of Jerusalem to be?
16. Who asked Him about it?
17. What was their question about?
18. What does their question reveal about their thinking on the destruction of Jerusalem and on the second coming of Christ?
19. What is the sign that will identify Christ when He comes?
20. Why was it unnecessary to be disturbed by false rumors of His coming at the time of the destruction of Jerusalem?
21. To what does "wars and rumors of wars" refer?
22. What was the sign of the approaching doom of the city?
23. To what may "terrors and great signs from heaven" refer?
24. What is the difference between this and "signs in the sun and moon and stars"?
25. To what does each of these refer?
26. What were the disciples to suffer before the destruction of Jerusalem?
27. How were they to regard persecutions?
28. What promise of providential protection did Jesus give them?
29. To what end did Jesus refer when He said, "He that endureth to the end shall be saved"?
30. Why did Jesus refer to those in Judea?
31. What is meant by "Jerusalem shall be trodden down by the Gentiles"?
32. What is meant by "the times of the Gentiles be fulfilled"?
33. To what does verse 38 refer?
34. How is "redemption" used in the New Testament?
35. What are the different readings of Matthew 24:33? Which is to be preferred?
36. What is meant by "this generation shall not pass away etc."?
37. Why did Jesus say, "Heaven and earth shall pass away"?
38. What does Matthew say about the time of Jesus' coming?
39. What should all do in view of the nature of Christ's coming?
40. How prepare for it?
41. What bearing does the parable of the Pounds have on the coming of Christ?
42. What was Jesus doing in the temple?
43. Where did Jesus and His disciples spend the nights of the final week of His ministry?
44. What was the attitude of the people toward Him at that time?

A. Luke told about the events that preceded the betrayal and arrest of Jesus (1-46).
1. The search for a way to kill Him (1-6).
    a) The time: Feast of unleavened bread, the Passover.
    b) The conspirators: Chief priests and scribes.
    c) The instigator and his agent: Satan and Judas Iscariot.
    d) The plan: Judas was to deliver Him to them for an agreed price. He was to do it without arousing the people.
2. The last Passover feast (7-38).
    a) Peter and John were sent to make the necessary preparations (7-13).
    b) Jesus and the disciples sat down to eat the Passover (14-38).
        (1) Jesus told of His desire to eat this Passover as it was to be fulfilled in the kingdom of God. (14-16).
        (2) He explained the significance of the Passover cup (17-18). He would not drink it again until the kingdom of God should come.
        (3) He instituted the Lord's supper which was to be kept in memory of Him (19-20).
        (a) The bread represents His body.
        (b) The cup represents the new covenant in His blood.
        (4) He pointed out the traitor (21-22). The disciples wondered which of them it would be.
        (5) He settled the question as to which of them was the greatest (24-30).
            (a) The standard of Gentile kings contrasted with His: Oppression vs. humble service.
            (b) The kingdom in which they would judge the twelve tribes of Israel.
        (6) He warned Simon Peter about Satan's desire to have them and predicted Peter's denial. (31-34).
        (7) He told the disciples what to expect on their next mission: The need for a sword (35-38).
3. The agony in Gethsemane (39-46).
    a) The disciples warned.
    b) The prayer for the cup to be removed.

c) The strengthening by the angels.

d) The sweat that became like drops of blood.

e) The warning repeated to the sleeping disciples: "Pray that you enter not into temptation."

B. Luke told about the betrayal and arrest of Jesus (47-65).

1. The traitor's kiss (47-53).

a) Jesus challenged Judas: "Are you betraying the Son of man with a kiss—a sign of friendship?"

b) The disciples offered to defend Him; Peter struck off the ear of the high priest's servant.

c) Jesus challenged the action of the priests, but it was their hour, the hour of darkness.

2. The arrest (54-65).

a) Jesus was led to the high priest's house; Peter followed from a distance (54).

b) Peter denied three times that he knew Jesus (55-60).

c) The Lord looked at Peter; he left, weeping bitterly (61-62).

d) Jesus was mocked and reviled by His captors (63-65).

C. Luke told about the trial of Jesus before the Jews (66-71).

1. The convening of the court of elders, chief priests and scribes (66).

2. The trial (67-69).

a) The court's question: "If you are the Christ, tell us."

b) Jesus' answer: "If I tell you you won't believe; if I ask, you won't answer."

c) Jesus statement of His position: "The Son of Man will be seated at the right hand of the power of God."

d) The court's second question: "Are you, then, the Son of God?"

e) Jesus' answer: "You say that I am."

3. Their verdict (70).

a) No further testimony needed.

b) "We have heard from his own mouth."

The Search for a Way

Scripture

22:1-6 Now the feast of unleavened bread drew nigh, which is called the Passover. 2 And the chief priests and the scribes sought how they might put him to death; for they feared the people.

3. And Satan entered into Judas who was called Iscariot, being of the number of the twelve.

4. And he went away, and communed with the chief priests and captains, how he might deliver him unto them. 5 And they were glad, and covenanted to give him money. 6 And he consented, and sought opportunity to deliver him unto them in the absence of the multitude.

Comments

Now the feast of the unleavened bread drew nigh.—This is one of the three principle feasts of the Jews. It lasted a whole week and came immediately after the Passover Feast. For this reason, Luke says it was called the Passover.

how they might put Him to death.—The chief priests and scribes had already decided that He must die. Jesus was well aware of their intention to kill Him. On one occasion He had asked, "Why seek ye to kill Me?" (John 7:19) While the Jews, of course, denied it, they had actually attempted to carry out their plot more than once. See John 8:9 and 10:31. This murderous plot crystalized in the minds of their leaders at the time of the healing of the lame man at the pool of Bethseda. It was at that time that Jesus had made it clear that He was equal with God. This, in their minds, was blasphemy and punishable by death. Their only problem was how to get it done. They, of course, would have to get permission from the Roman governor to have Him put to death, but this was no problem. The real problem was to carry out the plot without arousing the people. Luke had already indicated that the people were coming early in the morning to hear Him teach in the temple. The crowd had welcomed Him at the triumphal entry. But the search for the way would soon be over.

and Satan entered into Judas.—The plot of these conspirators was master-minded by Satan himself. It was both daring and clever, for Judas was one of the twelve. But it was the biggest mistake Satan ever made. In the Garden of Eden, God had said that the seed of the woman would bruise the head of the serpent. Evidentally, Satan did not believe Him, for he tried to overcome Jesus in the wilderness temptation and was now seeking a way to put Him to death. But it was through death that Jesus was to bring to nought this one who had the power of death; that is, the devil. (Hebrews 2:14).

Luke says that Satan entered into Judas. This is not demon possession. Jesus called Judas a devil (John 6:70-71), not a demon. He was a man who had deliberately given himself over to the control of Satan. It is not too difficult to see how this was done. Judas was a thief (John 12:6). He had charge of the treasury of Jesus and the apostles and had been in the habit of stealing from that fund. This unholy desire for money was his downfall. The thought of selling his Lord for thirty pieces of silver was too great a temptation for him to withstand. He bargained with the chief priests and the captains to betray Jesus into their hands. He knew how to get the deed done, for he knew that sacred spot in Gethsemane where Jesus and His disciples often went to be alone in prayer. There he could betray his Lord, without arousing the people.

The Last Passover Feast

Scripture

22:7-38 And the day of unleavened bread came, on which the passover must be sacrificed. 8 And he sent Peter and John, saying, Go and make ready for us the passover, that we may eat. 9 And they said unto him, Where wilt thou that we make ready? 10 And he said unto them, Behold, when ye are entered into the city, there shall meet you a man bearing a pitcher of water; follow him into the house whereinto he goeth. 11 And ye shall say unto the master of the house, The Teacher saith unto thee, Where is the guest-chamber, where I shall eat the passover with my disciples? 12 And he will show you a large upper room furnished: there make ready. 13 And they went, and found as he had said unto them: and they made ready the passover.

14 And when the hour was come, he sat down, and the apostles with him. 15. And he said unto them, With desire I have desired to eat this passover with you before I suffer: 16 for I say unto you, I shall not eat it, until it be fulfilled in the kingdom of God. 17 And he received a cup, and when he had given thanks, he said, Take this, and divide it among yourselves: 18 for I say unto you, I shall not drink from henceforth of the fruit of the vine, until the kingdom of God shall come. 19 And he took bread, and when he had given thanks, he brake it, and gave to them, saying, This is my body which

is given for you: this do in remembrance of me. 20 And the cup in like manner after supper, saying, This cup is the new covenant in my blood, even that which is poured out for you. 21 But behold, the hand of him that betrayeth me is with me on the table. 22 For the Son of man indeed goeth, as it hath been determined: but woe unto that man through whom he is betrayed! 23 And they began to question among themselves, which of them it was that should do this thing.

24. And there arose also a contention among them, which of them was accounted to be greatest. 25 And he said unto them, The kings of the Gentiles have lordship over them; and they that have authority over them are called Benefactors. 26 But ye shall not be so: but he that is the greater among you, let him become as the younger; and he that is chief, as he that doth serve. 27 For which is greater, he that sitteth at meat, or he that serveth? is not he that sitteth at meat? but I am in the midst of you as he that serveth. 28 But ye are they that have continued with me in my temptations; 29 and I appoint unto you a kingdom, even as my Father appointed unto me, 30 that ye may eat and drink at my table in my kingdom; and ye shall sit on thrones judging the twelve tribes of Israel.

31 Simon, Simon, behold, Satan asked to have you, that he might sift you as wheat: 32 but I made supplication for thee, that thy faith fail not; and do thou, when once thou hast turned again, establish thy brethren. 33 And he said unto him, Lord, with thee I am ready to go both to prison and to death. 34 And he said, I tell thee, Peter, the cock shall not crow this day, until thou shall thrice deny that thou knowest me.

And he said unto them, When I sent you forth without purse, and wallet, and shoes, lacked ye anything? And they said, Nothing. 36 And he said unto them, But now, he that hath a purse, let him take it, and likewise a wallet; and he that hath none, let him sell his cloak, and buy a sword. 37 For I say unto you, that this is which is written must be fulfilled in me, And he was reckoned with transgressors: for that which concerneth me hath fulfilment. 38 And they said, Lord, behold, here are two swords. And he said unto them, It is enough.

Comments

The day of unleavened bread came.—This day began on Thursday at sundown and ended on Friday at sundown. The passover meal was eaten on Thursday night. The crucifixion of Christ occurred on Friday. Luke says it was the day of Preparation and the sabbath was beginning (Luke 23:54-55). Mark says that it was the day of Preparation; that is, the day before the sabbath (Mark 15:42). John calls it Preparation of the passover (John 19:14). John was speaking of those Jews who didn't want to enter the judgment hall and become defiled, making them unable to eat the feast, meaning not the passover itself but the feasts of that entire week. They apparently had no thought of being defiled by their murderous plot to destroy the Son of God. John's reference makes it clear that the word "passover" was sometimes used synonymously with the expression "the feast of unleavened bread." Luke also adds that after the burial of the body of Jesus, the women prepared the spices and rested on the sabbath (Luke 23:55). John calls it a high sabbath because it was the sabbath of this passover week. (John 19:31).

Go make ready for us the passover.—Peter and John were given the task of preparing the passover meal for Jesus and His apostles. Jesus gave them detailed directions which they were to follow. Did this indicate His supernatural knowledge or had He previously spoken to the master of the house about the place where He and His disciples were to keep the feast? We are well aware of the fact that the Scriptures indicate that Jesus knew all things. Some of the things in the account suggest that Jesus had already contacted the owner of the house. Peter and John were to say, "Where is the guest chamber where the Teacher is to eat the passover with His disciples?" They were shown the large upper room, and they prepared for the passover.

And when the hour was come, He sat down and the apostles with Him.—This was not a hurried meal as some have suggested, but the regular passover at the regular time. Jesus had His heart set on keeping this passover because it was soon to be fulfilled in the kingdom of God.

until it be fulfilled in the kingdom of God.—Is this a reference to the eternal kingdom of God—heaven itself—or to the church? The slaying of the passover lamb looks forward to the sacrifice of Christ, the Lamb of God. The Lord's Supper, which was instituted at this particular passover feast, looks back to His crucifixion and forward to His coming again. It would seem, therefore, that this is a reference to the kingdom which began on the day of Pentecost; that is, the church.

and he received the cup.—This was the passover cup. He said, "Divide this among yourselves," for He would not eat again of the fruit of the vine until the kingdom of God should come; that is, the church.

He took the bread.—Having pointed out the significance of the passover, Jesus instituted the Lord's Supper by taking the bread and pointing out that it represented His body which was given for them. They were to eat it in remembrance of Him. After the supper, He took the cup and said, "This is the new covenant in my blood, which is poured out for you." The new covenant was sealed in the blood of Christ. Its blessing, the remission of sins, was made available through the shedding of His blood (Matthew 26:28). Paul calls it a cup of blessing because it represents the remission of sins. He also calls it a cup which we bless because we praise God for the thing which He did for us. It is a participation in the remission of sins through the blood of Christ (I Corinthians 10:16). See *Studies in First Corinthians,* Pgs. 187-191 and 208-212.

the hand of him that betrayeth me.—When Jesus indicated that the traitor was in their midst, the disciples began to wonder which one it was. Even Judas dared ask, "Is it I, Rabbi?" (Matthew 26:25) Did he assume that this would keep Jesus from knowing that he had already bargained to betray Him to the enemy for 30 pieces of silver?

which of them was accounted to be greatest.—Judas was not the only one who had mistaken notions about the kingdom of Christ. James and John had attempted to use family influence to gain a special position in that kingdom, but apparently all of them were wondering which one was to be the greatest. This attitude characterized the kings of the Gentiles, not the servants of the Lord. He was in their midst as one who serves; to be humble like Him was to be great.

I appoint unto you the kingdom.—Even though the task He had for them was to be performed with genuine humility, it was actually great. They were to sit at His table in His kingdom as His honored servants. The parable of the Pounds indicates that this is the church. The work of that kingdom was to be carried on through His inspired apostles.

thrones judging the twelve tribes of Israel.—See also Matthew 19:28. Paul mentions the authority that the Lord gave to the apostles (II Corinthians 10:8). The twelve tribes of Israel represent the church, for Paul indicates that the believers are the Israel of God (Galatians 6:16). Their activity was to be carried on during the "regeneration;" that is, during the period when men become new creatures through obedience to the gospel which they preached (Titus 3:3-5). In this Christian age, Christ exercises authority through His apostles. The New Testament is the record of the judgment of that court. It is as binding on the followers of Christ as the words spoken by Him in person.

Satan asked to have you.—Satan desired to sift all the apostles as one would sift wheat to separate it from the chaff. This may suggest that he believed that all of them were chaff just as Judas had demonstrated himself to be. But Jesus said to Simon Peter that he had made supplicaion for him that his faith fail not. While His prayer did not prevent Peter's denial, it did leave the way open for him to return to the Lord. Long after this experience, Peter wrote these words, "For hereunto were you called: because Christ also suffered for you, leaving you an example that you should follow in his steps: who did no sin" (I Peter 2:21-22).

both to prison and to death.—Paul had something to say about presumptuous boasting: "Wherefore let him who thinketh he standeth take heed lest he fall" (I Corinthians 10:12). No doubt Peter was sincere when he said to Jesus that he would go with Him both to prison and to death but he had not reckoned on the trial through which he was soon to go.

lacked ye anything.—The first mission of the apostles had been to the lost sheep of the house of Israel. They were to be shown hospitality by their own Jewish brethren. It was not necessary for them to take extra clothing or provisions for that journey. The first mission had been a training experience for them. Now they were being sent out into the whole wide world with the gospel. They were to face hardships of every sort. They would have to protect themselves against enemies. That is why Jesus said, "He that hath none let him sell his cloak and buy a sword." This, of course, did not mean that they were to go out and wage war. It did mean, however, that they would face situations in which it would be necessary for them to protect themselves. When they showed the Lord the two swords which they had, He said, "It is enough." Two swords would afford them some protection, but certainly would not equip them to wage literal warfare. They were to fight the good fight of the faith, preach the gospel of Christ, and tell the world torn by strife and faction about the Prince of Peace.

The Agony in Gethsemane

Scripture

22:39-46 And he came out, and went, as his custom was, unto the mount of Olives; and the disciples also followed him. 40 And when he was at the place, he said unto them, Pray that ye enter not into temptation. 41 And he was parted from them about a stone's cast; and he kneeled down and prayed, 42 saying, Father, if thou be willing, remove this cup from me; nevertheless not my will, but thine, be done. 43 And there appeared unto him an angel from heaven, strengthening him. 44 And being in an agony he prayed more earnestly; and his sweat became as it were great drops of blood falling down upon the ground. 45 And when he rose up from his prayer, he came unto the disciples, and found them sleeping for sorrow, 46 and said unto them, Why sleep ye? rise and pray, that ye enter not into temptation.

Comments

As his custom was unto the Mount of Olives.—John says that Jesus and His disciples went out of the city across the Brook Kidron and entered into a Garden (John 18:1). Matthew says it was called Gethsemane (Matthew 26:36). Jesus said to the disciples, "Pray that you enter not into temptation." He was well aware what Judas was about to do and that Peter, who boasted of his loyalty, would soon deny Him.

remove this cup from me.—Just before this prayer, He had said to the disciples, "My soul is exceeding sorrowful even unto death" (Matthew 26:38). His sweat became as great drops of blood falling down to the ground. Jesus was near death in the garden. Then angels came and strengthened Him, but He prayed the more earnestly that this cup might be removed.

It is generally believed that Jesus was asking that He might not have to go to the cross. It is assumed that human weakness caused Him to shrink from that ordeal. But Jesus had come into the world for the express purpose of giving Himself as a sacrifice for the sins of the world. He had reminded his disciples on several occasions that He had to go to Jerusalem and there to be put to death. He had also said that He had the right to lay down His life and take it up again; no man took it from Him. After His prayer in the garden, He said, "The cup which the Father has given me, shall I not drink it?" (John 18:11) Does this refer to the experience in Gethsemane or to the fact which He had announced on many occasions that He had come into the world to offer Himself on the cross?

Light is thrown on this problem by the remarks of Jesus at the time that the Greeks came saying, "We would see Jesus." He said, "Except the grain of wheat fall into the earth and die, it abides by itself alone; but if it die, it bears much fruit" (John 12:24). Then He said, "Now is my soul troubled; and what shall I say? Father, save me from this hour. But for this cause came I unto this hour" (John 12:27). But this passage is also punctuated so that it reads, "Shall I say, Father, save me from this hour?" In that case, He did not ask to be excused from death on the cross. Then He prayed, "Father, glorify thy name." John reminds us that the voice of God said I have glorified it and will glorify it again. It is also possible to interpret the prayer in Gethsemane to mean that Jesus was asking that He might not die in the Garden but that He might have the strength to go on and complete His earthly mission; that is, to die on the cross.

The Traitor's Kiss

Scripture

22:47-53 While he yet spake, behold, a multitude, and he that was called Judas, one of the twelve, went before them; and he drew near unto Jesus to kiss him. 48 But Jesus said unto him, Judas, betrayest thou the Son of man with a kiss? 49 And when they that were about him saw what would follow, they said, Lord, shall we smite with the sword? 50 And a certain one of them smote the servant of the high priest, and struck off his right ear. 51 But Jesus answered and said, Suffer ye them thus far. And he touched his ear, and healed him. 52 And Jesus said unto the chief priests, and captains of the temple, and elders, that were come against him, Are ye come out, as against a robber, with swords and staves? 53 When I was daily with you in the temple, yet stretched not forth your hands against me: but this is your hour, and the power of darkness.

Comments

Judas, one of the twelve.—The Satan-inspired traitor saluted Jesus with a kiss of friendship, little aware of the fact that Jesus knew exactly what he was up to. Jesus challenged him saying, "Judas, are you betraying the Son of Man with a kiss?" The little band of disciples drew close to Jesus, as if to protect Him. One of them— John says it was Peter—drew his sword and struck a blow in what he thought was in the defense of his Lord. All that he did was to strike off the ear of the high priest's servant. Jesus touched the ear of the high priest's servant and healed him.

Jesus had permitted them to go this far. They could arrest Him; they could sentence Him to death; they could nail Him to the cross; but they could not keep Him from arising from the dead. He turned to the captains of the temple and the chief priest and challenged them with these words, "Are you come out as against a robber with swords and with staves?" He reminded them that He had taught openly in their temple but they had not dared to touch Him. In the garden they were made bold by Satan whose strength was the power of darkness.

The Arrest of Jesus

Scripture

22:54-65   And they seized him and led him, away, and brought him into the high priest's house. But Peter followed afar off. 55 And when they had kindled a fire in the midst of the court, and had sat down together, Peter sat in the midst of them. 56 And a certain maid seeing him as he sat in the light of the fire, and looking stedfastly upon him, said, This man also was with him. 57 But he denied, saying, Woman, I know him not. 58 And after a little while another saw him, and said, Thou also art one of them. But Peter said, Man, I am not. 59 And after the space of about one hour another confidently affirmed, saying, Of a truth this man also was with him; for he is a Galilaean. 60 But Peter said, Man, I know not what thou sayest. And immediately, while he yet spake, the cock crew. 61 And the Lord turned, and looked upon Peter. And Peter remembered the word of the Lord, how that he said unto him, Before the cock crow this day thou shalt deny me thrice. 62 And he went out, and wept bitterly.

63 And the men that held Jesus mocked him, and beat him. 64

367

And they blindfolded him, and asked him, saying, Prophesy: who is he that struck thee? 65 And many other things spake they against him, reviling him.

Comments

and brought him into the high priest's house.—He was taken before Annas first and then to Caiaphas. (John 18:13-14).

but Peter followed afar off.—He had boasted of his loyalty to Christ. He had actually taken his life in his hands when he took the sword to defend Jesus. But Jesus rebuked him for doing so and meekly submitted to arrest. Peter's dream of the restoration of the kingdom with Jesus on the throne was over. But his lingering desire to see what was going to happen led him to follow at a distance and enter into the court where he sat down in the midst of those who were about to crucify his Lord. To the first one who said to him, "This man was with Him," he answered, "Woman I know Him not." A little later, another said, "You are also one of them." But he said, "Man, I am not." About an hour later, another one said, "You really are one of them, for you are a Galilean." Peter answered, "Man, I don't know what you are talking about."

and immediately while he yet spake, the cock crew.—Just then the Lord turned and looked at Peter. He remembered that the Lord had said, "Before the cock crows, you will deny me three times." What was the meaning of the look on the face of Jesus that caused Peter to go out weeping bitterly? Did it say, "I told you so?" Did it say, "You ought to be ashamed?" Or did it speak the message of love and forgiveness that made this once bold man repent of the awful thing he had done and determine that henceforth he would set the proper example before his brethren?

The Trial of Jesus Before the Jews

Scripture

22:66-71   And as soon as it was day, the assembly of the elders of the people were gathered together, both chief priests and scribes; and they led him away into their council, saying, 67 If thou art the Christ, tell us. But he said unto them, If I tell you, ye will not believe: 68 and if I ask you, ye will not answer. 69 But from henceforth shall the Son of man be seated at the right hand of the power of God. 70 And they all said, Art thou then the Son of God? And he said unto them, Ye say that I am. 71 And they said, What further need have we of witness? for we ourselves have heard from his own mouth.

Comments

If thou art the Christ, tell us.—This is actually the third phase of the trial before the Jews. It was held early in the morning to plan the presentation of the case before Pilate, for they had to get his permission in order to have the death sentence carried out. Their question was how to get a confession from Him that would justify them in doing what had already been determined to do.

Jesus answered, "If I tell you, you will not believe, and if I ask you, you will not answer." Jesus had told them before that He was the Son of God, but they did not believe Him (John 5:18; 10:36). There was no reason to suppose that if He should repeat the statement that they would believe Him. On the other hand, when He had asked them, "What think ye of the Christ; Whose Son is He?" they had refused to answer. Had they done so, they would have involved themselves in the confession that David's son was also his Lord.

But from henceforth shall the son of man be seated.—Jesus called attention to the fact that He was soon to be seated on the right hand of the power of God. In His final statement in the Jewish trial, the third phase of which was just then being hurriedly conducted, Jesus referred to Himself as "Son of Man"—that is, Messiah. But Messiah, of course, was not only the Son of man, He was also the Son of God. This is seen in Peter's confession when he said, "Thou art the Christ (Messiah) the Son of the Living God."

The Jews evidently understood that "Son of Man" means also that He was "Son of God," for their next question was, "Art thou, then, the Son of God?" He answered them affirmatively, "Ye say that I am." A similar answer was given to Pilate. Paul comments on it, saying that Jesus confessed the good confession before Pontius Pilate; that is, He acknowledged that He was the Christ, the Son of the living God (I Timothy 6:13).

What further need have we of witnesses?—This seemed to satisfy them; they had finally forced from Him the confession that justified them in condemning Him as a blasphemer; they had heard it from His own mouth.

Summary

The enemies of Jesus had long since determined that He must be destroyed. They were only searching for a way to get it done without arousing the people. The feast, they thought, would be a poor time. But Satan, the chief conspirator, showed them how it could be done even during the Passover. He entered the heart of Judas who bargained for the thirty pieces of silver to deliver Jesus into their hands. He knew the place; he knew how to get the thing done quietly.

Jesus, of course, was well aware of what was going on. He had told the disciples that He must die in Jerusalem. He was eager to eat the last passover with them, for He would soon become the Lamb that would be sacrificed for the sins of the people. At the feast He pointed out the traitor.

Jesus instituted the Lord's supper that the disciples might be caused to remember His death for them until He comes again.

But the disciples were still thinking of an earthly kingdom. They began to argue about which of them was to be the greatest. Jesus again reminded them that true greatness was to be found in the humble servant. He had set the example for them. And they would see times when they would need to remember this lesson. Satan had desired to have all of them. He must have thought that all of them could be bought as Judas had been. Jesus' supplication for Peter did not prevent his denying that he had ever known such a person as Jesus, but it did leave the way open for his return.

The agony of Gethsemane brought Jesus near physical death. He asked that the cup—was it the cross or death in Gethsemane?—be removed, but was willing to submit to the Father's will. Angels strengthened Him and He finished His work as He gave Himself to die that man might be saved.

After the arrest in the Garden, Jesus was taken hurriedly through a three-fold Jewish trial. The Jews convinced themselves that they had found the excuse for putting Him to death. In their minds He was guilty of blasphemy.

Questions

1. What is the feast of unleavened bread?
2. What is the relation of the Passover to the feast of unleavened bread?

370

CHAPTER TWENTY-TWO

3. When did the Jews decide that Jesus had to be put to death?
4. Why hadn't they carried out their plot to kill Him?
5. What were they looking for at this time?
6. How had Satan entered into the heart of Judas?
7. In the light of what God said to the serpent in the Garden, why did Satan use Judas to bring about the death of Jesus?
8. What was God's purpose in the death of Jesus?
9. Why had Jesus called Judas a devil? How different from demon?
10. What was Judas' motive in betraying Jesus?
11. Where did the betrayal take place?
12. What evidence according to the Scriptures is there to suggest that Jesus was crucified on Friday? On what day did the resurrection take place?
13. What is suggested as to the supernatural knowledge of Jesus in the account of the preparation for the passover?
14. What evidence is there to show that Jesus and the disciples ate the passover meal at the regular time?
15. Why did Jesus say that He had earnestly desired to eat this passover meal?
16. In what way was it fulfilled in the kingdom of God?
17. How is the significance of the Lord's supper suggested by the fact that it was instituted at the passover meal?
18. What is the meaning of the cup? the bread?
19. How was the traitor pointed out?
20. What caused the argument about the greatest in the kingdom?
21. How did Jesus settle it?
22. What is meant by the fact that the apostles were to sit on twelve thrones judging the twelve tribes of Israel?
23. Why had Satan asked to have the apostles?
24. What did Jesus' supplication for Peter do for him?
25. What instruction did Jesus give Peter in view of the trials through which he was to go?
26. What caused Peter to deny his Lord?
27. What may be said about Peter's loyalty?
28. Why did Jesus say that the two swords were enough?
29. How did Judas know where Jesus would be?
30. What was the condition of Jesus as He entered the Garden?
31. What were the words of His prayer?
32. To what cup did He refer? What are the various views?

33. What bearing does Jesus' prayer at the time the Greeks came seeking Him have on the meaning of the cup? (John 12:27).
34. Why did Judas betray Jesus with the kiss?
35. What did Jesus mean by asking Judas about the kiss?
36. How is the arrest accounted for?
37. What are the three phases of the Jewish trial?
38. What led Peter to follow and to deny his Lord?
39. What effect did Jesus have on Peter by looking at him?
40. What was the final decision of the Jews? On what charge?

CHAPTER TWENTY-THREE

Outline

A. Luke told about the trial of Jesus before Pilate and Herod (1-25).
1. The first trial before Pilate (1-7).
    a) The charge against Him.
        (1) Perverting the nation.
        (2) Forbidding to give tribute to Caesar.
        (3) Claiming that He is Christ the King.
    b) The investigation of the charges by Pilate.
        (1) "Are you the King of the Jews?" Jesus answered affirmatively.
        (2) His verdict: "I find no fault in this man."
    c) The urgent complaint: He stirs up the nation from Judea to Galilee.
    d) The governor's decision: Send Him to Herod, the ruler of Galilee.
2. The trial before Herod (8-12).
    a) The attitude of Herod: Delighted at this turn of events, for he hoped to see Jesus work some miracle.
    b) The investigation by Herod: He questioned Jesus at length, but Jesus refused to answer.
    c) The complaint: The priests and scribes pressed their charges.
    d) The outcome of the trial: Herod and soldiers mocked Jesus and returned Him to Pilate. Pilate and Herod became friends that very day.
3. The second trial before Pilate (13-25).
    a) The verdict: Pilate reviewed the case and again pronounced Jesus innocent.
    b) The verdict of Herod: Nothing worthy of death done by Him.
    c) The plan to release Jesus: Twice announced and twice rejected. The Jews said, "Release Barabbas; crucify Jesus."
    d) The third and final effort to save Him:
        (1) Pilate asked, "What evil has he done?" The Jews urged that He be crucified.

373

(2) Pilate gave in, passed sentence on Jesus, and released Barabbas.

B. Luke told about the crucifixion of Jesus (26-49).
    1. The circumstances leading to the crucifixion (26-32).
        a) Simon of Cyrene carrying the cross.
        b) The crowds following and lamenting Him.
        c) Jesus comforted them.
            (1) "Daughters of Jerusalem, weep not for me, but for yourselves and your children."
            (2) Trials of the days to come: Fortunate are the childless; asking the mountains to fall and cover them; this in the green tree, what of the dry?
        d) The other two who were also to be put to death.
    2. The crucifixion of Jesus (33-38).
        a) The place: "The skull"—Calvary.
        b) The prayer: "Father forgive them, for they know not what they do."
        c) The people:
            (1) Parting His garments among them.
            (2) The people stood looking on.
            (3) The rulers scoffed: "Let him save himself."
            (4) The soldiers mocked Him.
        d) The sign: THIS IS JESUS THE KING OF THE JEWS.
    3. The other two who were crucified with Him (39-43).
        a) One scoffed, and was rebuked by the other.
        b) The other said, "Remember me when thou comest in thy kingdom." Jesus said, "Today shalt thou be with me in Paradise."
    4. The death of Jesus (44-49).
        a) The thing that happened: Darkness and rending of the temple veil.
        b) The word of Jesus: "Father, into thy hands I commend my spirit."
        c) The end: "He gave up the ghost," that is, He died.
        d) The reaction of those who saw Him die.
            (1) The centurion: "Certainly this was a righteous man."
            (2) The crowds: They returned, smiting their breasts.
            (3) His acquaintances and the women from Galilee: They stood some distance away, seeing these things.

C. Luke told about the burial of Jesus (50-56).
  1. The facts about Joseph of Arimathea (50-52).
     a) He was a righteous man.
     b) He had not consented to the crucifixion of Jesus.
     c) He had been looking for the kingdom of God.
     d) He asked Pilate for the body of Jesus.
  2. The facts about the burial (53-56).
     a) Joseph prepared the body for burial and laid it in the tomb.
     b) The time: The day of Preparation, and the sabbath was about to begin. There was still time to prepare the spices before the sabbath actually began (56).
     c) The women prepared spices and ointments and rested on the sabbath.

The First Trial Before Pilate
Scripture

23:1-7   And the whole company of them rose up and brought him before Pilate. 2 And they began to accuse him, saying, We found this man perverting our nation, and forbidding to give tribute to Caesar, and saying that he himself is Christ a king. 3 And Pilate asked him, saying, Art thou the King of the Jews? And he answered him and said, Thou sayest. 4 And Pilate said unto the chief priests and the multitudes, I find no fault in this man. 5 But they were the more urgent, saying, He stirreth up the people, teaching throughout all Judaea, and beginning from Galilee even unto this place. 6 But when Pilate heard it, he asked whether the man were a Galilaean. 7 And when he knew that he was of Herod's jurisdiction, he sent him unto Herod, who himself also was at Jerusalem in these days.

Comments

and brought Him before Pilate.—In the three Jewish trials, the leaders had satisfied themselves that they had found an excuse to put Jesus to death. But what about the governor? Why should a Roman care if the God of the Jews had been blasphemed?

The Jews were well aware of this; they, therefore, brought an entirely different charge against Him when they appeared before Pilate. There were three counts against Him: (1) Perverting the nation, (2) Forbidding to give tribute to Caesar, and (3) He said that Himself is Christ the King.

375

The most dangerous of the three, they seemed to think, was the first—perverting the nation. But it was the last—making Himself a king—that finally caused the governor to give in. Against his better judgment, against the advice of his wife, and against the concurrance of Herod in his own opinion Pilate granted the Jews' demand that He be crucified. See John 19:12.

They may have thought that such evidence as the presence of large crowds following Him wherever He went, especially at the triumphal entry where they praised Him as king, would be sufficient evidence to sway Pilate's judgment. Roman governors were responsible for keeping the peace and putting down any uprising that might challenge the authority of Caesar. The charge about forbidding to give tribute to Caesar was plainly a perversion of the facts in the case. See 20:20-26. The third charge was true but not in the sense in which they presented it, for His kingdom was not of this world (John 18:26). Moreover, Pilate was well aware of the fact that they had delivered Him up out of envy (Matthew 27:18).

I find no fault in Him.—Pilate pronounced Jesus innocent three times; yet in the end, he acceded to the demands of the Jews and ordered the innocent Christ to be crucified.

He asked whether the man were a Galilean.—Jesus' ministry, for the most part, had been carried on in Herod's territory. Learning of this, Pilate eagerly sought to shift the responsibility of Jesus' case to Herod. But Herod, after examining Him, sent Him back to Pilate who announced that Herod had found nothing worthy of death in Him (23:15).

The Trial Before Herod

Scripture

23:8-12 Now when Herod saw Jesus, He was exceeding glad,: for he was of a long time desirous to see him, because he had heard concerning him; and he hoped to see some miracle done by him. 9 And he questioned him in many words; but he answered him nothing. 10 And the chief priests and the scribes stood, vehemently accusing him. 11 And Herod with his soldiers set him at nought, and mocked him, and arraying him in gorgeous apparel sent him back to Pilate. 12 And Herod and Pilate became friends with each other that very day: for before they were at enmity between themselves.

Comments

When Herod saw Jesus.—Herod at one time had been frightened by the reports of the miracles of Jesus. He concluded that Jesus was John the Baptism risen from the dead and, therefore, able to perform these signs. Later, a report was circulated that Herod wanted to kill Jesus. There was another shift in his attitude, by the time of His trial. He was delighted to see Jesus, for he wanted to see Him work a miracle. Jesus, of course, did not grant his wish. After he and his men had treated Him with every indignity, Herod returned Him to Pilate. On that day these two rulers who had been at enmity with each other became friends.

The Second Trial Before Pilate

Scripture

23:13-25   And Pilate called together the Chief Priest and the rulers, and the people, 14 and said unto them, Ye brought unto me this man, as one that perverteth the people: and behold, I, having examined him before you, found no fault in this man touching those things whereof ye accuse him: 15 no, nor yet Herod: for he sent him back unto us; and behold, nothing worthy of death hath been done by him. 16 I will therefore chastise him, and release him. 18 But they cried out all together, saying, Away with this man, and release unto us Barabbas:—19 one who for a certain insurrection made in the city, and for murder, was cast into prison. 20 And Pilate spake unto them again, desiring to release Jesus; 21 but they shouted, saying, Crucify, crucify him. 22 And he said unto them the third time, Why, what evil hath this man done? I have found no cause of death in him: I will therefore chastise him and release him. 23 But they were urgent with loud voices, asking that he might be crucified. And their voices prevailed. 24 And Pilate gave sentence that what they asked for should be done. 25 And he released him that for insurrection and murder had been cast into prison, whom they asked for; but Jesus he delivered up to their will.

Comments

I will therefore chastise him and release him.—Pilate may have believed that this cruel and inhuman beating would satisfy the Jews' desire for vengeance. But they noisily demanded that He be crucified.

377

and release unto us Barabbas.—Barabbas was a notable prisoner who had been guilty of all the things that had been charged against Jesus and more, for he was actually a murderer. But the misguided mob chose Barabbas and demanded the death penalty for Jesus.

On the day of Pentecost, the 3,000 reversed that decision—repented—and accepted Jesus as Lord and Christ. (Acts 2:36-38). See also Acts 3:18-15.

The Crucifixion of Jesus

Scripture

23:26-49   And when they led him away, they laid hold upon one Simon of Cyrene, coming from the country, and laid on him the cross, to bear it after Jesus.

27 And there followed him a great multitude of the people, and of women who bewailed and lamented him. 28 But Jesus turning unto them said, Daughters of Jerusalem, weep not for me, but weep for yourselves, and for your children. 29 For behold, the days are coming, in which they shall say, Blessed are the barren, and the wombs that never bare, and the breasts that never gave suck. 30 Then shall they begin to say to the mountains, Fall on us; and to the hills, Cover us. 31 For if they do these things in the green tree, what shall be done in the dry?

32 And there were also two others, malefactors, led with him to be put to death.

33 And when they came unto the place which is called The skull, there they crucified him, and the malefactors, one on the right hand and the other on the left. 34 And Jesus said, Father, forgive them; for they know not what they do. And parting his garments among them, they cast lots. 35 And the people stood beholding. And the rulers also scoffed at him, saying, He saved others; let him save himself, if this is the Christ of God, his chosen. 36 And the soldiers also mocked him, coming to him, offering him vinegar, 37 and saying, If thou art the King of the Jews, save thyself. 38 And there was also a superscription over him, *THIS IS THE KING OF THE JEWS.*

39 And one of the malefactors that were hanged railed on him, saying, Art not thou the Christ? save thyself and us. 40 But the other answered, and rebuking him said, Dost thou not even fear God, seeing thou art in the same condemnation? 41 And we indeed

justly; for we receive the due reward of our deeds: but this man hath done nothing amiss. 42 And he said, Jesus, remember me when thou comest in thy kingdom. 43 And he said unto him, Verily I say unto thee, Today shalt thou be with me in Paradise.

44 And it was now about the sixth hour, and a darkness came over the whole land until the ninth hour, 45 the sun's light failing: and the veil of the temple was rent in the midst. 46 And Jesus, crying with a loud voice, said, Father, into thy hands I commend my spirit; and having said this, he gave up the ghost. 47 And when the centurion saw what was done, he glorified God, saying, certainly this was a righteous man. 48 And all the multitudes that came together to this sight, when they beheld the things that were done, returned smiting their breasts. 49 And all his acquaintance, and the women that followed with him from Galilee, stood afar off, seeing these things.

Comments

Simon of Cyrene.—John says that Jesus went out, bearing His own cross; that is, He started to the place of the crucifixion carrying the cross (John 19:17). His agony in Gethsemane and the ordeal of the trial could easily have been the cause of His needing help to bear the heavy burden of the cross. Simon of Cyrene—Cyrene was a country in north Africa—was compelled to bear it after Jesus.

> Must Jesus bear the cross alone,
> And all the world go free?
> No; there's a cross for everyone,
> And there's a cross for me.

Daughters of Jerusalem.—Jesus spoke to the women who were following Him, trying to comfort them in this hour of His ordeal. He reminded them, however, that they were also facing an ordeal that would come at the time of the destruction of Jerusalem. The suffering of that day would cause some of them to say to the mountains, "Fall on us; and to the hills, Cover us." What they were suffering was likened to the green tree; He asked, "What shall be done in the dry?"

The place called "The Skull."—The other writers use the Aramaic name "Golgatha," which means "skull" or, when translated into Latin, "Calvary."

And Jesus said.—Luke gives three of the words Jesus spoke from the cross. The first is found in 23:34, "Father, forgive them; for they know not what they do."

The context seems to suggest that He was speaking of those who were actually nailing Him to the cross. The rulers and others were also there, but He had already indicated on several occasions that nothing but doom awaited them because their rejection of Him was final, and no repentence was to be expected. But, of the crowds who had become involved in their sins, many would reverse their decision and find forgiveness through repentence and baptism in the name of the one who prayed "Father, forgive them."

The second, given in 23:43, is, "Verily I say unto thee, Today shalt thou be with me in Paradise."

According to Acts 2:27, which is a quotation from Psalms 16:10, Jesus was in Hades while his body lay in the tomb. Paul speaks of Paradise and identifies it with the "third heaven" (II Corinthians 12:4). He also suggests that being absent from the body means being present with the Lord (II Corinthians 5:6-9). Jesus had indicated that Hades is the place where both the good and the bad are to be found after death. (Luke 16:23).

It is correct, then, to say: (1) That Paradise is the place where the righteous dead await the resurrection, and (2) that the dying thief was told that he would be there with Jesus.

The third statement, found in 23:46, is, "Into thy hands I commend my spirit" (23:46).

He had come from the Father. As He prayed in the shadow of the cross He said, "Father, glorify thou me with thine own self with the glory which I had with thee before the world was" (John 17:5). See also Philippians 2:5-11.

Matthew and Mark mention only one saying of Jesus from the cross: "My God, my God, why hast thou forsaken me?" (Matthew 27:46; Mark 15:34).

This is a quotation from Psalm 22:1. It reveals the real meaning of the death of Christ. It was more than physical death; it was separation from the Father. The answer to the cry of Jesus is found in Paul's statement, "Him who knew no sin he made to be sin on our behalf; that we might become the righteousness of God in him" (II Corinthians 5:21). As Son of Man—He was also Son of God—God made Him represent sin. "The death that He died, He died unto sin once for all" (Rom. 6:10). There will never be another sacrifice for sin (Heb. 10:14, 18).

The cross, then, is not only the symbol of God's love, it is also the symbol of God's punishment for sin. Let those who would know the meaning of hell look at the death of Him who was made sin on our behalf.

John records three of the sayings of Jesus on the cross. The first, found in John 19:26-27, is: "Woman, behold thy son." Jesus committed His mother to the care of John. Then He said to John, "Behold thy mother." There is reason to believe that John may have been her nephew. Just why Jesus put His mother in John's care rather than one of her own sons is not stated.

The second saying is: "I thirst" (John 19:28). This indicates something of the torture Jesus was suffering as He was dying on the cross.

The third is: "It is finished" (John 19:30). In His prayer before going to the cross, He had said, "I glorified thee on earth, having accomplished the work thou hast given me to do" (John 17:4). That work was finished at the cross. The final sacrifice was made. The new and living way into the refuge which He prepared was opened (Heb. 6:19-20; 10:19-22).

He saved others.—Although they spoke out of malicious wickedness, they spoke the truth. He had saved others, and His death would save the multitude that no man can number of those who wash their robes and make them white in the blood of the Lamb (Rev. 7:9-14). But He had to die in order to do it. In His death, He brought to nought him who has power of death, that is, the devil.

THIS IS THE KING OF THE JEWS.—John says that the sign over the cross was written in Hebrew, Latin, and Greek. Pilate wanted everyone to read the sign and know that Rome had thus disposed of the one who, the Jews said, made himself a king. He refused to change the wording of the sign so as to relieve the Jews of the ignominy of having their king die on a Roman cross. See John 19:19-22.

And one of the malefactors.—Two robbers were put to death at the time Jesus was crucified. Three crosses were planted on Calvary. The death of Jesus provided the only possible way of escape from eternal punishment (Acts 4:12). Calvary's crosses dramatize this gospel truth.

he gave up the ghost.—that is, He died. The evidence is conclusive: (1) The darkness and the earthquake provided the setting; (2) the temple veil was rent from the top to the bottom, suggesting that something unusual had happened that it should be torn in this manner; (3) the expression of the centurion who saw Him die (Mark 15:39). A Roman soldier knew death when he saw it. He said, "Truly this man was the Son of God." (4) The soldier pierced the side of Jesus' body from which there came blood and water. It was the soldiers' judgment that He was already dead, but this was done to make sure of it (John 19:33). (5) The enemies of Jesus were concerned only that the body be kept safely in the tomb; they did not question the fact of Jesus' death.

And when the centurion.—Soldiering was never considered a soft business. Execution of criminals—and, no doubt, many innocent people—was all in a day's work for Roman soldiers. But there was something different about the death of Jesus of Nazareth. When the centurion heard Him say, "Father, into thy hands I commend my spirit," and saw all the things that were happening, he glorified God and said, "Certainly this was a righteous man." Thus he concurred in the judgment of both Pilate and Herod that this man had done nothing worthy of death; He was innocent.

According to Matthew, the centurion said, "Truly this was God's Son" (Matt. 27:54). In doing so, he recognized the deity of Jesus.

Some have assumed that a pagan soldier could not mean by this remark that He was anything other than "a son of the gods—pagan gods." But what about the centurion who loved the Jewish nation and built their synagogue? Jesus commended his faith which was unlike anything He had found in all Israel. Cornelius was another exception. God heard the prayers of this devout, God-fearing man even though he was a Gentile (Acts 10:1-4).

There is no good reason to question the meaning of the centurion's confession. He believed that Jesus was God's Son. The resurrection of Our Lord proved him right (Rom. 1:3-4).

The Burial of Jesus

Scripture

23:50-56   And behold, a man named Joseph, who was a councillor, a good and righteous man 51 (he had not consented to their counsel and deed), a man of Arimathaea, a city of the Jews, who was looking for the kingdom of God: 52 this man went to Pilate, and asked for the body of Jesus. 53 And he took it down, and wrapped it in a linen cloth, and laid him in a tomb that was hewn in stone, where never man had yet lain. 54 And it was the day of the Preparation, and the sabbath drew on. 55 And the women, who had come with him out of Galilee, followed after, and beheld the tomb, and how his body was laid. 56 And they returned, and prepared spices and ointments.

And on the sabbath they rested according to the commandment.

Comments

a man named Joseph.—Another man named Joseph had watched over Jesus in His infancy. Now this good and righteous man who was looking for the kingdom of God boldly identified himself with Him in His death. That took courage. But Joseph had not consented to this wicked deed; he had agreed with Pilate and the centurion that Jesus was innocent. It is true that he had been a secret disciple (John 19:38), but he could no longer remain so. He asked Pilate's permission to take the body of Jesus from the cross. He prepared it for burial and laid it in his own new tomb.

Nicodemus, the inquiring Pharisee whom Jesus taught the lesson of the New Birth, the bold defender of Jesus who was being condemned by all his colleagues, brought spices and helped Joseph with the burial. See John 3:1-5; 7:50; 19:39-41.

And it was the day of Preparation.—That is, Friday, for the sabbath was about to begin. The women had only time enough to prepare the spices before sundown. They rested on the sabbath and came early on the first day of the week to complete their sorrowful task.

Summary

The Jews agreed that Jesus should be put to death because, as they said, He was guilty of blasphemy. But they knew that such a charge would mean nothing to Pilate. What could they say to the governor that would get him to consent to the death of Jesus? "He was perverting the nation of the Jews!" That would do it, for the governor had to keep peace. But just to make sure, they added two more charges, forbidding to give tribute to Caesar and saying that He was a king.

Pilate examined Jesus and three times pronounced Him innocent. When he learned that Jesus was from Galilee, he sent Him to Herod who questioned Him at length but found nothing worthy of death in Him. But the Jews pressed the issue and threatened to take the case to Caesar. When Pilate saw that he was getting nowhere, he ordered Jesus to be crucified.

Jesus went out bearing His own cross, but soon Simon of Cyrene was compelled to bear the cross to the place of crucifixion. Jesus tried to comfort the women of Jerusalem as they followed Him. They would suffer—perhaps at the destruction of Jerusalem—more hardships later on. They would cry for the rocks and the mountains to fall on them and cover them from that persecution.

On the cross, Jesus prayed, "Father forgive them, for they know not what they do." He said to the dying thief, "Today, shalt thou be with me in Paradise." Just before He died, He said, "Father, into thy hands I commend my spirit."

The centurion who commanded the soldiers that executed the three looked at Jesus as He died and said, "Certainly this was a righteous man." Later he said, "This was God's Son."

Joseph of Arimathea who had been a secret disciple of Jesus went to Pilate and asked permission to take the body of Jesus down an bury it. It was the day of Preparation and the sabbath was about to begin. The women prepared spices and ointments and rested on the sabbath.

Questions

1. Why did the Jews change their charge when they brought Jesus before the governor?
2. What are the three charges which they presented before Pilate?
3. What evidence could they present to support them?
4. What was Pilate's verdict after examining Jesus?
5. Why did he send Him to Herod?
6. What was the attitude of Herod when he saw Jesus?
7. What examination of the charges did he make?
8. What was the verdict of Herod?
9. Why did he and Pilate become friends at that time?
10. What plan did Pilate use to attempt to get the people to agree to the release of Jesus?
11. When did the people reverse the decision made at the trial?
12. Who was Simon of Cyrene? What did he do?
13. What was to happen to the Daughters of Jerusalem?
14. What does Calvary mean? Golgotha?
15. What did Jesus mean by His prayer: "Father forgive them"?

16. Why did He say to the thief, "Today you will be with me in Paradise"?
17. Where are the dead awaiting the resurrection?
18. What is the significance of Jesus using the words of Psa. 22:1?
19. How does Paul explain the reason for the death of Christ?
20. What was unfair about the remark, "He saved others, but he can't save himself"?
21. Why was the sign over the cross written in three languages?
22. Why did Pilate refuse to change what he had written?
23. What made the difference between the death of Jesus and that of two who were crucified with Him?
24. What proof is there that Jesus actually died?
25. What are the two statements of the centurion? What do they mean?
26. Who was Joseph of Arimathea?
27. What had been his attitude toward Jesus?
28. Why did he ask Pilate for the body?
29. Who helped him?
30. On what day was Jesus buried?

CHAPTER TWENTY-FOUR

Outline

A. Luke told about the empty tomb where the body of Jesus had lain (1-12).
   1. The women found it empty (1-7).
      a) Time: First day of the week at early dawn as they brought spices which they had prepared.
      b) Evidence:
         (1) The stone was rolled away, but the body of Jesus was not there.
         (2) Angels asked, "Why do you seek the living among the dead?"
         (3) The angels declared that He had risen as He said.
   2. The women reported it to the apostles (8-11).
      a) Their reason: They remembered His words about the resurrection.
      b) Their names: Mary Magdalene, Joanna, Mary the mother of James, and others.
      c) The reaction of the apostles: Idle talk; they didn't believe it.
   3. The apostle Peter inspected the empty tomb (12) .

B. Luke told how Jesus appeared to the two on the way to Emmaus (13-35).
   1. The circumstances (13-24).
      a) The two were talking about the crucifixion (13-14).
      b) Jesus joined them, but they didn't recognize Him (15-16).
      c) He asked what they were talking about; they were astonished that He didn't know (17-18).
      d) They reviewed the report of the resurrection of Jesus (19-24).
         (1) The fact of the crucifixion of Jesus the Nazarene, a mighty prophet.
         (2) The hope that He would redeem Israel.
         (3) The evidence presented by the women: empty tomb; angels said He had risen.
         (4) The investigation which confirmed the fact that the tomb was empty, but Jesus was not seen.

2. The explanation of the Scriptures (25-27). Jesus explained to the two what was written about His death and resurrection.

3. The Risen Lord revealed (28-32).
   a) Jesus accepted the hospitality of the two at Emmaus; He blessed the bread and gave it to them.
   b) As He did so, they recognized Him, but He vanished from their sight.
   c) Their hearts burned as they recalled His explanation of the Scriptures.

4. The report to the eleven in Jerusalem (33-35).
   a) They went to Jerusalem and found the eleven.
   b) The apostles said to them, "The Lord is risen indeed; He has appeared to Simon."
   c) They told how He was revealed to them in the breaking of the bread.

C. Luke told of His appearing to the eleven (36-49).
   1. The evidence that proved it was He (36-43).
      a) The circumstances (36-38).
         (1) He stood in their midst and said, "Peace unto you."
         (2) They were frightened, thinking it was a spirit.
         (3) He asked, "Why do questions arise in your hearts?"
      b) The evidence (39-43).
         (1) He told them to both see and handle the evidence of His hands and feet; this couldn't be a spirit.
         (2) He actually ate the broiled fish they gave Him.
   2. The Scriptures that had foretold His death and resurrection (44-47).
      a) He reminded them that He had told them that all that was written in the Law of Moses and the prophets and the psalms about Him would be fulfilled.
      b) He summed up what the Scriptures said about Him.
         (1) The Christ must suffer and rise the third day.
         (2) Repentance and remission of sins should be preached in His name to all nations beginning from *Jerusalem.*
   3. The Great Commission according to Luke (48-49).
      a) You are witnesses of these things.
      b) I send forth the promise of my Father upon you.

c) Wait in the city until you are clothed with power from on high.

D. Luke gave a brief account of the ascension of Jesus (50-53).
   1. Place: Over against Bethany.
   2. Blessing: He lifted up His hands and blessed them.
   3. Ascension: He was carried up into heaven.
   4. Worship: The disciples worshipped Him and returned to Jerusalem with joy and were continually in the temple blessing God.

The Empty Tomb

Scripture

24:1-12 But on the first day of the week, at early dawn, they came unto the tomb, bringing the spices which they had prepared. 2 And they found the stone rolled away from the tomb. 3 And they entered in, and found not the body of the Lord Jesus. 4 And it came to pass, while they were perplexed thereabout, behold, two men stood by them in dazzling apparel: 5 and as they were affrighted and bowed down their faces to the earth, they said unto them, Why seek ye the living among the dead? 6 He is not here, but is risen: remember how he spake unto you when he was yet in Galilee, 7 saying that the Son of man must be delivered up into the hands of sinful men, and be crucified, and the third day rise again. 8 And they remembered his words, 9 and returned from the tomb, and told all these things to the eleven, and to all the rest. 10 Now they were Mary Magdalene, and Joanna, and Mary the mother of James: and the other women with them told these things unto the apostles. 11 And these words appeared in their sight as idle talk; and they disbelieved them. 12 But Peter arose, and ran unto the tomb; and stooping and looking in, he seeth the linen cloths by themselves; and he departed to his home, wondering at that which was come to pass.

Comments

They came to the tomb.—All four Gospel writers present conclusive evidence that Jesus actually died on the cross. They also present conclusive evidence that He was actually raised from the dead.

The first point is that the tomb where His body had lain was found empty on the first day of the week by the women who came to complete the burial arrangements. It is evident that they had not anticipated this, for they were wondering who would roll away the stone from the entrance to the tomb. Roman soldiers had been guarding it to prevent anything happening to it until after the third day. The chief priests and Pharisees had said to Pilate, "Sir, we remember that that deceiver said while he was yet alive, 'After three days I will rise again.' Command, therefore, that the sepulchre be made sure until the third day lest haply his disciples come and steal him away and tell the people that he is risen from the dead and the last error shall be worse than the first." Pilate gave them a guard and told them to make it as sure as they could (Matt. 23: 63-65).

Seeing the stone rolled away, the women entered the tomb but did not find the body of Jesus. In their perplexity, they were startled by two angels who said, "Why seek ye the living among the dead?" These heavenly messengers were the first to announce that He was alive. At long last, His disciples were beginning to see what He meant when He told them that He would be delivered up into the hands of sinful men and be crucified and on the third day rise again.

The women hurried away to tell the good news to the eleven and the others. Mary Magdalene was one of those women. She had been faithful throughout Jesus' ministry. She was present as He died on the cross. She was among the first to hear the heavenly announcement, "He is risen from the dead."

as idle talk.—The apostles couldn't believe it; it was just idle talk, for they knew that He had died on the cross. But their attitude constitutes one of the strong points in the proof of the resurrection of Jesus. They had failed to understand His prediction, partly, no doubt, because of their concept of His kingdom. The idea of a spiritual kingdom—a kingdom that was not of this world—had never crossed their minds. There was no place for a cross in their concept of the kingdom.

They didn't believe that Jesus had risen until forced to do so by indisputable evidence. After they had investigated the evidence and had become convinced beyond a doubt that He was alive again, they did not hesitate to risk their lives to proclaim the Risen Lord. When commanded by the Jews not to do so, they said, "Whether it is right in the sight of God to harken unto you rather than unto

God judge ye for we cannot but speak the things which we saw
and heard" (Acts 4:19-20).

We may think it strange that the enemies of Jesus remembered
the prediction of His death while His disciples did not. His enemies
were interested in one thing only: His destruction. They rejoiced
over the fact that He died on thir cross. They did everything possible
to make sure that no one remove the body from the tomb. But
when the tomb was found empty, they felt compelled to explain
it somehow. So they bribed the soldiers and told them to say that
while they were asleep His disciples came and stole away the body.
They promised that if this should come to the ears of the governor
they would clear the soldiers.

Unbelievers have made many attempts to explain that empty
tomb. But none of them have improved the fabricated tale told
by the Pharisees. No court at any time or any place would accept
testimony from a witness who openly admitted that he had been
asleep when the incident being investigated had occurred.

but Peter arose and ran to the tomb.—Even though the story of the
women seemed as idle talk, there was something in that made Peter
hasten to investigate for himself. When he did, he found every
item of the account to be correct. The tomb was empty; the body
of Jesus was not there. He returned home wondering what had come
to pass.

The Appearance on the Way to Emmaus

Scripture

24:13-35   And behold, two of them were going that very day to a
village named Emmaus, which was threescore furlongs from Jerusalem. 14 And they communed with each other of all these things
which had happened. 15 And it came to pass, while they communed
and questioned together, that Jesus himself drew near, and went
with them. 16 But their eyes were holden that they should not know
him. 17 And he said unto them, What communications are these that
ye have one with another, as ye walk? And they stood still, looking
sad. 18 And one of them, named Cleopas, answering said unto him,
Dost thou alone sojourn in Jerusalem and not know the things which
are come to pass there in these days? 19 And he said unto them,
What things? And they said unto him, The things concerning Jesus
the Nazarene, who was a prophet mighty in deed and word before

God and all the people: 20 and how the chief priests and our rulers delivered him up to be condemned to death, and crucified him. 21 But we hoped that it was he who should redeem Israel. Yea and besides all this, it is now the third day since these things came to pass. 22 Moreover certain women of our company amazed us, having been early at the tomb; 23 and when they found not his body, they came, saying, that they had also seen a vision of angels, who said that he was alive. 24 And certain of them that were with us went to the tomb, and found it even so as the women had said: but him they saw not. 25 And he said unto them, O foolish men, and slow of heart to believe in all that the prophets have spoken! 26 Behooved it not the Christ to suffer these things, and to enter into his glory? 27 And beginning from Moses and from all the prophets, he interpreted to them in all the scriptures the things concerning himself. 28 And they drew nigh unto the village, whither they were going: and he made as though he would go further. 29 And they constrained him, saying, Abide with us; for it is toward evening, and the day is now far spent. And he went in to abide with them. 30 And it came to pass, when he had sat down with them to meat, he took the bread and blessed; and breaking it he gave to them. 31 And their eyes were opened, and they knew him; and he vanished out of their sight. 32 And they said one to another, Was not our heart burning within us, while he spake to us in the way, while he opened to us the scriptures? 33 And they rose up that very hour, and returned to Jerusalem, and found the eleven gathered together, and them that were with them, 34 saying, The Lord is risen indeed, and hath appeared to Simon. 35 And they rehearsed the things that happened in the way, and how he was known of them in the breaking of the bread.

Comments

a village named Emmaus.—The village was in the vicinity of Jerusalem. It will be forever remembered because of what happened to two of Jesus' disciples as they journeyed toward it on that resurrection day. As they talked about the death of Jesus and the report of the women that He was alive, Jesus drew near and went with them. They didn't recognize Him, for "their eyes were holden that they should no know him." Were they blind to His presence because of their knowledge of His death? The Stranger wanted to know about the things they were talking about. The disciples, their grief showing on their faces, said, "Are you the only one in Jerusalem who does not know what has come to pass in these days?"

Then they told the story of Jesus the Nazarene who was a prophet mighty in deed and word before God and all the people. They told about His crucifixion and said, "We had hoped that He would be the one to redeem Israel." Everyone was longing for the restoration of Israel to a place of dignity among the nations of the world. They thought this Son of David would surely be the one to make their dream come true, but that hope died at the cross.

and besides all this.—Three days had gone by since the death of the Prophet. The report was out that He had been seen alive. Was the light of hope beginning to show on the faces of these Emmaus disciples? They told the Stranger about those who had investigated and confirmed the report.

foolish men and slow of heart to believe.—Jesus chided them for being slow to believe all that the prophets had spoken. He said it was necessary for Christ to suffer and enter into His glory. That was the message of the Scriptures, was it not? Then He explained all that was written in the Scriptures about Himself. What a privilege those disciples had to listen to that message! The book of Matthew covers this very same material showing how Jesus fulfilled the prophecies about Messiah.

abide with us.—The disciples couldn't let the Stranger go on; they invited Him to stay with them for the night. As they sat at the table, the Stranger took bread and broke it and gave it to them. Their Guest did this; but they had seen Him do it before. Their eyes were opened and they knew that it was the Risen Lord. In that moment of recognition, He vanished from their sight.

was not our heart burning within us.—The story of the Scriptures stirred their hearts as nothing else could have done. It is still the most thrilling story known to man. There are millions whose hearts would be thrilled today if only someone would tell them of the Savior who died and arose that they might have eternal life.

that very hour.—The two had made the long walk from Jerusalem to Emmaus. The conviction that they had actually seen the Risen Lord banished all thought of being tired. They arose and hurried back to Jerusalem to share the good news with the eleven. There they discovered that the evidence of His resurrection was piling up, for the apostles said, "The Lord is risen indeed and has appeared to Simon."

Luke does not record all the appearances of Jesus. Some of them recorded by others are: (1) The appearance to the eleven when Thomas was absent and again when he was with the group (John 20:19-31; I Cor. 15:6). (2) The appearance at the sea of Tiberias (John 21:1-23). (3) The appearance to the five hundred at one time (I Cor. 15:6). (4) The appearance in the mountain in Galilee when Jesus gave the Great Commission (Matt. 28:16-20). (5) The appearance to James (I Cor. 15:7).

Luke summarized all this evidence in his second letter to Theophilus in these words: "to whom he also showed himself alive after his passion by many proofs, appearing unto them by the space of forty days, and speaking the things concerning the kingdom of God" (Acts 1:3).

Jesus' Appearance to the Eleven

Scripture

24:36-49   And as they spake these things, he himself stood in the midst of them, and saith unto them, Peace be unto you. 37 But they were terrified and affrighted, and supposed that they beheld a spirit. 38 And he said unto them, Why are ye troubled? and wherefore do questionings arise in your heart? 39 See my hands and my feet, that it is I myself: handle me, and see; for a spirit hath not flesh and bones, as ye behold me having. 40 And when he had said this, he showed them his hands and his feet. 41 And while they still disbelieved for joy, and wondered, he said unto them. Have ye here anything to eat? 42 And they gave him a piece of a broiled fish. 43 And he took it, and ate before them.

44 And he said unto them, These are my words which I spake unto you, while I was yet with you, that all things must needs be fulfilled, which are written in the law of Moses, and the prophets, and the psalms, concerning me. 45 Then opened he their mind, that they might understand the scriptures; 46 and he said unto them, Thus it is written, that the Christ should suffer, and rise again from the dead the third day; 47 and that repentance and remission of sins should be preached in his name unto all the nations, beginning from Jerusalem. 48 Ye are witnesses of these things. 49 And behold, I send forth the promise of my Father upon you: but tarry ye in the city, until ye be clothed with power from on high.

Comments

He himself stood in the midst of them.—He said, "Peace be unto
you." But the terrified disciples thought that they were beholding
a spirit. Important evidence of the resurrection is revealed in this
appearance. Jesus told the disciples to see His hands and feet for
themselves. Thomas, on one occasion, said he would not believe
unless he could see the prints of the nails in His hands and put his
hand into the wound in Jesus' side. Jesus gave him the opportunity
to do that very thing. When Thomas saw it, he said, "My Lord and
my God."

Their joy over what they had heard and seen still kept them
from believing what their eyes told them was true. Then Jesus took
a piece of broiled fish and ate it in their presence. That convinced
them that He was not a spirit, but the Risen Lord. See also John's
comment in I John 1:1-4.

these are my words.—Jesus had reviewed the Scriptures about His
death and resurrection for the Emmaus disciples. He repeated it for
the group in Jerusalem, reminding them that all that had been
written in the Law of Moses and the prophets and the psalms about
Him had to be fulfilled. He helped them to understand the Scriptures by saying, "Thus it is written, that the Christ should suffer
and rise again from the dead on the third day and that repentance
and remission of sins should be preached in his name unto all the
nations beginning from Jerusalem." This message of Christ is the
central theme of the Bible. When the apostles preached the Word,
they preached Christ. They did not hesitate to declare that in none
other is there salvation, for neither is there any other name under
heaven that is given among men wherein we must be saved (Acts
4:12).

beginning from Jerusalem.—The crucifixion had taken place at
Jerusalem. The evidence that proved His resurrection had been presented at Jerusalem. The preaching of the gospel that was based on
these facts was to begin in Jerusalem also. The eleven, and Matthias,
all of whom were eye-witness of these facts, began their ministry
of preaching and teaching on the Day of Pentecost immediately
after they were baptized in the Holy Spirit.

the promise of the Father.—That was the promise that the Holy
Spirit would be sent to enable them to bear accurate testimony
concerning that which they had seen and heard. They were to wait
in Jerusalem until they received that power from on high.

The Ascension of Jesus

Scripture

24:50-53 And he led them out until they were over against Bethany: and he lifted up his hands, and blessed them. 51 And it came to pass, while he blessed them, he parted from them, and was carried up into heaven. 52 And they worshipped him, and returned to Jerusalem with great joy: 53 and were continually in the temple, blessing God.

Comments

And he led them out.—He was soon to be taken from them, but He would continue to lead them through the Holy Spirit. He had promised the apostles that the Holy Spirit would guide them into all the truth (John 16:13-14).

and blessed them.—He had blessed them on other occasions; just before leaving them, He blessed them again. The memory of that blessing was to remain with them through their sufferings as they carried out the Great Commission, for He had promised to be with them always, even to the end of the age.

and was carried up into heaven.—In his second letter to Theophilus, Luke says that Jesus was taken up from the disciples and a cloud received Him from their sight. Heavenly messengers stood beside them with the encouraging word, "He will return again as you beheld Him taken up from you into heaven."

and they worshipped him.—The resurrection had convinced them that He was both the Son of Man and the Son of God. As He departed from them, they worshipped Him. Indeed, from that time on, their lives were a living sacrifice of real worship to the Lord Jesus Christ.

Their joy knew no limit. They returned to Jerusalem to await the day, not far distant, when they would begin the proclamation of the gospel. They were continually in the temple praising God while waiting for the signal to begin their world-wide mission for Christ.

In a very real sense, the story does not end here. A great climax was reached on the Day of Pentecost as the apostles preached the first sermon in that campaign. The three thousand who reversed the decision they had made at the trial got themselves baptized in the name of Christ for the remission of sins. They continued stead-

395

fastly in the apostles teaching and fellowship, in the breaking of bread and the prayers (Acts 2:38-42).

The story ends with the triumphant coming of Christ to receive His own unto Himself that they may be with Him always. Even so, "Come, Lord Jesus. The grace of the Lord Jesus be with the saints. Amen." Revelation 22:20-21.

Summary

Wicked men crucified Jesus at Calvary. There is abundant evidence that He actually died. There is equally positive proof that He arose from the dead.

The women found the tomb empty; the body of Jesus was not there. Angels announced that He was alive. With the startling news, the women hurried away to tell the apostles who thought it was idle talk. Peter·investigated and found the tomb empty just as the women had said.

During the period of forty days between the resurrection and ascension, Jesus appeared to the disciples by many certain proofs. They saw Him, they heard Him explain the Scriptures, they touched Him, and they saw Him eat a piece of broiled fish in their presence. Not only were the Emmaus disciples convinced that He was alive, but also all of the eleven. At one time, more than five-hundred had seen Him alive.

The Risen Lord summed up the Scriptures about the Christ by saying, "Thus it is written, that the Christ should suffer, and rise again from the dead the third day; and that repentance and remission of sins should be preached in his name unto all the nations, beginning from Jerusalem."

Having fully demonstrated the fact of His resurrection, and having instructed the apostles as to their duties, He led them out until they were near Bethany. Then He lifted up His hands and blessed them and was carried up into heaven.

Heavenly messengers had announced the birth of the Christ; now angels told the apostles that He was coming again.

"Now the God of peace, who brought again from the dead the great shepherd of the sheep with the blood of an eternal covenant, even our Lord Jesus, make you perfect in every good thing to do his will, working in us that which is well-pleasing in his sight, through Jesus Christ; to whom be the glory for ever and ever. Amen." (Heb. 13:20-21).

CHAPTER TWENTY-FOUR

Questions

1. On what day did the resurrection occur?
2. What precautions had the Jews taken to prevent anything happening to the body until after the third day? Why?
3. What did the women find when they came to the tomb?
4. What did angels tell them?
5. Who were some of the women at the tomb?
6. What did the apostles think of their report?
7. Why did Peter investigate it?
8. What evidential value is there in the fact that the enemies remembered Jesus' predictions of His resurrection while the disciples did not?
9. What evidence did Peter discover at the tomb?
10. Where was Emmaus?
11. What were the two disciples talking about?
12. Why didn't they recognize Jesus when He joined them?
13. What had they hoped for in Jesus?
14. What did Jesus say to them?
15. Why did they ask Him to abide with them?
16. How was He made known to them?
17. What did they mean by saying that their heart burned as He had spoken to them?
18. What did they do immediately after He was revealed to them?
19. What are some of the other appearances not recorded by Luke?
20. How did Luke summarize his report of the proofs of the resurrection?
21. Under what circumstances did He appear to the eleven?
22. What was their reaction? Why?
23. How did they become convinced that Jesus had actually been raised from the dead?
24. How did He help them to understand the Scriptures?
25. Why did He order them to begin their ministry in Jerusalem?
26. What is meant by the promise of the Father?
27. Where did the ascension take place?
28. What did the heavenly messengers say to the wondering disciples?
29. What did the disciples do at the time of the ascension?
30. Where did they await the fulfillment of the promise of the Father?